# THE
# SCRAP IRON
# FLOTILLA

Also by Mike Carlton

*Cruiser: The Life and Loss of HMAS* Perth *and Her Crew*

*First Victory 1914: HMAS* Sydney's *Hunt for
the German Raider* Emden

*Flagship: The Cruiser HMAS* Australia II
*and the Pacific War on Japan*

*On Air*

# MIKE CARLTON

# THE SCRAP IRON FLOTILLA

WILLIAM HEINEMANN: AUSTRALIA

## WILLIAM HEINEMANN

UK | USA | Canada | Ireland | Australia
India | New Zealand | South Africa | China

William Heinemann is part of the Penguin Random House group of companies
whose addresses can be found at global.penguinrandomhouse.com

Penguin
Random House
Australia

First published by William Heinemann in 2022

Cover photography courtesy of the Royal Australian Navy and
Shutterstock (planes)
Cover design by Adam Laszczuk © Penguin Random House Australia Pty Ltd
Drawings of HMAS *Stuart* and HMAS *Waterhen* by Colin Harvey
Maps by James Carlton
Author photograph © Carol Gibbons
Internal design by Midland Typesetters, Australia
Typeset in 11/14.5 pt Janson Text by Midland Typesetters

Printed and bound in Australia by Griffin Press, part of Ovato, an accredited
ISO AS/NZS 14001 Environmental Management Systems printer

A catalogue record for this
book is available from the
National Library of Australia

ISBN 978 1 76104 200 3

penguin.com.au

MIX
Paper from
responsible sources
FSC® C009448

We at Penguin Random House Australia acknowledge that Aboriginal and
Torres Strait Islander peoples are the Traditional Custodians and the first storytellers
of the lands on which we live and work. We honour Aboriginal and Torres Strait
Islander peoples' continuous connection to Country, waters, skies and communities.
We celebrate Aboriginal and Torres Strait Islander stories, traditions and living
cultures; and we pay our respects to Elders past and present.

# CONTENTS

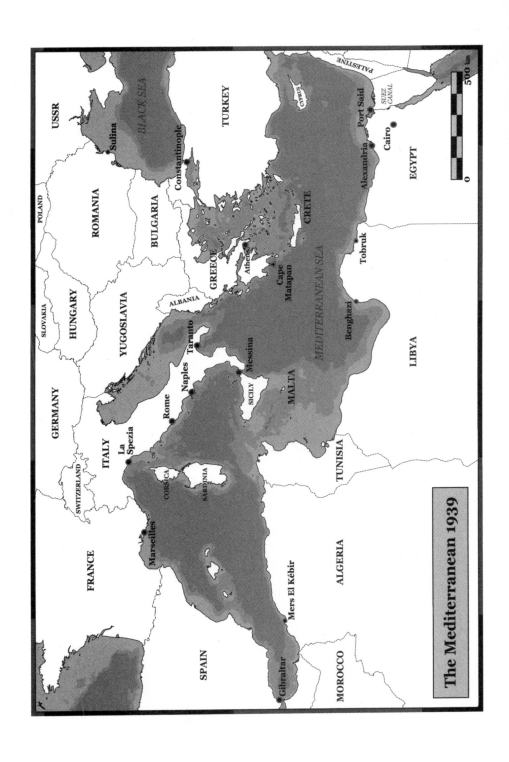

# The Mediterranean 1939

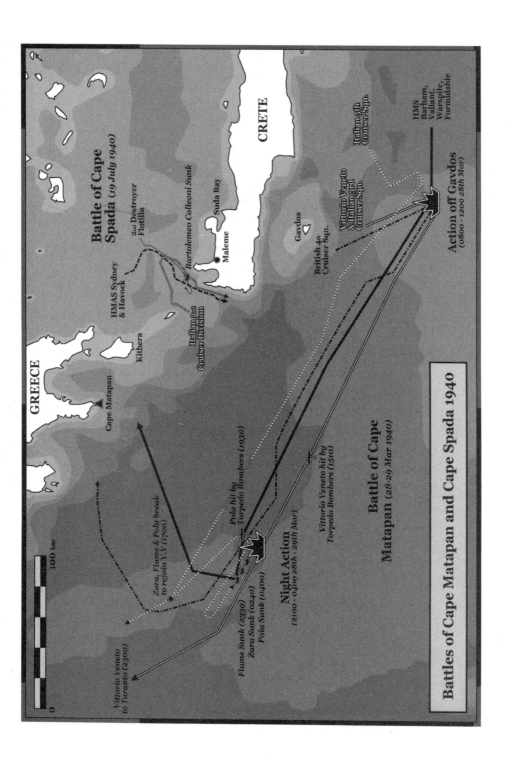

**Battle of Cape Spada** *(19 July 1940)*

GREECE

Cape Matapan

Kithera

CRETE

HMAS Sydney & Havock

2nd Destroyer Flotilla

*Bartolemeo Colleoni Sunk*

Maleme

Suda Bay

Italian 2nd Cruiser Division

Gavdos

British 4th Cruiser Sqn.

*Vittorio Veneto & Italian Cruisers Sqn.*

Italian 5th Cruisers Sqn.

HMS Barham, Valiant, Warspite, Formidable

**Action off Gavdos** *(0800 - 1200 28th Mar)*

*Vittorio Veneto to Taranto (2300)*

*Zara, Fiume & Pola break to rejoin V.V (1700)*

*Pola hit by Torpedo Bombers (1930)*

*Fiume Sunk (2330)*
*Zara Sunk (0240)*
*Pola Sunk (0400)*

**Night Action**
*(2100 - 0400 28th - 29th Mar)*

*Vittorio Veneto hit by Torpedo Bombers (1510)*

**Battle of Cape Matapan** *(28-29 Mar 1940)*

100 km

**Battles of Cape Matapan and Cape Spada 1940**

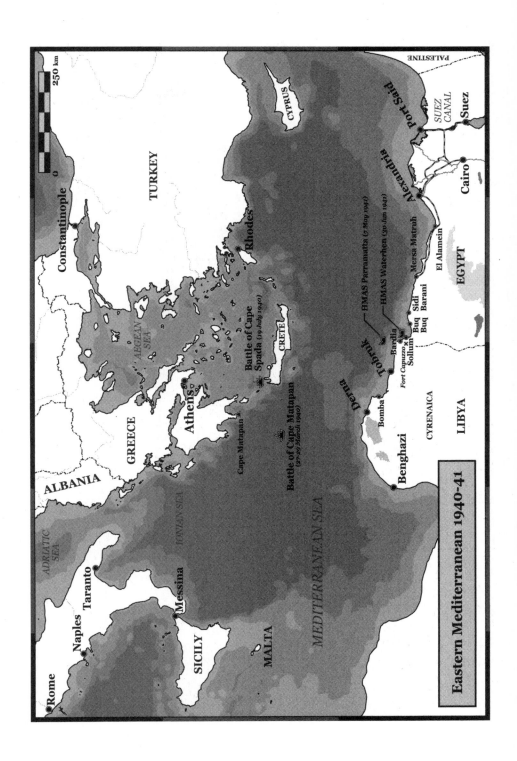

Eastern Mediterranean 1940-41

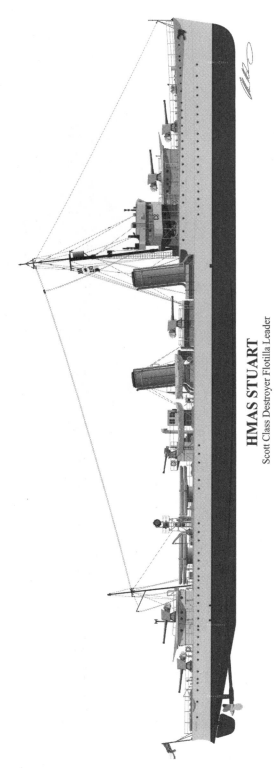

**HMAS STUART**

Scott Class Destroyer Flotilla Leader

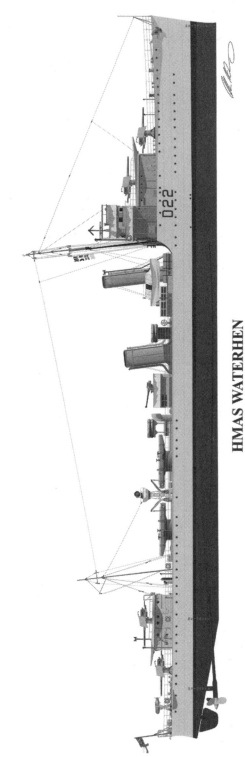

**HMAS WATERHEN**
V and W Class Destroyer

# NOTES ON THE TEXT

The map of the Mediterranean has changed radically since 1945. New countries have emerged – Lebanon and Israel to name just two – and many cities and ports now have different spellings or, in some cases, new names entirely.

For example, Sollum, on the Egyptian coast, is now Sallum or El Salloum, while Bardia, in modern-day Libya, is now Bardiyah. To keep it simple, I have mostly stuck with names, places and spellings as they were known during the Second World War. Then again, for clarity, I have sometimes done the reverse: Tripolitania and Cyrenaica were well enough known in 1940. Libya works better today.

Measurements of length and distance have been converted to metres and kilometres, except where they occur in direct quotations. Where it does crop up, a nautical mile is 1.8 kilometres. A knot is a measure of speed at sea, one nautical mile per hour. Thus a ship travelling at 30 knots is doing 30 nautical miles per hour or 55.5 kilometres per hour (km/h). This might not seem much to a car driver on land, but at sea – especially in a big sea – it is tearing along at a great pace.

Gun calibres are also tricky. In the Allied navies they were measured in inches; in the Italian and German navies in centimetres.

I have retained inches. HMAS *Stuart*'s main armament of 4.7-inch calibre guns fired a shell of that diameter, or 11.9 centimetres. A 6-inch cruiser had main guns of that calibre, or 15.2 centimetres. The bigger the shell the more explosive it carried and the further it went.

'Port' is the left-hand side of a ship as you look forwards towards the bow. 'Starboard' is the right-hand side. They remain the same, though, even if you turn to face the rear. 'Fo'c'sle', an abbreviation of the old 'forecastle', is the front section of a ship, including the upper deck there and decks immediately below. The quarterdeck is on a ship's stern, the rearmost part. The 'head' is a toilet, a name from the days of sail when seamen used the head of the bow (the front of the ship) as a latrine.

To be captain of a ship is a job description or an appointment, not a rank. Some ships' captains might be commanders, lieutenant commanders or even lieutenants. The crew would refer to them as 'the captain' even though they might not hold that captain's rank of four gold stripes. Today, the second in command of a ship is usually known as the executive officer, or XO. In the destroyers of the Second World War he was the First Lieutenant. A 'flag officer' is one who holds the rank of rear admiral or above. A kapitänleutnant in the German Kriegsmarine held the equivalent rank to a British or Australian lieutenant.

Not all warships are 'battleships', which is a specific term. A battleship was a large, heavily armoured warship carrying a navy's biggest and most powerful guns. It had no means of detecting or fighting submarines, having to rely on a surrounding screen of destroyers and cruisers for that protection. Battleships were designed to fight other battleships or to bombard targets ashore. A battlecruiser was similar, about the same size as a battleship and also with big guns, but carrying less protective armour and designed for more speed. Neither of these exists today outside maritime museums, their place taken by aircraft carriers and nuclear submarines carrying ballistic missiles.

Finally, this is not a history of every Australian ship that served in the Mediterranean in the early years of the Second World War. That book would have to be twice as long as this one. I have focused on the five old destroyers of the 'Scrap Iron Flotilla' – *Stuart, Vampire,*

*Vendetta*, *Voyager* and *Waterhen* – because their stories are unique and magnificent, as I hope will become apparent. At the same time, a couple of other ships found their way in. The cruisers HMAS *Sydney* and *Perth* and the sloop *Parramatta* have an honoured place as well.

# CHAPTER I

# THE THEATRE

Yea, and if some god shall wreck me in the wine-dark deep,
Even so I will endure …
For already have I suffered full much,
And much have I toiled in perils of waves and war.
Let this be added to the tale of those.

Homer, *The Odyssey*

War at sea began in the Mediterranean, the centre of the earth. In myth and legend, Greek and Roman gods and heroes rowed and sailed its waters to fight their battles. Odysseus and Achilles, Ajax and Hermes, Aphrodite and Artemis, Jason and his Argonauts all furrowed its waves or strode its shores. Zeus, the God of War, and Poseidon, the wrathful God of the Sea, held the fate of men and women in their hands. Paris, son of Zeus, abducted the beautiful Helen of Troy, 'the face that launched a thousand ships' of the Trojan Wars.

Down the centuries before and after Christ, great cities and nation states, republics and kingdoms and caliphates and empires rose and fell on the Mediterranean littoral of Europe, Africa and the Middle East. Minoans and Greeks, Romans and Carthaginians, Persians and Byzantines, Phoenicians and Ottomans, Genoese and Venetians hurled their fleets at each other in sea fights evermore violent as their ships and weapons and tactics grew more capable of slaughter.

Triremes and galleys rowed by banks of slaves gave way to sailing galleons. The armoured ram on the prow of a warship was superseded by the catapult hurling mighty rocks at the enemy, to be supplanted in turn by gunpowder and cannon firing iron balls.

As navigation became more sure, more distant thrones lunged for the spoils. The Norman kings of France seized the rich prize of Sicily in the eleventh century. England's Richard I, The Lionheart, took Cyprus on his way to the Crusades at the beginning of that clash of faiths and civilisations still playing out in the twenty-first century. In 1571 at Lepanto, off the western coast of Greece, the largely Spanish and Venetian armada of the Holy League of Pope Pius V met and routed the Ottoman Empire in the biggest naval engagement ever fought; some 400 ships in a conflict so bloody that artists would later paint the sea in crimson.

Inevitably, the Mediterranean became the cockpit in which France and England vied for the supremacy of their empires. Reputations rose and fell. In 1757, the English admiral John Byng was court-martialled and executed by firing squad on his quarterdeck after failing to relieve a British garrison from a French attack on the island of Majorca. The British, wrote Voltaire, '... think it good from time to time to shoot an admiral to encourage the others'.[1]

In the spring of 1798, Napoleon Bonaparte sailed from the southern French naval port of Toulon for Egypt to menace British India and – for entertainment – to plunder the treasures of the pharaohs. Pausing briefly to seize the island of Malta from the ancient order of the Knights of St John, he landed in Egypt that July. 'Soldiers!' he thundered to his army at Cairo. 'From these pyramids, forty centuries of history look down upon you!'

It didn't work. Nemesis met him but a month later, in the diminutive, one-armed and one-eyed form of Rear Admiral Sir Horatio Nelson, whose Mediterranean fleet of battleships of the Royal Navy trapped the French fleet at anchor in Aboukir Bay at the mouth of the Nile Delta. It was an annihilating British triumph climaxing in the spectacular destruction of the giant French flagship *Orient* when her magazines exploded, an apocalyptic vision which seared itself into naval history. For generations, British schoolchildren would recite a poem that limned the heroism of the young son of the *Orient*'s captain:

The boy stood on the burning deck
Whence all but him had fled;
The flame that lit the battle's wreck
Shone round him o'er the dead.[2]

The Mediterranean, though, did not lie entirely subdued. In the first five years of the nineteenth century, pirates of the four Barbary states of North Africa – Tripoli, Tunis, Algiers and Morocco – were seizing merchant ships at will, including many Americans, and holding the crews as infidel slaves and demanding ransom and tribute from their governments. Eventually, President Thomas Jefferson sent in the United States Navy. In May 1805, after the Battle of Derna in what is now modern Libya, the splendidly named Lieutenant Presley O'Bannon of the newly forged United States Marine Corps raised the Stars and Stripes at the first-ever American military victory on foreign soil, a feat enshrined in the opening line of the 'Marines' Hymn' – 'From the halls of Montezuma to the shores of Tripoli'.

Thrilling though that was to the young United States, in the grand scheme of things the Barbary War was a sideshow. Greatness arrived in October that same year when Horatio Nelson – by then a vice admiral and a viscount – sealed Britain's supremacy at sea. In a climactic battle off Cape Trafalgar in the Atlantic just outside the Strait of Gibraltar, the western entrance to the Mediterranean, he crushed a combined French and Spanish fleet. Nelson was shot and killed by a French marksman at the height of the fighting but that famous victory, still toasted by the Royal Navy – 'The Immortal Memory!' – ushered in Pax Britannica to rule the waves for the remainder of the nineteenth century.

And so the show went on. With glorious pomp and circumstance – battleships and cruisers trailing sulphurous clouds of coal smoke in fleet exercises, guns thundering, brass gleaming, bands playing, flags flying – the navy of Queen Victoria commanded the Mediterranean from the island rock of Gibraltar off southern Spain to the Turkish Dardanelles some 4000 kilometres to the east. Mighty, unchallenged, absolute. The Royal Navy's Commander-in-Chief Mediterranean, gleaming in an admiral's finery of blue, white and gold, sat on the right-hand side of an Anglican God.

The guns of August 1914 ended all that. In the opening days of the First World War, two warships of the Kaiser's navy, the modern battlecruiser *Goeben* and the cruiser *Breslau*, boldly evaded an incompetent British pursuit in the Mediterranean – *Das Mittelmeer* – to fetch up in Constantinople, where they were hastily commissioned into the Ottoman navy and renamed *Yavuz Sultan Selim* and *Midili*. A few weeks later, flying the Turkish flag but still with their German crews on board and a German admiral in command, they sortied into the Black Sea to bombard five Russian ports, a masterstroke which emphatically plunged Turkey into the war on the German side. Two British admirals had their careers wrecked for their failure, and rightly so. The *Goeben*, wrote Winston Churchill after the war, 'brought more slaughter, more misery, and more ruin than has ever before been borne within the compass of a ship'.[3]

That flourish was a typical piece of Churchillian exaggeration, but not by much. The waves reached all the way to the southern hemisphere. They brought Australians to the Mediterranean for the first time, the Anzacs to die on the fatal beaches and cliffs of Gallipoli; the 4th Australian Light Horse to charge into immortality at the Battle of Beersheba. His Majesty's Australian submarine *AE2* penetrated the Dardanelles on 25 April 1915, 'to run amok' in the Sea of Marmara,[4] in 'the finest feat in submarine history'.[5] Her hull still lies there on the bottom.

A quarter of a century later, Australia's sons would be in the Mediterranean once again.

# CHAPTER 2

# COMMENCE HOSTILITIES AT ONCE WITH GERMANY

In the late winter of 1939, the destroyer *Stuart* lay alongside a wharf at Sydney's Garden Island naval base, preparing for war. Tired and old and not a little shabby, like some once dazzling actress grown grey and fallen on hard times, for more than a year she had been quietly retired in mothballs across the harbour at Athol Bight, a cove below Taronga Zoo. In due course she would have been torn apart by the oxyacetylene torches in some shipbreaker's yard.

But with the news from Europe growing increasingly dire, a tug had towed her back to Garden Island to be pressed into service again. Now, this August, her decks were abuzz with the urgency of making ready for sea.

There was no denying her age. *Stuart* had been built on the River Tyne in the north of England to a First World War design known to the Admiralty as the Scott class. She and her eight sister ships had resounding Scottish names – *Bruce, Douglas, Campbell*, and so on – and, although the phrase had not been coined then, they were state of the art, the most powerful destroyers afloat. Officially they were 'destroyer leaders', meaning that they were a little bigger, faster, and more heavily gunned than other ships of their type, with extra space to accommodate a captain and a small staff in command of a squadron or flotilla of other destroyers.

*Stuart* was commissioned into the Royal Navy in December 1918, just too late for the war, and she never fired a shot in anger. As HMS *Stuart* she had spent many of her early years in the Mediterranean, with some time in the Black Sea in 1919 as a part of the eventually futile British effort to bolster the White Russians against the advancing Bolsheviks. In her heyday they'd called her the 'White Lady of the Med'.

She had come to Australia in 1933. On a request from Canberra, the British transferred her and four other destroyers – *Vampire*, *Vendetta*, *Voyager* and *Waterhen* – on a permanent loan to the Royal Australian Navy (RAN), to spend the rest of their lives respectably ageing in southern seas.

At the beginning of the twentieth century, destroyers were a relatively new idea in the world's navies. When they first appeared in the late nineteenth century they were called 'torpedo boat destroyers'. Fast and manoeuvrable, they were intended to beat off attacks by small craft which might swarm from an enemy coast to launch torpedoes upon a fleet of ponderous, slower-moving battleships. Soon enough, captains and admirals realised there was a lot more that torpedo boat destroyers could do – in scouting ahead for a fleet, dashing into enemy ports for a swift attack, fighting off other destroyers, escorting merchant convoys, generally fetching and carrying and, eventually, meeting the new and increasing menace of submarines.

They were versatile and, better still, they were fun. They were also glamorous. Battleships were all very well and good and no doubt necessary, but they moved in squadrons or fleets, in stately parade like great grey whales. Destroyers dashed about like dolphins. Energetic young officers yearned to command one. It was exhilarating, sublime, unique; a wild ride to balance on the open bridge of a destroyer at full speed, seas green over the fo'c'sle, stern buried deep in a white wake, buffeted by the wind and spray, shouting helm and engine orders. Destroyers they would be. The name stuck, as it does to this day.

Aged or not, *Stuart*'s bones still looked well and weatherly to a sailor's eye. Even in repose she seemed ready to pounce. Her lines were low and lean: 101 metres long, with a beam or width at her widest part of 9.6 metres, and displacing just over 2000 old tons full load. She was fast too. Brand new on her speed trials off southern England, her four Yarrow boilers and two Brown-Curtis turbine engines had pumped out 40,000 shaft horsepower to her twin propellors, sending her racing over a calm sea at a thrilling speed of 36.5 knots. Age had cut that back a bit over the years, perhaps to 32 knots at an optimistic best, but still a handsome gallop. Her old machinery, though, would need careful nursing.

Weapons she had aplenty. For her main armament she carried five 4.7-inch guns (120 millimetres), mounted singly, 'A' and 'B' for'ard of her bridge, 'Q' amidships between her two tall and slender funnels, and 'X' and 'Y' aft of her mainmast. Another old but tried and true design, handled by a well-trained crew the 4.7s could fire a 22.7-kilogram semi-armour piercing shell over a maximum range of 14,450 metres, at a rate of six rounds per minute.

There was a 3-inch anti-aircraft gun, effective enough in service against the slow-moving biplanes of the First World War but utterly useless against the far swifter aircraft of the conflict to come. A couple of 2-pounder, quick-firing pom-pom guns beefed up her anti-aircraft armament, weapons impressively noisy in action but still more miss than hit even with a gunner who truly knew his trade. Four .303 Lewis machine guns, another Great War relic but still serviceable for close action, sat to port and starboard of the bridge. Six 21-inch torpedo tubes – in two triple-mounts – lay just aft of her second funnel. Finally, she carried two rails for the depth charges to be sent tumbling over her stern against a submarine below. The size of her crew varied, but she would normally carry five or six officers and about 130 sailors.

It was enough to take to war. If a war there would be. The last alarm, the Munich crisis of September 1938, had fizzled out after the British prime minister, Neville Chamberlain, handed Czechoslovakia to the German Führer and flew back to London to promise 'peace for our time'. Yet Herr Hitler was now making the same belligerent noises about Poland. And in a stunning and worrying new development, in Moscow on 23 August, Germany and the Soviet Union had signed a non-aggression pact. The newsreels in Australian cinemas had shown the oily Nazi foreign minister, Joachim von Ribbentrop, and his dour Soviet counterpart, Vyacheslav Molotov, signing the treaty with a beaming Josef Stalin watching over their shoulders.

The newspapers had all agreed that this gave Hitler a free hand to wage war in Western Europe. They did not know that the Nazis and the Soviets had secretly agreed to carve up Poland between them.

—

On Thursday 31 August, *Stuart* stirred to life in a dawn that promised a cheerful end to winter and a sunny start to spring, with a light south-westerly breeze along the coast.

'Trees have already blossomed and gardens are now gay with exotic blooms,' said the *Sydney Morning Herald*, forecasting a day 'mostly fine with scattered cloud, but tending to an occasional shower' with a temperature of 68° Fahrenheit.[1]

Across Woolloomooloo Bay from Garden Island, people were walking their dogs, and swimmers in the faded Edwardian grandeur of the Domain Baths were getting in their morning laps.

*Stuart*'s new commanding officer, Commander Hector Waller RAN, breakfasted early and quickly in his cabin, served by his steward. The newspapers offered a faint whiff of optimism, with the *Daily Telegraph*'s special correspondent reporting:

> The outlook in Europe has brightened during the last twenty-four hours, because Hitler's reply to the British Note of Monday last is said to leave the door open for further discussions ...[2]

Commander Waller had little time for that and less for exotic blooms or an early swim. The ship was due to commission tomorrow, to formally rejoin the navy, and there had been a daunting amount of work to get through, much of it reams of paper which had been arriving in an unending torrent for weeks. The navy's bible, *King's Regulations and Admiralty Instructions* – KR and AI as everyone called them – contained commandments upon everything from the punishment of mutiny to the correct courtesies for greeting a visiting archbishop. There were the newly revised and impressively named *Fighting Instructions, Confidential Book 04027–39*, with no fewer than 649 separate clauses: 'The advanced forces will endeavour to prevent enemy flotillas and cruisers from reaching a position favourable for torpedo attack on the British battlefleet'.

*Admiralty Fleet Orders*, issued to 'all Commanders-in-Chief, Flag Officers, Senior Naval Officers, Captains and Commanding Officers of H.M. Ships and Vessels, Superintendents or Officers in charge of H.M. Naval Establishments and Admiralty Overseers concerned', ran to an eye-watering 829 pages. In *Fleet Orders* their Lordships fretted over an infinity of matters major and minor, including such gems as modifications to the Mark VIB searchlight lamp; the Marriage Allowance – Stoppage on Estrangement of Husband and Wife; Gyro Compass Repeaters for submarines; the correct use of anti-gas respirators, and the regrettable disappearance of mislaid or stolen binoculars.

And there was more, much more, in the *Commonwealth Naval Orders* issued from Navy Office in Melbourne specifically for the RAN. Although nominally the independent fleet of a self-governing dominion, controlled and directed by the Minister for the Navy and the Commonwealth Naval Board, the RAN was in practice a branch of the mother Royal Navy and proud to be so. In 1939 its two senior commanders were both British, simply because no Australian officer yet had the experience or rank to do the job. It was a fact of life: graduates of the Royal Australian Naval College would not reach flag rank, an admiral's gold braid, until 1947. So Admiral Sir Ragnar Colvin RN, Chief of the Naval Staff, was the Australian government's principal adviser on all things naval, and Rear Admiral John Crace – Australian-born, but also a Royal Navy officer – commanded the ships at sea under the quaintly colonial title of Rear Admiral Commanding Australian Squadron.

The paperwork piled up. Clearly, if any war with Germany were to be fought with paper alone it would be a British victory to dwarf Trafalgar. The trick was to know what to ignore and what actually mattered. With tact and common sense the system largely worked to everyone's satisfaction, directing a naval enterprise of hundreds of ships and tens of thousands of men far flung from the north of Scotland to Cape Town, Hong Kong to the Falkland Islands.

Hector Macdonald Laws Waller was born 4 April 1901 in the pleasant little river town of Benalla in Victoria's Ned Kelly country, a half-day's journey by steam train north-east from Melbourne. His father Bill and his mother Helen ran a grocery store on Bridge

Street. They named their tenth and last child after a Scottish hero of the Boer War, Major General Sir Hector Archibald MacDonald, a humble crofter's son who had enlisted in the Gordon Highlanders as a private at the age of fifteen and ascended to glory with derring-do military exploits in the far corners of the Empire.

Perhaps it was the general's singular triumph over his lowly origins that inspired young Hec to leave the bush shop to seek a life in the new Australian navy. In 1914, not old enough to shave, he entered the RAN College (RANC) in its second year, at its first home at Osborne House in Geelong. It was a feat a similar youngster might not have achieved in Britain. In those days, the Royal Navy drew its cadet midshipmen from the upper classes. If you were the grandson of an admiral or the nephew of an earl you were in, one's family happily paying for the education and the uniforms as if the young chap were at Eton or Wellington. Hons and hyphens were scattered like leaves. Much against the paternal advice of the British, the Australians after Federation very firmly laid down that entrance to the RANC would be not by social class but on aptitude and medical fitness alone, and that the education would be free. It was a marked distinction and it worked.

The competition was stiff, with a quota for each state, but Hec made it through and took to the spartan regime like the proverbial duck to water. He sailed through mathematics, physics, chemistry, history, geography, English, French, German, seamanship, gunnery, navigation and pilotage with nautical astronomy, engineering, Bible study, gymnasium and drill. He won his colours for rugby and when he passed out in 1917 he carried off the coveted King's Medal for 'gentlemanly bearing, character, good influence among his fellows and officer-like qualities'. It was a dazzling start.

Every newly launched Australian midshipman was packed off to Britain to be polished in the gunroom of an RN battleship, a rite of passage. In 1918 Midshipman Waller fetched up in HMS *Agincourt*, a coal-burning colossus originally intended for the Turkish navy and so richly furnished, carpeted and wood-panelled that everyone called her 'the Gin Palace'. He was too late to hear her guns in action, but he was on *Agincourt*'s upper deck on a bleak November day that year to witness one of the most epic spectacles of naval history. Beaten and broken, their crews hungry and mutinous, some of them flying the red flag of revolution, no fewer than seventy ships of the Kaiser's High Seas Fleet steamed out of the North Sea haze and into Scotland's Firth of Forth to a humiliating internment beneath the guns of the victors. Hec had travelled a long way from Benalla.

In the grand scheme of Empire, the British and Australians had sensibly agreed that their naval ships and people should be seamlessly interchangeable. Officers and men learned and did the same things.[3] Ranks and uniforms were identical down to the last button, and His Majesty's Australian ships flew the British White Ensign with the red cross of St George on a white field and the Union Jack in the top left-hand corner.[4] Every RAN ship had been built in Britain or to a British design. It made sense. The Victorian and Edwardian swank had largely evaporated, but the Royal Navy was still far and away the biggest and best, the gold standard for the rest. With Japan still nominally an ally, the Imperial Japanese Navy copied the British assiduously, its officers doggedly improving on what they had learned.

Climbing steadily up the ladder, young Hec straddled both hemispheres. In 1924, a year after his marriage in Sydney to Nancy Bowes, a clergyman's daughter, he topped the Royal Navy's long signals course, an ordeal known as 'the Dagger', scoring record marks to beat the previous prodigy, none other than that gleaming aristocrat Lord Louis Mountbatten. Back home he did spells in the RAN's cruisers, the old *Melbourne*, *Sydney* and *Adelaide*, and he taught for a while at the Naval College. The Depression of the early 1930s wrecked not a few naval careers as defence cuts bit hard, but Hec survived with his promotion to commander in 1934, a stint behind a desk at the Admiralty Intelligence Department in Whitehall and a sea posting as executive officer of HMS *Resource*, a 12,000-ton heavy repair ship that was a virtual floating dockyard.

Then came a ship of his own, his first command. HMS *Brazen* was a destroyer less than eight years old when he got her in November 1937. Attached to the 4th Destroyer Flotilla of the Royal Navy's Home Fleet, she was fast and well-armed. It was a blue-ribbon job, a brilliant opportunity. And he almost blew it. The first official report on his abilities, signed by his commanding officer, gave him a score of two out of ten for shiphandling, and just three for both judgement and reliability.

His ability in handling a ship, in spite of much instruction and advice, is far below the average and, at sea, his erratic movements upset the whole flotilla. In consequence of his lack of judgement and his lack of ability in handling his ship ... I am unable at present to recommend him for promotion.[5]

It was a heavy hit, but Hec Waller took it on the chin and knuckled down. It worked. When he left *Brazen* in April 1939 to return to Australia, his final report marked his performance as:

Very good ... he handles his ship and division well and appears to be quick to act and interpret his senior officers' intentions and has a good knowledge of destroyer duties.[6]

His admiral recommended him for promotion.

Now, this last day of the Sydney winter, he was at Garden Island with his first Australian command. There would be more learning to do, a great deal more. He had been away from home for almost three years. He barely knew his ship for, unusually, he had not served before in *Stuart* nor, for that matter, in any of the other four Australian destroyers. His first task on stepping aboard had been simply to find his way around, from stem to stern, from bridge to boiler room, for the captain had to know it all. Many if not most of his ship's company were strangers, with more still to arrive, men whose strengths or failings would only become apparent as he got to know them over time and – with war imminent – there was very little time. To add to the load, he had also been appointed Commander (D), the initial between the parentheses meaning that he was senior officer for all five destroyers, whose captains were junior to him and would expect leadership from him. For all his years of experience, Commander Waller was starting again on a new page. His customary pipe clenched between his teeth, he went to it with the zeal the navy expects of its officers and which would be his hallmark.

—

That same Thursday, Signalman Les Clifford threaded his way through the hassle and hustle of Garden Island to find his ship. There she was, berthed just ahead of another destroyer, *Waterhen*. Smart in his best blue uniform, cap at a proper angle, kitbag slung over a shoulder, he mounted the gangway that linked *Stuart* to the wharf and saluted the Officer of the Day as he stepped onto the deck. His experienced eye saw that the ship was a mess, still far from a going concern. The place was littered with ropes and hawsers, crates and boxes containing who knew what, sacks of potatoes, cartons of tinned food, and various metal bits and pieces obviously destined for the engine room. He could hear the clink and thump of that most hated chore for the ordinary sailor, the filthy job of chiselling away at rust patches in the ship's steel. Up for'ard on the fo'c'sle, men in overalls were passing ammunition through a hatch to the magazines below.

Les was thirty-nine, the same age as Hec Waller, born in the Borough of Lambeth south of the Thames in London. In 1918, in the last year of the war, he'd enlisted at the Chatham dockyard in Kent as the lowest of the low, a boy second class. The navy sent him first to HMS Ganges, the notoriously hard-knuckle training school for youngsters at Shotley in Suffolk, but someone must have seen something in him, for he was plucked out of the scrum to be trained as a signalman.

This was to join an elite caste. Signalmen were the eyes and voice of a warship. 'Bunting tossers' they called themselves, with some pride. Even long after the arrival of wireless at sea, much of the communication between ships by day was still done with hoists of multi-coloured flags whipping up the halyards on the foremast. It was secure, it was secret, there could be no enemy eavesdropping, it had worked well for 200 years and more. Each rectangle or triangle or swallowtail flag represented a letter of the alphabet, or a numeral, or when grouped together, a specific coded message or order, in bewildering array. There were exactly 201 flags and pendants in a ship's flag locker, and the trained signalman had to know – instantly – the use or meaning of each one or combinations of them. Sometimes that might be a matter of proper seamanship or courtesy, sometimes captains merely chatting socially to each other. Usually it was more serious. Admirals used flag signals to manoeuvre an entire fleet, where a mistake could mean anything from harmless but red-faced embarrassment to – quite literally – accident, collision, disaster and death at high speed.

By night or in filthy weather it was different again. Ships had powerful lamps that could project their light to the horizon. Usually known as an Aldis projector after the man who had invented them, they had shutters opened and closed by a hand-operated lever. Aiming the projector at the recipient, clacking at the lever, working the shutters furiously, the signalman would transmit his message in Morse Code, *dit dah dit*, another job that required considerable practice when both sending and receiving messages. Semaphore was a third though not so common trick, waving hand-held flags in a different position for each letter of the alphabet.

All of this was hard enough to learn and perform on dry land. At sea, in ships heaving and pitching and rolling in heavy weather, it was hard enough just keeping your balance. In cold weather, bending a hoist to the halyards could leave your hands numb, blue and bloody. Even with powerful binoculars, the signals you were trying to read from many miles away were small scraps of colour, still more difficult to discern if a gale was blowing the flags directly away from you. On a howling night with the rain bucketing down, a distant Aldis projector would be a pinprick of light glimpsed through binoculars smeared with spray and salt, the signalman's eyes red-rimmed with fatigue. It was a job for a quick brain, perfect vision, a steady hand, and an iron constitution. There were no excuses.

Les Clifford clambered down the hatch where the ammunition was being passed and onto the for'ard mess decks where the sailors lived, slept and ate. His mess was a cramped compartment running along one side of the ship, a space about 10 metres long by about 3 metres wide. There were wooden lockers for clothing and a few personal belongings, one for each man, some of them fixed to the bulkheads at either end, others used for seating around the plain wooden table where meals were served. Light entered via a couple of portholes, or 'scuttles' as the navy called them. There were a few sailors seated at the table. Les introduced himself.

'How many blokes down here?' he asked.

'About ten,' they said.

Part of the space was already taken up by a low-power generator and the wireless telegraphy transmitting motor, which were making a quiet hum. It was going to be noisy and cramped. Couldn't be helped.

Les had not been in time for the Great War. He first went to sea in 1919 in the cruiser *Danae*, serving in the grey, dreary Baltic Sea in that dogged but confused attempt to thwart the Bolsheviks. Unofficially known as Cowan's War after the British admiral in command,[7] it had been a nasty business, much of it fought in bitter midwinter and only partly successful in guaranteeing the independence of the Baltic states of Latvia, Lithuania and Estonia. There were ships lost and men killed on both sides. Mutinies by war-weary crews in several British ships were harshly put down.

After four years, Les left the Royal Navy in 1923 when his last ship, the ancient cruiser HMS *Gibraltar*, was sold off for scrap. More accurately, the navy left him, in the savage cutbacks to Britain's defence budgets in the 1920s when thousands of officers and men were thrown on the civilian unemployment scrap heap. Australia had seemed a better prospect and he emigrated to Melbourne, where – a literate man – he found work as a jobbing journalist. In 1936 he enlisted in the Royal Australian Naval Reserve as a part-time sailor, both to keep up his signal skills and for the very welcome £3 a month it paid him. There was not much promotion, though, not for the 'Rockies', as they called the reserves. At his age he should have been no mere low-ranked signalman but a petty officer, a yeoman or even chief yeoman of signals in the navy's hallowed terminology, pulling down a wage of eleven shillings a day. But no such luck.

All his time at sea Les kept a diary. Technically it was forbidden for security reasons but a few men did it secretly, scratching away in the mess decks at night. In the last year of the war he put it all down in a small book, *The Leader of the Crocks*. It is a delightful eye-witness account.

After dumping his belongings in the mess, Les climbed up the ladders to the bridge to find his new boss, Chief Yeoman Clem Page, sorting through still more paperwork.

On reporting myself for duty, I was greeted with a broad smile. Evidently I was welcome.

'We are due to commission tomorrow,' said the C.Y.S., 'and so far we are the only two of our staff on board. Our appropriated complement is ten.'

He added, 'I hope the rest arrive before we go to sea, or we'll be taking our meals up here.'[8]

Page was an old-timer, born in 1897, enlisted in 1922. He had served in cruisers and destroyers, just about every ship the navy had to offer, taking the rough with the smooth. He had a good point. The RAN was scrambling to crew its ships and *Stuart* was struggling for men. More kept arriving each day, some of them kids as fresh and green as grass from the training school at the Flinders Naval Depot, officially known as HMAS Cerberus, lying some 70 kilometres south-east of Melbourne on Western Port Bay, but none of them 'bunting tossers'. Hec Waller was short of officers too. He had been promised a navigator as soon as one could be found but no one had turned up yet, which very likely meant, for the time being, that he would have to share the job with his executive officer, Rupert Robison, another burden for the two of them.

Lieutenant Robison was the son of a clergyman, born in Springwood in the Lower Blue Mountains west of Sydney. A tall young man of thirty, newly married to his wife Jenny, his career had taken the usual route from the RANC in 1922 to a brace of British battleships – *Barham, Royal Sovereign, Resolution* – and then back home to whatever the peacetime RAN had to offer including, usefully, a previous spell in *Stuart*. He knew her. Now, as her second in command he was officially known as the First Lieutenant, unofficially by his fellow officers as 'Number One', and still less officially to the ship's company as 'Jimmy the One', or just 'the Jimmy'.

It was the First Lieutenant's job to present his captain with the ship and her crew as a going concern, clean and efficient, 'in all respects ready for sea', as the official phrase had it. Even in such a small ship as *Stuart*, hallowed naval custom and practice required captains to live in Olympian isolation, not standing a regular watch on the bridge, taking their meals alone, not dining in the officers' wardroom unless they were specifically invited. Captains gave their orders and let their demands and wishes be known but it was the First Lieutenant who ran the show, with the heads of the ship's departments: the Chief Engineer, the Chief Bosun's Mate, the Torpedo Gunner, the Gunnery Officer, the Paymaster Chief Petty Officer, the Chief Yeoman, and other assorted odds and sods. For Rupert Robison on 31 August 1939, it meant still more paper: list after list of this and that, of sailors to be assigned to their messes and watches and action stations, cipher logs, dockets and receipts to be checked and signed, lists of punishments and promotions: it went on and on. If there was a break in the paper, there was a constant patrol to be done on the upper deck and down below, checking the work underway, assigning men to some new task that had suddenly sprung up. It was gradually getting itself sorted, in fits and starts, order appearing out of seeming chaos.

Much of the heavy lifting fell on the Chief Engineer, Lieutenant Commander (E)[9] Walter Herbert Stanley Rands, born in the little mining town of Lithgow west of the Blue Mountains. He had graduated from the college a year after Hec Waller with the prizes for gunnery and engineering theory. Since the end of sail, seaman officers had liked to joke about engineers as grubby mechanics, a lower breed, but everyone knew that without them the ship did not move, as simple as that. Wal Rands ruled his own kingdom deep in the bowels below the waterline, a hot, stifling, cramped, deafeningly noisy and mysterious realm of engine and boiler rooms, with their valves and dials and wheels and ladders and steel gratings and miles upon miles of asbestos-clad piping winding here, there and everywhere.

On those rare occasions that First Lieutenants or even Captains entered this kingdom they knew their place and behaved with due deference. The denizens of the engine spaces – stokers and engine room artificers – were known as the 'Black Gang', a hangover from the days when working in the stokehold of coal-burning ships left them almost perpetually smeared with coal dust. *Stuart* was oil-fired, but the name had stuck to the breed. Stokers were a knockabout mob who kept to themselves, who messed together, and who were more likely than not to be at the centre of any brawl on a run ashore or to return late from an evening's leave hopelessly drunk. As the ship made ready this day, two or three of them would appear on deck every so often with their chief at their head, clad in oily overalls and squinting in the sunshine, to seize some newly arrived item of their trade and lump it below again. In *Stuart*, they had a hard, exacting job ahead. The raw truth was that her machinery was old and worn, as tired as the ship herself. Held together with chewing gum and string, was the wry joke. It would require dogged, unremitting nursing to keep it going.

—

As the sun began to lower west of the Harbour Bridge, the civilian dockyard workers who had been plying their various trades on *Stuart* downed tools and headed for the Woolloomooloo pubs, leaving behind their usual clutter of lunch wrappers, old newspapers and cigarette butts shockingly stubbed out on the deck. Much of the chaos of the day had subsided and by the time the First Lieutenant made his evening rounds of the mess decks things were in tolerable shape, as good as could as you could expect. *Stuart* and her ship's company slept quietly that night.

Others did not. In Germany, the Nazis were readying an act of deceit cynical even by their own depraved standards. After months of belligerent threats to Poland, Hitler needed a *casus belli*, a reason for war. Operation Himmler, named for the SS chief Heinrich Himmler, would launch a series of false flag attacks on the German–Polish border, choreographed to convince the world that the Poles had fired the first shots.

At Gleiwitz, a small frontier town on the German side, a squad of seven SS thugs dressed in Polish uniforms had been waiting for a fortnight for the order to go into action. It came at 8 pm Berlin time, a coded telephone message: '*grossmutter gestorben*', 'grandmother died'.

In two cars the SS men stormed the grounds of a local radio station, brandishing pistols, shooting into the air and terrifying the staff. One of them, a Polish speaker, barged into a studio, seized a microphone, and bellowed that the station was in Polish hands. A technician shut down the studio before any more could be heard, but it was enough. And the SS had a few more theatrical touches to add realism.

The squad had captured a local Polish farmer known for his out-spoken hatred of Germany. He was drugged with a hypodermic needle, dressed in a Polish army uniform and dragged into the radio station where he was shot several times and his body left on the steps of the building. In half a dozen similar stunts along the border, at customs posts and railway stations, another grisly operation tagged as *Konserve* (canned goods) saw prisoners from the Dachau concentration camp also drugged, clad in Polish uniforms and shot, their faces disfigured to avoid any chance of recognition.

The next day, Friday, 1 September, American foreign correspondents in Berlin were invited to view the locations of these treacherous Polish attacks upon the sacred soil of the Third Reich, complete with corpses still in place. Duped, they duly reported them. The truth of Gleiwitz would not emerge until after the war.

For most of August, the Führer had been deftly juggling a handful of moving parts, all of which had to slot into line before he could march on Poland. Britain and France had agreed to guarantee Poland's territorial integrity, but Hitler believed he could keep them on the back foot and hesitating, with every chance that they would stop at the brink as they had at Munich. That strategy seemed to be working. Critically, the Russians had been squared away with the diplomatic coup of the Molotov-Ribbentrop Pact. The Luftwaffe and the army were poised and awaiting the word.

The war at sea was another consideration. All of the Kriegsmarine's available U-boats had begun sailing from 19 August into their assigned patrol areas in the Atlantic. Two of the three commerce-raiding heavy cruisers that the British called 'pocket battleships', the *Admiral Graf Spee* and the *Deutschland*, had also slipped secretly into the Atlantic to await orders. The cruisers could stay out indefinitely for they had supply tankers with them, but the U-boats had limited endurance and the war would have to start well before they had to return home to refuel.

With Operation Himmler done and dusted the stage was set. Hitler was in a buoyant mood. He had all he needed. He had set the timetable for the invasion of Poland in April and kept it to the day. General Franz Halder, Chief of Staff of the Army High Command, noted in his diary:

Führer calm, has slept well ... he expects France and England will not take action.[10]

At exactly 4.40 am Berlin and Warsaw time, the Wehrmacht hurled itself across the Polish borders, blitzkrieg from the south, the west and the north.

—

In peacetime, commissioning a warship is a moment for ritual and celebration. The ship's company is in best uniform, officers with swords and medals, and very likely there are family, friends and VIP guests watching on from the wharf with a band playing. There might even be an admiral for added glamour as a gleaming new White Ensign is raised on the flagstaff at the stern.

This day there was no time for all that. *Stuart*'s ship's company, or those who could be spared from essential jobs, were hastily assembled on the quarterdeck. Hec Waller said a few words, now lost to history; the flag went up, and the job was done. Once again she was His Majesty's Australian Ship *Stuart*. Much the same happened on the destroyer *Waterhen* lying astern, where her commanding officer, Lieutenant Commander Jim Swain, an Irishman on loan from the Royal Navy, was also readying for sea. Then it was back to work again, with the familiar navy routine humming smoothly.

With Berlin eight hours behind Sydney, news of the onslaught on Poland did not reach Australia until early that Friday evening, for those who might have been listening to the BBC on short-wave radio. It burst with its full flood in the newspapers of Saturday morning, 2 September, in the blackest of triple-decker headlines. In Sydney, the Labor *Daily News* put out an extra edition:

BOMBERS RAIN DEATH ON POLAND
Our Own Cable Service, London, Friday
Details of stark warfare come seeping through the mass of cable news of the German offensive in Poland.

The German army is attacking on three fronts – East Prussia, the Moravian border, and from Breslau.

It is reported that fifty German planes made the first raid on Warsaw, which was continued until 9.40 a.m.

Hundreds of civilians – men, women and children – were burnt to death by a merciless rain of incendiary bombs from German planes, a message states.

German forces are smashing their way towards Warsaw ...[11]

War was nearer than ever. In Australia, life went on in an almost surreal calm tinged with apprehension. The Great War, just twenty years earlier, had been fought to end all wars. Yet here it was again. People clung to the safe, to the comfortingly familiar, as if that might somehow deflect the worst. The exciting new Australian tennis champions John Bromwich and Adrian Quist were due to play the Americans Bobby Riggs and Frank Parker in the opening round of the Davis Cup in Philadelphia this Saturday, with their coach, Harry Hopman, telling the newspapers, 'I'm certain we'll win'.[12]

Sydney's Rugby League final was that afternoon at the Cricket Ground, South Sydney versus Balmain, with the experts picking Balmain, although Mr Arthur Frizelle, vice president of the New South Wales Rugby League, quixotically chose Souths because the players often wore dinner suits.

'When they're not playing football team members are constantly in each other's company,' he told the *Daily Telegraph*. 'This makes them combine better on the field. Souths were called the "Rabbitohs" until they began to wear dinner suits. That's all over now.'[13]

Twenty-six thousand people went to see Balmain beat the dinner suits 33–4. In Melbourne, the Victorian Football League was playing its final round before the semis, with the match of the day between Collingwood and Richmond and the secretary of the League, Mr L. H. McBrien, assuring fans the games would certainly go on:

We feel that in keeping the game going we are performing a public service. I read the other day a statement by the Prime Minister [Mr Menzies] that we should be calm. We can rely on our leaders doing everything possible in the present crisis, and we, as a sporting body, are behind them.[14]

That afternoon, even as the games were under way, the prime minister broadcast to the nation on the ABC.

This has proven a most disturbing and anxious night. You have heard the news of the attack by Germany on Poland.

At present I have no official confirmation of these matters, though the frequency and character of the reports would appear to leave little doubt that hostilities have begun.

I do know the British Cabinet has met, that it is in urgent consultation with the French Government, and that we are on the very brink of war.[15]

History was tumbling over itself, a headlong rush. Sunday 3 September was fine and cool again, with work on board *Stuart* eased back and leave granted for some of the crew. In the mess decks and the wardroom the radios were tuned for the latest. That evening they heard the reedy voice of Neville Chamberlain announce that Berlin had not replied to the British ultimatum for Germany to withdraw from Poland. War it would be.

An hour later, at 9.15 pm, Menzies made another broadcast:

Fellow Australians, it is my melancholy duty to inform you officially that in consequence of a persistence by Germany in her invasion of Poland, Great Britain has declared war upon her and that, as a result, Australia is also at war ...

At 9.50 pm the British Admiralty's war telegram arrived at Navy Office in Melbourne, the order to go to all-out war. It was coldly succinct: TOTAL GERMANY. That was repeated to Australian ships, wherever they might be, followed a short time later by another signal somewhat more discursive: COMMENCE HOSTILITIES AT ONCE WITH GERMANY.

Until the very last minute, Les Clifford – one of millions – had hoped and believed that war might be avoided. 'My firm conviction was shattered,' he wrote.[16]

At 11 pm, the shrill of 'Pipe Down' echoed through *Stuart* at Garden Island and she fell into an uneasy sleep. That night, on the other side of the world, the Kriegsmarine's *U-30* stalked and then fired two torpedoes into the British liner SS *Athenia*. She sank off Northern Ireland with the loss of 117 of her passengers and crew.

The war at sea had begun.

# CHAPTER 3

# TRAVELLING NORTH

Being in all respects ready for sea, slip at 1100 and proceed in accordance with previous orders.

*Stuart* had been awake since 0600 hours, the men's hammocks lashed and stowed, breakfast eaten; the destroyer vibrating gently to the hum of the blowers and the rumble of her engines as Wal Rands raised steam to get under way. A blue haze wafted from her funnels. She had passed the last few days completing her stores and ammunition, scrubbing up to a respectable naval cleanliness and receiving a few more late arrivals to join the ship's company, including a couple of extra signalmen scraped together from other ships at the base and a young officer from the Reserve, Sub Lieutenant Robert Scott, who told the captain he knew how to navigate. Still no full-time navigator, though. *Stuart* was now as ready as she could be in the time allotted to her. The captain had spent hours planning a rigorous program of drills and exercises to test the ship and to begin the long, exacting job of welding her crew into a well-trained, disciplined fighting unit.

It was Friday, 8 September 1939, another glorious spring day. In his tiny sea cabin just behind the bridge, Hec Waller had cleared his mind of the ties of home to concentrate on his departure: his sailing plan, exactly how he would leave the berth, what to do in case of a sudden engine breakdown or a steering failure, say, within the confines of the harbour, or perhaps someone just cocking up an order. You prepared for anything and everything. On schedule, he received the formal word from the first lieutenant and the chief engineer that *Stuart* was ready to proceed. No matter how experienced a captain might be, this was always a testing time in an unfamiliar ship with a new crew; a moment of acute awareness. The men would be watching him like seagulls at a bag of chips to see if he knew his business, to see if he got the ship neatly away from the dock or whether he backed and filled uncertainly in a hasty flurry of helm and engine orders. Reasonably enough, sailors like to know they are in the care of a competent ship-handler. They are keen and unforgiving judges. The bosun's call split the air and the PA began to crackle.

'Hands to stations for leaving harbour. Special sea duty men close up. Close all scuttles and X and Y doors ...'

*Stuart* echoed to the stamp of boots on steel ladders as the men took their assigned positions and more orders snapped out in succession. Up on the bow the fo'c'sle officer began singling up his wires, one by one releasing the bonds that held *Stuart* to the continent of Australia until there was just one wire spring running aft from the starboard bow to the wharf. Out on the starboard wing of the bridge Hec judged his moment.

'Slow ahead port. Starboard twenty.'

The bells of the engine room telegraph jangled and after a few seconds a froth of white water began churning beneath the stern. The captain moved to check the rudder indicator and the revolution gauges, to see if his orders had been obeyed correctly. They had. The destroyer's bow, still held by the spring, nudged inwards towards the heavy coir rope fenders hanging over the side to protect her hull, pulling the stern gently outwards. More orders.

'Midships. Slow astern both.'

The fo'c'sle crew ran the last wire in through the fairleads and she slipped cleanly from the wharf and backed out towards the finger piers in Woolloomooloo Bay.

'Stop both main engines.'

She was free.

'Slow ahead both, port ten.'

She was under way.

*Waterhen* followed her down the sunlit harbour in line astern, past the foremast of the first HMAS *Sydney* mounted on Bradleys Head off to port. *Stuart* had carried the Governor-General to the dedication of that mast just five years before, a memorial to the old cruiser's battle with the German raider *Emden* in 1914, the RAN's first victory. Further on down the harbour then, a sharpish turn to starboard and out into the Tasman Sea. With *Waterhen* under Hec's orders as Commander (D), the two destroyers cruised off the coast that day, beginning the working-up program that would turn them into a going concern and patrolling for submarines possibly lurking off Sydney Heads that night.

—

Early the next afternoon, *Stuart* received a signal that electrified them all. Two boys at Terrigal, a sleepy beach village some 30 kilometres north of Sydney, had reported to the local police that they had seen a submarine surface out at sea. *Stuart* was ordered to the scene at full speed. The captain sounded action stations, the first for the war. The excitement was intense, men closed up at the guns, the torpedo tubes, the depth charge rails, on the signal deck. For a few hours they slowly criss-crossed the spot, back and forth, *Stuart*'s Asdic giving off its insistent, searching *pings*.

Asdic – known today as sonar – was a British invention developed by Admiralty scientists in the deepest secrecy after the First World War. It was both an electronic sender and receiver, projecting a sound-wave from a transmitter encased in a metal dome beneath a ship's hull, *ping … ping*. Slowly turning a small wheel, the Asdic operator could direct the transmitter through an arc of about 45 degrees either side of the ship. If that soundwave struck a solid underwater object it would bounce back an echo, *ping … bip, ping … bip*. You could then get a bearing on your target and, judging by the strength and frequency of the echo, an estimate of the range and, if it was moving, its speed and direction. But Asdic was by no means foolproof. It did not give you the depth of the submarine. The soundwave could also bounce an echo off rocks or wrecks on the seabed, whales, and even shoals of fish or schools of dolphins. Sometimes it could be confused by different thermal layers of water or a strong current below the surface.

A skilled operator could work out which was what but it took a lot of practice to get there.

As night began to fall, *Stuart* got her first contact.

'Echo bearing green one-five, sir!'

That meant something just off the starboard bow. The Anti-Submarine Officer, Lieutenant Geoffrey Corlett, another loan from the Royal Navy, clapped his headphones to his ears and stared intently at the small circular screen in front of him where a moving white line was pulsing to the sound. *Ping ... bip ...*

'Range 800 yards. Definitely a submarine, sir!'

Aft on the quarterdeck, the Commissioned Torpedo Gunner, Frank 'Shorty' Ley, and his men began to prime the depth charges ready on the stern.

'Range 500 yards!'

A depth charge looked like an oil drum. The 1939 version, the Royal Navy Mark VII, packed an explosive charge of 130 kilograms of Amatol, a mixture of TNT and ammonium nitrate. It could be set to explode at various depths and was, in theory, lethal to a submarine so long as it detonated within about 12 metres of the sub's pressure hull. The trick was to deliver it to the right spot; no easy task. Les Clifford, who was on the bridge, takes up the story:

> Excitement was now running high throughout the ship at the prospect of not only having a crack at the enemy but of being the first ship to do so within Australian territorial waters.
>
> 'Full ahead both,' was the next order given.
>
> The engines pulsated in reply to the telegraph, and every nerve in the ship was tense with anticipation.
>
> 'Fire one,' ordered the captain.
>
> A few seconds later the stillness of the night was shattered with a 'crumph crumph' as the depth charges exploded beneath the waters astern of the ship, shaking the old vessel from stem to stern and throwing columns of water high into the air ... *Stuart* had struck her first angry blow of the war.[1]

Eager eyes scanned the boiling sea, hoping for a slick of oil rising to the surface or perhaps some debris to indicate a sinking or damaged enemy, but there was nothing. Hec brought the destroyer around and made another run, the Asdic still in contact, and again the depth charges rolled over. Back on shore, *Stuart*'s signal that she was engaging a submarine caused a sensation. Cooler heads might have thought it highly unlikely, even fanciful, that a U-boat could turn up on Australia's doorstep this early in the war. It would not have the range to get there from Germany, for a start.[2] But no one was taking chances. Sydney Harbour, Newcastle and Port Kembla were closed for outbound shipping.

*Stuart* kept up the attack all night at slow speed, the residents of Terrigal lying sleepless as the depth charges exploded with a dull *woomph*. The next morning *Waterhen* joined to help in the search and an RAAF aircraft flew over to look for any floating wreckage, but the sea surface was calm and clear. Disappointed, they gave it up as a bad job.

A few days later, *Stuart* headed back to the scene with a motor launch and some navy divers who went down for a look. They found a large outcrop of rock on the seabed with a sheer face about 4 metres high. A strong current swirling past it might well have given the impression of a moving object. It was a lesson well learned and known forever after, with wry good humour, as the 'Battle of Terrigal'.

For the rest of the month, the two destroyers hurled themselves into the schedule of training and exercises that Hec Waller had drawn up, sometimes singly, sometimes in company, and a couple of times with the heavy cruiser *Canberra* off Jervis Bay south of Sydney. The program for 25 September was typical:

Range and inclination tests.
Sub-divisional dummy torpedo attacks
Sub-calibre firing day and night.
Single Ship torpedo firings.
Officer of the Watch manoeuvres.
High Angle firing at kite target.
PM anchored in Jervis Bay.[3]

It was hard, it was testing, it was exhausting. There were drills for fighting a fire anywhere from the galley to the engine room, for lowering a boat, for shoring up a bulkhead in damage control, for dealing with a steering breakdown, for hustling casualties below to the sickbay, and any other accident or incident the captain could devise, all suddenly called without a moment's notice and done at the double. For the old-timers in the crew it was nothing new, nothing to get excited about, something in which they could take a professional pride. For the green-as-grass recruits it was daunting, sometimes mystifying. For two days off Twofold Bay on the New South Wales south coast the weather turned foul, with driving rain, high winds and heavy seas pounding over the fo'c'sle. Most of the crew were laid low with seasickness, even some of the hard-bitten veterans, and the misery was compounded by newly revealed leaks which sent streams of water sloshing through the mess decks. Hec Waller allowed them a few hours leave in the fishing port of Eden, recording later that ...

> There were no absentees, but *Stuart* had one case of drunkenness. It is worthy of reporting that this rating, Stoker O. H. Sharpe, ON 19391, in his drunken state sang 'The Red Flag'. I am not familiar with this song, but I am assured by one of my officers that such was the case.[4]

Gradually, steadily, they came together as a crew. Some things that had seemed impossible at the beginning were now done with newly acquired learning and often some sense of accomplishment. Some of it was even enjoyable, like banging away on the pom-poms or the Lewis machine guns. There was satisfaction in getting it right, in not copping a blast from the First Lieutenant or a petty officer for some sin real or imagined. *Stuart*'s men were no longer a collection of individuals but forming into a cohesive, coherent ship's company, an efficient fighting unit, and the same went for *Waterhen*. This was the first test and they had come through it. Back at Garden Island, now busier than ever, the ship had some minor engine and machinery defects to be fixed. But they were ready, they thought, for what might come their way.

—

In the mills of power in Canberra and London and at Navy Office
in Melbourne, wheels were slowly grinding. As peace evaporated,
Australia cabled London on 30 August:

> In the present international situation the Commonwealth Govern-
> ment desire to place the ships of the R.A.N. and their personnel
> at the disposal of the United Kingdom Government, but find it
> necessary to stipulate that no ships (other than HMAS *Perth*)
> should be taken from Australian waters without prior concurrence
> of Commonwealth Government.[5]

In short, and unlike in the First World War, Britain would have to
request permission to deploy Australian warships. The reason lay in one
word: Japan. Looking north, white Australia saw a modern, powerful
Japanese navy and the Imperial Japanese Army locked in a long, brutal
war with China. Japan was notionally neutral but it had aligned itself
with Hitler's Germany in the Anti-Comintern pact of 1936, ostens-
ibly directed against the spread of global communism. Over time, the
public pronouncements of the Japanese emperor's politicians, generals
and admirals had become increasingly unfriendly towards the demo-
cratic west, particularly the United States and Australia.

With the war less than a week old and the Royal Navy already hard
pressed in the Atlantic, Britain made her first request, in a cable on
8 September from the Secretary for the Dominions, Anthony Eden, to
the British High Commissioner in Canberra, Sir Geoffrey Whiskard.
Assuming that Japan remained neutral – and H.M. Government was
confident it would – perhaps a cruiser and five destroyers could be …

> lent for service other than on the Australian Station. So long as
> Japan remains neutral it is considered that Australian waters may
> be regarded as unlikely to suffer submarine attack.[6]

The High Commissioner passed it on. Following that up a few
days later, Eden wrote that:

> the Admiralty would not propose in the first instance to employ
> the second cruiser and five destroyers west of Suez.[7]

The Menzies War Cabinet of senior ministers considered the request on 2 October. There were misgivings. The government was not convinced that the British were fully alive to the menace of Japan. But eventually the cabinet agreed that a cruiser, HMAS *Sydney*, could be offered up, and that the five destroyers of the Scrap Iron Flotilla would be sent to the newly built naval base on the island fortress of Singapore, the Empire's impregnable bastion against any Japanese expansion in the Far East.

The die was cast.

—

Saturday, 14 October 1939. A misty morning rain dimmed the harbour as *Stuart*, *Waterhen* and a third destroyer, HMAS *Vendetta*, slipped at Garden Island. Off and away again. The men had been up well before the dawn. Colours had been piped in the drizzle at 0800 hours. An hour later they were on their way out to sea, fading into the grey horizon.

Emotions run high when you know you will be away for a long time. Some men are nervous, some are anxious, some are excited, spanning a gamut from apprehension to anticipation. Some are keen to get to sea again. Others are too busy to feel too much at all – here we go again, job to do – and some perhaps are just plain hungover from a last run ashore the night before. Some worry about the onset of seasickness. Some with wives and children feel sadness or an emptiness, sometimes a lurking sense of guilt at leaving them behind.

This time there were no farewells, no families waving goodbye at the wharf, no streamers from ship to shore as there might have been in peacetime. Here was the real thing at last. Not another training exercise, not a jaunt down to Jervis Bay but a departure for the war.

Over in the west at Fremantle, two more destroyers, *Vampire* and *Voyager*, sailed the same day. Despite the supposed wartime secrecy, word had got around, and their leaving was a little more colourful. To the surprise and amusement of her captain, Lieutenant Commander James 'Copper' Morrow, *Voyager* sailed beneath a barrage of rotten tomatoes and abuse hurled by some ladies of the port angry at being left unpaid for services rendered.

No one save the ships' commanding officers had any idea of their destination, just that they were heading north. *Stuart*'s Supply Chief Petty Officer, Ken Sprague, had crammed the galley and every conceivable locker, store and nook and cranny with as much fresh and packaged food as he could squeeze on board, a sure indication that they would be away for a long time. Some of the buzz on the mess decks suggested they might be off to Singapore but the Rockies, the reservists, thought that wasn't on. They'd signed on to serve only in Australian waters, they said hopefully.

*Vampire, Vendetta, Voyager* and *Waterhen* were sister ships of the Admiralty's V and W class destroyers of about the same vintage as *Stuart* but a little different. From 1916, English and Scottish shipyards had been turning out V and Ws by the dozen, as fast as they could go. Sixty-seven of them were built in all, with another forty cancelled after the war ended. Like *Stuart*, they were advanced for their time, a design so successful, so tough and seaworthy, that it would set a benchmark for succeeding classes built for the next twenty years.

They had that singular destroyer look about them, a long and low silhouette of unmistakable purpose and power. At 1470 tons full load, a length of 95 metres and a beam of 9 metres, they were smaller than *Stuart*, and not quite so fast or well-armed. Three boilers and two Brown-Curtis turbines pumped out 27,000 shaft horsepower to twin screws for a best speed of 34 knots, although that had wearied a little with age. For a main armament they had four 4-inch guns, two fore and two aft; a 2-pounder four-barrel pom-pom anti-aircraft gun; one .303 Vickers machine gun and four of the old .303 Lewis guns. There were six torpedo tubes and space to carry fifty depth charges. The crew would be around 130 men, depending.

*Vendetta*, the oldest of the four sisters, was the only one to have fought in the First World War, at the Second Battle of Heligoland Bight in 1917, an inconclusive scrap of cruisers and destroyers and two or three bigger ships a little south of that corner of the North Sea where Germany meets Denmark. At one time or another, she and the other three had been involved in Cowan's War in the Baltic. Royalty had also graced *Vendetta*'s deck. In March 1925 she escorted the sailor king, George V, on a tour of the Mediterranean. The arrival of the four in Australia in 1933 was somewhat less glamorous, like a quartet of retired old warriors put out to a colonial pasture. In this year, 1939, *Vendetta* had ceremonially carried the flag- and flower-covered coffin of Prime Minister Joe Lyons back to his home in Tasmania after his death in Sydney in April.

—

The trip north was almost a pleasure cruise, or as close to one as you would ever get in the navy. The weather stayed fair in both oceans, the Indian and the Pacific, and as it grew warmer towards the tropics the men off watch could laze about on deck in a pair of shorts, enjoying a smoke and soaking up the sun for a much-prized tan.

The Commander (D) himself would appear on *Stuart*'s bridge in shorts and a crumpled, open-necked shirt, feet in leather sandals, a battered old cricket hat on his close-cropped head and the inevitable pipe clamped between his teeth. The ship's company were getting the measure of him now, knowing his whims and ways, his likes and dislikes, as you had to do with a captain.

Ean McDonald was a twenty-one-year-old ordinary signalman in *Stuart*, a reservist from Perth called up for the war. Smart and alert, he would serve in all five of the destroyers and eventually gain a commission and command a ship. He too kept a diary and wrote a memoir in which he included a sketch of Hec:

> He was a virile man, quietly confident, calmly inspiring, and usually good for a chuckle. Always crisp and definite in orders, he was unforgiving of fools but very knowledgeable of his craft and in my own field of signals.
>
> Once trying to repair a rope binding around the bridge ladder rail, Hec came up behind me to mount to the bridge. I went to scuttle aside but he stopped and said, 'Well, McDonald, do you know how to finish off that lashing?' When I replied 'no' he said, 'Well let me show you' and he did it with skill.[8]

Hec was a holy terror if you got on the wrong side of him, they told each other, but he was a fair and reasonable man if you did your job. Sometimes when you told him something you might get just a grunt in return. There were times when he appeared far away, lost in

thought. But he was not arrogant or haughty, far from it, and sometimes he could surprise by suddenly starting up an amiable chat with
a bridge lookout or the man on the wheel. Not that he treated you
as an equal; that could never be. A naval ship was not a democracy.
But he did not look down on you, either. You were more than just a
name or a number to him, and subtly he let you know it. The bonds
of loyalty began to form.

*Vampire* and *Voyager* headed directly for Singapore at an easy
15 to 20 knots, up the Indian Ocean and through the Sunda Strait
between Java and Sumatra. *Stuart*'s group steamed northwards off the
Queensland coast, calling briefly at Brisbane and Townsville to show
the flag. Robert Scott, the young sub lieutenant in *Stuart*, proved his
worth as navigator by taking them through the Barrier Reef at night,
no mean feat. They went west around Cape York through the Torres
Strait, called at Darwin to take on more stores and refuel and sailed
off north-west again to pass through the passage between Bali and
Lombok in the Netherlands East Indies.

The crews stood four-hour watches, normal navy routine, with the
two 'dog watches' of two hours each between 1600 and 2000 hours.
Action stations was sounded each day at a different time, to keep
them sharp, and there were constant drills and exercises for the same
reason. One day it might be gun drills or fire drills or man overboard,
the next day streaming paravanes for minesweeping, a complex piece
of seamanship involving floats and wires that was easy to get wrong.
Their wits grew sharper, their bodies fitter. The new men had put the
gut-wrenching horrors of seasickness behind them and they had their
sea legs now, the ability to move easily along a deck or up and down a
ladder with the motion of the ship.

Yet the living conditions were atrocious. A lot of custom and
practice in these destroyers had not changed since Nelson's day of
wooden ships and sails. The messes where the sailors ate and slept were
overcrowded and reeking, crawling with cockroaches and colonies
of rats. Les Clifford's small mess in *Stuart*, intended for perhaps ten
sailors, now had nineteen men and their belongings jammed in there,
sleeping wherever they could find a space to sling a hammock from the
deckhead. If there was no space you would have to curl up on a bench,
the mess table or even the deck itself. At sunset came the pipe to

darken ship, which meant closing all the scuttles, deadlights, hatches and doors so that not a glint of light might betray their presence to a prowling foe. There was a ventilation system which blew supposedly fresh air through the interior of the ships, but it was feeble at best and in the tropics it gave off only more stifling heat. These destroyers had been designed for the North Atlantic and the North Sea, and cooling had not come into it. Clifford described it in his memoir:

> The night air on the lower mess decks became polluted and acted as a mild anaesthetic on the personnel sleeping there. Clothed only in bathing trunks, one would perspire freely at the slightest exertion. The atmosphere was almost white-hot, and one could sense the thickness when descending from the purer air above decks. Added to these discomforts, the low-power generator in our mess kept up a continual noisy hum, occasionally squeaking for oil. At times the W/T transmitting motor would also be operating, and together they would drown all attempts at conversation.[9]

Many men preferred to take their hammocks and sleep out on the upper deck beneath the stars, which was officially frowned upon but unofficially condoned. Officers had cramped cabins with bunks in the after part of the ship, still small and smelling but something of an improvement, and they did have the wardroom to retreat to with an armchair or two to collapse in and a steward to serve their meals.

For the sailors, meals were another primitive routine, again largely unchanged since Nelson. There was no central dining area, no cafeteria. Each mess was issued its own rations. For the main meal, in the middle of the day, the mess would appoint its own cook, who would take the raw ingredients to the central galley. Ean McDonald's description cannot be bettered.

> In the galley were the full-time cooks. About once a week each sailor acted as a mess cook, appointed by each mess. Early in the forenoon the supply bloke would yell down the little hatch that led down the vertical steel ladder to our mess. The mess cook had to be alert enough to catch the allocated stores for the day as they were dropped and fell where they may. The daily batch could be a

great lump of frozen beef or tins of Bully or even the hated Spam.
The day's chunk of beef would be laid on the table and become the
subject of earnest consideration and finally an executive decision
was made as to what to do with it.

'Roast, stew, steaks, pie?'

The mess cook would set about hacking the meat accordingly.
Meantime, from under the hammock bin, another team would
drag out the bags of veggies stacked below and begin to peel and
chop as directed. Very occasionally we would have a creative mess
cook but generally meals were just something to eat. What could
anyone do with that horribly bland, tasteless junk after you'd tried
it cold in slices, warm in rissoles, hot wrapped in batter and fried,
or minced into a gluggy stew?

The food assemblage would be taken up a couple of decks to
the galley and handed to the ship's real cook. His job was simply
to follow its progress and take it out of his oven once cooked.
Returning with the cooked meal, the mess cooks would dole out
the portions, fend off the back-chat and collect the ditties. A couple
of deck levels above they would wash up in a tin basin, to be emptied
over the side, and finally return to their normal duties on watch.[10]

Keeping clean was another daily struggle. The Admiralty's naval
architects, serenely aware of the infrequent and reluctant bathing
habits of the British lower classes, had not troubled to provide baths
or showers for the sailors in the destroyers.[11] There were two open
spaces below decks at the break of the fo'c'sle, port and starboard,
each about 3 metres by 2, with a tiled floor and a drain and a line of
four chipped ceramic wash basins mounted on gimbals so they would
stay more or less level when the ship rolled. That was all, for 100 men
and more. There was no privacy, and there were no taps, either. You
drew a bucket of cold water from a hand pump on the upper deck,
gave it a quick blast from a steam pipe to heat it, then poured it into
one of the basins. Stripped naked, you shaved, then soaped up and
quickly sloshed more water over your body, wiping yourself down
with a washcloth and doing your best not to splash or bump into the
men next to you who were doing the same thing. At sea, many preferred to wash themselves from their bucket out on the upper deck

where at least there was a bit more space, but that was not permitted in harbour.

Washing your uniforms and underwear was yet another burden, another hot water and soap job in a bucket on the upper deck. There was no laundry. If you had a few shillings you could pay one of the 'firms' to do it for you, as the officers usually did. The firms were a uniquely shipboard institution, two or three men who would set themselves up to provide a service for their shipmates and make a quid at it. Laundry was known as *dhobying*, a Hindi word picked up by the Royal Navy back in the mists of time. Other firms would cut your hair, write your letters, or sell you filthy French postcards. Moneylending was known as 'jewing'. Most prized were the tailors who could take your Number One uniform with its swaggering bell bottom trousers and render it 'tiddly' as the saying went: skintight around your bum and your groin and a plunging neckline on your jacket that displayed your manly chest.

They took this life stoically, as a matter of course, the way things were. This generation of Australians was not accustomed to much in the way of comforts. A twenty-year-old sailor in 1939 had grown up a child of the Depression, quite likely with the cold reality of a father out of work, a mother not knowing where the next meal might come from, of going to school hungry in ragged shorts and bare feet. In the navy you got regular pay: seven shillings a day for an able seaman, with a little extra if you had a wife and kids. And these destroyer men were allowed an extra sixpence a day as compensation for the tough conditions; 'hard lying money' it was called. Harsh though the navy life could be, for a lot of men it was a good bargain, a deliverance from the uncertainties of civilian life for which they were grateful. They repaid it in full measure.

—

*Vampire* and *Voyager* arrived at the big Sembawang naval base on the north of Singapore island on 21 October 1939. *Stuart* and her consorts turned up a week later, berthing alongside the monitor HMS *Terror*, a slow, ugly lump of a ship that was basically a floating artillery battery, boasting two enormous 15-inch guns in a turret beneath her bridge. They would meet her again later, in very different circumstances.

The trip had been uneventful, though enlivened by the traditional, rollicking arrival of King Neptune on board as they crossed the equator. Off Borneo, Hec Waller had spiced things up by putting a shot across the bows of a small tanker that had not replied to his demands for a recognition signal. That produced a flurry of action. She turned out to be British and very apologetic.

Singapore was an eye-opener. Everyone got leave, a turn at a run ashore, with a hair-raising, white-knuckle 40-kilometre taxi ride over a winding, teeming road from the base to the city. Les Clifford found it confronting:

As we stepped out of the car, half a dozen rickshaw 'boys' swarmed around us. 'Me take you to Number One Girl,' they would chant. But according to their statements the 'Number One Girl' could be anything from French to heathen Chinese: the variety was apparently unlimited. This was definitely the Cesspool of the East. The 'boys' would follow us for miles, constantly pestering us to ride in their carriages; their patience seemed to be inexhaustible. The odour of the native cooking, added to the repugnant stench of the Singapore River was nauseating.[12]

It seems unlikely that everyone was as fastidious. Singapore then was a raw, feisty, colonial fleshpot that had been welcoming sailors for more than a century in the bars and brothels of the infamous Bugis Street, where the locals had a well-honed judgement of the demand for goods and services and the ways and means to supply them. The navy pragmatically issued condoms and sex was cheap and easily obtainable.

But there was work to do too, a rigorous program of engine and boiler room maintenance and exercises at sea in the coming days which, at last, included a real submarine to play with, HMS *Parthian*. For many, she was the first sub they had actually seen in the flesh. Each of the destroyers took turns at hunting her, groping in the dark at first, then gradually sharpening their skills to hold her in the Asdic pulses and run her down. And there was a welcome surprise: *Stuart*'s much promised navigating officer finally arrived. Lieutenant Norman Joseph Macdonald Teacher RN appeared on board out of the blue, just like that, sent over from a nearby British destroyer. A tall and lanky twenty-five-year-old Scot, the son of a British army officer, he sported a piratical black beard much admired and eventually copied by some of *Stuart*'s sailors.

Back at home, so far away now, the mills were grinding again. On 30 October, the day after *Stuart* arrived in Singapore, the British High Commissioner in Canberra formally wrote to Prime Minister Menzies to ask if the five destroyers might now be sent on to the Mediterranean. It would be abandoning the agreement struck just weeks before, that they would not be required 'west of Suez', but, to compensate, the Admiralty would send two cruisers to Australian waters to deal with any enemy surface raider that might appear.

There was no doubt that Britain was hard pressed at sea. The Battle of the Atlantic was growing fiercer each week, with losses mounting on both sides. Shockingly, on 14 October, *U-47* had penetrated the defences at the Royal Navy's northern base at Scapa Flow in the Orkney Islands, sinking the old battleship *Royal Oak* with the death of 835 of her crew. Yet Germany had made no serious attempt to carry the war to the Mediterranean. The Middle Sea was, in effect, a backwater. The Admiralty began withdrawing battleships, cruisers and destroyers from the Mediterranean Fleet for service in the North Sea and the North Atlantic. The five Australian ships would help plug the gaps they had left. The Menzies War Cabinet considered the request the next day and agreed to it.[13]

—

The five sailed from Singapore on 13 November, through the Strait of Malacca and into the Indian Ocean, bound for Ceylon. Again the destination remained secret, although the buzz on the mess decks was tipping the Med. There was some discontent from the Rockies, some of them still believing they had enlisted to serve only in Australian waters. That was how it was if you'd joined the army militia, they said. They could not send you overseas. Not entirely sure himself, Hec Waller sought a ruling from the Navy Board, which replied that, no, RAN reservists were required to go wherever their ships were sent. After some tactful handling, the grumbling eventually died away.

Then, once more, the game changed. On 15 November came the news that a small British tanker, the *Africa Shell*, had been sunk in the Indian Ocean by a German pocket battleship thought to be *Admiral Scheer*. It was in fact *Admiral Graf Spee*, which had already sunk five British merchant ships in the Atlantic before doubling around into the Indian Ocean to create a little havoc there. When they arrived in Ceylon the Australian destroyers were split up again, to be drawn into the hunt. *Stuart* was despatched on a long and solitary journey more than 3000 kilometres to the south-west across the Indian Ocean towards the African coast, where she was to join forces with a British cruiser and a French frigate.

It was yet another idyllic voyage across a calm, deep-blue ocean with barely another ship sighted, ploughing along at an easy speed and relaxed cruising stations, where ...

> an occasional bird swooped overhead, feathers glinting in the sunlight, and men scorched in the sun on deck or dripped sweat from their semi-naked bodies below decks.[14]

It took them a week, the pleasure of it fading when the fresh food began to run out, forcing the mess cooks to work their magic on rations of tinned salmon and the much-loathed Maconochie's Bully Beef Stew, another canned concoction of stringy, gluey meat and mushy vegetables. Maconochie's, a British firm, had been supplying rations to the fighting services of the British Empire since the Boer War, and the stuff tasted as you would expect. Fresh water began to run out too, so much so that the first lieutenant had a sentry posted on the upper deck pump. And overlaying it was a certain nervousness about what might happen if they did run into *Admiral Scheer* or *Graf Spee*, whichever it was. At 16,000 tons full load, a German pocket battleship – a Panzerschiff – carried six 11-inch guns and eight 6-inch guns and God alone knew how many torpedo tubes. If it came to trouble, *Admiral Graf Spee* could sit back at long range and safely and serenely blow *Stuart* out of the water.

They reached the French-owned island of Madagascar in December, berthing in the little harbour of Diego Suarez near a handsome colonial sloop, the *Rigault de Genouilly*, whose *matelots* happily introduced their new Australian allies to ridiculously cheap and plentiful champagne in the local bars. The French port authorities, though, were much less helpful with supplies. It was puzzling at first, then infuriating. Promised deliveries of food simply did not arrive and Ken Sprague, the Supply Chief Petty Officer, had to tell the captain he had been frustrated at every turn. They christened the place 'Dago Squares'. When the news came that *Graf Spee* had returned to the Atlantic, *Stuart* resumed her long haul to the Mediterranean, sailing north again for Aden at the mouth of the Red Sea, the ship's company gloomily resigned to subsisting on more Maconochie's and the jaw-breaking, weevilly hard tack they called 'Pusser's biscuits'.

Two days into their journey the bridge lookouts sighted smoke on the horizon. The captain ordered action stations and the men tumbled to their posts, guns loaded and training as they closed the stranger, an oil tanker. When *Stuart* demanded her identity she began to turn away in a heavy cloud of smoke. The captain ordered a shot across her bows, which brought her to a quick standstill and sent her signal letters flapping up her foremast. She was friendly, identifying herself as the *British Chivalry*, bound from Cape Town to the Persian Gulf. Apologising profusely, she said she had thought *Stuart* was German. Hec had a sudden thought. 'Signal her again,' he said. 'Do you have any food to spare?'

She did. British chivalry indeed. She offered a carcass of mutton, and fresh beef and potatoes as well. Salvation! *Stuart* lowered a boat in record time, with Ken Sprague on board carrying a wad of cash to pay for it. The Battle of the Indian Ocean, they called it later. They ate like kings on the way to Aden.[15]

From there it was up through the scorching heat and blinding light of the Red Sea, an ordeal all the more horrible when an engine breakdown forced them to a standstill, the ship drifting listlessly on a calm sea while the engineers battled to fix the problem and a big shark lazily circled them. To entertain the crew, Hec emptied his revolver into the shark's head and the beast was hauled aboard, where its jaws were eventually cleaned and hung as a trophy on the fo'c'sle. After a few hours they got going again, plodding up the Suez Canal to call at Port Said and then into the Mediterranean proper, the weather now much cooler and kinder.

In the early afternoon of Sunday, 17 December, the fortress island of Malta appeared on the horizon. HMAS *Stuart* made her number to the Castille signal station and eased her way past the ancient and spectacular stone ramparts guarding Grand Harbour, Valletta. That same day brought a triumphant close to the first great naval victory of the war, far away across the Atlantic. Harried by British cruisers, the beaten *Graf Spee* sailed from the refuge she had taken in the Uruguayan port of Montevideo and scuttled herself in a Wagnerian funeral pyre in the estuary of the Rio de la Plata, the River Plate at the border of Uruguay and Argentina.

Three days later in Buenos Aires, her captain, Hans Langsdorff, wrote letters home to his family and naval superiors:

> I can now only prove by my death that the fighting services of the Third Reich are ready to die for the honour of the flag. I alone bear the responsibility for scuttling the panzerschiff *Admiral Graf Spee*. I am happy to pay with my life for any possible reflection on the honour of the flag. I shall face my fate with firm faith in the cause and the future of the nation and of my Führer.[16]

Lying on *Graf Spee*'s red, black, and white battle ensign, Langsdorff shot himself with a pistol.

Remarkably, the ship's last days and hours were seen by millions. Newsreel cinematographers had been filming ever since her arrival in Montevideo, with all the comings and goings of diplomats and Langsdorff himself. On the day she sailed, the British Gaumont company had an enterprising cameraman in a light aircraft above. He captured the explosions, the flames and pillars of smoke, the breaking hull, the collapsing superstructure, everything.

The films were flown around the world for a British propaganda coup, reaching Australia in mid-January. Thousands queued in the cities and every country town with a theatre. It was:

> One of the most remarkable, and certainly the most dramatic, newsreels ever seen on the screen ... No verbal account of the episode, no matter how vivid, can give any adequate idea of the terrific spectacle.[17]

Everyone was entirely satisfied. The long arm of the Royal Navy had reached out to seize and destroy the enemy, as was only to be expected, as it had always done.

*Stuart* and her sisters prepared to join the Mediterranean Fleet.

# CHAPTER 4

# THAT FIRST CHRISTMAS

In the very centre of the Mediterranean, some 150 kilometres south of Sicily, the island of Malta is a jewel prized by conquerors down the ages. In the sixteenth century, the Holy Roman Emperor, Charles V, gave the island to the Knights Hospitaller of St John of Jerusalem, a religious order of chivalry. They held it for 250 years, building its little cities and its churches, its formidable forts and grand castles. Napoleon Bonaparte briefly took Malta from the knights until it was ceded to Britain under the Treaty of Paris in 1814.

Through the nineteenth century and into the twentieth, Britain secured Malta and the Grand Harbour at Valletta as the base for the battleships of its Mediterranean Fleet, the Royal Navy's most prestigious command, the guardian of the sea routes to the Empire east of Suez. For generations, men of the great Maltese family clans – the Borgs, the Micallefs, the Zammits, the Attards – found secure work in the dockyards and provision stores. Others served as civilian canteen staff in ships of the Royal Navy, the positions jealously handed down from father to son. Some of them worked in canteens for the RAN too.

But by the end of 1939 the Mediterranean Fleet had all but evaporated, the battleships and most of its cruisers and all its destroyers withdrawn for the Battle of the Atlantic. That October, an attempt by the Kriegsmarine to pass three U-boats through the Strait of Gibraltar ended in fiasco when *U-53* ran short of fuel, *U-25* cracked its pressure hull and the third – *U-26*, which did make it through – unaccountably found nothing to sink and returned home. For a while,

Germany lost interest. With Italy still officially neutral and France still in the fight, the Mediterranean was a backwater in the war.

The Royal Navy's Commander-in-Chief Mediterranean was a Scot, Admiral Sir Andrew Browne Cunningham. Like any admiral of his day he had done his time in battleships but, unusually, he was at heart a destroyer man. As a young officer he had commanded the three-funnelled destroyer HMS *Scorpion* for seven years, taking her right through the First World War and mostly in the Mediterranean, where he had been in the attempt to force the Dardanelles at the Anzac landing in 1915. By the end of the war he was a commander and had won the DSO, the Distinguished Service Order, three times. Of slightly less than average height, with a pink complexion, rheumy eyes and a persona often crusty in the Scottish manner but leavened by an acid wit, he knew the Mediterranean as well as his much-loved back garden at home in Hampshire. Known as 'ABC' by his staff, he was one of the brightest minds in the service.

With no flagship to call his own, Cunningham had moved ashore on Malta, setting up his headquarters in the Castille, a Spanish baroque mansion at Valletta. Starved of resources, he still had to provide escorts for the great convoys of merchant ships carrying troops and weapons, ammunition and vehicles, fuel and food, back and forth across the Med. He was glad, very glad, to see the Australians, and if he was worried about the age of their ships and the inexperience of their crews, he never gave a hint of it.

The night they arrived, *Stuart*'s men were given a run ashore to sample the delights of Valletta's Stretta Strada, or Strait Street; a long and narrow cobbled alley of bars, cafés and brothels pithily known to generations of British sailors as 'The Gut'. It was a welcome break, although no compensation for the disappointment in finding that Malta had no mail for them from home. They had heard nothing from family and friends since they had left back in October, a sorry state of affairs which could lead to almost unbearable longing in a man alone in his hammock or bunk at night when the pangs of homesickness hit. Getting mail to Australian sailors in ships at sea would remain a hit-and-miss business for the rest of the war. At least here in Malta they could now post the letters many had written while at sea. But any hopes of a few days' leave with Christmas just a week away were torn the next day. After a hurried round of fuelling, taking on stores and replacing her old torpedoes with a newer Admiralty version, *Stuart* sailed the following afternoon to pick up a troop convoy in Marseille.

The weather was foul; cold and raining. A heavy sea met them as they cleared the harbour and it grew relentlessly worse as they headed north-west towards France, the ship labouring against a strong, icy headwind and walls of green water breaking over the bow and crashing aft as high as B gun with thunderous explosions. The captain slowed the ship to 8 knots, barely enough to keep steerage way, and still she pitched and rolled, creaking and groaning, plunging into a deep trough one minute and then heaving up to the next towering, terrifying peak. On the bridge, the watch clung on with hands frozen despite their heavy gloves, their woollen duffel coats sodden and their eyes stinging from the salt spray that lashed them. Their world had become a menacing, enclosing cauldron of sea and a patch of grey, lowering sky glimpsed dimly through the spindrift. The mast above them lurched in crazy arcs, the aerials and halyards thrumming like some hellish orchestra. The noise was another assault on the senses. In the wheelhouse the quartermaster struggled to keep on course. Bill Reeve, an Engine Room Artificer from Hobart, just nineteen years old, would write long after the war that these were the roughest seas he ever encountered:

> The inclinometer on *Stuart* was graduated 0–50° on either side and it was hitting the stops. The guardrails were eight to ten feet under water when rolling and the mess decks were always awash. At times it was impossible to keep the galley fire alight so we had cold meals. It was quite a contrast with the Red Sea two weeks earlier.[1]

Below, it was a different sort of misery. In the engine room they were warm enough but they still had to battle to keep their feet. For the men off watch in the messes trying to get some sleep or just sitting there glumly waiting for their next turn on watch it was a seemingly endless assault upon their bodies and their senses. The forced air heating failed, the decks were slimy with water sloshing this way and that and the air was heavy with the stench of seasickness.

They had not expected this in the Med. Tourist poster visions of calm blue seas and sunny beaches were a world away from the grim reality they were enduring.

On the third day as they approached the coast of France the seas eased a little, offering them a respite. But then came a new menace, a dense fog as they neared Marseille. From the bridge you could see forward as far as A gun and then nothing but a wall of clinging, clammy vapour. Eventually it cleared a little, into banks and then wisps, and Hec Waller took them into the harbour at dead slow, every eye on the bridge straining to see through the haze. Entering an unfamiliar foreign port can be a test at the best of times; the fog was an unwanted addition to the captain's burden. It was 21 December. At 1130 hours Hec and Norm Teacher the navigator found the berth they'd been assigned and the ship eased alongside. The lines soared to the wharf. 'Finished with main engines.' It was almost a benediction.

There was more leave and the French welcomed them gladly. It was the worst Mediterranean winter in memory, they said. Despite the evening blackout, some of the men found their way to the fish market in the Old Port for a seafood feast that night. The officers discovered le Restaurant Basso on the Quai des Belges, the most celebrated fish café in Marseille, famous for its bouillabaisse. They were pleasantly surprised to run into some RAAF officers who had also arrived that day in the liner *Orontes*, bound for England.

The respite did not last long. Next day they were back at sea, escorting two troopships carrying 2000 British soldiers and nurses to Haifa in Palestine and then on to Port Said. The weather worsened for a couple of days, a reprise of the trip out, but the seas calmed by the time they reached Malta to refuel on Christmas Eve. Hopes rose again that they might have Christmas Day ashore but *Stuart* spent just three hours in port. Only the mess caterers were allowed to hunt up whatever Christmas food they could find and that evening they were on their way again into yet another bout of filthy winter weather, the ship tossing and corkscrewing once more. There was no let-up on the day. Traditionally in the navy the ship's officers serve the men their Christmas dinner and *Stuart*'s officers made a dogged attempt at it, but the festive spirit was thin.

We were looking forward to our roast goose which, we hoped, was browning nicely in the galley. 'Whacker', our caterer, had bought wisely during his short visit ashore in Valletta.

Our Christmas dinner was eventually served, but it called for some effort to prevent one's plate from sliding off the mess table and into the salt water that partly flooded the deck. No, it was not the Christmas Day to which we had been looking forward. We lamented that the RN at least had a tot of rum with which to toast the festive season; we had to be content with tea.

For the next three days we wallowed through the heavy, wind-swept seas. The nights were dark and long, and we yearned for the sight of Haifa ...[2]

*Voyager* had it a little better in her corner. Like *Stuart*, all the destroyers had been criss-crossing the Med since their arrival, escorting convoys here, there and everywhere in that same vengeful winter. *Voyager* found herself butting and battling through atrocious seas in company with *Vampire* on the way up from Port Said with five troopships full of Indian soldiers destined for Europe. Her captain, 'Copper' Morrow, and the first lieutenant, Alan 'Strangler' Lewis, were rarely off the bridge, willing the ship through each mountainous wave as it descended upon them.

Morrow's shock of red hair had won him his nickname at the naval college and it had stuck with him through his career. He had been in command of *Voyager* since 1938 and his sailors admired him for his flair as a shiphandler. 'Copper' would approach a wharf or a buoy at a speed which gave port admirals and nearby captains apoplexy, dashing up at full tilt before coming to a neat stop in a flurry of perfectly judged helm and engine orders. It was the naval equivalent of screeching to a halt in a squeal of car tyres and a shower of gravel, and his crews loved it. Some, though, said he was hard on his junior officers. In one famous moment, in front of the entire bridge crew, he had humiliated a downy-cheeked young sub lieutenant by very scornfully ordering him below to get a shave.

'Strangler' had earned his name for other reasons. It was an era that enjoyed giving men nicknames, the navy more than most, some of them ritual. No one knew why, but Millers in the navy were known as 'Dusty', Clarks were inevitably 'Nobby', Webbs were 'Spider', Martins were 'Pincher', Whites were 'Knocker' and Wilsons were 'Tug'. 'Strangler' got his for his prowess as a boxer. As a sub lieutenant studying in Britain he had won the Royal Navy and Royal Marines Officers' Middleweight Championship in 1927 and again in 1928, a reputation that preceded him. Like his captain, he was a lieutenant commander, an unusual arrangement, although he was four years Morrow's junior.

*Voyager* and *Vampire* struck it lucky with their convoy. On Christmas Eve they handed it over to *Vendetta* and *Waterhen* to take on to Marseille and returned to Grand Harbour that afternoon. Most of the men were allowed ashore to the bars of The Gut. Christmas lunch in the messes was a handsome feast topped off with a proper plum pudding and beer to drink as well.

*Vendetta* and *Waterhen*, on the other hand, had a glum Christmas at sea:

'Cold and grey for the most part,' wrote Fred Thompson, a petty officer in *Vendetta*. 'Spotted a portion of Corsica. Cake and a glass of beer, just to make it feel a bit like Christmas.'[3]

They berthed in Marseille on the afternoon of Boxing Day, in the teeth of a winter gale so fierce that no leave was allowed until it blew itself out two days later. The two captains, Glen Cant in *Vendetta* and Jim Swain in *Waterhen*, arranged to turn on a Christmas dinner of sorts on 27 December, but the weather grew more insistently miserable with temperatures dropping below zero and snow encrusting the upper deck.

—

Gordon Hill grew up in the Sydney beach suburb of Maroubra, another child of the Depression. He began to study accountancy when he left school but after a few years he tired of sitting at an office desk. His father was a petty officer in the navy and, despite some family misgivings, Gordon went to follow in his wake. He joined up in April 1938 at the age of nineteen, and after his recruit training at Flinders, the navy decided he could be a supply assistant. That September he was posted to *Vendetta*. Intelligent and observant, Gordon kept a diary and later wrote a rich and humorous memoir. He was in Marseille that first New Year.

I went ashore with Stoker POs Robbie and Bunting and joined the French men and women in their New Year's Eve celebrations. We visited a French brothel where we were ushered into a little theatrette where we watched some 'blue' pictures. Then two girls came on stage and play-acted having sex in various situations. Some girls came and sat with us and invited us to their boudoirs, but not me. They said I was too young, just a 'petit garcon', a pretty little boy. We left without partaking of their favours and went to the English/French club and got warmed up with a few rum and beer chasers instead.

Marseille was not a very safe place, especially around the dock area, and our permit to go ashore restricted us to certain areas. On the 2nd of January it stopped snowing so I went for a walk and took some photos. Dull grey buildings, cobblestone roads and antiquated trams made a depressing sight. The women walked along pleasantly smiling and, exuding the refreshing smell of perfume, brightened up the scenery.[4]

One of Gordon's shipmates, Thomas 'Paddy' Doyle, was an amateur poet. He put it a little more pungently:

To France we went on duty bent,
'Twas Christmas thirty-nine.
We took a chance with gay romance
While drinking sparkling wine.
The French girls there enchanted us
With their bewitching arts.
For when we sailed away again
We all had dented darts.[5]

'Paddy' was a cheerful, pipe-smoking Irishman, born in County Cork in 1900, and still speaking with a Gaelic brogue. After thirteen years in the Royal Navy, he had enlisted in the RAN in 1926. By the outbreak of war, nearly forty years old, he was a type familiar in the service: a three-badge able seaman, meaning that he had never once been promoted and was never likely to be. The three gold badges, worn on the sleeve and looking like an army sergeant's stripes, were for twelve years' good conduct or, as they always said, undiscovered bad conduct. Older than all of them, including the captain, 'Paddy' was a popular figure who took the new young blokes under his wing. He was Captain of the Heads, a job rather less grand than it sounds, meaning he was responsible for cleaning the toilets. His poems and his talent with a harmonica cheered them all.

—

The opening months of 1940 brought no relief, just more of the same evil winter, still with no glimpse of the enemy. It was at around this time that Lord Haw-Haw's sneer about scrap iron and 'the consignment of junk' began to percolate among them. Germans were not permitted to listen to the BBC on pain of severe punishment, but Allied troops frequently tuned in to Berlin Radio for the entertainment value of its absurd Nazi propaganda. Haw-Haw's affected attempt at an upper-class English accent, an adenoidal drawl, was especially amusing. 'Jair-many calling, Jair-many calling,' he would honk at the start of his diatribes. The scrap iron jibe tickled the Australians no end. They adopted it with glee.

On 2 January they stopped being 'those Australian ships' and became the Royal Navy's grandly named 19th Destroyer Division, with Hec Waller still in command. In Malta, their new boss, Rear Admiral John Tovey, called the ships' companies together for a pep talk, telling them they had much work to do, and would get 'a crack at the enemy when circumstances permit'. In truth, Tovey, as Cunningham's second in command, was dismayed at what he had been handed. In his memoirs, Cunningham wrote that:

> Tovey's command as Rear Admiral (D) was reduced to five Australian destroyers, manned by the most stout-hearted of ships' companies, but in old ships of a 1918 vintage. In consequences, Tovey was rather downcast.[6]

The enemy was not the Germans but the weather, cruel and capricious, a foe you could not fight but just endure. They became resigned to the worst the elements might throw at them and more sure in their capacity to withstand its torments. They were more sure in their seamanship, too. It showed in the small things, like effortlessly keeping your footing as the ship rolled; like a signal smartly sent in the teeth of a screeching gale; like cooking dinner in the galley with the pots and pans jumping on the stove; or the bigger things, such as battling on an icy deck to secure a boat dislodged by a freak wave. The kids who had been green recruits fresh from the Flinders Naval Depot just five months earlier had grown into the job and went about their work with the confidence of gathering experience. In the beginning, escorting a convoy had been exacting, exasperating. The slowest ship set the convoy speed, perhaps as little as 8 knots, crawling over a seemingly endless expanse of ocean. The escorts would zig-zag at a faster speed, but not by very much, and the strain was heavier at night when all the ships were darkened and, in the days before radar, the Officer of the Watch had to keep station on the black bulk of a troopship or the low silhouette of a tanker only dimly visible through the murk. That too had become second nature, almost a matter of intuition, performed with practised efficiency. Mugs of hot cocoa kept them going in even the darkest, dirtiest night; cocoa so thick you could stand a spoon in it: kye or kai it was called, an old Royal Navy word. The most junior sailor on watch would have the job of fetching it from the galley and carrying it up the ladders to the bridge, in a big sea a feat of acrobatic courage and dexterity. But best of all and at last, mail had begun to arrive from home, eagerly anticipated with every return to Malta.

In the engine rooms and boiler rooms the men of the Black Gang went about their business, quietly performing miracles. They kept their elderly machinery going against all the odds, nursing it with meticulous care. In a beam sea, with the crests of the waves breaking parallel to the ship and smashing into its sides, the failure of even one engine and the loss of power might prove fatal, sending the ship rolling over, never to rise again. It did not happen. And if the ship were punching headlong into a coming sea, burying her bows deep, the stern could rise out of the water with the propellor shafts racing. Unchecked, that could tear the heart out of the turbines.

On the engine room control platforms the stokers on watch remained glued to their various dials and wheels and throttles, ready to react in an instant. And in port there was little rest for them, either, with constant maintenance and the dirty, hated job of cleaning the boilers.

Much of the life was monotony, enlivened in finer weather by the occasional bit of gun drill or an anti-submarine exercise. In *Voyager* they found that the 3-inch anti-aircraft gun kept jamming after every third or fourth round; not a pleasing prospect. They stripped and reassembled it a few times but discovered in the end that the solution was to whack it with a heavy wooden mallet. Yet there were moments out of the ordinary, incidents of the unusual, or the extreme, or the downright perilous, and not to be forgotten. On one trip to Marseille that January, in mountainous seas, *Voyager*'s decks and her guns were thick with ice, with the men on the bridge peering through sleet hurled at them on a biting wind. When they berthed it was snowing. At about the same time, *Vampire* found her torpedoes had frozen solid in their tubes; the steam pipes that were supposed to prevent that had been disconnected back in Australia.

On 17 January, *Stuart* sailed from Malta to escort the heavy repair ship HMS *Resource* to Gibraltar. *Resource* was a familiar figure, at least to Hec Waller. He had been her executive officer back in the mid-1930s during his long stint with the RN. She was a handsome vessel, just ten years old and virtually a sea-going dockyard. At 12,300 tons full load and 155 metres long, she dwarfed the little destroyer.

The first day out the weather was calm, but the barometer was dropping and the next began with a rising gale that by evening turned into a full-blown storm. The next day it was worse, and the day after that worse again. *Stuart* was pitching headlong into the waves. The conditions below were the usual horrible shambles, the upper mess decks running with water. Ean McDonald recalled the ordeal of coming off watch and returning to his mess:

> As you went down one of the ladders your body felt the hot, foetid air rising. Like a rasping band of rottenness it then reached your nose, and you had to breathe it or suffocate. I preferred to stay above it. I could not bear more than a few minutes of being down below. It was impossible to breathe the air or eat the lousy cold

food on offer either. I could not sleep in the coffin-like atmosphere and only ventured down long enough to grab a change of underwear or socks. This went on for days. Everything below stank and everything above was soaking wet and as cold as ice ...[7]

He found somewhere else to sleep, a small companionway or passage below the bridge running from side to side of the ship. There were supposedly watertight doors at either end, but water from each new wave streamed through them anyway, swilling back and forth.

After I came down from my watches on the bridge I sought out an empty place in the companionway among other prone bodies and lay down to whatever rest I could claim. I literally snatched only moments of sleep on the deck of the companionway. I wore my underwear under my pyjamas, under my uniform blues and under my woollen jumper. For windproof comfort over this I wore my Burberry overcoat and my heavy watch-keeping duffel coat with its half inch thick felt. Over that I wore my oilskin, plus my balaclava and a knitted scarf. My socks were covered by extra thick sea boot stockings, topped off with heavy rubber sea boots. Had I gone overboard I would have sunk gratefully in seconds.

As the ship rolled constantly, the six-inch deep water in the companionway sloshed back and forth, forming a wave nine inches high. I was lying in the way of this. Each roll sent a wave of water rushing up, around and over my unresisting body. One way, then the other way, each wave ran into my sea boots or into my balaclava, then down my collar into my neck and down my back. In no time I was soaked through and cold with it. Somehow I slept, that is my body took its rest.[8]

In the early morning of 20 January, not long after the change of the watch at midnight, *Stuart* was labouring at a bare 7 knots through crests so high and troughs so deep that they had only fleeting glimpses of *Resource* through the pitch-black and the flying spray. For long periods she would disappear altogether. The first lieutenant had the watch, Rupert Robison, and he and the bridge crew were hanging on for dear life. Les Clifford was the duty signalman, struggling to keep his balance and his binocular lenses clean.

Climbing a giant wave, glancing astern, they suddenly saw the dark mass of *Resource* bearing down on them, barely 50 metres away off the port quarter. It was a nightmare vision of extreme peril. In a collision, the bigger ship could crush the destroyer like an empty tin. Robison sprang to the voice pipe connecting the bridge to the wheel-house, yelling into its brass mouth, 'Hard a'starboard!'.

It was the maximum turn for a destroyer, spectacular in a calm sea, hazardous in these conditions, but perhaps the only instinctive way to escape from under the oncoming menace. The helmsman wrenched the wheel around. It did not work. *Stuart* did not respond. She would not answer her helm, she would not turn. A freak combination of wind and wave – a following sea – had rendered her rudder useless and they had not noticed it. The destroyer was out of control. *Resource* was closing them, drawing nearer. There was only one thing left to do, one last desperate chance.

'Full ahead both engines!'

In the wheelhouse and below in the engine room the telegraph jangled and the stoker of the watch threw open the throttles. The old turbines whined, the revolutions picked up, the shafts turned faster. Slowly, agonisingly slowly, the ship began to lift, to gain speed. It was enough, just enough to take her out of harm's way. The captain, dozing fitfully in his sea cabin, heard the clang of the telegraph and raced up the ladder to the compass platform to see his old ship wallowing past them astern, a monster in the night. A signal lamp was blinking high on her bridge. Les Clifford read it to the captain.

'What appears to be the trouble?'

'Tell her we lost steerage way,' said Hec coolly.

It had been a close-run thing, lethally close. By coincidence, in an intriguing footnote to history, a collision might have been an embar-rassing all-Australian affair. The officer of the watch on *Resource*'s bridge that night was her Australian first lieutenant and navigator, Robert 'Oscar' Rankin, a lieutenant commander born in Cobar in western New South Wales, a graduate of the RANC in 1924 and on loan to the RN. It would be nice to think that he and Waller enjoyed a drink together when their ships docked in cold and rainy Gibraltar the next day. Perhaps they did, perhaps they did not. Both men were still in their thirties. Hec could be remote on the bridge but he was a famously convivial figure over a beer at a wardroom bar. Rankin was a rising star, a brilliant and personable young officer showered with praise by his superiors, recommended for accelerated promotion. Almost exactly two years later, in February 1942, in command of the sloop *Yarra* in the Timor Sea, he gallantly turned his ship into the teeth of an overwhelming Japanese force of cruisers and destroyers to shield a convoy he was escorting. He was killed on his bridge as *Yarra* went down beneath him. One of the navy's immortals, like Hec Waller, his name is carried today by a Collins class submarine.

—

The harbours they visited, ports that had seemed so foreign at first, became familiar havens of rest and recreation, even if only for a few hours. Marseille had an edge of danger to it; sailors had been beaten up and robbed and some areas were off limits. But it was perhaps the favourite, for the food and the cafés and bars were good, the French were generally hospitable and the girls – it was agreed – were the prettiest and friendliest of any in the Med.

Alexandria, Gibraltar, Haifa and Port Said had their own attractions. Alexandria, Egypt's ancient seaport, had been battleground and playground for kings and queens, conquerors and pharaohs down the centuries. Named for its founder, the Greek general Alexander the Great in 331 BC, it had once been the largest city in the ancient world, famed for its towering lighthouse and its wondrous great library, its commerce and culture. Persians and Greeks, Romans and Turks had ruled from its palaces, and there both Julius Caesar and Mark Antony had succumbed to the charms of the wily Queen Cleopatra. In the nineteenth century Napoleonic France and Georgian Britain had contended for mastery of Alexandria, the French surrendering after a mighty battle in 1801.

In the mid-twentieth century the city was both queen and whore, nominally Egyptian but in fact controlled by Britain. Grand, gated mansions stood on broad boulevards within sight and sound of teeming, filthy slums. Arabs, Greeks and Jews mingled in its streets. The infamous red-light district, Rue des Soeurs, or Sister Street, lay in wait with its bars and brothels, and nightclubs where the girls danced with naked breasts. Egypt was a carnival of erotica for young kids not long out of Sydney or the bush, as it had been for their forefathers, the Anzacs of the 1st AIF a quarter of a century before. A few of the more expensive whorehouses boasted cleanliness, French girls and pretensions of elegance. Others provided quick sex on a production line, with queues at the door. As in Marseille, there was more than an edge of the wild side to Sister Street, an aura of danger, where a fight might erupt at any minute, with fists or knives. British army military police patrolled day and night, with local Arab police on horseback.

Not every sailor sought these thrills, far from it. As the weather improved, many simply looked forward to a swim at the harbour's pleasant sandy beaches with a cold beer afterwards, or a film at one of the cinemas. Others did the sights, photographing themselves in the ancient Roman catacombs or at the monumental Pompey's Pillar, a Corinthian column built 300 years before Christ. Some who scored a longer leave would venture the 220 kilometres inland to Cairo to see the pyramids and buy souvenirs to send back home. They would get to know Alexandria very much better in the coming year.

Haifa was different, not so volatile, not so awash with sex and sin. A commercial city of both Arabs and Jews and the chief port for the British protectorate of Palestine, it was clean and relatively modern and – miracle of miracles – it offered cheap oranges and other fresh fruit for the ships' messes. Nazareth and holy Jerusalem were within striking distance if you had a couple of days' leave. Port Said was universally judged to be dull, apart from the bazaars where you could snap up cheap cameras, radios or jewellery for a song.

Malta, with its naval dockyard, was the cornerstone of life ashore, the best and most welcoming of all. It was splendid to enter Grand Harbour, gliding past the three great forts of St Elmo, St Angelo and Ricasoli, their majestic ramparts and battlements of tawny limestone towering above the little destroyers. The Knights of Malta had built well. You berthed in either Dockyard Creek or French Creek on the south-eastern shore of the harbour, the two separated by the fortified little city of Senglea with its warren of lanes and alleys. The dockyard had a NAAFI canteen[9] which offered the exquisite luxury of hot baths and real soap; a magnet for the Australians before they set off in their best tiddly suits for a night on the town. The Gut, with its raunchy nightlife, lay across the harbour in the capital, Valletta, which you could reach by the liberty boat or by spending a few pennies to hire a *dghaisa*, a watercraft very like a Venetian gondola. And there you could get pretty much anything a sailor far from home might want: cafés, restaurants, bars, music, and sex in considerable variety. So narrow that the balconies on either side almost touched each other in places, the street was thronged night and day with sailors and sometimes a few British army or RAF men, pursued by touts and pimps. 'Hey Jack, come inside, Jack, big eats here, Jack, you want nice girl, Jack?' Most of the bars would have hostesses, girls who would bring your beer and sit down to join you, making small talk. 'You very handsome, Jack.' They'd ask you to buy them a sherry, which duly arrived and turned out to be some sort of sweetened, coloured water.

> For the purpose of purchasing this famous – or infamous – sherry, you are charged the sum of eightpence, and on enquiry you discover that sixpence of this sum is presented to the hostess – for her only remuneration – the remaining twopence entering the coffers of the establishment ... it did not take the lads long to dub these hostesses 'Sherry Bandits' and the refreshment 'Lolly Water'.[10]

The Gut did not radiate that air of latent trouble that you sensed at Sister Street in Alexandria. You could get a fight there if you wanted to pick one, and some did just for the hell of it, but for most it was enjoyable entertainment, a safety valve to release the tensions acquired at sea.

> 'I had a memorable evening with two shipmates and two English squaddies in a room over Dirty Harry's Bar,' wrote Gordon Hill. 'We sang and danced and one girl did the Dance of The Seven Veils. One soldier who had a magnificent voice sang "My Prayer" and "Indian Summer", two songs I will never forget.'[11]

Overlaying it all, difficult to ignore, was the growing sense that Italy might soon enter the war. On 18 March, Hitler and Mussolini took their private trains to a meeting at a small rural railway station at the Brenner Pass on the Italian alpine border with Austria. With much heel clicking and fascist saluting in a flurry of snow, they embraced for the newsreel cameras and then met for two hours in Il Duce's carriage. With Hitler doing most of the talking as always, Mussolini was pressured into going to war against Britain and France. His foreign minister and son-in-law, Count Galeazzo Ciano, kept notes:

> 'When the enemy has been smashed in northern France,' Hitler told him, 'the moment will come for Italy to intervene actively … the war will be decided in France. Once France is disposed of, Italy will be mistress of the Mediterranean and England will have to make peace.'[12]

Ciano recorded that Mussolini was nervous and hesitant, but eventually agreed that he would intervene 'when the time was right'. Hitler had him hooked. None of this was reported. The meeting of the two dictators was portrayed by their propaganda machines as a fraternal encounter of fascist solidarity. In the months that followed, Mussolini's speeches and the tone of the subservient Italian press became distinctly more belligerent. Strutting atop the Palazzo Venezia in Rome, posturing as the reincarnation of the Caesars, Il Duce would whip up the cheering throng of *fascisti* below with the cry of *Mare Nostrum*! Our Sea.

—

Eventually the Admiralty began passing ships into the Med to strengthen the fleet. A posse of destroyers brought the elderly aircraft carrier *Glorious* to Malta for a refit and training in January. In the last week of March, with the weather a little warmer but still vile, *Voyager* put out from Gibraltar into the Atlantic to meet that most glamorous of carriers, the brand-new, 27,000-ton HMS *Ark Royal*. Like most of the Australians, Petty Officer Arthur Cooper, *Voyager*'s Gunner's Mate, had never seen a ship quite so stately in a hammering, punishing sea.

> Waves were sweeping over everything. The whaler filled with water and was going rapidly, so we risked our necks and put an

axe through two planks to let water out, otherwise we would have lost it. Went around upper deck, securing everything we could ... 'A' gun badly knocked about, weather shield bent and folded up generally. Chiefs' and POs' mess flooded out and galley flat awash ...

... opened up to 25 knots, turned our stern to the sea and commenced zigzagging. Peculiar motion of ship in stern sea at high speed. I was watching the stern of the ship springing up and down. Some day soon she will crack up. Twenty-two years is a fair age ...[13]

The next day, 26 March, was worse:

Still a very high sea running astern, and as our speed is 22 knots, it is very uncomfortable. 'A' gun shield bent a little more during forenoon when we turned around into sea during high speed. Once we rolled over to an angle of 50 degrees and I thought we were right over. Cases of ammunition were torn from their racks and careering around the deck. Les and I donned oilskins, sou'westers and sea boots and risked our necks again securing everything that had broken loose. The decks were awash. *Ark Royal* is so big she is hardly rolling.[14]

That same day and in much the same weather, *Stuart* was exercising with *Glorious* north of Malta when a thick fog rolled in, blanketing the two ships from each other. After midnight, halfway through the middle watch, the carrier signalled through the gloom that a Shell oil company tanker, the *Trocas*, had broken down some miles away and was adrift. *Stuart* made the best speed she could to the tanker's position and found her a couple of hours later, two red lights atop her mast shining through the fog to indicate that she was not under control. The water was too deep for her to anchor and she was drifting slowly towards the unfriendly coast of Sicily.

Hec Waller had been told simply to stand by while a tug arrived from Malta but, characteristically, he made the bold decision to take her in tow. At a thin, cold and thoroughly miserable daybreak, as the two ships heaved and rolled, *Stuart* tried and tried again to heave or shoot a line across, and again and again the sea and the winds defeated them. Late that morning Hec decided to lower a boat, the ship's whaler, to carry a line over. A whaler was a heavy, clinker-built timber craft, a little over 8 metres long, powered only by the muscle of five men at the oars and a coxswain steering in the stern. Every young sailor had rowed one in training, but to take one in a sea like this would require near superhuman strength and, beyond that, raw courage. Les Clifford watched from the signal bridge:

> Then began a struggle between man and the mighty sea. It is no mean task to navigate a whaler in mid-ocean, and in weather such as we experienced on that morning the labours of the whaler's crew were enhanced a hundredfold. Sometimes they appeared to be gaining ground, then a particularly heavy swell would carry them back again. For hours, the men struggled against the elements, and eventually *Trocas* was reached and the line passed inboard. A few minutes later the hawser was secured. But alas! No sooner had we taken the strain than the manila [rope] parted. The arduous task of the whaler's crew had been in vain.[15]

The captain could have given up then but he persevered. The only way to do it now, he thought, was to nudge *Stuart*'s bow as close as he could to the tanker, try with yet another line, and then make the tow stern first. In the fog it was hazardous, almost reckless, with waves rising 2 metres and more, and lookouts posted in the bows. One misjudgement and the ships could have crunched into each other. But it worked. Each ship heaved a light line to the other, the heavier hawsers followed and were secured, and by 1600 hours *Stuart* was slowly hauling her charge on a course for Malta at a battling 2.5 knots. Disaster almost struck again just after 1800 hours into the second dog watch, when the tug *Respond* arrived and surged suddenly out of the fog, almost cutting the tow. But by nine o'clock she had taken over and the trio lumbered back towards Grand Harbour, *Stuart* in the rear like a cattle dog. It was a feat of extraordinary seamanship,[16] recognised in a signal from Sir Andrew Cunningham:

HMAS *Stuart* has again showed her mettle in the way in which she brought help to SS *Trocas*. I am very glad to have the Australian destroyers under my command. [This] has shown how ready they are to seize any situation and cheerfully carry it through to a successful conclusion.[17]

Cunningham was a hard marker who suffered fools not at all and did not lightly dispense praise. You had to earn it. Any early doubts about the abilities of these five little ships and their young crews had been swept away.[18] A month later he demonstrated his confidence in an unmistakeable way. He placed four Royal Navy destroyers under Waller's wing: *Dainty, Diamond, Decoy* and *Defender*. Hec was now Commander (D) of the new 10th Destroyer Flotilla.

The Australians had emphatically arrived.

# CHAPTER 5

# 'A MORNING NEVER TO BE FORGOTTEN'

The European summer of 1940 saw the Nazi river of death in full, dark flood. After months of watching and waiting, of skulking like a jackal on the banks of that river, Mussolini finally decided to plunge in, to snap up what pickings there might be. 'I need only a few thousand dead so that I can sit at the peace conference as a man who has fought,' he told his army Chief of Staff, Marshal Pietro Badoglio.[1] Italy declared war on Britain and France on 10 June.

Many of Mussolini's generals and admirals feared they were not ready, and the feeble Italian economy was straining to supply the war machine with oil, steel and coal. Hitler remarked acidly and accurately of the *fascisti* that, 'First they were too cowardly to take part. Now they are in a hurry so that they can share in the spoils.'[2] President Roosevelt was scathing. 'On this tenth day of June, the hand that held the dagger has stuck it into the back of its neighbour ...'[3]

In London, they were less than surprised at the arrival of a new enemy. The British had cracked the Italian diplomatic code and were able to read some of the air force and naval codes as well, cementing the belief that Mussolini was readying for war. It was not a matter of if but when. They had done their best to prepare for it.

But both Britain and France were struggling, and at sea the Battle of the Atlantic was running strongly for the U-boats. In February Hitler had unleashed them for unrestricted submarine warfare, to sink any ship without warning. There were some moments of light, though. The British scored a cheering victory that same month when the destroyer HMS *Cossack* stormed into an icy Norwegian fjord and rescued 303 merchant seamen – 'The navy's here!' – who had been captured by *Graf Spee* and were being carried back to Germany on the prison ship *Altmark*.

But in early April Germany seized Denmark in a land invasion which lasted less than six hours and then moved on to snatch Norway. At sea, the Royal Navy put up a spirited fight. In later years, marine painters would be inspired by the image of the mighty battleship HMS *Warspite* thundering into Narvik fjord, 15-inch guns blazing as she descended to wreak havoc upon a cornered squadron of German destroyers. Trading blows, the battleships *Scharnhorst* and *Gneisenau* sank the carrier *Glorious* and two destroyers in the North Sea on 8 June, with the loss of 1519 lives. On land, the bold Norwegians fought with might and main but they were no match for the Wehrmacht and they surrendered on 10 June, the same day that Italy entered the war.

May was the darkest month and Friday 10 was its darkest day. Hitler lunged to crush western Europe. The blitzkrieg descended upon Belgium, France, Holland and Luxembourg, the panzer generals Erwin Rommel and Heinz Guderian vying with each to see who could cover the most ground in a day. Nothing could stop them. In London on that same day Prime Minister Neville Chamberlain, sick and exhausted, finally realised that his time was up. Winston Churchill became prime minister. Three days later, on Monday 13 May, in the House of Commons, he made the first of his great wartime speeches:

> I have nothing to offer but blood, toil, tears and sweat. We have before us an ordeal of the most grievous kind. We have before us many long months of toil and struggle.[4]

As the towns and cities of France fell like wheat before the whirl-wind, the British army, much of the French army and some of the Belgians retreated to the French channel port of Dunkirk. Operation Dynamo, that heroic, desperate evacuation, began on 26 May. In his first big tactical and strategic error, Hitler halted his army to allow Hermann Göring's Luftwaffe to finish off the rats in the trap. It failed.

When Dynamo ended on 3 June, 224,686 British and 121,445 French and Belgian troops had been extracted from the bombed and burning beaches, carried across the Channel and landed safely in England. The next day, Churchill gave perhaps his most celebrated speech to the Commons:

> We shall not flag or fail. We shall go on to the end. We shall fight in France, we shall fight on the seas and oceans, we shall fight with growing confidence and growing strength in the air. We shall defend our island, whatever the cost may be. We shall fight on the beaches, we shall fight on the landing-grounds, we shall fight in the fields and in the streets, we shall fight in the hills. We shall never surrender.[5]

—

*Vendetta* was first to feel the fire. She had gone into the Malta dockyard on 3 June for a long and much needed refit, her boilers taken apart and her engines silent. Early in the morning of 11 June, the day after Mussolini's declaration of war, the Italian air force – the Regia Aeronautica – launched a bombing raid on Malta that would begin two and a half years of agony for the island and its 250,000 people. Petty Officer Fred Cooper was still asleep:

> A morning never to be forgotten. Awakened at 0700 by George Stent shouting 'Air Raid!' and then came the bombs. They landed less than 200 yards from the ship, accompanied by shrapnel, machine gun bullets, dust and terrific noise. Spent the rest of the day in No. 65 tunnel. No wash and very little food. Another bad raid at 1930. Damage unknown. Bombs fell close to dockyard in Cospicua. Eight raids in all today. Slept in Refuge behind sandbags.[6]

This would be the pattern of their lives for the next month under their new captain, Lieutenant Rodney 'Dusty' Rhoades, who had taken over from an ailing Lieutenant Commander Cant on 30 March. A Sydneysider, and with a young wife at home there in Woollahra, Rhoades had been *Vampire*'s First Lieutenant. At the age of thirty-one,

'Dusty' was and probably still is the youngest and most junior officer ever to be given command of an Australian destroyer. He took to the job with gusto. Half the ship's company, those not needed for the refit, were sent off to Fort Ricasoli at the mouth of Grand Harbour, where they were handed .303 rifles and told to prepare for a possible landing by Italian paratroopers. The fear of invasion was real. 'Dusty' dubbed them 'The Ricasoli Rifle Range Expeditionary Force', and took to leading them about the countryside on route marches like so many common soldiers.

The rest of the crew, about fifty men, remained working in the dockyard, enduring the bombing and strafing by day and long nights of sleepless misery and squalor. At first when the ship docked they had been put up in the NAAFI canteen, which was uncomfortable enough. They slept there on wooden tables or bare floorboards. But when the air raids began they were moved into the dark, dank and stinking tunnel No. 65 hollowed out beneath a rocky cliff in the dockyard near the ship. It was safe enough from the bombs, but infested with fleas and rodents. Gordon Hill jotted in his diary:

Thursday, 13th June 1940. We are living ashore in our tunnel. It is damp and dirty and we live like rats. There have been eight air raids today and if we are working on the ship we run like hell to our pillbox near the tunnel to guard against parachutists. The *Vendetta* was bombed, unsuccessfully, the bombs landing about 150 yards away. A fighter plane strafing the dockyard anti-aircraft gunners shot at Mick, and did he run!

The Regia Aeronautica did not have dive-bombers. The Italians' chief weapon in the air was the Savoia-Marchetti SM.79 Sparviero or 'Sparrowhawk', a three-engined medium bomber of such a stumpy, ugly design that its crews christened it *il gobbo maledetto*, 'the damned hunchback'. It carried a crew of six. Flying from Catania in Sicily to Malta, a trip of just 187 kilometres or about forty minutes, they first bombed from a height of 18,000 feet, which made any accuracy almost impossible. After a few weeks they brought that down to around 9000 feet. Usually they would be accompanied by a protective screen of fighters, the single-engined Macchi C.200 Saetta or

'Lightning', which could strafe the ground with two wing-mounted machine guns.

Malta lay almost helpless beneath the onslaught. Before the war there had been occasional talk in London of strengthening the Crown Colony's defences with more anti-aircraft guns but, scandalously, nothing ever came of it. There was only a handful of guns and searchlights dotted here and there and the air defences were equally scant. The grandly named Hal Far Fighter Flight, based at the Hal Far RAF base on the south of the island, consisted of a dozen crates of ancient Gloster Sea Gladiator biplanes, six of which were eventually unpacked and assembled. A shortage of pilots meant that only two or perhaps three could be airborne at any one time. The last of Britain's open cockpit fighter biplanes, the Sea Gladiator was obsolete even as it came into production in 1934, but it was simple to fly and agile in the air and for Malta it was better than nothing, perhaps. A Maltese newspaper christened the three *Faith*, *Hope* and *Charity*.

Day after day, night after night, the air-raid sirens howled, the aircraft engines throbbed above, the bombs rained down with their chilling, eldritch scream and the thunderous *crump* of the explosions. Some 50,000 people lived and worked in Valletta on the northern shore of Grand Harbour and in the Three Cities around the dockyard on the southern shore, packed into an area of about 2 square kilometres. The Regia Aeronautica, the most ardently fascist of Italy's three services, unconscionably targeted the civilians of urban Malta in a deliberate policy of dealing death and destruction to lower their morale. There was some refuge for the people in cellars and in the warren of tunnels beneath the streets and lanes, but when they emerged again on the all clear they would find homes and shops, offices and their precious, historic churches reduced to smoking rubble.

Somehow, *Vendetta* escaped harm. There was damage all around her on the docks, and at times she was showered by shrapnel and rubble, but not a bomb struck her. Excerpts from Gordon Hill's diary capture the essence of these bleak and frightening days:

These lumps all over me are caused by fleas. There are thousands of them in the rocks and the dirt floor. 2000 (8 pm) and we have just witnessed a thrilling air duel overhead between an Italian bomber and two of our fighters. It lasted only a short while and the bomber was brought down ... there was no sleep for me last night. The bugs nearly drove me mad. I was fairly crying in anger at not being able to get away from it all ...

... 15th June. Three air raids today and many casualties in the dockyard. No planes brought down. Sunday two more raids on the dockyard. One worker blown in half and another only his booted feet were left ...

... The bugs are causing me many wild moments and every morning I am bitten all over. Lumps from head to feet. The only relief is a swim in the harbour ...

... 26th June. The day started off well with an air raid at 0700 and four more at short intervals. Each time flights of bombers flew over. At about 1200 an unsuccessful attempt was made to bomb our ship. I was running for shelter when a plane started to machine-gun the dock. I dived for a pillbox and the others threw themselves down on the ground. Six bombs landed about 200 yards away from us ...[7]

Towards the end of the refit, the strains and tensions were spilling over:

It is sometime in the morning of Tuesday and I cannot sleep, so I shall write the unhappy events of yesterday. The boys came back from the rifle range and got drunk. Fights were caused and the Petty Officer Cook hit an ordinary seaman. The boys swam naked in the dock and wanted to drown a dockyard policeman who annoyed them. The Coxswain put one chap under arrest and tomorrow will see the result of drunken foolishness ...[8]

That same day, 1 July, 'Dusty' Rhoades celebrated his promotion to lieutenant commander, buying drinks in the NAAFI canteen for his officers and petty officers. A week later, on 9 July, *Vendetta* was ready to leave. No ship's company was ever happier to slip and put to sea, to leave behind the bombs and the bugs, to feel the deck vibrate beneath their feet, to see the wake boiling at the stern, to find their sea legs again as the destroyer bowed once more to the Mediterranean swell. The Vice Admiral Malta Sir Wilbraham Ford farewelled them with a grateful signal:

> The amount of good work of every description done by Lieutenant Commander Rhoades and the ship's company of *Vendetta* since war broke out with Italy has been beyond praise. They have turned their hands to everything in true Australian fashion and produced astonishing results.[9]

—

As the summer drew on, and despite the reverses in Norway and the Atlantic, the Admiralty had been working to strengthen the Mediterranean fleet, scraping together what ships it could find. Andrew Cunningham had also decided, reluctantly, to move his fleet base from Malta to Alexandria, taking it further away from Italian bombing raids. The Regia Aeronautica could still reach Alexandria but not as easily. A floating dock had been sent out from Britain, and there were some civilian repair facilities there as well. It was far from an ideal solution, but it also put the naval Commander-in-Chief in better touch with his RAF and army opposite numbers in the Middle East, who were based in Cairo.

Notionally, Egypt was an independent nation, but it was in every way a British fiefdom largely ruled by the British Minister in Cairo, the suave and domineering Sir Miles Lampson. The Egyptian monarch – His Majesty Farouk I, by the grace of God, King of Egypt and the Sudan – was a spoiled boy barely twenty years old. After failing the entrance exam for Eton, Farouk ended up at the Woolwich Military Academy before assuming the kingship at sixteen on the death of his father. Fabulously wealthy, he passed his days flitting between his five palaces and playing with more than 200 cars and two lavish yachts he owned. Lampson alternately flattered him with florid compliments and bullied him with schoolmasterly reproofs – 'You're a very naughty boy,' he told him once. Farouk resented it but sullenly submitted. In Egypt, the British did pretty much as they pleased.

By the time Italy declared war the Mediterranean Fleet was – at least on paper – a formidable force. There were four battleships – *Warspite*,

*Malaya*, *Ramillies* and *Royal Sovereign* – and an aircraft carrier, *Eagle*. The 7th Cruiser Squadron had five modern cruisers, including the 6-inch-gun HMAS *Sydney* which had arrived from Australia on 26 May under the command of Captain John Collins, one of the first graduates of the RANC and a year senior to Hec Waller. There were four older cruisers in the 3rd Cruiser Squadron, a dozen submarines, and what Cunningham called a mixed bag of twenty-five destroyers, including the five Scrap Iron Flotilla ships. Appearances were deceptive. All the battleships mounted the big 15-inch guns but they were of Great War vintage and only *Warspite* had been properly modernised. *Royal Sovereign*, in particular, could squeeze out a bare 20 knots at best, which gave the admiral the awkward choice of leaving her behind to catch up or slowing the rest of the fleet to match her. As Cunningham's deputy, the newly promoted John Tovey had command of the cruisers and destroyers under the catch-all title of Vice Admiral Light Forces. With the RAF stretched to the limit in the Middle East, the fleet was seriously short of air cover. On the plus side of the ledger, the Royal Navy had learned from the mistakes of the First World War and had trained in fighting at night – which the Italians had not – and Cunningham had complete freedom to deploy his forces as he wished.

Italian admirals at sea did not have that discretion. They were rigidly controlled from Supermarina, navy headquarters ashore, and rarely able to use their own initiative, a failing that would have grim consequences in the coming months and years. Inter-service rivalries and a clogged chain of command meant that Supermarina and air force headquarters, Superaereo, were barely on speaking terms. An Italian admiral calling for air support at sea might wait all morning for it to arrive, if it turned up at all.

Yet the Regia Marina was still a formidable instrument. It had a substantial network of bases and ports west, south and east along the Italian coast at La Spezia, Naples, Messina, Taranto and Brindisi. It had five battleships, three of them elderly, but two of them – the strikingly elegant sister ships *Littorio* and *Vittoria Veneto* – were newly completing. At 45,000 tons full load, they mounted nine 15-inch guns and could whip along at a spanking 30 knots, enough in theory to run rings around the British fleet. There was an impressive force of heavy and light cruisers, squadron upon squadron of destroyers and motor torpedo boats and, at the outbreak of the war, no fewer than 100 submarines.

The Italians, though, also had to contend with the powerful French navy, led by the gleaming new battlecruisers *Dunkerque* and *Strasbourg*, which were almost as fast as the two *Littorio* class ships. The weight of the French tipped the scales against Italy. And so, in that first month of the northern summer, the stage was set for war at sea. It was an Italian submarine, *Bagnolini*, that scored first blood, torpedoing and sinking the old cruiser HMS *Calypso* south of Crete on 12 June, with the loss of thirty-nine lives.

—

As *Vendetta* entered her purgatory in Malta, the other Scrap Iron destroyers had been plying their trade from one end of the Med to the other. Most impressively, they found themselves escorting the newly arriving capital ships for the fleet, an imposing spectacle for young Australians who had never beheld anything so grand. For others, they were a familiar sight. Rupert Robison, *Stuart*'s first lieutenant, and 'Dusty' Rhoades had both been midshipmen in *Royal Sovereign* in the 1920s. *Stuart* had escorted the carrier *Glorious* out into the Atlantic and as far as Cape Finisterre on the north-western tip of Spain, raising everyone's hope that they might be heading for Britain, but there they were sent back to the Med again.

The dire winter had passed, but the Middle Sea still had surprises in store. On the morning of 12 May, *Stuart* was just off Alexandria when she was ordered to rescue an observation seaplane from the cruiser *Neptune* which had made a forced landing and was adrift some 30 miles away. Hec Waller ordered full speed and they found the aircraft at 1100 hours, a small Fairey Seafox biplane bobbing on her floats in a calm sea, with her pilot and observer still on board. The recovery looked to be simple enough. *Stuart* lowered her whaler to take a line out to the plane and when that was secured they brought the two airmen back to the ship to begin the slow tow back to port.

All went well for an hour or so until the weather turned upon them with a new and different ferocity. The sky darkened with ominous speed, the wind stiffened and the seas began to whip up. Suddenly they were steaming into the teeth of a Khamsin, one of the Mediterranean's great dust storms of fable and legend whipping up out of the deserts of the Middle East and North Africa. A Khamsin can blow at up to 140 km/h, but it is the fine, hot, powdery dust which wreaks havoc, making it hard to see or even breathe. On *Stuart*'s bridge, coughing and spluttering, their eyes smarting, there were moments when the crew literally could not see beyond the rail through the gritty orange cloud. And there was no relief below. The dust penetrated everything. It smothered the mess decks, found its way into the men's clothing lockers, left its filth all over the galley and, sucked in by the fans, reached as far down as the boiler and engine rooms. The wind had brought on a heavy swell, too, with every chance that the little Seafox might nosedive and be lost. The captain slowed down to some 3 knots, and a couple of times stopped the ship altogether, although with visibility down to nil the only way they could tell if they still had their charge was to see if there was tension on the tow line. Once they spread oil on troubled waters, hoping that its viscosity would smooth the seas a little. They made it back to Alexandria just after the change of watch at eight o'clock that evening, when a tug turned up to take the plane from them. A 'well done' signal from Vice Admiral Tovey was small consolation. It took another day to clean the ship of the desert dirt.

—

Well before the war began the Italians had been sowing minefields around the larger Mediterranean and the Adriatic to their east. At first they were defensive, to protect their coasts and harbours on the mainland and along the African shores of Italian Libya. The Regia Marina had a fleet of submarines specifically designed for laying mines and they set about doing it. The big Foca class submarines, 1600 tons and with a long range of up to 14,000 kilometres, could carry thirty-six mines, released through chutes in the stern. Mines were cheap to make and deploy, an important consideration for the struggling Italian defence budget and, better still, they were effective. They had caused great loss on both sides in the First World War, to warships and merchant ships, and would do so again in the Second World War. They also had a profound psychological effect.

The discovery of a single enemy mine could disrupt shipping in and out of a busy port for days. At the great Battle of Jutland in the North Sea in 1916, the British Commander-in-Chief, Sir John Jellicoe, had been haunted by the fear that the withdrawing German High Seas Fleet would lay mines in his path as he pursued it.

Unlike some of the more technically advanced German mines which could be detonated by the noise of a ship's engines and pro-pellors, or by a ship's magnetic field, the Italian mines were not sophisticated. They were contact mines which had to be touched to explode. The most common type was a simple, black-painted iron sphere of a metre or more in diameter with an explosive charge of around 125 kilograms of TNT or Amatol, more than enough to blow the bows off a warship large or small. They had six or eight protrud-ing spikes known as 'Hertz horns'. When a ship hit one of those horns and crushed it, a small stream of sulphuric acid would run down a tube and activate a lead acid battery which in turn detonated the explosive. The mines could be left to float with wind and waves, but more commonly they were tethered to the seabed by a weight with a chain up to 300 metres long.

With war declared the Italians redoubled their efforts with offen-sive minelaying along all the shores of Italy, off Malta, off Libya and off Egypt. Hundreds and hundreds were sown. The Royal Navy's *Mediterranean War Diary* for 12 June warned of a minefield just 30 kilometres north-west of the tall column of the Ras el-Tin light-house which guarded the entrance to Alexandria Harbour.[10]

They found it because *Stuart* ran into it. That day they had been patrolling the Boghaz Pass, a regular job for the Australian destroyers assigned to keep clear one of the channels which led through the shoals into the port. With wry humour, the sailors called it the 'Bughouse Patrol'. It was usually a tedious job of back and forth, back and forth at slow speed, searching for possible submarines. That evening Hec Waller took the ship a little further out to sea. At 1940 hours, in the gathering dusk, they sighted the sinister shape of a mine bobbing in the water ahead of them off to port. The alarm gongs clattered through the ship; the men ran to their action stations. *Stuart* came to a dead slow with the Asdic searching, and very soon they heard the chilling *ping ... bip* echo from more mines below the surface all around them. The danger was immediate, the fear and tension on board icy, silent, palpable. Somehow they had to find a way through. Only one man could do it. The life of everyone on board depended on the skill and caution of the captain, and they looked to him to save them. Hec had a buoy thrown overboard to mark the spot of the mine they saw, doubled the lookouts on the bridge and up in the crow's nest on the foremast, reported the find back to Alexandria, and began the delicate, nerve-wracking task of extricating them from the danger, gingerly steering with the rudder and both engines as he crept further out to sea. *Ping ... bip. Ping ...* eventually the Asdic returned no echoes and they were free. *Stuart* continued her patrol in the hope of perhaps discovering the submarine which had done the deed.

But there was more to come. A couple of hours later they ran into yet another minefield some 8 kilometres or so from the first, and then a third 5 kilometres further on. The submarine had been busy. Lieutenant Corlett, the Asdic Officer, and his operator Harry Warr, a twenty-eight-year-old able seaman from Sydney, fortified by mugs of kye, spent a long and exhausting night reporting each new find to the bridge.

'Contact green twenty, sir. Contact red ten.'

Much depended on these men. The thought of them missing a mine was too awful to contemplate. The Asdic squawked from the loudspeaker behind the compass platform, its incessant, maddening *pings* drilling into the brains of the watch. *Stuart*'s ship's chronicle recorded the action:

While backing and filling to get out of the danger area all hands not actually employed elsewhere were ordered to remain amidships, the captain saying: 'If we hit a mine, I'll see to it that it is our bow or stern.' Next morning we returned to the buoyed mine.[11]

With the men still huddled on deck in the waist, the widest and hopefully safest part of the ship, Hec tried to sink the mine by rifle fire. It did not work. And then ...

another mine was discovered alongside the ship, floating just under the water. The feeling of the ship's company watching over the side an easily visible and wicked looking mine, swaying to and fro from the ship only a couple of feet away, may be more easily imagined than described.

Their luck held. Ever so slowly the black sphere disappeared astern, bobbing in their wake. Two minesweepers eventually turned up from Alexandria with their paravanes streamed, all bustling competence, and methodically began to clear the field with a series of impressive *whoomps* and fountains of dirty brown seawater. *Stuart* headed back to the harbour for the captain to report to the staff ashore and to redeploy his flotilla patrol, and that afternoon, 13 June, they were back at sea again in the same area.

It was to be an exciting, turbulent night of the most intense action they had yet encountered. As Commander (D), Waller now had four more of his flotilla at sea: *Vampire* and *Voyager*, and the British destroyers *Decoy* and *Dainty*. The stakes were high, and not only for the safety of their own ships and their own lives. On Italy's declaration of war Cunningham had taken his fleet, battleships and cruisers out of Alexandria on a probing sweep to sea. It was now the job of the 10th Flotilla, and the minesweepers, to ensure their safe return.

As night began to fall, just before 1800 hours, *Stuart*'s lookouts spotted the flash from a gun over the horizon. It was *Voyager*, who reported seeing a submarine some 20 kilometres to seaward. Waller rang for full speed and headed to the spot, only to find himself in yet another minefield. It was maddening, but there was nothing for it except to slowly try and free himself yet again. *Voyager*, though, was in clear water, her Asdic searching. Not long after *Stuart*'s arrival, *Voyager*'s operator, Leading Seaman George 'Nut' Cooper, reported a contact. Definitely a submarine.

The officer of the watch, Harry Burgin, ordered action stations. The Captain, 'Copper' Morrow, who had briefly left the compass platform, raced back to take charge. On the bridge the first lieutenant, Alan Lewis, readied his gun crews. On the quarterdeck, the Torpedo Gunner, Harry Edmondstone, another RN man, and his depth charge crew waited for the word to send their canisters overboard. It was exhilarating, the adrenalin running, everything they had trained for. The Asdic *pings* were growing louder and closer together as *Voyager* forged into the attack at almost 20 knots.

'Starboard twenty ... midships ... depth charge pattern ready ...'

Morrow now had to judge his moment for in the last minute of an attack at speed and with the destroyer virtually on top of her quarry the Asdic would lose contact in the turbulence. A skilled sub captain knew that and could take quick evasive action.

'Fire!'

The buzzer sounded. Four depth charges tumbled over the stern. *Voyager* shot off a calcium flare which rose high in the night and in its eerie white light they watched as the sea erupted behind them. The captain swung around on a reciprocal course with the Asdic *pinging* again and the depth charge crews straining to reload as the destroyer ran in on the contact once more. They made four attacks in all, and on the final one, after the charges exploded, a black shape rose briefly to the surface like a breaching whale. It must be, it could only be the hull of a submarine, they told each other. Alan Lewis ordered his 4-inch guns to shoot and it seemed, in the turmoil and the dark, that they might have scored a hit or two. They were sure they had. The shape submerged, and shortly afterwards they heard and felt some heavy but muffled explosions at some distance and some depth. Cheers echoed through the ship. *Voyager* would have the honour of the Australians' first kill.

There was more to come that night and into the early hours of the morning of 14 June. *Voyager* made another underwater contact and *Stuart*, who had escaped from her minefield, joined her in a concerted attack. So did the destroyer *Decoy*, which had turned up at the scene. *Voyager* expended all her depth charges and, as dawn rose, they saw a long slick of oil gleaming on the surface. It seemed to be evidence of yet another kill. Back in Alexandria that night, they celebrated long and hard. Harry Edmondstone wrote home to friends in Fremantle 'from a Mediterranean port', a letter published in the *West Australian* and newspapers around Australia.

Since Italy entered the war, we have been more or less isolated here as far as mails have been concerned, both inward and outward.

However, having dealt faithfully with our dear enemy, things are getting back to normal once more, and we shall soon have a more or less normal service running again.

We have been allowed to divulge a certain amount of news, so here goes to tell you. You probably read in the papers how one of the Aussie destroyers collared an Italian submarine directly after Italy declared war. Well that was our ship, and a grand reviver it was for all hands after months of soul-destroying monotony escorting convoys and so on. It was first blood, but we have had a lot of fun since. Naturally, we spend a great deal of our time at sea, on patrols, etc, especially as, according to the Italian Press, Italy controls the Mediterranean. As a matter of fact, 'Musso' said he was coming here to rake us out, and we all shook at the knees. So, of course, not wanting to put the Italians to such a lot of trouble, we sent a few ships out to see if we could form a welcoming committee. That jaunt cost 'Musso' several subs and a destroyer, which must have fallen to pieces trying to meet us.[12]

Only after the war did the facts emerge, when the Supermarina archives became available. There had certainly been a submarine there, very likely their Foca class minelaying boat. But she had not been sunk. Shaken up, yes, but she had escaped. Yet it had been a victory and an important one, for the flotilla had done the job it was assigned to do, thwarting an enemy attack. Cunningham was able to bring his fleet back safely to Alexandria. As the official Australian navy history put it:

the work done by the flotilla in discovering and determining the position and extent of the minefields was invaluable. Throughout the 14th, all the available ships of the flotilla sought out an approved channel for the main fleet returning in the afternoon from its four days' sweep; and the Italian expenditure of effort and mines to block the approaches to the base and to cause ship casualties went for nothing.[13]

Alexandria had become pretty much home base. Comings and goings developed their own routine, with a run ashore eagerly anticipated and the chance for a couple of days' leave if there was a boiler clean to be done. There were the carnal attractions of Sister Street, to be sure, but most of the men with liberty were just as happy to get a few cheap beers with mates, a square meal and a bed for the night at the handsome Royal Navy Fleet Club just a few blocks back from the beach. There was sport if you wanted it. Tennis was popular, and some of the ships prided themselves on their water polo teams, *Stuart* once famously defeating *Voyager* 8–0. Alexandria also boasted an attractive cricket club with the wicket and outfield so lovingly watered and manicured that, but for the surrounding palm trees, it might have been transplanted from Surrey or Hampshire. Quite a few ships formed their own teams, where rank did not count, and winners and losers would share a cold beer on the pavilion verandah after the game. On a 'make and mend' afternoon, when the men got time off to do anything or nothing and the temperature could reach the old Fahrenheit century mark, there might be diving competitions off the fo'c'sle, a swim over the side and sunbaking. Air raids, though, were becoming more frequent, at any hour of the day or night. The sirens wailed, the searchlights stabbed the dark to pick out the bombers high overhead, the harbour anti-aircraft guns opened up and every ship joined in, like fireworks night. This too became routine, almost not worth commenting on. It happened and you dealt with it.

*Voyager* sailed again from Alexandria at dawn on 27 June in company with *Dainty*, *Decoy* and *Defender* from their 10th Flotilla, and *Ilex* from the 2nd. They were line abreast, plunging like a school of porpoises into a heavy green sea at 25 knots, when Able Seaman 'Buck' Rogers was washed overboard as he attempted to secure some cases of ammunition on the fo'c'sle. He was lucky to have been spotted. The whaler picked him up, shaken but unharmed.

From the end of June and into July, Britain's decoding experts could read signals to Italian submarine commanders in real time, as they were sent and received. The intelligence had suggested the Italians were placing a submarine patrol line from Crete to the African coast. That evening, 27 June, in a pearly sunset, about 150 kilometres south-east of Crete, *Voyager* sighted a submarine on the surface, wallowing in heavy seas. It submerged in a hurry as the five converged on the position. *Voyager* stood off while the four British destroyers took turns at depth charge runs in the fading light.

The submarine was the *Console Generale Liuzzi,* a big and modern ocean-going boat of 1500 tons, named for one of Mussolini's fascist Blackshirt commanders and launched only in September 1939. She had left La Spezia on 24 June for her first patrol. Gesuino de Montis was a young engineer also on his first trip:

I was in the bow when I heard the alarm siren. We descended with a rapid dive to 100 metres but were bombarded with ten depth charges. We continued to descend to a depth of 120 metres and another pattern of ten bombs arrived ...

*Era il finimondo!* It was the end of the world! We continued the descent to 150 metres, but more depth charges arrived: we counted a total of sixty. The submarine was now unmanageable, all the instruments on board were destroyed as we had lost all the equipment. When we reached 190 metres our commander, Capitano di Corvetta Lorenzo Bezzi, decided to surface. The situation was very critical: we were immersed in total darkness, with unusable instruments and equipment smashed, a scary thing.

The captain and the chief engineer gave the order to surface, and since we were no longer able to defend ourselves, he ordered us to leave the submarine through the conning tower because it was about to sink. Those of us in the bow got out last. Then the captain ordered us to jump overboard because no one wanted to abandon the submarine; with his order 'throw yourself all into the sea' we were forced to obey and to dive into the water. Immediately the destroyers bombarded us with a couple of cannon shots: one hit the bow. The captain, when he saw that we were all in the water, returned to the inside of the submarine and locked himself in, going to the bottom with it.[14]

Someone in the top of the conning tower waved a small white light in surrender, the shooting stopped, and the destroyers lowered boats in the rough seas to rescue the survivors. A few men, crying and wailing, refused to leave the illusory safety of the submarine's deck and had to be coaxed, persuaded and ordered to jump. *Voyager*'s whaler collected thirteen men. Most of them had stripped naked for the swim, and were shivering with cold, shock and fear. It was the first time the Australians had seen the enemy up close, in flesh and blood. They were not Mussolini's invincible legionaries, nor some abstract concept of enmity to be hated, but blokes like themselves, some of them still teenagers like themselves, all sailors like themselves. Smartly, but with a rough kindness, the Italians were helped on board. A couple of hours earlier they had been intent on killing each other. Now there they were on *Voyager*'s deck, the winners and losers together. The battle was done. It was not like the end of a football game, three cheers and handshakes all round, but nor was there any evident hostility. One boy, who gave his name only as Vito, told them he was seventeen and had left school just a month before. Another man, a petty officer who spoke fair English, talked enthusiastically of a trip he had made to Hobart before the war. There but for the Grace of God ... *Voyager*'s crew took pity:

> The poor devils were sick and didn't know what was going to happen to them. Some were injured. We took them into the galley flat and changed them into some dry clothes, gifts from the ship's company. We gave them cigarettes, coffee and sandwiches.[15]

Two days later, almost incredibly, it happened again, in a turbulent encounter about 200 kilometres due west of Crete. A little before dawn on 29 June, *Voyager* sighted the small, dark shape of a conning tower about 15 kilometres away. The enemy saw them almost simultaneously and dived. *Voyager* and three of the other destroyers took turns to attack with depth charges, but they lost contact and it apparently escaped. Almost an hour later, *Ilex* spotted a second submarine, which also crash dived and was depth charged without luck. An hour later again – it seemed almost comical – a third boat appeared. This was the small, 800-ton *Uebi Scebeli*, which rapidly submerged to periscope depth to make a torpedo attack but was quickly run down by *Voyager* and *Defender*. She blew her tanks and surfaced, wallowing in the swell. Again the destroyers opened fire, sparks flying from a couple of hits on the conning tower until the crew scrambled out onto the deck and surrendered with hands up. Some of the Italians began to throw the secret books into the sea, but an armed boarding party from *Dainty* managed to capture the *Sommergibili Italiani SM 19/S* submarine code book, a treasure beyond price. The sub was sunk by gunfire, all done and dusted in a brisk morning's work. The code book was passed to *Voyager*, for she was low on fuel and would be first to return to Alexandria.

> Sunday, 30 June 1940. Quiet day, weather nice, prisoners sunning themselves. Very talkative. As we neared Alex we fell them in on the Pom Pom deck. Alongside the oiler, boats came with an armed guard, and after we bade them farewell they were taken away.[16]

There were celebrations at the Fleet Club that night for the sailors who had done the job, and in the wardroom for the captain, 'Copper' Morrow, who learned that evening he had been promoted to the brass hat of a full commander. Later, there were medals in it too. In London that coming September, the Admiralty announced that Hector Macdonald Laws Waller and James Cairns Morrow had been awarded the DSO, the Distinguished Service Order. Geoff Corlett, *Stuart*'s Asdic officer, got the DSC, the Distinguished Service Cross. In those class-conscious days there were different decorations for sailors. The two Asdic operators, George Cooper and Harry Warr, won the DSM, the Distinguished Service Medal.

The parties and gongs were well justified. In that first fortnight of July another eight Italian boats were sunk. Only then did Supermarina suspect what had happened and change the codes. The war was hotting up.

# CHAPTER 6

# 'YOU ARE GOING ON A VERY DANGEROUS MISSION'

Back in the first week of March, with *Stuart*, *Vampire* and *Voyager* berthed together in the Malta dockyard, the crews were surprised one morning to find an unusual notice pinned up in the mess decks.

VOLUNTEERS WANTED FOR A SPECIAL SERVICE OPERATION.

Intrigued, keen for a change from the dull routine of convoy here and there, a lot of men put a hand up. Mostly the younger blokes. Twelve were chosen, told to pack their gear quick smart and get ready to go ashore. Two were officers: Robert Scott, the sub lieutenant RANR who had joined *Stuart* in Sydney as a temporary navigator, and another sub, twenty-five-year-old Bill Milne from Adelaide, a watchkeeper from *Voyager*.

The rest were young seamen or stokers. Terry Van Prooyen, a youngster from Melbourne, had been promoted to able seaman in *Voyager* just a few weeks before. Fair-haired and fresh faced, he had grown up in the tough streets of suburban Kensington, where he had made a name for himself as a sporty, active sort of kid who didn't mind a bit of a fight occasionally. Cricket was his particular passion. Looking for a steady job, he joined the navy in 1938, where his foreign-sounding surname landed him the nickname 'Dutchie', a handle he did not particularly like but was stuck with.

'Being only twenty years old and a bit adventurous or a little stupid I volunteered and was chosen,'[1] he recalled long after the war. His shipmate Robert 'Zack' Lardner, a year older and a stoker from Sydney, was picked with him. On 10 March they and the other Australians humped their kitbags into the ancient Fort St Angelo, a Royal Navy barracks on the southern shore of Grand Harbour, where they found fifty or so British sailors equally in the dark about what was going on.

It didn't take them long to find out. For the next two weeks they were put through a punishing round of physical exercise and intensive training on machine guns, pistols, grenades and the handling of explosives. On one truly startling day they found themselves paraded before none other than the Commander-in-Chief himself, who descended from on high to give them some 'real British stiff upper lip stuff',[2] as Terry called it.

'You are going on a very dangerous mission,' Cunningham told them. 'If it goes wrong, you may not get back, and we will deny all knowledge of you. If anyone wants to step out now you may do so, and we will think no less of you.'

Nobody moved.

'Then good luck to you all,' said the Admiral.[3] And off he went.

Towards the end of their training each man was handed the enormous sum of £10 – about three months' pay – and told to go shopping for civilian clothes. They bought slacks, shirts, some snappy sports jackets, socks and shoes. They had their photographs taken for new passports and were given forged merchant seamen's discharge papers. They were handed a suitcase to pack their new gear in, along with one navy uniform and a cap with a tally band that simply read 'HMS' with no ship's name on it. All top secret, say nothing to no one, they were endlessly told. They still had no idea where they were going or what they were supposed to do when they got there.

—

On 7 March, a long way from the Mediterranean, a steamship of the Ellerman Line, the SS *Mardinian*, quietly left the Liverpool Docks

on England's west coast, eased her way down the Mersey River into
the Irish Sea and then turned south for the Atlantic. With her rusty
black hull, cargo derricks and tall buff funnel she was small, slow and
entirely unremarkable, the sort of British merchant tramp familiar in
ports around the world.

She had been selected for just those reasons. In the *Mardinian*'s
hold was a cargo of ninety-five sealed wooden crates which appeared
on her manifest as motor car spare parts, addressed to the agent of the
Chrysler car company in the Hungarian capital, Budapest. A list of
the contents of those crates still exists:

| | |
|---|---|
| 4 | .303 Vickers machine guns with spare parts |
| 12 | Lewis machine guns |
| 20 | .303 Lee Enfield Rifles |
| 50 | Revolvers |
| 14,000 | Rounds of.303 ammunition |
| 10,000 | Rounds of incendiary ammunition |
| 1,000 | Rounds revolver ammunition |
| 600 lbs | High Explosives |
| 49 | Limpet mines |
| 5 | Boxes of canisters.[4] |

Plodding along at her best speed of 10 knots, the *Mardinian* slipped
unhindered past France, Portugal and Spain. In the middle of March
she passed eastwards through the Strait of Gibraltar and, hugging the
African shore, headed for a rendezvous at sea off the coast of Tunisia.

—

*Stuart* sailed from Malta on 20 March, on a course to the south-west.
Hec Waller told the crew only that they were looking for a certain
ship. Two days later they found one, a small freighter loitering off
Tunis as if she too had been looking for them. To mounting curiosity, the captain called away *Stuart*'s motorboat, scrambled up a ladder
over the side of the stranger and disappeared. On *Stuart*'s bridge they
could read the name on the stern of the newcomer: *Mardinian*. Less
than half an hour later the Captain emerged, rejoined the destroyer,
then ordered full speed back to Malta.

The mystery deepened. *Stuart* secured in the dockyard. There was no leave given. As dusk fell, some lighters came alongside bearing wooden packing cases labelled 'agricultural machinery', which were laboriously loaded on deck and lashed down. That done, a group of sixty-eight silent, purposeful men in civilian clothes trooped up the gangway with their luggage, and by 2000 hours the destroyer was heading back out to sea again at speed. To general astonishment, *Stuart*'s men recognised some of the civilians: Sub Lieutenant Scott ... 'Dutchie' Van Prooyen ... 'Curly' Sutton and Frank Peade, two of *Stuart*'s stokers ... Dom Owens, a three-badge able seaman from *Voyager* ... and more. They were warned not to talk to them.

Waller offered a prize of £1 to the first man to sight the *Mardinian* again. At ten o'clock on the morning of 24 March a keen-eyed signalman spotted smoke on the horizon, and there she was. *Stuart* closed her once more and the two sailed slowly along in company as first the agricultural machinery – in fact more weapons and ammunition – and then the solemn and silent civilians were transferred across. By midday the job was done and *Stuart* turned home for Malta.

'During the return passage Commander Waller cleared lower deck,' wrote Les Clifford. 'And in an address to the ship's company, stressed the point that no mention of the ship's latest venture must be made ashore, or reach the ears of anyone outside the ship, as it would not only endanger the lives of the men we had disembarked but would be disastrous for the Allied cause.'[5]

Cunningham sent Waller a letter, which he read to the ship's company:

On the conclusion of the important operation which was entrusted to HMAS *Stuart*, I wish to convey my appreciation of the way in which this duty was carried out. The interception of the ship concerned and the subsequent embarkation of the personnel and stores and their final disposal was carried out in a manner which reflects great credit on all hands.[6]

The little *Mardinian* steamed east for another day and then turned north-west to pass between mainland Greece and the island of Crete and up into the Aegean. Then north-east again, with the fatal shore of Gallipoli off to port; through into the Sea of Marmara, where lay the sunken wreck of the First World War Australian submarine *AE2*; up through the Bosphorus, that narrow strait of legend that bisects north-western Turkey and opens into the Black Sea. Only then did Terry and Zack and the rest of them find out where they were going. On 29 March, the *Mardinian*, with her lethal cargo of men, guns and munitions, dropped anchor at Sulina, a small port in the Balkan kingdom of Romania on the estuary where the mighty Danube River ends, at last, its long and winding journey through Europe to the sea.

—

Famed for its brooding Transylvanian castles and forests, its fictional vampires, and its very non-fictional fifteenth-century ogre Vlad the Impaler, Romania also boasted a more modern blessing: oil, and lots of it. The vast oilfields at Ploesti, north of the capital Bucharest, were some of the most productive in Europe, second only to those of the Soviet Union.

One of the largest customers was Germany. In peacetime, Romania supplied more than one third of all Germany's oil, some of it sent by train but most of it carried up the Danube in fleets of river tankers. The outbreak of war and the British sea blockade of Germany meant that maintaining and increasing that flow of Ploesti oil became of crucial importance to the Reich's economy and war machine. With their usual combination of threats, bribery and flattery, in December 1939 the Nazis persuaded Romania to agree to export to Germany 130,000 tons of oil each month.

The Romanians were not particularly enthusiastic about this arrangement. The Kaiser's Germany and the Austro-Hungarians had ravaged their country in the First World War, and they had not forgotten it. But their ruler, King Carol II, an absolute monarch, was trapped in a maze of competing pressures of a uniquely Balkan confusion. A notorious playboy whose chief interests were fast cars, an exotic mistress and a wardrobe of evermore gorgeous uniforms dripping with stars, plumes and medals, he was inclined towards friendship with Britain and France. They had given Romania much publicised, although largely meaningless, guarantees of territorial security in April 1939.

But on Romania's long northern border lay the haunting menace of the Soviet Union, which might at any time invade and seize as much territory as it wanted. Commercial agreements with Germany, Carol thought, might forestall any Russian aggression. At home, the king indulged in a personality cult which portrayed him to the peasants and working classes as the fount of all goodness. The elite revered all things French. Waiting in the wings was the Iron Guard, a rising political movement of religious mystics, fascists and anti-Semites who despised the king and idolised Hitler. It was an almost impossible juggling act, but for the first year of the war Carol pulled it off and Romania maintained an uneasy neutrality.

Long before the war the British had mulled plans for choking off the flow of Romanian oil if the need arose. They did not know the fine print of the new agreement with Germany but they knew it existed, and stopping that oil had now become imperative. If that was successful it would cripple the Wehrmacht. The bureaucracies of Whitehall set to work. The mandarins at the Foreign Office piously believed that traditional British diplomacy of appeals to decency, logic and reason might induce Carol to see things their way. If that didn't do the trick, they would tighten some economic screws of their own. Rather more practically, the Secret Intelligence Service – known then as MI6 – wanted to bust heads and break things. It had already set up a new department known as Section D – supposedly D for 'Destruction' – which would run spies and agents to carry out acts of sabotage big and small. And the Naval Intelligence Division, with its secret rooms at the Admiralty, had some exotically salty ideas of its own which it jealously guarded.

Some of the proposals were weird and wonderful, almost cartoonish. In the first months of the war an operation to blow up a giant cliff on the Yugoslav side[7] and topple it into the Danube had to be scrapped when Yugoslav military intelligence got wind of it. Plans to send a flotilla of motor torpedo boats dashing about, shooting at everything German were abandoned when no boats could be found. Another idea was to offer all the Danube river pilots three years' pay to stop work and somehow disappear, bringing tanker traffic to a halt. Cables flashed back and forth between the British Legation in Bucharest and Section D in London and a list of names was drawn up with the cash allotted, but it too fell over simply because the pilots weren't interested. Section D's sabotage on the ground was marginally more effective. Agents sent from London and locals working on oil trains in the railway yards cut brake cables and couplings and poured sulphuric acid into axle boxes.

The most complex scheme of all was to buy up as many of the Danube tankers, tugs and barges as possible to deny them to the Germans. Section D set up the grandly named Goeland Transport and Trading Company and sent one of its men from London to splash money around and build the fleet, which he did with some success. Then somebody suggested it would be a terrific idea to fill some of these vessels with rocks and concrete and to sink them to block the river at its narrowest part ...

At this point, enter the Naval Intelligence Division at the Admiralty. One of its brightest lights was a newly recruited former journalist and stockbroker named Ian Fleming. An Old Etonian, independently wealthy, suave and witty, chain-smoking, exquisitely well-tailored with impeccable manners, with a string of impressive sexual conquests and knowing all the right people, Fleming was offered a job in early 1939 with the rank of lieutenant commander in the Royal Navy Volunteer Reserve. There he began the career in intelligence and espionage that would lead him, after the war, to create the stratospherically successful James Bond, Agent 007, licensed to kill.

Fleming seized the idea of blocking the Danube and – it so happened – he knew just the chap to help out. Merlin Minshall, aged thirty-three, was another rich and personable scion of the upper classes, educated at another posh school, Charterhouse, and at Oxford. Disdaining the tedious business of working for a living, in the 1930s Minshall dashed about Europe as a racing driver, rode a motorcycle across the Sahara Desert and went on safari in Africa. In the mid-1930s he sailed a Dutch canal boat down the length of the Danube from its beginnings in Germany to its finish in Romania, a trip on which he claimed to have met Reichsmarschall Hermann Göring and to have been seduced by a beautiful blonde German spy who hitched a ride with him. Fleming took him on as a lieutenant in the RNVR.

In the best Whitehall tradition, an interdepartmental committee of the Foreign Office, Section D and Naval Intelligence pored over what to do. Instead of merely sinking boats full of concrete, why not cram them with explosives and blow them up? Section D would provide the bang, the Navy would provide the manpower and the Foreign Office would provide the money, with the operation controlled on the ground by the naval attaché at the Bucharest Embassy.

But where to do it? After much study, with input from the helpful Minshall, the committee chose a gorge where the Danube rushes down between the Carpathian Mountains on the Romanian side and the Balkan Mountains of Yugoslavia. There the river narrows to some 150 metres, with swift currents. Long and spectacularly wild and grand, the gorge is known as the Iron Gates. It would be a simple exercise to block it there, everyone agreed. All that had to be done was to pack some of the Goeland Company vessels with explosives and send them up the river with crews of stout-hearted British sailors. The scheme was put to the War Cabinet, where it gained the enthusiastic backing of the then First Lord of the Admiralty, Winston Churchill, always keen for a novel adventure and the more luridly theatrical the better. Blow up the Iron Gates! It was new, it was clever, it was daring. If it worked, it might just bring Germany to her knees and shorten the war. Minshall was sent out under diplomatic cover to get things moving.

Thus the stage was set for Able Seaman 'Dutchie' Van Prooyen, Stoker 'Zack' Lardner and their mates from the Scrap Iron Flotilla to make their mark on history.

—

There at Sulina to meet the *Mardinian* was the man who would lead the expedition, Commander Alexander Gibson RN. A month earlier Gibson had been the 7th Cruiser Squadron's torpedo officer in the Mediterranean Fleet, presumably chosen for this new task for his professional knowledge of explosives. He had arrived in Romania a week before with a party of ten sailors to get the show under way. Another group, led by Merlin Minshall, was upriver at a small port named

Braila, preparing the Goeland Company vessels to receive their crews and cargoes.

Things now began to unravel slightly. Gibson had brought with him to Sulina two Goeland Company tugs, the *Britannia* and the *Princess Elizabeth*, and a big river barge, the *Termonde*. Unloading the crates of Chrysler spare parts from the *Mardinian* onto the *Termonde* took ages, understandably exciting the interest of Romanian customs officials who wanted to know what was in them. Swift talking and a suitable bribe fixed that, but then came the intriguing question of the sixty-eight fit young civilians, all of whom had brand-new passports issued on the same day a few weeks before and with no old visa stamps. As Cunningham wrote much later in his letter to the Admiralty:

> This rather blatant arrival was necessitated by the apparent urgency of the operation at that time, and it was hoped that dislike of the Germans and a little judicious bribery might cause the Romanian officials to shut their eyes to what was going on … the organisation of these illegal expeditions is much hampered by the difficulty of obtaining satisfactory bogus passports and the lack of experts in forgery.[8]

Gibson solemnly explained that the young chaps were tourists on holiday, more money changed hands, and the next day the group set off on the 170-kilometre journey through the Danube delta and up the river to Braila, followed at a distance by a little Romanian gunboat. Even in late March it was cold. The Australians could see chunks of ice still coming downstream and the basin at Braila itself was only just beginning to thaw. It was startling, too, to pass the occasional vessel flying the red, black and white swastika flag.

The news that met Gibson when they arrived at Braila was disastrous. Two British consular officials were waiting to tell him that Lieutenant Minshall had been arrested by the Romanian police. He was out on bail, but the troubles were only just beginning.

It was common gossip that Romania was seething with spies from all the belligerent nations. German agents of the Nazi intelligence service, the Abwehr, were everywhere. Some French agents reported to the British that they had overheard Minshall and another man loudly and drunkenly discussing the Goeland plan at 2 am in a bar of Bucharest's best hotel, the Athénée Palace. That was shocking enough, but there was worse. The police had arrested Minshall after he had drunkenly pulled a gun on a German doctor in a Braila brothel where, according to one of the consular officials, he had been 'thrilling the ladies of easy virtue' with lurid tales of British sabotage. Gibson was outraged, incensed. Everyone was joking about 'the Battle of the Braila Brothel' and 'Two-Gun Minshall'.

> 'Stories have been broadcast of wholesale British schemes of sabotage against the interests of the government with which we were on friendly terms,' reported the consular man to the Foreign Office. 'The fantastic posturing of some of the young men involved gave every excuse for gossip if not for credence, particularly as some of the wildest versions can be traced to the amateur Guy Fawkes themselves.'[9]

There was nothing for it. Minshall had to be got out of the way, and quickly. Commander Gibson sent him back to Britain in disgrace. Long after the war, when Ian Fleming was safely dead, Minshall produced a 'memoir' bragging of fantastical exploits in Romania and elsewhere, dashing escapades that painted him as the inspiration for James Bond. It was a tissue of lies.[10]

Still, Gibson decided to press on with the fleet of two tugs, six small river tankers and the barge *Termonde* loaded with the explosives. The Iron Gates were a distant 750 kilometres upriver and with the ice beginning to melt the traffic was picking up, especially the German traffic. The local pilots actually skippering the Goeland Company vessels, mostly Romanians or Greeks, were anxious to get moving. 'Zack' Lardner was assigned to the *Princess Elizabeth*, which also carried Gibson. Sub Lieutenant Scott and Terry went on board the tanker *King George*, and Sub Lieutenant Milne travelled in another tanker, *Scotland*. They set off from Braila on April Fool's Day. The next stop would be Giurgiu, a bigger river town that was the terminal where the crude oil from the Ploesti fields was pumped into the tankers for Germany. In peacetime it might have been a leisurely

trip past green farmland and sleepy villages, with the occasional
glimpse of a grand Baroque church or castle. But Terry Van Prooyen
was beginning to have his doubts:

> How the hell we could ever expect to get out of Romania after-
> wards I'll never know. It looked like a one-way trip for sure.
> We thought it would be a firing squad for all of us, and it damn
> near was. Romania was neutral at this stage, but it seemed full
> of Germans, and every second ship tied up along the riverbank
> seemed to carry a swastika. But up the river we went, tailed by a
> Romanian gunboat. We tied up at one stage with a Nazi ship on
> either side of us.[11]

More disaster awaited them at Giurgiu, as Gibson recounted in his
Report of Proceedings:

> The ships arrived at about 1500 on the 3rd April. I have since
> learned that our reputation had preceded us and that while we
> were still at Braila people in the street were openly talking about
> the arms and explosives that the Englishmen were bringing into
> the country. The authorities duly arrived and searched the ships
> properly. They found uniforms, arms and money; the latter
> appeared to excite them as much as anything. We had about
> £500 in Romanian lei in *Princess Elizabeth*, which was apparently
> very wrong.[12]
> … Throughout this episode the customs authorities were well
> disposed towards us and were all in favour of turning the blind eye.
> Unfortunately in Romania the authority who actually conducts
> the search is the Captain of the Ports Department, and the
> Captain of the Port at Giurgiu is pro-German and a scoundrel.[13]

The game was pretty much lost but not quite over. There was more
to play out. Trying to salvage something from the wreckage while his
sailors remained stranded on the ships, Gibson spent the next few
days locked in discussions at the British Legation in Bucharest. In his
absence, the Giurgiu Port Captain and a search party swooped again
and thoroughly turned over the *Termonde*, where they discovered the

machine guns, the rifles, the ammunition, the explosives, everything. Hoping to postpone the inevitable, a British consular official who was there tried to convince the Romanians the explosives were too dangerous to be handled by amateurs, but the next day they were confiscated and unloaded. Done, gone. The daring expedition to the Iron Gates was no more.

Terry's doubts about an exit from Romania were well founded. Bizarre as it seems, there had been no real idea of what to do if the Iron Gates had been successfully blocked, and no specific plan to bring the team back down the Danube and safely out of the country. Presumably they would have shot their way out with the machine guns, rifles and pistols if need be, but that was never specified. Now, with their weapons gone, even that was no longer possible. The only way forward was negotiation, which Gibson left at first to the diplomats.

The British Minister at Bucharest, Sir Reginald Hoare, had been infuriated by the naval chaos on the river. It threatened to wreck his careful diplomacy aimed at keeping the Romanians neutral and notionally pro-British, and he had complained forcefully in cables home to the Foreign Office. But he was also an old Balkan hand, urbane and at least outwardly imperturbable, and he began the rounds of various government ministries to try to limit the damage and to secure the sailors' release. It cannot have been an easy brief to argue. Under international law, Romania clearly had every right to seize the ships, arrest everyone and throw away the key, a course the Germans were quite understandably pushing hard. Hoare's unenviable task was not helped when German propaganda seized the moment, upped the ante and went public on 8 April with a series of news broadcasts in English and several European languages from Deutschlandsender, Berlin Radio.

> Danube plot! The criminal terrorists of the English Secret Service have carried out a monstrous outrage against the peace of South-East Europe in an attempt to dislocate Danube shipping …

It went on to list, with disturbing detail, the names of the Goeland Company vessels and a description of their contents.

Through an indiscretion of the members of the English crew, the following became known about the tasks, cargoes and crews of these ships. On board the English ships were quantities of revolvers, signal pistols, hand grenades, machine guns, depth charges, mines, empty shell cases and several thousand boxes of dynamite. The crews consisted of over 100 English special soldiers with special passports, disguised as sailors ...

... competent quarters in Romania consider the act of destruction was to be aimed at the Iron Gates. England makes herself guilty of a monstrous violation of neutrality with this attempt at a military action against Germany on neutral soil ...[14]

It was essentially accurate, and repeated yet again in even greater and more sensational detail the next day. King Carol's foreign minister, the pro-British politician Grigore Gafencu, under pressure from the German ambassador, had no choice but to make at least a gesture. He publicly ordered the British to send ten sailors out of the country which, with some difficulty, Gibson managed to do. That left the rest of them still sitting on the boats at Braila, virtually imprisoned, battered by bitter, late winter gales and with no idea of what their future might hold. The Romanians then demanded that thirty more sailors be put on a train, under guard, and sent to Bucharest. One of them was 'Zack' Lardner. At the Bucharest railway station they were publicly paraded as saboteurs for a few hours and then, inexplicably, loaded back on another train and returned to Braila, where they were locked in the hold of the *Termonde* for five days under guard until Gibson secured their release with yet another fat bribe.

The Commander found himself trapped in an almost surreal web of diplomatic and political intrigue and Balkan bureaucracy, frustrated at every turn. 'The gloves are off,' the diplomats warned him. Told one day to expect a German attack – wrongly, as it turned out – Gibson ordered the men to throw their uniforms overboard and he jettisoned his confidential papers. A few of the Australians thought Gibson was aloof and arrogant, but it is clear from his report to the Admiralty that he stuck tenaciously to the job of caring for his men and getting them out of Romania, at one stage asking for a doctor to be sent to them. A surgeon lieutenant duly arrived and discovered eleven cases of venereal disease, 'due to the extremely high local incidence, which is estimated at between 80–95 per cent of the population', he reported sternly.[15]

Weeks passed. Boredom hung heavy. There was none of the usual naval harbour routine, no colours at 0800 hours, no change of watch, no First Lieutenant's rounds in the evening to break the monotony. The men lolled on deck by day and slept by night on thin mattresses on hard wooden bunks, not the familiar comfortable hammocks. The food, much of it tinned, was prepared by local hired cooks, some of whom were perpetually drunk. Sometimes the Romanians allowed them ashore, sometimes they did not, but there was little to do in Braila anyway. Several times 'Dutchie' Van Prooyen and 'Zack' Lardner found themselves drinking in a bar with Germans at nearby tables. The war and the world passed them by, far away. They heard of the fall of Norway, of the German invasion of Belgium and France, but there was no news from home and no way of sending letters back to Australia.

Port captains, police officers and shipping officials bore down upon Gibson with new and maddening demands, restrictions, rules and regulations every day – and increasingly pro-German they were, too, as the war swung in Germany's favour. If the Commander lost heart, though, he did not show it. Eventually he concluded that the only way to leave the country was on some of the Goeland Company tugs and tankers. It was a desperate decision, for these were lightly built river vessels with a low freeboard – their upper decks only a few metres from the water – and entirely unsuitable for a passage across the Black Sea. Even a moderate swell could easily capsize them or, perhaps, simply break their backs. Most of them had no navigation equipment, not even a compass. But there was no alternative.

In the first week of May, the Romanians at last told Gibson he could take his ships and men back downriver to Sulina where they had first landed. There he tried to begin the heroic task of stiffening his vessels, of strengthening or shoring up the tankers' hulls with baulks of timber to render them a little more seaworthy. A Yugoslav contractor proved helpful, but he could not begin work until the middle of May and he estimated the job would take three weeks. The Commander combed the local stores for old compasses and sextants for navigation, and did his best to keep up morale:

Exercise was difficult to obtain. On occasions it was possible to kick a football about and for most of our stay at Sulina we were able to bathe in the river: until some official discovered that it was prohibited to bathe within the precincts of the port. There is usually good sea bathing to be had but what was once the plage is now a prohibited area owing to the presence of an anti-aircraft gun.[16]

In the end, with delay after infuriating delay, the tankers never got to be strengthened. But by 2 June three of them were fuelled, stored, and as ready as they ever could be to leave and sail for Turkey. Others would follow later. To their tremendous relief, the Australians were all on board one or the other, with Robert Scott from *Stuart* commanding *King George*, Bill Milne from *Voyager* in charge of *Scotland*, and a Royal Navy officer in *Lord Byron*. Terry, too, was in *King George*, and Zack was in *Scotland*.

At last they could put cursed Romania behind them. The voyage south down the Black Sea was choppy and nerve-wracking, the tankers wallowing and lurching, but they survived it and in two days they had reached the relative safety and security of the Bosphorus, passing down the winding narrows and dropping anchor at a little port and beach resort called Beikos just north of Istanbul on Turkey's Anatolian shore. Commander Gibson, in the tug *Princess Elizabeth*, arrived a week or so later. They were there when Italy entered the war.

At first, Beikos was a haven. The neutral Turks were friendly enough, and the men were freely allowed ashore. But the weeks began to drag by again, with no sign of them leaving and no idea of where they might be going. June turned to July. Zack caught a painful case of shingles. Terry celebrated his twenty-first birthday on 9 July. Gibson was in contact with Cunningham's Mediterranean Fleet headquarters, through the British Consul in Istanbul and after more delay – never explained – he was ordered to take his charges to sea again, heading for Alexandria via Athens. Resourceful as ever, he found a supply of mattresses to hang about the ships' bridges as 'anti-machine gun protection', and some neutral flags – Greek and Panamanian – in case they might come in handy. On 25 July the ships moved down to Chanak (Cannakale) opposite the Gallipoli Peninsula, where they regrouped again for the 300-kilometre voyage south to Athens. They sailed again on 27 July, skirting the Turkish islands of Imbros and Lemnos in kindly weather and into the Aegean Sea between the Greek islands of Skyros and Skiathos in the southern Sporades. There – to the surprise of the Australians – they encountered none other than HMAS *Stuart*.

It was no coincidence, for *Stuart* had been slowly patrolling there, back and forth, for a couple of days after escorting a convoy from Alexandria to Athens. Les Clifford gives a glimpse of the meeting:

> Our position was quite close to enemy bases, and had the Italians learned of our presence in these waters they might have been tempted to despatch a much superior force to deal with us. We could not afford to allow this to happen as we still had an important mission to perform and secrecy of our movements was vital to the success of this mission …
>
> … That afternoon, two specks were sighted on the horizon. As they drew nearer they were noted to be two barges. The leading barge, on sighting *Stuart*, flashed a signalling lantern and called us by our distinguishing signal.
>
> 'Who on earth can this be?' queried Captain Waller.
>
> On answering the call, we discovered that the officer in charge of the barge was none other than our late navigating officer, Sub Lieutenant Scott, who had been a member of the special mission in connection with our 'Hush Hush operation'.[17]

And there he leaves it, with no further explanation. *Stuart*'s log says nothing either, but we do know it happened, for Commander Gibson records an exchange there with Hec Waller as well. The likely explanation is that *Stuart* had been told from Alexandria that the tankers were on their way in the area and had been asked to keep an eye out for them.

Had they but known it, there were echoing footfalls to be heard in the halls of myth and history here. In these very wine-dark waters the hero Ulysses had searched for and found the noble Achilles on Skyros itself. Together they had sailed for the Trojan War. On Skyros, too, there lay Rupert Brooke, the celebrated British poet of the First World War, dead on his way to Gallipoli and buried by his friends in some foreign field that is forever England.[18] On their own long odyssey, the Australians from Romania had happened upon their own countrymen and their own ship once more. But that done they parted, and Gibson took his charges on to Piraeus, the port for Athens. There they rested again for three days to prepare for the most dangerous leg of their journey, down the open Med to Alexandria. The British naval attaché in Athens rustled up a few sub-machine guns with ammunition to put on board, and the RAF attaché found them some recognition silhouettes of Italian military aircraft.

They set off again on 3 August, with their course set by Fleet Headquarters. They were to stick as far as possible to the coast of mainland Greece, then go south around Crete, then south-east to Alexandria, a journey of some 1200 kilometres. In fair weather at their best speed of 9 knots it should take about four days. The *Princess Elizabeth* was flying the flag of neutral Yugoslavia. At first, luck held. The weather was good, the seas were calm and they made steady progress. But it did not last.

The Italians found them halfway along the south-east coast of Crete. At 10 am on 6 August, a lone flying boat appeared out of a cloudless sky and dived towards *Princess Elizabeth*, flying so low they could clearly see the Italian colours. It circled them a couple of times. Gibson ordered the crew below decks:

> I did not know whether she had any bombs or not so, after the ship's company had taken cover, I endeavoured to preserve a grudging, benevolent neutrality towards Italians, at the same time keeping the well-padded wheelhouse between myself and the aircraft. Eventually he fired one burst ... *Princess Elizabeth* replied with a Tommy gun and he flew away.[19]

There was nothing for it but to keep going. Two hours later, at around 1 pm, at the point where they were about to turn south-east for Alexandria, the Italians were back. This time it was six Savoia-Marchetti bombers, coming in slowly from the west at about 2000 feet, engines growling as they turned to aim. Gripped by fear, the men raced again for cover. For every one of them it was the first time under air attack. Italy had not been in the war when they left Malta

five months before. Save for the few sub-machine guns acquired in
Athens they were naked and defenceless, in frail river craft which
could capsize at even a near miss.

> The raid lasted for about forty minutes. The first salvo straddled
> *Scotland*, who altered course further inshore. *Princess Elizabeth*
> increased to full speed and altered course continually, at the same
> time endeavouring to get further inshore, although she was well
> within territorial waters at the beginning of the raid.
>
> My general idea was to alter in the direction of the reciprocal
> of the plane's course as soon as I saw a bomb leave the aeroplane.
> Two or three salvoes were eventually aimed at *Princess Elizabeth*,
> none of which fell particularly close, until finally a single plane
> dropped a single bomb which fell 20 or 30 yards from the star-
> board side amidships.[20]

That bomb threw up a mighty fountain of dirty brown sea,
sending shock waves that tossed the tug like a bathtub toy. Water
sloshed below decks, a bulkhead cracked, sheets of glass were broken
and a hatch cover was blown off, but somehow she survived and kept
ploughing along. *Scotland* was not so lucky. She was not hit either, but
in the confusion of twisting and turning to avoid the falling bombs,
blinded by smoke and deafened by the noise, Bill Milne took her too
close inshore. She ran gently aground. With the Savoias still circling
as menacing as ever, some of the *Scotland*'s men, including 'Zack'
Lardner, dived overboard and swam ashore.

At this moment – at this excruciating moment – the gods of war
played their hand again. Incredibly, the cavalry arrived over the
horizon. Despatched from Alexandria, the destroyers HMS *Jervis* and
HMS *Hostile* came steaming towards them at full speed, bow waves
curling, anti-aircraft guns blazing, all fight and fury, deliverance
itself. The Italians wheeled away, whether out of bombs or frightened
off, it didn't really matter.

Gibson turned to worrying about how to get *Scotland* off her shoal,
hoping to get a line across to her and begin a tow, but again fortune
intervened. Slowly, carefully, Sub Lieutenant Milne managed to go
astern and she eased herself free, undamaged. The ships formed up

once more with *Jervis* and *Hostile* fussing around them like sheep-dogs, and they set course for Alexandria. The bombers returned a couple of hours later but, with the destroyers there, they dropped from a much greater height and hit nothing.

On the morning of 8 August the odyssey ended. They sighted the tall pillar of the Ras el-Tin lighthouse and entered Alexandria at last.

———

'It must be admitted that the expedition was ill-conceived, badly organised, and proved a dismal and costly failure,' wrote one of the British consular officials in a report to the Foreign Office.[21] Terry Van Prooyen was pithier: 'the Grand Fiasco', he called it.[22]

Cunningham, applying balm to the wound, wrote to the Admiralty that:

> All the officers and men who were selected from the fleet for this enterprise carried out their duties in a most able manner and their loyalty and cheerfulness under most adverse conditions were beyond praise.

He urged their Lordships to show 'some recognition' of Commander Gibson's 'most valuable services on the Danube'.[23]

In the clear light of hindsight, it is a wonder that anybody ever thought the scheme would work. The expedition could hardly have been more obvious, to the Germans and everyone else, if the boats had gone up the river with a brass band playing 'Rule Britannia'. If anything, it helped the Nazis to foment the rise of fascism in Romania. King Carol was forced to abdicate in September and Romania joined the war on the German side in November.

After a spell of leave in Alexandria, the Australians returned to their ships of the Scrap Iron Flotilla, with orders not to talk about their adventures. Promoted to leading stoker, 'Zack' Lardner spent his entire war at sea, serving in the new destroyers *Napier* and *Quickmatch*, and then in corvettes in the Pacific islands until 1945. Robert Scott and Bill Milne, both promoted to lieutenant, also served in the Pacific and left the navy in 1946, Milne as a lieutenant commander. Terry 'Dutchie' Van Prooyen finished up as a pom-pom gunner in the fleet flagship, the heavy cruiser HMAS *Australia*, where he was credited with shooting down two Japanese kamikaze aircraft. After the war he lived quietly in Melbourne, working on the wharves. At the beginning of their trip to Romania there had been talk of medals if the expedition had been a success, but failure has no fathers and nothing ever came of it. There is not a word of their mission or their exploits in the official history of the RAN, and the only records in Australian archives are copies of a few British documents.

Ian Fleming stayed on in Naval Intelligence until war's end. Merlin Minshall was eventually packed off to New Zealand and then Fiji, out of harm's way.

Commander Alexander Gibson was given leave to return to the UK and he sailed from Alexandria for Gibraltar as a passenger in *Hostile*. On 23 August she struck a mine off Cape Bon on the Tunisian coast and he was one of five men killed. He was awarded a posthumous Mention in Despatches.

## CHAPTER 7

# OLD MEDITERRANEAN
# HANDS

France fell on 22 June 1940. Hitler, exultant and vindictive, ordered
that the armistice be signed in a forest clearing at Compiègne in
the north of the country, on the very same spot and in the very same
Wagons-Lit railway carriage in which Germany had surrendered in
1918. The country was carved up. Germany would occupy most of
metropolitan France, with a puppet French government installed in
the spa town of Vichy. At dawn the next morning the Führer flew to
Paris to see the capital he had conquered, spending an ostentatiously
reverent moment at the tomb of Napoleon Bonaparte in the Invalides.

The French capitulation changed everything in the Mediterranean.
Britain was now on her own. The future was bleak and perilous. At
best, Cunningham and the Mediterranean Fleet could no longer
count on the support of the Marine Nationale or the use of French
ports, shifting the balance of power decisively in favour of the Italians.
At worst, the French fleet, including its seven powerful battleships,
might fall into German hands. The French Minister of Marine,
the devious and scheming Admiral François Darlan, had given his
word of honour that French ships would not be sailed to German
ports or come under German control, but the British did not trust
him to deliver.

Winston Churchill grasped the moment with characteristic
boldness. Plans had already been drawn up, with the code name

Operation Catapult. French ships, wherever they were, must be disarmed, or seized or, if necessary, destroyed by force. It was, he wrote after the war:

> a hateful decision, the most unnatural and painful in which I have ever been concerned.[1]

On the night of 2 July, armed British sailors and soldiers swooped on French ships in Plymouth and Portsmouth, overwhelming their crews and taking control. Three British sailors and one Frenchman were killed.

In the Mediterranean the situation was more delicate, more difficult and very much more dangerous. In the west, a strong French fleet including the old battleships *Provence* and *Bretagne*, and the very much newer battleships *Dunkerque* and *Strasbourg* of the powerful Force de Raid, lay at anchor in the harbour of Mers-el-Kebir on the Algerian coast. Outside the harbour, patrolling slowly back and forth, waited the Royal Navy's Force H from Gibraltar: the battlecruiser HMS *Hood*, the battleships *Valiant* and *Resolution*, the carrier *Ark Royal*, and their escort of cruisers and destroyers. The Force H commander, Vice Admiral Sir James Somerville, had detailed proposals from London to put to the French commander, Admiral Marcel-Bruno Gensoul, and he sent a French-speaking officer on a destroyer to open the negotiations. Broadly, Gensoul should sail his ships to British ports; or to French ports in the West Indies; or to the United States; or he could scuttle them where they were. Failing any of these alternatives, a reluctant Somerville was explicitly ordered:

> to use whatever force may be necessary to prevent [Gensoul's] ships from falling into German or Italian hands.[2]

The negotiations failed, due largely to the wounded *amour propre* of the French admiral. He would not be dictated to. At 1755 hours, with a heavy heart, Somerville ordered his ships to open fire. *Hood* was the first to shoot at a range of 17,000 metres, quickly followed by the other two capital ships. The French were still at their berths, sitting ducks, with most of their guns either facing inland or masked by other ships. After just three minutes the second British salvo hit *Bretagne*, which blew up in an appalling mushroom cloud and sank, taking 977 of her crew with her. There was chaos in the harbour with other ships also hit but largely concealed from the British by the drifting smoke from *Bretagne* and the shell explosions. At 1804 hours Somerville ordered a ceasefire to allow the French crews to leave their ships if they could. *Provence, Dunkerque* and three destroyers were run aground, but under cover of the smoke the battleship *Strasbourg* and five destroyers managed to slip out to sea and across the Mediterranean to Toulon. In all, 1250 French sailors were killed. One of the ships lost was the colonial sloop *Rigault de Genouilly*, whose *matelots* had drunk with *Stuart*'s sailors in Madagascar. She was torpedoed and sunk by the British submarine HMS *Pandora* off the Algerian coast. Admiral Somerville wrote to his wife that Operation Catapult was:

the biggest political blunder of modern times and will rouse the whole world against us. We all feel thoroughly ashamed.[3]

There were also French ships at Alexandria: the battleship *Lorraine*, four cruisers, three destroyers and a submarine. Under Catapult, Sir Andrew Cunningham received much the same orders as Somerville, and he viewed them with the same distaste, not least because he had formed a close professional friendship with the French commander, Vice Admiral René-Émile Godfroy.

'Suddenly and without warning to attack and board his ships, and in the course of it probably to inflict many casualties upon his sailors, appeared to me to be an act of sheer treachery which was as injudicious as it was unnecessary,' he wrote.[4]

Cunningham decided that he could resolve things by negotiation and he set about it with a tact and patience that grew more determined as he heard of the tragedy at Mers-el-Kebir. Wracked by indecision, Godfroy played for time and, as that day of 3 July dragged on, Cunningham waited. His situation was different to Somerville's. All the ships, French and British, were within the harbour. A gun battle between them, at point-blank range, could be nothing short of catastrophic for both sides. The night passed uneasily. In the morning, to his dismay, Cunningham saw that the French were raising steam to go to sea and that their guns were cleared for action.

*Stuart* was berthed in the harbour alongside the small net-laying ship HMS *Protector*, lying quietly but warily in the oppressive July heat. Ean McDonald, the observant young signalman from Perth, feared that all hell might break loose:

> One hundred yards away was the French *Duguay-Trouin*, a beautiful modern cruiser carrying eight 6-inch guns as her main armament. We were fully closed up at action stations. Our three aft-bearing 4.7-inch guns were trained directly at the bridge, control tower and decks of the Frenchman. His Y-turret with its two 6-inch guns was trained directly at us. I shall never forget the two black open holes of those two 6-inch barrels pointed at me from one hundred yards away.
>
> Tension mounted as the hours passed. About 0800 *Duguay-Trouin's* anchor cable was shortening in, with her fo'c'sle crew actually hosing the mud off the cable as it came up from the bottom in that simple but so out of character routine among all the tension. The moment her anchor came clear of the water we were to open up on her: she in turn would fill those ominous black muzzles of hers with living death.
>
> Just then the blessed Italians took a hand as over came a group of raiding aircraft. Both British and French forgot their differences and opened up against the Italians overhead. *Stuart* was straddled by a stick of bombs that blew the wharf shed apart and punched some fair-sized holes in the side of *Protector* alongside. The final bombs of the stick exploded close to us and covered us with shrapnel, fortunately with nothing actually hitting us. Tension broken, the two fleets settled back to rethink the situation ...5

Perhaps it was the Italian air raid that did it, perhaps not. Taking a different tack, Cunningham sent some of his senior ship's captains to reason with their French opposite numbers, and it soon became apparent that they were keen on a peaceful resolution. That afternoon,

Godfroy yielded. His ships would discharge their fuel oil and the firing mechanisms for their main guns. Cunningham, for his part, guaranteed to permit as many French sailors as possible to return to their homeland. The crisis was over. The French admiral and a skeleton crew remained in Alexandria, immobile, until the Italian surrender in 1943. Churchill viewed Operation Catapult as a political success, painful though it had been. It had demonstrated British resolve to the world – and particularly to President Roosevelt in Washington. 'It was made plain that the British War Cabinet feared nothing and would stop at nothing,' he wrote.[6]

—

By now the Australians were old Mediterranean hands. Only six months had passed, but it seemed they had been there forever, knowing the sea in all its moods and perils. They were proud to be destroyer men, too, confident that they were a special breed. 'Gimme the boats,' they told each other. It became a catchphrase, almost a war cry. They held a certain amused disdain for sailors in the supposed comfort of bigger ships, the cruisers and battleships.

The Italian bombing was almost a daily occurrence in harbour at Malta or Alexandria and always frightening, but at the same time so constant, such an inevitable part of the routine, that you just dealt with it as best you could and got on with the job in hand. It was less likely at sea, depending where you were, but there was always the chance of a few dark specks appearing out of the blue on the horizon to set the alarms clattering, the fear rising, the adrenalin running. The miracle was that the Scrap Iron ships were so far largely unscathed; there had been shrapnel sometimes, and a good shaking up occasionally, but very little damage from near misses, and no injury or death.

Hec Waller was promoted to captain on 30 June. He had been in the navy for twenty-seven years, man and boy, and a commander for six. The shopkeeper's son from Benalla had risen to this exalted rank with the four gold stripes on his jacket sleeves and become a fighting sea captain in command, as if he had been made for war. The writer and seafarer Joseph Conrad put it best:

Only a seaman realises to what extent an entire ship reflects the personality and ability of one individual, her commanding officer. To a landsman, this is not understandable, and sometimes it is difficult for us to comprehend – but it is so.

A ship at sea is a distant world in herself and in consideration of the protracted and distant operations of the fleet units, the navy must place a great power, responsibility, and trust in the hands of those leaders chosen for command.

In each ship there is one man who, in the hour of emergency of peril at sea, can turn to no other man. There is one who, alone, is ultimately responsible for the safe navigation, engineering performance, accurate gunfire and morale of his ship. He is the commanding officer. He is the ship.

This is the most difficult and demanding assignment in the navy. There is not an instant during his tour as commanding officer that he can escape the grasp of command responsibility. His privileges in view of his obligations are almost ludicrously small; nevertheless, command is the spur which has given the navy its great leaders.

It is a duty which most richly deserves the highest time-honoured title of the seafaring world: 'CAPTAIN'.7

*Stuart* was at Alexandria when the news of the promotion came through and it is reasonable to assume there were celebrations, for everyone knew that Hec loved a party or a dinner. Cunningham certainly offered his congratulations, for the two were sharpened from the same steel and they had hit it off. Once, at a meeting of fleet captains, Hec had been bold enough to query one of the admiral's edicts. 'Get out of my cabin, you bloody Australian,' Cunningham had barked. But then he invited him back to drink gin. Rather less formally, his sailors had given him the nickname 'Hard Over' Hec, a tribute to his vigorous shiphandling. One of his officers, Commander Phillip 'Polo' Owen, left this picture:

Most men try to mould at least their exterior personality to their chosen idol or idols: not so Waller. He never failed to be himself. He was humble. He was firm: forthright and to the point, perspicacious and uncomplicated in expression. He was without any frills: always fair and without favourites. He was a definite character with a flair for making the best of the material and conditions offering. How else could the Scrap Iron Flotilla have persisted in its predatory pursuits so successfully and so long? I hear his voice now, as clearly as a ship's bell striking, saying to me, 'Polo, it's the rub o' the green.'

Not only did he have a sense of humour but also of the ridiculous ... The mutual understanding between Waller and his captains was excellent. The destroyer captains themselves were all outstanding men. He knew all the officers in the flotilla and often surprised them by the depth of his knowledge of them and their interests. Loyalty, for him, was a two-way switch.[8]

Another of his officers, Captain Norman 'Knocker' White, was less glowing:

I was a cadet when he was Commandant of the Naval College. He was terribly tough on officers and he gave me a very hard time. He was tough, especially on young, untrained officers who did not have a watch-keeping certificate, which I didn't have then. As Second Officer of the Watch I copped Hec's very abrasive tongue on more than one occasion.[9]

Domestically, Hec was the loving husband of Nancy Bowes, the clergyman's daughter he had married as a lieutenant in 1923 and the mother of their sons Michael and John. Nancy had gone with him around the world in peacetime, but now she was at home in the Melbourne suburb of Hawthorn, bearing the solitary lot of the naval wife with cheerful fortitude: running the house, paying the bills, dealing with the domestic ups and downs and the family decisions that had to be taken on the spot in the days when a letter took weeks to arrive. She nurtured the boys at Scotch College, where two of Hec's brothers were teachers. In his long spells away at sea their father had delighted in sending them carefully coloured sketches and cartoons of his adventures – 'Here is Daddy shooting a crocodile' – often with a playful rhyme attached:

What Ho! For the sea
Sailors they'll be
As Michael and John climb
Onboard.
How happy they seem
Like a wonderful dream
Although the great ship is still
Moored.[10]

At war, he would snatch a few precious hours of relaxation by going for a sail in a little dinghy he kept lashed to the guard rail aft on *Stuart*'s quarterdeck. The ship would hardly have berthed or secured to a buoy in Alexandria before the captain was over the side and away, with a packet of sandwiches and one of his sailors chosen to act as a for'ard hand. Richard 'Gerry' Garrard was one of them:

I can't remember how I, an ordinary seaman, was chosen to be the crew, but on numerous occasions for the next two years I was 'piped' to report aft, to go sailing with the captain. I have never forgotten him and the special times we had together.[11]

As happens in the navy, the dits gathered around him, 'dit' being sailor speak for a yarn or an anecdote. There was the dit about shooting the shark in the Red Sea; the dit about Hec seizing the gardener's secateurs to prune the roses at Government House in Malta; the dit about the truly atrocious cocktails he would mix; the dit about Hec lying flat on the deck under some heavy bombing and finding himself next to a young sailor newly arrived in the ship. 'Not so bad, is it, son?' said the captain. 'Not so fucking good, either, sir,' said the boy.

All these things were the measure of the man. The navy had found in Hector Macdonald Laws Waller qualities of leadership and burnished them to a high shine. They would be tested to the full in the year to come.

—

Despite his promotion, Hec was no longer the senior Australian officer in the Med. That place had been taken by Captain John Collins, who brought the cruiser HMAS *Sydney* up from Australia in late May to join the fleet's 7th Cruiser Squadron.

Another country boy, from the Tasmanian town of Deloraine, the son of an Irish doctor who died seven months before he was born, Collins had been in the very first class of the Naval College when it opened in 1913. Slight and wiry, he scooped his share of the glittering prizes on offer there. His career at sea began with the customary spell as a midshipman in a Royal Navy battleship, HMS *Canada*, in the last year of the First World War, an eye-opening experience as it turned out. *Canada*'s increasingly eccentric captain, nicknamed 'The Quail',[12] took to challenging his sailors to a fight, famously hoisted his chair atop his dining table to serenade his officers with a banjo and once, in the middle watch, ordered Collins to stand beside him and pop cough lozenges into his mouth whenever he sneezed. The Quail eventually lost it altogether, suddenly ordering a potentially disastrous wrong turn in a fleet manoeuvre and was placed under arrest by his executive officer.

After that it was onwards and upwards for young John, with a scorching performance to take top marks at the RN's long gunnery course at Whale Island in Portsmouth in 1922. He went from ship to shore, back and forth, once finding himself in the nerve-wracking position for a naval officer of having to ride a horse at the opening parade for the new Parliament House in Canberra in 1927. His first command in 1930 was the ancient three-funnelled destroyer HMAS *Anzac*. He was promoted to captain in December 1937. That made him two and a half years senior to Hec Waller, and at the outbreak of war he was the Assistant Chief of the Naval Staff and the Director of Naval Intelligence at Navy Office in Melbourne, an officer marked for higher things.

Collins took command of *Sydney* in November 1939. He already knew every nut and bolt, for he had been her first executive officer when she was commissioned in 1935. And a handsome ship she was, modern and powerful, with strong, muscular lines. She had started life as HMS *Phaeton*, laid down for the Royal Navy on the Tyne in northern England, but while she was still building she was bought by the Australian government in the belated drive to re-arm the RAN in the late 1930s. Two sister ships, *Hobart* and *Perth*, would join her later.

The three were on the books as modified Leander class light cruisers, 'modified' meaning that they had been improved and updated from the original design of five earlier ships. The noticeable difference was that the Australian version had two funnels, instead of a large central one, and better armour protection. *Sydney* displaced 8900 tons full load, over a length of 171 metres. Four Admiralty 3-drum boilers and four Parsons geared turbines turned out an impressive 72,000 shaft horsepower to four shafts, for a best speed of 32.5 knots. Her main armament was of eight 6-inch guns mounted in four turrets, two fore and two aft, complemented by four 4-inch anti-aircraft guns and a host of heavy and light machine guns mounted here, there and everywhere. She boasted eight 21-inch torpedo tubes, depth charges, and a catapult and crane mounted amidships to launch and recover the small reconnaissance aircraft she carried, a boxy Supermarine Seagull biplane. She carried a crew of more than 640.

*Sydney* and the Scrap Iron ships were chalk and cheese. The cruiser was spacious, almost luxurious compared to the cramped and rickety-rackety old destroyers. In effect, she was five times the size of *Stuart*. Her machinery was new and smooth running. Unfortunately for the men, discipline in a cruiser was distinctly more rigid and impersonal than the relatively easy-going, cheek-by-jowl life in a destroyer. A cruiser was proper 'Pusser', as the sailors would say; everything done by the book.[13] In the destroyers, in the early days of the war until a fleet order forbade it, the gun crews in a sweaty summer would often go to their action stations wearing only a pair of shorts, an unheard-of liberty in a cruiser. The destroyer men took to calling their ships 'the boats', a very un-naval term but one they used with a perverse pride. To be 'in the boats' was unique, a distinctive badge of honour.

At forty-one years of age, John Collins was proper Pusser too. He was a stickler for rules and regulations, a keen observer of proper naval ceremony, and it would never have occurred to him to turn up on his bridge dressed like Hec Waller, as if he were going fishing. His white uniforms were immaculate, the gold braid gleaming, and he expected the same polish from his officers and the crew. On his appointment to *Sydney*, his boss at Navy Office in Melbourne, Admiral Sir Ragnar Colvin, offered high praise in his confidential report:

One of the most able staff officers I have met. Keen, enthusiastic and fertile of ideas. Has a most orderly mind and is at the same time a rapid worker. Sometimes apt to be overkeen and to tread on toes, but this I feel will be corrected by experience. His subordinates work both with him and for him.[14]

*Stuart* and *Sydney* first came together in late June 1940, just days before the French collapse. The land war with the Italians in North Africa had begun as a fitful affair of a feint here and a jab there, almost as if neither side could summon the energy to do much more. The British army had crossed the Egyptian border into Libya and captured the small Italian outpost of Fort Capuzzo, which they set about destroying. There was the occasional desultory skirmish of tanks and armoured cars. The Italian army concentrated on building up its supplies further west along the Libyan coast, running convoys into Tobruk.

Sir Andrew Cunningham decided the fleet would lend a hand by bombarding the little port of Bardia, some 500 kilometres west of Alexandria. Bardia would later become famous as the site of the first victory for the Australian army's 6th Division in the Western Desert campaign, but at this stage of the war it was no more than a fortified desert supply dump with a small Italian garrison. Cunningham put together a force of three ships from the 7th Cruiser Squadron – *Orion*, *Neptune* and *Sydney*; the French battleship *Lorraine*; and the destroyers *Stuart*, *Dainty*, *Decoy* and *Hasty*, all under the command of Vice Admiral Tovey. They left Alexandria at 1130 hours on 27 June, in weather so calm and sunny, and at such a leisurely pace, that some of *Stuart*'s sailors passed the time doing their washing on the upper deck. Tovey's plan was to approach Bardia just after dawn the next day, with the sun rising behind him and hopefully dazzling the Italian defenders.

It worked perfectly. Paymaster Lieutenant Walter Ross was a twenty-four-year-old from the sleepy New South Wales country town of Gilgandra. Known to everyone as 'Jack' Ross, he had joined the navy as a cadet in 1934 and had already been on a round-the-world cruise in the fleet flagship, the heavy cruiser HMAS *Australia*. Now he was eager to see his first shots fired in anger:

As the action buzzers sounded throughout the ship before day-break and all hands hurried away to their stations it was with feelings that the next hour or so might produce all kinds of unfore-seen happenings. However, conditions for the bombardment were as near perfect as could be desired, a slight mist veiling the sea and allowing us to approach within about six miles of the shore before the sun rose to clear the atmosphere and give us good visibility.[15]

Tovey's plan for surprise had worked. His flagship *Orion* led the line, opening fire just before o6oo hours at a range of about 13,000 metres, followed by *Lorraine*, *Neptune* and *Sydney*. The destroyers took their assigned positions, with *Stuart* ranging her 4.7-inch guns on a barracks and some wireless masts to the left of the town. It was almost like an exercise, a practice shoot in friendly waters. The guns thundered smoke and flame, the shells whined through the air and exploded in balls and mushrooms of smoke and dust all along the rough, bare red cliffs on which Bardia stood. The Italians made no reply, nothing. From *Stuart*'s bridge they could see dimly through the smoke some troops running for cover.

'The first the Italian garrison knew of the impending attack was when *Sydney*'s amphibian [the Seagull aircraft] came chugging overhead to spot for us,' wrote Jack Ross. 'Then before they had rubbed the sleep from their eyes and were completely alert to what was happening our cruisers had opened fire and the first salvoes of 6-inch "bricks" were falling amongst their buildings. *Sydney*'s objective was the military barracks situated on top of the escarp-ment, and after a couple of ranging salvoes we hammered away, bringing the whole place down like a pack of cards and leaving only a pile of dust and rubble.'[16]

Ironically, the only casualty was the Seagull, or the 'Pusser's duck', as she was invariably known. She was jumped by a trio of Macchi fighters which appeared from nowhere and hit her with a burst of machine-gun bullets that riddled her rudder and some of her ailerons. Her RAAF pilot, Flight Lieutenant Tommy Price, put her into a steep dive of some 7000 feet which apparently convinced the enemy she was crashing, for they sheered off and left her to her fate. Price had been grazed on the backside by a bullet which had penetrated his seat, but his observer and gunner were unharmed, and he managed to nurse the aircraft to a British airfield at Mersa Matruh on the Egyptian border. They just made it, on the proverbial wing and a prayer. On landing, with one flat tyre, the undercarriage collapsed and the plane skidded sideways to a crunching halt, so badly damaged that it was a write-off. Tommy Price, though, received the Distinguished Flying Cross for his efforts.

It had been, said Cunningham, 'a useful minor operation in which the damage caused fully justified the ammunition expended'.[17]

For Hec Waller the chance to get an unanswered crack at the enemy was a useful morale boost for his ship's company.

—

In its first month, the balance of the war at sea had tipped towards the Mediterranean Fleet. Italy lost ten submarines in the three weeks to the end of June, a high toll which surprised both sides. Curiously, most of those boats had been first sighted on the surface in daylight, suggesting a carefree approach to life in contested waters.[18] On the plus side for the Italians, on the second day they had sunk the elderly British cruiser HMS *Calypso* to the south of Crete, with the loss of thirty-nine lives.

An imperative for the Regia Marina was to run supplies of men, materiel and food from mainland Italy south across the Med to the army at the Libyan ports of Tripoli, Benghazi and Tobruk. It was hazardous, and it provoked the first surface clash of the war at sea.

Shortly after midday on 28 June, a patrolling RAF Sunderland aircraft from Malta reported sighting a convoy of Italian destroyers west of the Greek Ionian island of Zakynthos. Vice Admiral Tovey's 7th Cruiser Squadron, including *Sydney*, was already at sea south of Crete to cover a convoy. They swung into the hunt. Another Sunderland saw the Italians again at 1640 hours, reporting their course and speed towards Benghazi, in a position just 35 miles to the west of Tovey. Turning south-west, Tovey prepared his trap. At 1830 hours, one of his cruisers, HMS *Liverpool*, sighted the Italians starkly outlined against the lowering sun, by now about 100 miles north of Tobruk. Three minutes later *Liverpool* opened fire at a range of 20,000 yards. Tovey formed his squadron into two divisions, the sister ships *Orion*, *Neptune* and *Sydney* of eight 6-inch guns each, to pursue the Italians on their starboard quarter. The two more powerful Town class cruisers, *Liverpool* and *Gloucester*, brand spanking new and each with twelve 6-inch guns, would chase from the port side. The weather was fine and visibility good, with a distinct breeze and some surface chop to the sea, although evening was closing in.

There were three Italian destroyers, *Ostro*, *Zeffiro* and *Espero*, sailing from Taranto on the Italian east coast, their decks loaded with the men and equipment of one of Mussolini's crack Blackshirt anti-tank units. Recognising that he was hopelessly outgunned, the convoy commander, Capitano di Vascello Enrico Baroni in *Espero*, first attempted to make a run for it, but the fortunes of war were against him. His ship had one of its three boilers out of action, which limited him to just 25 knots, and the other two, of about the same vintage as the Australian V and Ws, were so heavily laden that they could not make their best speed, either. Steadily, the British cruisers closed them in a storm of gunfire. Baroni laid down a heavy pall of thick black smoke which shrouded the sea for a while and allowed *Ostro* and *Zeffiro* to keep making their escape while, with dogged courage, he turned *Espero* on a zigzag course to meet the onslaught.

First he fired a spread of torpedoes. An alert lookout in *Neptune* spotted their streaking, grey-green wakes and Tovey ordered a change of course to 'comb the tracks', as it was called, turning towards them so as to make a narrower target. It worked, the torpedos shooting harmlessly past and beyond. *Espero* began shooting and scored a minor hit on *Liverpool*, which turned away with *Gloucester* and began to pursue the two fleeing destroyers. *Orion*, *Neptune* and *Sydney* poured still more fire into *Espero*, shell after shell after shell, and then joined the chase south until Tovey ordered *Sydney* to return and finish off Baroni's now immobile ship. Jack Ross recorded the scene:

We approached slowly from astern, noting that she was still flying her colours, and as we came up she opened fire again, several shells falling uncomfortably close by. Captain Collins now had no option but to re-engage at what to us was point-blank range, and practically every shell found its mark, blasting great pieces out of the destroyer and demolishing what little remained of her super-structure. Nothing daunted by the hopelessness of her position, she continued to fire on us with her little 4.7s, game to the last, for as long as they could be fired and sufficient crews found to man them, and, even in her death throes, she tried to torpedo us, but all her 'fish' were wide of the mark and easily avoided ...

... as *Sydney* slowly approached to a position about 2000 yards astern her forward magazine blew up, completely demolishing her bridge and, according to survivors, killing her captain. To us gathered on deck to see the end she was a horrible, flaming mass, belching great clouds of black smoke and listing at an acute angle as her battered hull slowly filled with water. We watched her in silence, somewhat awed and dismayed, I think, at the terrible sight of our handiwork, and then with a last crackle of flames and a hissing of steam she lurched over onto her beam ends and slid from sight.[19]

It was 2100 hours, with night drawn in. The shocked, awestruck silence that followed *Espero*'s sinking was broken first by several loud underwater explosions, probably her boilers blowing up or perhaps her depth charges. Then came the cries of the survivors in the water, some loud and near, some faint and distant.

John Collins faced a hard dilemma. These were men like them-selves, sailors like themselves, whose lives he knew he could save and wanted to save. And he knew instinctively that his crew wanted them saved too. Yet the scarlet funeral pyre of the burning *Espero* would have been visible for miles, well beyond the horizon, a magnet for any prowling enemy submarine. Should he risk the safety of his own ship and his own men – his first charge and responsibility – to linger on the scene and rescue the enemy? It was a choice between duty and humanity and the decision was his alone to make, a moral question, a captain's call that Joseph Conrad would have recognised. He pondered it on his bridge that fateful night while the routine of the watch went quietly on around him, the lookouts scanning their arcs of the horizon, a small knot of officers standing at a discreet distance, the midshipman awaiting an instruction, the Chief Yeoman and the

Coxswain awaiting an order. To his resounding credit, Collins chose humanity.

'Stop all engines!'

The telegraphs jangled and the cruiser glided to a halt. The pipe echoed through the ship. 'Away seaboats!'

*Sydney*'s crew had been anticipating the order, awaiting the moment. The two cutters were in the water in an instant and pulling towards the distant shouts. The description by Jack Ross is matchless:

> From all around us in the darkness we could hear the pitiful sound of men, most of them wounded and burnt in varying degrees crying out to us, and yet we were forced by circumstances to show the minimum of light, the boats working in the dark. On board, the sick bay was cleared ready to receive the wounded, warm blankets prepared, stretchers laid out on the upper deck and every man ready to do as much as was humanly possible to relieve the distress of the survivors. As many ladders and lifelines as could be rigged were hung over the side and groups of us stood ready around them to help the swimmers inboard. As each sea boat picked up its load it came alongside and willing hands soon had the men into the hands of the surgeons and sick berth attendants. Odd groups of Italians, not far from where we had hove to, managed to paddle their rafts and pieces of wreckage to the ship's side and groups of our chaps climbed down to help them up the ladders. Some were beyond human aid, and their bodies, still supported by their lifebelts, were left to float by while we concentrated our efforts on rescuing the living.[20]

*Sydney* stayed there for nearly an hour and three quarters, slowly drifting, although it must have seemed longer as the night wore on. The two cutters plied back and forth with more survivors, some evidently unharmed, others burnt or wounded or covered in stinking oil fuel, some whimpering piteously, others in silent shock, a few putting up a brave front. They were treated with tender care, enemies no more.

Running short of ammunition, Admiral Tovey and the rest of the squadron had given up the pursuit of the other two destroyers as a lost cause and were heading back to Alexandria. Tovey had signalled several times asking *Sydney* to rejoin him, and eventually gave a direct order which Collins could only obey. Forty-seven Italian sailors had been rescued and yet, as he wrote in his memoirs:

> The ship's company kept reporting that cries for help could still be heard, giving the bearing. It was obvious they were reluctant to leave the remainder to their fate, and tended to overlook the submarine threat in their enthusiasm, but the initiative allowed a subordinate commander had already been stretched to the extreme, so we had to proceed.
>
> However, a happy inspiration came to me. One cutter, with oars, sails, provisions and water, was left at the spot so that the remaining survivors could get aboard. The boat was illuminated for a few seconds in the beam of the 10-inch projector to enable those left in the water to see it. I never heard whether any of them got into the cutter, or what happened to the boat. But it was worth sacrificing a cutter for the morale of the ship's company. They naturally would have been distressed had we just steamed away with cries for help still to be heard.[21]

*Sydney*'s captain had done all he could and more. He ordered a course for Alexandria. Above and below decks, the Executive Officer, the English-born Commander Tom Hilken, and *Sydney*'s senior doctor, Surgeon Commander Henry Gault, were methodically sorting order from chaos. Most of those rescued were uninjured, some of them in shock from their ordeal, but others were in dire straits. There was a sailor so badly burned that the doctors worked for hours upon him, eventually bandaging him from head to foot like some Egyptian mummy.

One of the three Italian officers rescued was *Espero*'s doctor, Capitano Medico Lorenzo Lotti, who was unhurt and, better still, spoke enough English to help diagnose the troubles of the wounded. Dr Lotti worked through the night on his countrymen. The other two were Sottotenenti di Vascello, sub lieutenants Gaetano Giussano, with a broken arm, and Gualtiero Corsetti, with a smashed foot. Corsetti had directed the last salvo of *Espero*'s guns and, despite his wound, had supervised the abandon ship. After the doctors had done what they could for him, he was bedded down on a stretcher in the cabin of *Sydney*'s Chief Engineer and given a gramophone and some records to amuse himself. Corsetti would spend six months in hospital in Egypt and five years in a prisoner-of-war camp in India. After the war he was awarded the *Medaglia di Bronzo al Valor Militare* for his 'display of serene courage and high war spirit'.[22]

Remarkable as it seems, the ship's company treated their captives as if they were welcome guests. The walking wounded were plied with hot cocoa and cigarettes when they arrived on deck and offered food and warm showers. Piles of spare clothing and old uniforms were unearthed for them with much mutual grinning and waving of hands in sign language.

For the return journey, the unwounded prisoners were kept under guard in the recreation room. They gave no trouble and were allowed on deck in the sunshine for certain periods each day, and here they were usually joined by groups of our chaps off watch, bringing them ice cream and drinks from the canteen and teaching them to sing some of the popular songs of the period.[23]

Three men died during the night. In fine, sunny weather, their shipmates were permitted on deck for a proper naval funeral service the next day, the bodies sewn into canvas hammocks beneath the Italian flag and then committed to the sea over *Sydney*'s stern ...

to be turned into corruption, looking for the resurrection of the body when the sea shall give up her dead.[24]

The cruiser had not received a scratch from the enemy but she had taken a beating nonetheless, entirely self-inflicted by the blast and concussion from her 6-inch guns, fore and aft. Glass and light-bulbs had been shattered everywhere below decks, with furniture and lockers overturned in the messes and even a couple of heavy steel doors blown off their hinges. One officer's cabin very near X-turret lay in ruins, most of the wardroom crockery was in pieces and, worst of all, the hot water system in the bathrooms finally gave up the ghost.

At first light the next morning they found that paint had stripped from the overheated muzzles of the guns and was hanging in grey-red streamers, like the dead petals from some exotic flower.

*Sydney* arrived back in Alexandria on the morning of 1 July 1940. Her uninvited guests were almost reluctantly sent ashore with emotional farewells on both sides, including a speech of thanks to John Collins from Dr Lotti, and three rousing Australian cheers for the bandaged burns victim, who managed a grateful wave to the watchers on deck as his stretcher was lowered into the ambulance boat. Humanity had triumphed.

Collins wrote after the war, rather wistfully, that he never found out if any survivors had reached the cutter he left for them. By the hand of providence, some did. It was an epic tale of hunger, thirst, injury, madness and death, illuminated only by indomitable courage and eventual salvation. *Espero* had been able to lower only one small boat and three rafts, and most of those who abandoned ship that night drifted away in the dark and were never seen again. A cruel sun rose upon a lone raft carrying thirty-six men, the badly wounded sprawled upon it, the unharmed or lightly injured taking turns in the sea to cling onto the loops of rope strung around its sides. There was no food, no water. Men began to die of their wounds and were pushed overboard. Others, tormented by thirst, drank seawater and went insane, screaming and hallucinating and writhing in delirium. The only officer on the raft kept shouting for his servant to bring him mineral water from his cabin and eventually threw himself into the water to drown.

After three days of this agony there were just fourteen men left, and by the fifth day that number had halved again to seven, with the raft circled by waiting sharks. Later that day, under a high sun, another mirage appeared before them: a ship's boat. Feebly they paddled over, and found it to be real, solid, tangible. It was *Sydney*'s cutter, wallowing empty on a calm sea. Clambering on board, they discovered oars, four 50-litre water kegs, a battery-powered signal projector and a compass, candles, wet-weather jackets, a Very pistol with thirty flares, and – best of all – some bananas and packets of jam and honey.

The senior sailor, Secondo Capo Franco Lo Mastro, took command, rationing the water and the bananas. And still they drifted, day after day, night after night. Another man died, and then there were six. On the tenth day an Italian seaplane sighted them and they signalled it with the projector: '*Siamo Italiani, naufraghi dell'*Espero'. 'We are Italians shipwrecked from the *Espero*.'

The plane acknowledged them, circled and flew off. The next day another aircraft appeared, saw them too, then also left. Their hopes of rescue rose, then fell again as more long and empty days passed. With the bananas and the jam long gone and starvation upon them once more, a man shot a Very flare into a flock of seagulls and brought one down, which they half-cooked in a steel helmet over a fire kindled with wood from an oar. Another man caught a fish, which they ate raw, and some tried to chew the leather of a belt.

Deliverance came on 12 July, a full fourteen days after the loss of their ship. Sprawled in the cutter, their skeletal figures burned black, their eyeballs sunk in their sockets above cavernous cheeks and filthy matted beards, limp at the very edge of death, they heard the noise of diesel engines. The Italian submarine *Topazio* had surfaced near them. One by one they were carried on board, and all survived.

In all, of the 255 sailors and Blackshirt soldiers who had sailed in *Espero*, just fifty men lived on. One way or another, John Collins had saved them all. One last man was found. The body of Seaman Antonino Russo, aged twenty, was washed ashore on a beach near Tobruk and buried at first in the Italian military cemetery at the coastal town of Derna, to be finally returned to his home town of Sorrento in 2012. Captain Enrico Baroni, who had so gallantly turned his ship to defend the convoy, was posthumously awarded Italy's highest decoration, the *Medaglia d'Oro al valor militare*.

The British and the Australians came to call the encounter The Battle of the *Espero* Convoy. The Italians know it today as *La Tragedia dell'Espero*, and honour the memory still.

## CHAPTER 8

# 'IN THE ROYAL AUSTRALIAN NAVY THINGS ARE SLIGHTLY DIFFERENT'

For all its visceral human drama, *Espero* was a thin and tepid victory. There were celebrations in Alexandria when the cruisers returned, Brits and Aussies sharing beers in the Fleet Club, but in truth there was nothing much to drink to. Five modern, fast and powerful cruisers, bristling with no fewer than forty-eight 6-inch guns, had sunk just one limping Italian destroyer and allowed two others to escape. It appalled Andrew Cunningham to learn that his men had fired more than 5000 6-inch shells for such a negligible result; a reckless waste of ammunition that exposed an embarrassing failure of accuracy in their gunnery and left the fleet's cruiser squadrons dangerously short of ammunition for three weeks until more could be convoyed in. The Commander-in-Chief was not happy, and it is safe to assume that he made this plain to Vice Admiral Tovey and his captains.

There was a brief pause in the naval surface war – partly because of the ammunition shortage – with the gap filled by the Fleet Air Arm. On 5 July, nine Swordfish torpedo biplanes, commonly known as 'Stringbags', attacked Italian shipping in the harbour at Tobruk, sinking the *Zeffiro*, which had sailed there after dropping her cargo of soldiers at Benghazi. Another four ships were badly damaged, including a large troop transport.

His miserable confrontation with the French now settled, Cunningham was eager to get to grips with the Italian fleet. He knew there had been murmurs in political circles in London suggesting he was too much on the defensive, not aggressive enough, which he found insulting, for his natural instinct all his career had been to go on the attack. He laid his plans.

The Regia Marina, on the other hand, was not quite so keen to come to grips with the British, chiefly because their newest battleships, the *Littorio* and *Vittorio Veneto*, were not yet fully worked up, and partly because Mussolini himself indulged the notion that the most fascist of his services, the Regia Aeronautica, would be the triumphant spearpoint of victory.

It was the need to convoy that brought the two forces together in what would be the Mediterranean's greatest modern clash of capital ships. The Italian army in Libya depended on a constant flow of supplies just to sustain itself without moving even a metre, but with Il Duce now dreaming of an assault eastwards on the British in Egypt there was a new urgency. On 6 July a convoy of four large merchant ships sailed from Naples carrying 2200 troops, more than 300 tanks and vehicles, and 16,000 tons of food and other equipment. It passed through the narrow Strait of Messina which separates Sicily from the Italian mainland, collected another heavily loaded freighter which had sailed from Catania, then headed south towards Benghazi. At this stage of the war, the Italians were able to understand some, if not all, of the Mediterranean Fleet's communications, with help from B-Dienst, the German Navy's code-breaking service. Two days before the convoy sailed, a noticeable increase in British signal traffic led them to the correct conclusion that the British might be about to put to sea. Supercommando, the Italian supreme command, pulled out all the stops to meet the threat, deploying both the Regia Aeronautica and the Regia Marina in force. There was a close escort of cruisers and destroyers in visual touch with the convoy and a distant escort of another four cruisers, some 55 kilometres to the west, to meet any possible attack from British cruisers the Italians believed (wrongly) to be in Malta. The Italian Main Fleet also sailed from Taranto heading south, its commander Ammiraglio di Squadra – Vice Admiral – Inigo Campioni flying his flag in the battleship *Giulio Cesare* with another battleship, *Conte di Cavour*, and a host of heavy and light cruisers and destroyers. Submarines were placed on a patrol line that began off Alexandria. It was an impressive display of Italian sea power.

Andrew Cunningham faced a different problem. As the bombing of Malta grew ever heavier it became harder to keep the island supplied with food and the essentials for everyday life. The British naval families and civilians living there – *bouches inutiles*, as the admiral delicately phrased it* – were anxious to get away to greater safety. The unnecessary mouths included his wife Nona and two nieces. There would be two convoys to carry them all to Alexandria, one of three fast ships code named MF1 to leave on 9 July, and a slower convoy of five ships, MS1, to sail a day later, each of them to be escorted by fleet destroyers. Cunningham's intelligence people could also read something of what his enemy was up to, helped immeasurably by the codebook which had been retrieved from the submarine *Uebi Scebeli* ten days before. He believed that the Italian fleet was out, although he did not know in what numbers nor where it might be heading. The admiral laid his plans and gave his orders for Operation MA5, as it was coded. The convoys would be supported and, if luck would have it, the Italian fleet would be engaged.

On 7 July, the harbour at Alexandria was alive with the Mediterranean Fleet making ready for sea. The ships had been raising steam since late that morning in a haze of funnel smoke, with a last-minute flurry of liberty boats returning, stores being loaded, signal flags fluttering up and down halyards. They began to leave early that evening, a long grey line of ships great and small steaming out past the Ras el-Tin lighthouse in three divisions as carefully orchestrated and choreographed as any grand ballet. *Stuart* was among the first to depart, to take her station as a screening destroyer in the van of Force A, which was Tovey's 7th Cruiser Squadron, including *Sydney*. Next came Force B, which was *Warspite*, the flagship, escorted by five destroyers; then Force C, the two slower battleships *Malaya* and

---

\*    Useless mouths

*Royal Sovereign* with the aircraft carrier *Eagle* and another eleven destroyers, including *Vampire* and *Voyager*. *Malaya* was of the same Queen Elizabeth class and vintage as *Warspite*, but she had not been reconstructed between the wars and was a few knots slower. *Royal Sovereign*, also unmodernised, was slower still. The last ship cleared the harbour by midnight and Cunningham ordered a course nor'west at a brisk 20 knots. There was a brief scare when the destroyer *Hasty* made two separate submarine contacts and depth charged both of them but with no apparent result: except that one of the submarines radioed back to Supermarina a report of sighting the fleet at sea. Far to the west, the Royal Navy's Force H, based at Gibraltar under Admiral Somerville, sailed with the battlecruiser *Hood*, the battleships *Valiant* and *Resolution* and the carrier *Ark Royal* to harry the Italians with a diversionary air attack on the airfield at Cagliari in Sardinia.

So the stage was set, the actors in place for what would become known as the Battle of Calabria. The British fleet passed a quiet night in sombre anticipation of an encounter the next day. The Italians had a rather livelier time when a handful of their destroyers launched a torpedo attack against some darkened shapes which turned out to be their own cruisers, fortunately without result. The Italian convoy plodded south at a steady 14 knots.

As the sun rose on 8 July on a calm, clear summer sea, the central Mediterranean south of Italy, west of Crete and east of Malta was alive with warships, neither fleet sure of the other's course or intentions but each commander trusting that intelligence and reconnaissance would bring some clarity as the day wore on. They would not have long to wait. Early that morning, an Italian aircraft flying over Alexandria confirmed that the harbour was empty; that the British fleet had indeed left. Cunningham received his first solid piece of information just after breakfast, when the submarine HMS *Phoenix* reported seeing two enemy battleships and four destroyers heading due south in a position about 800 kilometres to the west of *Warspite*. *Phoenix* fired torpedoes at long range, but unsuccessfully. The Commander-in-Chief and his staff put their heads together and surmised, correctly, that the Italian warships were very possibly shepherding a convoy to a Libyan port. Cunningham requested surveillance by long-range Sunderland aircraft from Malta. If the enemy kept at it, the Mediterranean Fleet might well be able to position itself off the Italian mainland to come between the enemy and his bases. For the moment, he held his nor'west course.

The bombers found them a little after 1000 hours, Savoias from airfields on Leros and Rhodes in the Dodecanese, flying so high that nobody saw them until a stick of bombs exploded in the sea astern of *Stuart*. The fleet opened up in a storm of anti-aircraft fire rather more optimistic than lethal, for at 12,000 feet the bombers were well out of range. And all day they came, glinting specks in a cloudless sky in five separate waves. At one stage the cruisers opened up on a speck that turned out to be the planet Venus. *Stuart* recorded the attacks at 1015, 1135, 1437, 1817 and the last in the gathering dusk at 1845. The ships wheeled and weaved beneath the onslaught.

'To us at the time it appeared that they had some squadrons especially trained for anti-ship work,' Cunningham wrote in his memoirs. 'Their reconnaissance was highly efficient, and seldom failed to find and report our ships at sea. The bombers invariably arrived within an hour or two. They carried out high-level attacks from about 12,000 feet, pressed home in formation in the face of the very heavy anti-aircraft fire of the fleet, and for this type of attack their accuracy was always very good …

… There was some consolation in realising that there was always more water than ship. Nevertheless, one felt very naked and unprotected.[1]

The last wave drew blood. Targeted at the cruisers, it disturbed a game of mah-jong being played in one of *Stuart*'s messes, sending the air attack alarm squawking. A line of bombs followed the wake of the cruiser *Gloucester*, dirty fountains drawing ever closer until the last landed directly on her bridge with devastating effect, killing Captain Frederick Garside and seventeen men there with him, and wounding another nine.[2] *Gloucester* yawed out of line to port, with a small fire burning, until her executive officer, in the ship's after control position for just this reason, took command and she resumed her station, her speed unaffected. After a while she was sent back out of the cruiser line to join *Eagle*'s escort.

As the evening drew in, the plot was changing. The Italian convoy reached Benghazi unscathed, so Campioni turned his cruisers and battleships to head back nor'west and then nor'east again to where he believed he might find his enemy, which seemed to have grown stronger. A message from the German B-Dienst reported that there were four British battleships at sea, twice as many as the Italians had. When Mussolini heard this he had a fit of nerves and ordered Campioni to refrain from any attack on the enemy until the Regia Aeronautica had been given a crack first. Supermarina told Campioni to group his forces at a position about 100 kilometres south-east of Punta Stilo, a prominent headland with a lighthouse on the Ionian coast of Calabria, Italy's southernmost mainland region. Close to home there would be plentiful air cover.

Cunningham, for his part, kept on nor'west for a while then, at midnight, he turned almost due west to 260 degrees, also aiming for the Italian coast, intent on blocking his enemy from the Gulf of Taranto. The two fleets were drawing together, each of them enjoying a quiet night. Some had an early start. At 0400 hours, the beginning of the morning watch, the flight deck of *Eagle* awoke to the splutters and bangs of the Bristol Pegasus radial engines of three Fairey Swordfish biplanes warming up for launch, the pilots and observers in their open cockpits leather-clad against the cold. Half an hour later they were airborne and heading west to find the Italian fleet, the sun rising behind them.

The dawn of 9 July promised another beautiful day, and so it turned out. A British army officer, Captain Francis Gerard, was hitching a ride to Malta in *Vampire*, put up in the captain's cabin.

In the Royal Australian Navy things are slightly different to what they are in the Royal Navy. The Captain's servant was a very pally sort of cove, and he woke me with a cup of tea and the remark: 'I shouldn't lie around all day if I was you. Get upon deck. You'll like it. There's going to be a battle.'

'A battle!' I echoed stupidly. 'What sort of battle?'

'Just an ordinary bloody battle,' he replied. 'The sea's lousy with ships. Looks like all the Med. Fleet's here.'

I went on deck as I was, in a pair of pyjama trousers, with a cup of tea in my hand. Remember, it was mid-July in the Mediterranean.

The morning was fresh and glorious, with a brilliant young sun painting the new sky with the effulgence of his coming. The sea was sapphire, set with diamonds. The wake of *Vampire*'s passing was like coiled ropes of pearls. It was a morning for poesy. It was also a morning for something grimmer. The young Australian rating was right. The sea was lousy with ships.[3]

At the centre of it all was *Warspite*, one of the crown jewels of the Royal Navy and the sixth ship to bear the name. The first *Warspite* had been a 29-gun galleon of the Tudor navy of Elizabeth I, the Virgin Queen, which had fought the Spanish and sailed with Sir Walter Raleigh in search of treasure. The Tudors had coined the name, laced with symbolism in their customary florid fashion: 'Despight' was an Old English word meaning defiance or contempt. *Warspight*, as it was originally spelled, would treat war with contempt. 'Spight' was also the Elizabethan word for a woodpecker, a sharp-beaked, belligerent bird which appeared on the ships' unofficial crest for centuries, along with the Latin motto *Belli dura despicio*, 'I despise the hard knocks of war'.

Andrew Cunningham's *Warspite* had been built as one of five Queen Elizabeth class fast battleships. 'Super dreadnoughts' they were called, the first British capital ships to be fuelled entirely by oil, designed to maintain Britain's superiority in the turn-of-the-century naval arms race with the Kaiser's Germany. She was commissioned in 1915 with an intended speed of 25 knots although, overweight at 33,000 tons deep load like all her sisters, she never got past 23 knots in her early days. Her great guns, though, were the navy's pride: a brand-new 15-inch design, eight of them, then the biggest in the world, capable of firing a shell of 879 kilograms over a maximum range of 30,000 metres. To back them up there was a secondary armament of no fewer than fourteen 6-inch guns, the same as those carried by the light cruisers, including *Sydney*.

It was an awesome display of might and power and *Warspite* employed it in the First World War in the Battle of Jutland in 1916, where she gained a reputation for having a cantankerous mind of her own when her steering jammed, forcing her to make two complete circles hard to port under the guns of the pursuing German battleships. She was lucky to escape, and that unpredictable quirk of her steering stayed with her. Disconcertingly, she did it again several times over the years.

In the 1930s she was virtually reconstructed from the bottom up in a three-year modernisation project that gave her entirely new boilers and engines, more armour and a new and imposing bridge structure. In addition, her main guns were upgraded to a higher elevation of 30 degrees, meaning a longer range, her anti-aircraft weapons were beefed up, and a catapult and hangar space for two reconnaissance floatplanes were added. With new masts, and the two funnels of her original design now trunked into one, in 1940 she was unrecognisable from the North Sea super dreadnought she had once been. Cunningham had especially requested her as his flagship. 'The Grand Old Lady' he called her, and he walked her decks with unconcealed pleasure.

There was, though, a flaw in this impressive array. *Warspite* did not have the new-fangled radar, not to see beyond her horizons, not to direct her guns. No ship in this coming battle did, not on either side. If the enemy were to be found, it would be only by air reconnaissance.

*Eagle*'s Swordfish drew a blank that morning. They saw only empty sea. At 0600 hours, evermore anxious for information, Cunningham rearranged the fleet into a new daytime cruising position, led by the five ships of Tovey's 7th Cruiser Squadron in line abreast, the A–K line as it was called, with *Stuart* riding shotgun. Twelve kilometres back were *Warspite* and her destroyer screen, and then another 12 kilometres astern were the slower battleships *Malaya* and *Royal Sovereign* and more destroyers – *Vampire* and *Voyager* among them – with *Eagle* acting more or less independently. The Australians, too, were impressed by the majesty of that morning, recording the swelling scene before them in *Stuart*'s 'chronicle':

> The British force, steaming at full speed in battle trim, was a sight not even seen at Jutland. In the perfect visibility, blue sea and cloudless sky, the cruisers on the wing, and the destroyers in semi-circular formation screening in front of the battleships, made a picture no one who ever saw it can ever forget …

... A few flags would flutter up to the flagship's yardarm and answering pendants to the yardarms of the other ships [showing they understood the signal].

Then in unison, down would come the flagship's signal and the answering pendants and, as if directed by a magician's wand, over all helms would go together and the fleet would alter course like so many well-drilled soldiers, the destroyers leaning over with the sea creaming from their bows, the battleships more ponderous but not the less spectacular, moving around more slowly in their restricted circle to take up their new course.[4]

Cunningham's prayers were answered at exactly 0732 hours when two RAF Sunderlands from Malta found Campioni for him. The Italians were where he had judged they might be, 230 kilometres to the west and steering north. The excitement on *Warspite*'s admiral's bridge and her compass platform was intense. Signal flags soared up the foremast. The Commander-in-Chief brought the fleet up to 18 knots and turned north-west again, still with the aim of blocking the enemy from his bases.

For four hours the Sunderlands shadowed the Italians, sending constant and accurate sighting reports. Campioni could only watch in increasing anger as they circled out of range of his anti-aircraft guns. Without an aircraft carrier of his own he was powerless, and his repeated requests for fighters from Messina – or anywhere – to deal with these tormenters produced no result whatever. It was the beginning of a total collapse in cooperation between the Regia Marina and the Regia Aeronautica. By now the air force should have found Cunningham and been bombing him ferociously in wave after wave but, inexplicably, the Savoias and Cants were searching too far south and discovered nothing. Cunningham drew ever closer, until by 1115 hours he knew he was just 140 kilometres from his quarry. He ordered an air strike from *Eagle*.

The carrier turned into the wind and nine Swordfish from the Fleet Air Arm's 813 Squadron laboured into the air, each carrying a 21-inch torpedo slung beneath the fuselage. It would be a slow flight. The Swordfish was a sturdy aircraft that would achieve some spectacular successes in this war, but it was almost comically obsolete.

Its best speed with a torpedo was about 160 km/h and it was well after 1300 hours that *Eagle*'s pilots hit their mark. By this time Campioni had turned his force south again, the two battleships in the van, followed by his heavy cruisers and their destroyer escorts. The Swordfish missed the battleships but found the four cruisers and split into three wings for an attack from three different directions. With extraordinary skill and courage, they dived almost vertically from 8000 feet to just 50 feet (15.5 metres) above the sea surface. Precision was everything: too high or too low and the torpedo would either dive straight to the bottom or break up on impact. Then, flying level at that best speed of about 160 km/h, they braved a storm of fire, not least from the cruisers' 8-inch guns firing at point-blank range. On they came, pressing home their attack through a hell of bright orange muzzle flashes, dark gunsmoke, the uniquely Italian red, white and green anti-aircraft tracer shells, and explosions in the sea which sent dirty fountains of water towering in front of them and over them. They released their torpedoes at a range of about 1000 metres and then, engines straining to the utmost they climbed again, curving away over their targets. Almost unbelievably, nobody scored a hit, not the British nor the Italians. Unscathed, the Swordfish returned safely to their carrier. And still the Regia Aeronautica had not appeared.

By now each admiral had a fair knowledge of his opponent's whereabouts, the Briton perhaps better than his enemy. Cunningham brought his entire fleet due west, 270 degrees, at 22 knots, although *Malaya* was struggling to keep up and *Royal Sovereign* was slipping further and further behind. Campioni turned back northwards again at 15 knots in some confusion until his battleships, cruisers and destroyers sorted themselves out. The two were converging. On the port wing of the cruisers, *Sydney* was the first to catch a smudge of enemy smoke on the horizon, but it was an eagle-eyed lookout in *Neptune* who sighted two unidentified enemy vessels at 1452 hours, at a distance of about 25 kilometres. Tovey pressed his cruisers onwards and 15 minutes later *Neptune* made a signal unseen and unheard in the Mediterranean since the days of Nelson: *Enemy battle fleet in sight.* They had found *Conte di Cavour* and *Giulio Cesare*. A fight was now inevitable. The sky had clouded slightly, but visibility was still excellent, on a sea ruffled by a fresh breeze. The cruisers began exchanging fire at an extreme range of some 23 kilometres, the British both out-numbered and outgunned but swinging north again to open up their A-arcs, bringing all their guns to bear. Jack Ross in *Sydney* was in the thick of it:

> *Sydney* had been able to squeeze a fraction of a knot more out of her turbines than the rest of the squadron and was therefore slightly in the lead and one of the first to come under the return fire. Firing steadily our cruisers struggled gamely to close the range still further and, succeeding, we were soon hotly engaged, not only by the opposing cruisers but by the two battleships as well.
>
> All around, salvoes of 8-inch and 12-inch shells began to churn up the sea and it seemed only a matter of time, in spite of our zig-zagging courses, before one or more of our number was hit.[5]

*Warspite* rode to the rescue, loosing off ten salvoes from her 15-inch guns and forcing the enemy cruisers to turn away. From now on, around 1530 hours, the battle would be fought with both sides heading more or less north, the Italians to the west, the British to the east, occasionally drawing closer, occasionally moving apart. Each admiral suffered his individual frustrations: Campioni, infuriated by the non-appearance of the Aeronautica; Cunningham, perturbed that *Malaya* was still struggling to keep up and that *Royal Sovereign* was hopelessly behind, almost out of sight. Up on the open compass platform where he had moved from his admiral's bridge for a better view, Cunningham paced back and forth – his 'caged tiger act' his staff called it – and ordered *Warspite*, steaming at 24.5 knots, to make a complete circle to starboard that would give *Malaya* time to join him.

The battleships began firing at each other at a range of about 25 kilometres. It was imposing, awe-inspiring, tumultuous, the shells sounding for all the world like the roar of a steam locomotive at full speed as they soared in. *Cavour* and *Cesare* mounted a smaller gun than the British ships, at 12.6-inches, but they carried twelve each. *Stuart*'s diarist recorded the action:

> On the starboard wing of our forces the British cruisers [includ-ing *Sydney*] were churning up the ocean at top speed, belching

flame and smoke as they fired rapid salvoes. Further back were our destroyers, line after line of them, in perfect formation, shuddering under their speed and firing every gun that would bear.

Behind, the majestic battleships, imperturbable, their grey bulk hidden every now and then in flame and dark yellow smoke as their great guns sent huge projectiles across the miles that separated them from the enemy. Last but by no means least came the *Eagle* ...

... the crash of main armament, the rattle of close-range weapons, the sharp crack of larger A.A. pieces, the towers of spray as enemy shells fell around *Warspite* and the battleships, acrid fumes of cordite, blasts of flame on firing and the trembling of the ship under high speed can never be reproduced on canvas or celluloid. Only the eye that saw it and the mind that recorded it can encompass it.[6]

*Warspite* was straddled several times, meaning that some of the Italian shells landed on either side of her, port and starboard, under and over, but she straddled the Italians, too. *Malaya* joined in, though she was too far away to have any effect beyond smoke and noise, her shells falling short. The turning point of the battle was not long coming. At 1600 hours, watchers on *Warspite*'s bridge saw one of their shells explode in a brilliant orange flash on *Cesare*, Campioni's flagship. It struck at the base of the after funnel, followed by a rising, spreading column of thick black smoke. Shrapnel flew about the battleship's deck and some twenty-two men were killed instantly with more wounded. The turbo fans sucked the smoke down into the boiler rooms and, deprived of air, four boilers had to be shut down, which gradually slowed the ship to 18 knots. All electrical power was lost for almost a minute and *Cesare* slewed off course. Campioni had had enough. He ordered his two battleships to turn due west, away from the British, and began laying down a curtain of smoke to conceal his withdrawal from the field while his cruisers and destroyers covered his rear. *Warspite* fired seventeen salvoes in all, but gave it away as the smoke thickened and the two Italian battleships disappeared behind it. Cunningham would later write that:

the enemy's smoke tactics were impressive and the smokescreens laid by his destroyers were very effective in completely covering his high-speed retirement.[7]

Now the smaller ships came into their own. There was another ten-minute gun duel between the cruisers, with a hit on the Italian *Bolzano* that jammed her rudders for a short time, and another bold but again ineffective air strike from *Eagle*'s Swordfish. A couple of shells landed within 100 metres of *Stuart*. After a few minutes the Italian cruisers began retiring behind a smokescreen as well, leaving their destroyers to sortie in and out through it to launch torpedo attacks on whatever targets they could find. Which they did but rather half-heartedly, the British thought, although a few torpedo tracks were seen and avoided. At 1614 hours, Cunningham ordered his destroyers to take them on. Hec Waller hurled *Stuart* into the fray, the little destroyer leader almost bounding through the water at 30 knots, a big battle ensign flying from her foremast and an even bigger Australian flag at the main. In typical Waller fashion she was the first to open fire, hammering away as fast as she could from her for'ard 4.7s. Her first salvo appeared to hit an enemy ship. Ean McDonald was on the flag deck:

*Stuart* had one gun mounted amidships. At this sharp approach angle that gun pointed just over our heads on the flag deck. At each blast of the gun we were all belted backwards, only feet away from that gaping muzzle, and we got faces full of hot cordite. When we got close enough to the Italian ships our Captain ordered the torpedo turn and around we went. Each destroyer in succession down the line reached the turning point and around it went following us and loosing its torpedos as it turned. The sea must have been thick with vengeful 'fish'. Each destroyer at that moment was at its most vulnerable position. The Italian gunners had Aunt Sally shots and they had our range. Why they didn't knock us off like dolls at a circus I will never know. Perhaps it was just the vagaries of shell flights that saved us. Sure they tried. The water around us was in continual eruption. The sound was all engulfing and very scary.[8]

It was an historic moment for the RAN: the first time an Australian destroyer had taken part in a classic fleet action, although not everyone got to see it. Bill Reeve, a twenty-year-old from Hobart who had joined up in 1939, was an engine room artificer in *Stuart*:

Calabria was the first time we had seen real action, and down below in the engine room you could hear the gunfire. Flakes of paint from the deckhead and asbestos dust from the lagging descended like a snowstorm, but we were too busy to worry about what was going on outside. If a forced lubrication pump broke down at high speed you lost oil pressure and had one minute to get things going before the main engine and thrust block bearings started to seize. Likewise, if you lost an air pump and you lost the vacuum in the condensers the build-up of water would strip the blades at the end of the low-power turbine in thirty seconds.

You were kept busy, eyes wandering around gauges all the time, and never had time to worry about what was happening on deck. At action stations, two ERAs were on watch in the engine room and two were close by on deck for damage control or fire party. Only if you were not on watch below did you have a chance to observe what was going on.[9]

With his enemy disappearing as he watched, Andrew Cunningham had more decisions to make. He knew what they were up to. For some inexplicable reason the Italians had been talking to each other in plain language, uncoded, and a translator in *Warspite* had picked up some of the chatter and relayed it to him. One had revealed that Campioni felt 'constrained to retire', which caused some mirth to Cunningham and his staff. Another morsel had discussed an Italian submarine patrol line which was indeed lying to the south of the battlefield in the hope that the British might stumble into it. More to the point, one of *Warspite*'s Walrus reconnaissance planes was in the air, reporting that the Italians were now heading south-west at high speed, although in some confusion, evidently making for the Strait of Messina. Cunningham could have plunged in through the smoke and gone after them but he held back, fearing that it might be a trap to draw him over those submarines. He knew also, to his chagrin, that both the Italian battleships and the heavy and light cruisers had the legs of his own ships by as much as 5 knots, making it highly unlikely that he could chase them down. And a lot of his destroyers were running low on fuel. Instead, he decided to work around the smokescreen to the north and west again.

At which point, the Regia Aeronautica finally turned up and, with magnificent impartiality, began to bomb both British and Italian ships alike. From 1640 until 1925 hours there was an almost continuous rain of bombs from on high on the British fleet, to Cunningham's considerable unease:

> All ships received attention, though perhaps the *Eagle* and *Warspite*, being unmistakeable, were rather specially singled out as targets, each being attacked five times. It was most frightening. At times a ship would completely disappear behind the great splashes, to emerge as though from a dark, thick wood of enormous fir trees. I was seriously alarmed for the old ships *Royal Sovereign* and *Eagle*, which were not well protected. A clutch of those eggs hitting either must have sent her to the bottom.[10]

*Eagle* sent up the only fighter aircraft she had on board; two old Gloster Gladiators that had been loaded in Malta. There were no trained fighter pilots to fly them, but a couple of the Swordfish pilots volunteered to have a crack at it and, splendidly, they managed to shoot down two bombers. For all its intensity and some frightening near misses, the bombing caused no damage to the British fleet. Campioni's ships were bombed almost as heavily and for almost as long for, remarkably, his ships and the aircraft had no means of communicating with each other. Eventually, in exasperation, the Italian ships began shooting back and brought down another bomber. Campioni and the lightly wounded *Giulio Cesare* reached Messina at 2100 hours that evening.

Thus ended the Battle of Calabria or, as the Italians would know it, *La Battaglia di Punta Stilo*, after the landmark just over the horizon. Essentially it was a draw, unsatisfactory to both sides. The Italians had achieved their aim of getting their supply convoy safely through to Libya but had not been able to use their edge in speed, guns and sheer numbers of ships to take on and beat the British. In coming days the disastrous lack of cooperation between the Marina and the Aeronautica exploded into a first-class row in Rome, dragging in almost everybody except Mussolini himself, who blindly believed the pilots' entirely fanciful claims of British battleships and cruisers crippled or sunk. His son-in-law, Count Galeazzo Ciano, rather more realistic, wrote acidly in his diary that:

> *La vera polemica in materia di combattimenti navali, non è tra noi e gli inglesi, bensì tra l'Aviazione e la Marina ... Confesso che anche io sono incredulo ...*
> The real controversy in the matter of naval combat is not between the British and us, but between the Air Force and the Navy ... I confess that I am incredulous too.[11]

Cunningham's despatch to the Admiralty was sober and downbeat, beginning with that time-hallowed phrase, 'Be pleased to lay before their Lordships the accompanying narrative ...'

> The meagre material results derived from this brief meeting with the Italian fleet were naturally very disappointing to me and all under my command, but the action was not without value. It must have shown the Italians that their Air Force and submarines cannot stop our fleet penetrating into the Central Mediterranean and that only their main fleet can seriously interfere with our operating there. It established, I think, a certain degree of moral ascendency, since although superior in battleships, our fleet was heavily outnumbered in cruisers and destroyers, and the Italians had strong shore-based air forces within easy range, compared to our few carrier-borne aircraft.
> On our side the action has shown those without previous war experience how difficult it is to hit with the gun at long range, and therefore the necessity of closing in, when this can be done, in order to get decisive results. It showed that high level bombing, even on the heavy and accurate scale experienced during these operations, yields few hits and that it is more alarming than dangerous.[12]

The night brought relief, most of all to the weary gunners above decks and to the hands who had been toiling deep in the magazines and the ammunition handling rooms. *Stuart* alone had fired sixty-seven rounds from her main armament. It was punishing physical labour heaving the shells into the hoists below decks, trying to keep your feet as the ship twisted and turned, everyone crammed into confined spaces so hot and airless that, drenched in sweat, they usually wore only shorts or underpants and just a pair of boots. It saved on your laundry.

Cunningham brought the fleet within 40 kilometres of the Calabrian coast and then turned south-west towards Malta, sending a handful of destroyers on ahead to refuel. *Stuart* entered Grand Harbour before dawn on 10 July with just 15 tons of oil remaining, a little too close for comfort. As if to atone for its failure of the previous day, the Aeronautica greeted them with a couple of heavy raids on Valletta but again damaged not one ship. They also failed to find the rest of the fleet, which was cruising south of Malta while the destroyers refuelled before returning to Alexandria. No doubt to make a point, Cunningham sent in *Eagle*'s Swordfish again to make an evening attack on the Sicilian port of Augusta where, with more luck this time, they torpedoed and sank a destroyer.

Of the two convoys carrying civilians from Malta, the fast MF1 had already sailed for Alexandria on 9 July, with *Vendetta* one of the escorting destroyers. *Stuart* and the damaged cruiser *Gloucester* chased after them and joined on 11 July. The slower convoy, MS1, sailed on the evening of 10 July, with *Vampire*, *Voyager* and *Dainty* as escorts. A little disappointed, *Vampire* and *Voyager* had been assigned to escort *Eagle* in the rear during the battle and had taken no active part, although they had been heavily bombed and once or twice machine-gunned, their captains dodging and weaving successfully.

There was more action to come, though. Early on the morning of 11 July, at the tail of the slow convoy, *Voyager*'s Asdic picked up a submarine contact. Commander Morrow dropped five depth charges but it came to nothing. Then the bombers returned in the forenoon, unseen at first, until a stick of eight bombs crashed into the sea near *Vampire* out to starboard of the convoy, a couple of them just 5 or

6 metres away. The destroyer plunged through the spray but could do nothing to avoid the shrapnel which peppered her from every direction. Jagged splinters of steel ripped and smashed into her superstructure, into some of the boats and both funnels, and made five holes in her hull, including two underwater. Men on the bridge and the fo'c'sle were thrown off their feet.

The ship's commissioned torpedo gunner, John Endicott, was on the pom-pom platform checking some empty ammunition belts and the splinters slashed him too. He fell to the deck, bleeding heavily. Another man with him was also wounded. *Vampire* did not have a doctor on board, but the sick berth attendants did what they could for him, while the captain, Lieutenant Commander John Walsh, turned the ship at full speed towards the fleet over the horizon to get better medical attention. It was the journey of nightmares, with more bombs plunging down around them, but there was a brief lull in which *Vampire* found the destroyer HMS *Mohawk*, which had a doctor on board. Mr Endicott, still conscious, was placed gently into the whaler and rowed across, where *Mohawk*'s surgeon was waiting for him. As the boat returned to *Vampire* the bombers came back once more, and the pom-pom and Lewis gunners fired away like men possessed, futile though it was. The Italians were far beyond their reach. Each time a new stick came down it seemed certain to be the one that would finally hit them, but Walsh judged his helm orders with consummate skill. With the wheel hard over, the destroyer would sheer away and the bombs would smash into the sea, some of them showering more shrapnel but with no material damage.

John Endicott died of his wounds that evening, still young at the age of thirty-two, leaving a wife, Dorothy, and a son aged just four. An Englishman, born in Devon, he had been on loan to the RAN from the RN since 1938. *Mohawk* gave him a naval burial the next morning. His death had a unique, sad significance. Commissioned Gunner Endicott was the first fatal casualty on board an Australian naval ship in this war.

The bombing continued all the way back to Alexandria, with mounting ferocity, in wave after wave. Cunningham had split the fleet into its component parts to separate them, battleships here, cruisers there, and taken a more southerly course towards the African coast, but still the Aeronautica found them. On 12 July, the worst day of all, *Warspite*'s group was attacked seventeen times between 0900 hours and midday, with more than 300 bombs dropped. *Sydney* was with her and, after one particularly fierce attack, it looked for all the world as if she had been lost, as Cunningham recounted:

> Particularly do I remember a most virulent attack on 12 July during our return passage to Alexandria when twenty-four heavy bombs fell along the port side of the ship simultaneously, with another dozen on our starboard bow, all within two hundred yards, but slightly out for line. Other ships had much the same sort of experience. On this day I saw the *Sydney*, which was in company, completely disappear in a line of towering pillars of spray as high as church steeples. When she emerged I signalled: 'Are you all right?' to which came the rather dubious reply from that stout-hearted Australian, Captain J. A. Collins: 'I hope so.'[13]

In his report, John Walsh would write of the bombing:

> The blast effect when we were straddled blew everyone on the upper deck and bridge flat, some ratings finding themselves yards from where they had been standing. The moral effect of the bombing was negligible until the straddle occurred on 11 July, after which there were signs of irritation at not being able to reply, and a slight nervousness when the penetrating power of the splinters was observed.[14]

The inability to hit back was galling. The cold, raw truth was that the anti-aircraft weapons on *Stuart* and the four V and W destroyers were useless, and the men knew it and resented it. A few weeks later, back in Alexandria, it led to trouble on *Voyager* one morning when a handful of sailors refused to leave their mess for the job of ship painting assigned to them. Petty Officer Cooper noted in his diary:

Alex, Tuesday, 23 July. Painted ship's side, otherwise quiet, boys had sit down strike. Air raid warning. News that they are thinking of mounting captured Breda guns on us.

Another version had it:

We were ready to start work, but we could not get out of the forward mess. Half a dozen or so of the older blokes had sat themselves outside the mess and would not let us out on deck. Strangler [First Lieutenant Alan Lewis] came down but he could not get them to move. It seems they were not going to start work or take the ship to sea unless something was done about the lack of anti-aircraft guns …

… the guns had no elevation so they were just useless against planes. To get a decent shot with our 4-inch guns the skipper would make a sharp turn to heel over so we could get some elevation to them …[15]

Technically it was a mutiny, for which the men refusing duty could be arrested, charged and punished. Sensibly it did not come to that. Commander Walsh evidently resolved it with tact and discretion, for the ship's side did indeed get painted as ordered and the men got leave to go ashore that evening as usual. Sometimes it was better to turn a blind eye to the black-letter law of naval discipline.

Arthur Cooper, *Voyager*'s gunner's mate, had heard a current buzz about the Italian Breda guns. In two different models, they were an anti-aircraft weapon very much better than anything the British had on offer. Captured guns were highly prized and a few had already been seized from the enemy. Later in 1940, as the British and Australian armies swept up the Italians in the Western Desert, literally hundreds of Breda guns were taken with seemingly endless supplies of ammunition. The Australian army used them as an effective anti-tank weapon and several eventually did find their way onto Australian warships, entirely unofficially.

By 15 July, the warships and the two convoys were all securely in Alexandria Harbour. Operation MA5 was over. The Australians had come through the worst the enemy could throw at them, battered but unbeaten. Hec Waller and John Collins had earned the Commander-in-Chief's respect for their handling of their ships in battle, a reputation they quietly prized. Within weeks, the stout-hearted Collins would seize an opportunity for deeds that would make his reputation as an energetic and intuitive fighting captain. *Vampire* and *Vendetta* would get the chance to prove their mettle and *Stuart*, too, would carve her name.

# CHAPTER 9

# 'STAND TO THE DAWN'

Lorna Walsh had been waiting at Alexandria for the return of her husband. She and John Walsh had been married just three years, time enough for her to become accustomed to the uncertain comings and goings of a naval officer, but the war had added a sharp new edge of anxiety to his absences. One of the few flotilla wives to brave life in the war zone overseas, she had left their flat in Sydney's Elizabeth Bay to make a domestic haven for him away from his ship, but it did not lessen the worry when he was at sea. She was waiting, too, for the Malta convoys, for she had friends on board.

A slender and elegant brunette, the daughter of a prominent Adelaide doctor, Lorna had been a popular actress in theatres in Sydney and Melbourne under her maiden name Lorna Dawson, and in the mid-1930s she had scored good reviews in supporting roles in London's West End. Her doings at balls, parties and suppers were often in the newspapers, and her wedding to the very eligible Lieutenant Commander Walsh had been one of the glamorous hits of the Adelaide season in 1937, admiringly reported in the society pages.

The bride wore a gown of ivory velvet over the palest gold taffeta, and it had a bodice softly gathered to the centre and outlined with pearls.[1]

John's 1919 term mate from the naval college, 'Copper' Morrow, had been the groomsman. Now, here were the two of them, both thirty-five years old, commanding destroyers in the Med. Lorna wrote chatty letters to her mother back in Adelaide, one after John's return from MA5.

> John was desperately strained and tired after no sleep for many days and nights. His gunner was killed and he was knocked about by flying shrapnel. Bombs had fallen across the ship between the mast and the bridge, and altogether he reckons about 1000 bombs were dropped round the escort.
>
> He had been escorting a convoy. There were a couple of convoys – one fast and one slow. Some of the wives coming from Malta were in the fast convoy. John had been with the slow one, but was fortunately signalled [sic] as he had been having such a bad time, and so he arrived on Saturday.
>
> We went round to the Metropole, and the wives were the heroines of the hour. They had had the time of their lives in Malta! They had seventy-four air raids, and bombs dropped all round them. They were the only occupants left in their huge block of flats, with no one for about a mile on either side of them. They had really stood up to it marvellously – that four days' trip across couldn't have been much fun, and they had had to get up at five o'clock that morning.[2]

The bombing was as much an attack on the mind as the body, for it took iron reserves of will for men on the upper deck to carry on and stick to the job as those menacing geysers of water erupted around them. Fear was ever-present, held in check by the urge to conceal it from your mates, to not let the side down. Below decks it was a little easier, perhaps, because you could not see the explosions, although you could certainly hear and feel them as the shock waves from a near miss hammered the hull. The weight of it all lay heaviest upon the captains, who bore the responsibility for the safety of the ship and every soul on board. In the destroyers they snatched what sleep they could in the tiny box of a sea cabin behind the wheel-house, subconsciously aware of every change of course or engine revolutions or sea state, nerves always on edge for the cry down the voice pipe of 'Captain to the bridge', or the shattering intrusion of the air alarm. 'Aircraft bearing red one five zero, angle of sight 50 degrees …!'

It could go on like that for days on end, when life blurred into a numbing weariness. Drained by fatigue, they would haul themselves back to the bridge to make the existential decisions, sometimes in a matter of seconds, as the bombs whistled down – port or starboard, life or death. Over time, and with practice, most captains became skilled at it. Some leaned back in their bridge chairs, others took to lying flat on their backs on the open compass platform, the better to see the black specks growing ever bigger as they plummeted towards you. It demanded intense concentration, exquisite timing. You picked your moment, you gave the order, and if you got it right the ship heeled safely away under full helm unscathed, to await the next onslaught. Getting it wrong did not bear thinking about.

As a captain must, Walsh cared for the health of his crew, a constant concern in these old ships. During that month of July he reported:

> One advanced case of pulmonary tuberculosis was discovered among the ship's company and several suspects were examined in the course of an inspection of all ratings. There is no doubt that this discovery, combined with poor ventilation and cracks in the deck which have appeared lately, and which allow water to enter the mess decks in head seas, have had a worrying effect on the ship's company. Steps taken to improve the morale in this direction include:
>   1. Stopping as many leaks as possible.
>   2. Opening as much ventilation as is safe.
>   3. Encouraging sleeping on the upper deck.
>   4. Spraying and scrubbing of mess decks with disinfectant, especially when closed down.
> These steps have had the desired effect, although nobody is looking forward to winter and rough seas.[3]

That brought him a stinging reproof from Admiral Tovey:

> Your statement that the discovery of this one case had a worrying effect on the ship's company is most improper; either it is unfounded, or it indicates that you allowed your ship's company,

through ignorance which you took no steps to dispel, to become unjustifiably apprehensive over a perfectly normal occurrence.[4]

It was a harsh response to a commanding officer raising an entirely legitimate issue, and Tovey comes out of it badly. He should have known better. But then he, too, was under strain. Even admirals were not immune.

—

When she came back, *Sydney* refuelled and replaced her ammunition, then went into Alexandria's floating dry dock for a couple of days to get her hull scraped and painted and her propellors cleaned; a pleasing respite. A clean bottom should be good for another couple of knots, they knew. Most of the ship's company got some quick leave ashore. John Collins squeezed in a couple of games of the tennis that helped him relax, but the war did not let up. As the cruiser undocked on 17 July there came the inevitable air raid to set nerves jangling again, fortunately without any damage. She was ready for sea once more.

Well before dawn the next morning two groups of ships slipped quietly out of the harbour, through the anti-submarine boom, down the swept channel and out to sea. Whenever possible, sailings from Alexandria were done in the dark to avoid air reconnaissance or the eyes of spies ashore; the British suspected, with good reason, that the Japanese Consul-General in Alexandria was regularly reporting comings and goings to the Italians.

In the first group were four fast, modern ships of the 2nd Destroyer Flotilla: HMS *Ilex*, *Hero* and *Hasty*, under the orders of Commander Hugh Nicolson in HMS *Hyperion*. Zigzagging at a steady 16 knots they headed nor'west for the Kaso Strait, which would take them around the eastern end of the island of Crete that evening. Nicolson's task was to make an anti-submarine sweep from east to west along the north coast of Crete and then, at 0600 hours, to complete the circle by returning south to Alexandria down the channel which runs between the island of Antikythera and western Crete.

A few hours later *Sydney* and the destroyer *Havock* sailed from Alexandria in the same direction. They were to follow Nicolson's course along Crete's north coast to support the four destroyers in case of trouble. Then they would turn away further north into the Gulf of Athens to pursue any Italian merchant shipping they might find. John Collins thought this through carefully. In the days before radar, sunrise and the couple of hours after it were reckoned to be the most dangerous time in the war at sea, the moment when an unexpected enemy might suddenly emerge as a smear of smoke on the horizon or a distant gleam of aircraft wings coming out of the sun. You had to be prepared for it. It was why ships 'stood to the dawn', as they called it, why they went to action stations as a matter of routine before the first glow appeared in the east. Weighing it up, Collins decided that his original orders, obeyed to the letter, would take him too far north to be of any rapid assistance to Nicolson if trouble did indeed arise that next morning. So he told the navigator, Lieutenant Commander Clive Montgomery, to keep steaming due west until sunrise. Maintaining a prudent radio silence, he did not tell Commander Nicolson or Alexandria what he was doing.

On that same morning, 19 July, two Italian ships were heading north from Tripoli, on a course which would take them up through the Antikythera Channel west of Crete towards the Aegean and, incidentally, towards Nicolson's destroyers. The *Giovanni delle Bande Nere* and the *Bartolomeo Colleoni* were light cruisers, each mounting eight 6-inch guns, similar in size, power and punch to *Sydney*, although thought to be perhaps 5 knots faster. Under the command of Ammiraglio di Divisione (Rear Admiral) Ferdinando Casardi, they too were due to enter the Channel at 0600 hours, from the southern end. Neither side knew anything of the other.

The morning dawned fine and sunny, although Casardi reported strong winds and a heaving sea which prevented him launching a reconnaissance float plane to scout ahead. Collins, in calmer seas, had no aircraft to send up, for *Sydney*'s Seagull lost at Bardia had not been replaced. In *Hyperion*, the leading destroyer, they had just stood down from dawn action stations and the watch on the bridge was savouring the smell of breakfast bacon wafting up the voice pipes when the starboard bridge lookout spotted the enemy. It was 0720 hours.

'Two cruisers on the starboard bow, sir. And they're Italian too!'

The alarms rang again for action stations. The men ran to their places, breakfast abandoned. Recognising that he was outgunned and outranged, Nicolson sensibly decided to run for it towards the protection of *Sydney*, wheeling his ships around to the north-east under full rudder and ordering a speed of 30 knots as the battle ensigns were hoisted up the masts. The Italians were about 16 kilometres away, far out of range of the destroyers, but *Hyperion* and *Ilex* opened fire anyway as they turned and sped off. Nicolson radioed an enemy sighting report.

The next move was Casardi's. He hesitated briefly, wondering if the destroyers might be the advance guard of a larger and more powerful force out of sight, but then swung around to chase them, opening fire a few minutes later. This placed the two sides on more or less parallel courses nor'east, the Italians to the west or to port of the British and gradually opening the distance to about 19 kilometres to avoid the chance of a torpedo attack. The cruisers' shots hit nothing, for their gunners were firing on a heaving sea and staring into the glare of the rising sun. They forged on.

Out of sight to the north, Collins received Nicolson's first enemy sighting report of two cruisers and then, very quickly, a further signal giving the destroyers' position, course and speed. He immediately swung *Sydney* and *Havock* to the south, working up to full speed to meet Nicolson as soon as possible, then went on the loudspeaker system to tell the ship's company what was happening. Petty Officer Richard Curtis, a thirty-two-year-old from Melbourne, readied his gun crew in A-turret.

The news of the attack on the destroyers acted like an electric shock on the ship's company. All signs of panic were conspicuous by their absence. There was a fight in sight. Soon everyone was in full battledress, closed up at action stations, and during the lull 300 pairs of eyes searched the horizon, vainly endeavouring to discover if they were light cruisers like us, or heavy.[5]

Jack Ross had conflicting emotions:

The murmurs of excitement, the cheers and whoops which followed this dramatic announcement left no doubt about the morale of our lads. They were itching for a private fight with something about their own weight and now they seemed as happy and excited as a crowd of schoolboys setting off on their Christmas holidays.

I'm afraid I didn't take such a cheerful view of the whole business. I was rather perturbed about the possibility of getting a shell into my cabin and losing all my clothing and gear, not to mention treasured letters and photos and, furthermore, on the face value of the facts it looked as if we were in for some heavy punishment, if not complete disablement. The odds on paper were two to one against us of being able to fight two cruisers of equal armament, and should they turn out to be 8-inch cruisers, well, we had our chance and Buckley's.[6]

The fears were well founded. *Sydney*'s 6-inch guns had a maximum range of 23,000 metres, firing a 51-kilogram shell. If the enemy were indeed 8-inch cruisers of the Regia Marina's Zara class, they could send a shell of 125 kilograms over 31,000 metres. It would be no contest. Two of the big Italian ships could stand off and destroy *Sydney* at their leisure. This must have occurred to John Collins as he planned his encounter, but he dismissed it. His orders were to support the destroyers and support them he would, for to decline action would be disobedience and cowardice, with a court martial and professional ruin to follow. His chief thought was that his hunch, his judgement, his decision to keep to the south had paid off. He might have been some 300 kilometres to the north but, instead, he was some 60 kilometres away from the destroyers, within easy striking distance. Nicolson did not know this, though, and nor did Andrew Cunningham back in Alexandria, and Collins very deliberately did not tell them. Breaking radio silence to acknowledge Nicolson's by now regular reports would have alerted the Italians to his presence and quite possibly have prompted them to turn and escape. He sketched the scene in his memoirs:

It was at this stage, with the Italian cruisers hot on their heels, that *Hasty*, the rear destroyer, made to *Hero*, her next ahead: 'Don't look now but I think we are being followed.'

From the plot it was obvious that we could not get into action until about 8.30, so opportunity was taken to pipe 'hands to breakfast'. Everyone feels better after breakfast. All stations reported closed up again at 8.20, just before we sighted smoke and hoisted battle ensigns.[7]

Casardi, meanwhile, had been jockeying for position but without success. He caught only rare glimpses of the target, for a light mist had closed in and the racing destroyers were also making smoke, disappearing into the murk, and he did not resume firing for about half an hour. He was also calling for air support from Rhodes, with the customary lack of response from the Aeronautica.

*Sydney* was north of Cape Spada, a long promontory on the north-west coast of Crete, when her lookouts found the Italians at 0826 hours, about 20 kilometres away on the starboard beam. They saw that *Colleoni* was astern of *Bande Nere* and heading east. Sharpened by much practice, the cruiser's gunnery teams started into action, a performance as intricately scored as any symphony concert. In the turrets fore and aft the men were waiting and ready, their guns loaded with semi-armour piercing shells designed first to enter a ship and then explode. As *Sydney* steamed on, Collins gave the bearing and an approximate range of the enemy to the Gunnery Officer, Lieutenant Commander Michael Singer, who was in the director control tower (DCT) high above the bridge, where he and a crew of seven had a sweeping view of the surrounding sea and could train to port or starboard towards a target. The range taker in the DCT measured the distance from the enemy and sent that range electronically to the transmitting station deep in the ship's bowels. There, an Admiralty fire control table, an early form of analogue computer, calculated the complex equations of course, speed and range to correctly aim and elevate the guns, and sent this to the range to elevation operator up in the DCT, who in turn passed it on to the turret officer in each turret. The turrets trained into position – each one marginally different – and the guns raised to the required elevation. The 'gun ready' lamps flickered on and the fire gongs in the DCT gave their tinny *tong tong* warning.

Now was the moment. It had been just three minutes since the first sighting of the enemy. The Captain bent to the voice pipe and gave the order to fire on the leading ship, *Bande Nere*. Singer repeated the order to the director layer, who pulled a trigger which sparked a cordite charge in each gun breech, punching the shell up the barrel to emerge at a speed of 840 metres per second. The for'ard turrets, A and B, thundered in unison, *Sydney* shuddering beneath the force. Concealed by a low bank of sea mist, Collins achieved exactly what he had hoped for: complete surprise. The first Casardi knew of him was the startling sight of bright orange muzzle flashes in the distant haze, then the screech of shells and the great plumes of water as they landed near him. Commander Nicolson learned the same way that salvation had arrived.

> At 8.29 bridge lookouts in the destroyers – who could still discern nothing to the northward except the island of Milo gradually taking shape over the haze – saw, on the port bow, the orange flashes of the *Sydney*'s opening salvo – the most welcome sight in the world. She came rushing to the southward, on the port beam of the Italian, guns flashing, battle ensign streaming, and such a smother of foam at bow and stern that from the destroyers one seemed almost to hear the high-tensioned scream of the machinery driving her across the water.[8]

In *Sydney*'s DCT, the spotting officer and First Lieutenant, Lieutenant Commander Edmund Thruston, peered through stereoscopic binoculars to see whether those first shots were over the target, short of it or straddling. That information went to the transmitting station where the fire control table made the necessary adjustments, and the guns roared again. An efficient ship – and *Sydney* was very efficient – could fire eight broadsides per minute.

After a short, shocked pause, Casardi returned fire on *Sydney* but skittered away, first to the south-east and then further around to the south-west around Cape Spada, with *Sydney* and *Havock* in furious pursuit. Only then did Collins identify the enemy as two 6-inch cruisers, not the 8-inch which would have made life so much more difficult. The race was now on in the opposite direction with the roles reversed; the Italians the quarry. At 0835 hours *Sydney* scored her first hit, a lucky shot that struck *Bande Nere* in her forward funnel, killing four men but causing no significant damage. Commander Nicolson, who could barely believe his good fortune, joined *Sydney* as soon as she came into sight and together, in line abreast, the six ships pursued the enemy sou'west, a classic stern chase at 30 knots. With the haze lifting, for half an hour and more they tore across a glittering blue sea like hounds at a hunt, guns firing, ensigns streaming in the breeze, a giant Australian flag at *Sydney*'s foremast, Collins once shifting his line to open the A-arcs to bring all his guns to bear. *Colleoni* and *Bande Nere* were now about 16 kilometres ahead, firing regularly but slowly from their rear turrets.

More shells appeared to hit *Colleoni*. By 0915 hours they could see on *Sydney*'s bridge that she was losing speed while *Bande Nere* was drawing further away. At 0921 hours *Sydney* herself was hit in her for'ard funnel, causing what Collins later described as a spectacular hole but only superficial damage. It could have been nasty: steel splinters splattered down into A-boiler room and the for'ard engine room was briefly filled with choking fumes, but no one was hurt; electric power stayed on and the turbines kept turning. One sailor on deck was lightly grazed by a splinter and a couple of the ship's boats were riddled with holes. It was the only hit she received.

The battle turned just four minutes later. Another of *Sydney*'s shells struck *Colleoni* and jammed her rudder in the midships position, followed by another two, one of which exploded in the bridge structure and the other – infinitely more damaging – smashing low into her hull and putting two boilers out of action. Her main steam line ruptured, her ammunition hoists lost power and fires began to break out. She slumped to a halt, dead in the water, shells still falling around her and one or two more hitting her, all hope gone. Richard Curtis watched the destruction:

> It must be hell in there now. All our guns are now bearing and broadside after broadside pours into her. Her bows have been blown away and she's sinking by the head. At 9.25 she fires one last salvo but Y-turret answers it and finally silences her. Two of our destroyers help her on the way with torpedoes which blow her to pieces.[9]

One of *Colleoni*'s engineers, Lieutenant Gino Gallupini, said later that her crew 'lost heart'[10] at this point and her firing ceased.

Casardi in *Bande Nere* turned back as if to come to the rescue but evidently thought better of it. It would be his one ship against six others, and still the Aeronautica had not arrived. He decided that discretion was the better part of valour and continued the turn in almost a complete circle to head off again to the south at full speed.

Collins ordered Nicolson in *Hyperion* to torpedo *Colleoni* while he set off in pursuit of *Bande Nere*, with *Hero* and *Hasty* leaping ahead of him. At the same time he signalled Cunningham:

> One cruiser sunk. Ammunition practically finished. Another cruiser course 200 degrees am following.[11]

The Commander-in-Chief had been pacing the deck in *Warspite* for what seemed like an age, evermore anxious for news:

> I was on tenterhooks. The enemy cruisers might well be 8-inch gunships, in which case the *Sydney* and her destroyers would be heavily outmatched. All I knew was that the destroyers were being chased, and that Collins, regardless of any odds, was closing them at full speed. After that, dead silence.
>
> It must have been quite two hours later that our feelings of anxiety changed to those of triumph when the *Sydney* reported that she had hit and stopped one of the cruisers, which was badly on fire, and that she was chasing the other to the southward with her, the *Sydney*'s ammunition running low.[12]

*Sydney* was indeed running out of shells. Most of her firing had been from her for'ard turrets, and Commander Singer, improvising quickly, had rounds brought up from the after magazines. One more shell struck *Bande Nere*, penetrating her fo'c'sle and killing four men. The Italian kept firing back but scored not a hit as she began to pull away, leaving her pursuers falling further behind. At 1040 hours, some 20 kilometres ahead, she disappeared into the distant Mediterranean haze still heading south, and the chase was over. Cunningham ordered Collins to return to Alexandria.

*Bartolomeo Colleoni* died a slow death. With dozens of men dead or wounded, some of them flayed by escaping high-pressure steam from the boiler rooms, a pillar of flame and smoke rising from beneath the bridge structure, more fires burning fiercely below and the upper deck a shambles as some of the high-angle ammunition exploded, the order came to abandon ship. The crew, those sailors who could, began jumping into the water. The captain, Umberto Navaro, also badly wounded, told his officers that he would go down with the ship, but was helped into a life jacket and over the side. A midshipman bravely hauled down the ensign and tied it around his body.

Only then did the Regia Aeronautica show itself. With their customary exquisite timing, a small wave of bombers came over as the rescue began. The destroyers fired at them with every anti-aircraft weapon they had and escaped unscathed, but the bombs landed near enough and it is almost certain that they killed Italian seamen in the water. When the aircraft had been driven off and he was sure that every last man had left, Nicolson in *Hyperion* fired three torpedoes into the stricken cruiser and missed with all of them. *Ilex* fired another three, one of them striking her a little for'ard of A-turret and blowing off the bow. *Hyperion* fired a fourth which hit amidships, and at 1000 *Colleoni* rolled over to starboard and slowly sank.

Hundreds of men were struggling in the sea, and the three destroyers set about saving them. Scrambling nets, ladders and ropes were slung over the sides, boats were lowered, and one by one they were plucked from the water. Many were injured, a few badly burned. Captain Navaro was among them. Some were ashen-faced in defeat, or fear, or perhaps relief, shaking uncontrollably as they were hauled onto the decks. One or two were foolish enough to make the fascist salute, which won them a rough push or a heavy seaman's boot on a bare foot. The rescue was an extraordinary feat of seamanship, bold in the risk to the ships themselves and remarkable for its success, for no fewer than 545 men were saved. Another 121 were lost. With prisoners jammed into every conceivable space above and below decks, Nicolson's three ships set off at speed to join Collins on the way home.

—

Another three waves of bombers from Rhodes came over that afternoon and early evening, finding the destroyers first. Again there were no direct hits, but a near miss damaged *Havock*, putting one of her boilers out of action and slowing her to 24 knots. Turning back to assist, *Sydney* was caught in a fourth wave and straddled, but with no harm. And that was that. *Hero* and *Hasty* had gone on ahead. *Sydney*, with *Hyperion*, *Ilex* and the wounded *Havock* headed for home as night brought down the curtain on the Battle of Cape Spada. Petty Officer Curtis, a thoughtful man, reflected on his part in it:

> It's all sort of mixed up. Before the ship opens fire you're all keyed up. Sometimes you find yourself trembling – not with fear but with the strain of waiting. Then when the action begins it's all excitement. If you know you're hitting the enemy there's a feeling of elation. Then you see the hits smack into the other ship, with the flashes and the smoke and the red hot steel and you try to think what you'd be feeling. That's where discipline and training come in. For a brief period you want to stop, but it passes. So you continue belting away, but you do it mechanically. The feeling of elation is gone. It's been replaced by a sort of cold efficiency. And then you seem to do your best work.[13]

———

They made a triumphant entry to Alexandria the next morning, 20 July 1940, like victorious Caesar returning in laurels to Rome. With the destroyers preceding her and the ship's company lining the decks, the barrels of her for'ard guns once again blackened and blistered, *Sydney* glided through the boom in the late forenoon and steamed up the harbour to a rapturous welcome from the fleet and crowds lining the foreshores. Andrew Cunningham had spread the word, with a signal that ended, 'Give her a rousing cheer'. Every ship had cleared lower decks and the hoorays rang out as they passed by, with Nicolson's destroyers, in a generous gesture, hauling out of line to let *Sydney* take the lead.

On her quarterdeck, the ship's band played 'God Save the King' and 'Waltzing Matilda' and the trills and flourishes of the 'Royal Australian Navy March'.[14] For Jack Ross it was one of the great events of his life:

Naturally we were simply bursting with pride at such a stirring and heart-warming gesture and wouldn't have changed places with the King himself. It was a moment I will never forget. The cheering seemed a continuous roar for about fifteen minutes. Just inside the boom a gentleman fishing from a tiny skiff stood up and solemnly clapped us. Tugs and steamboats hooted their heads off and on shore we could see crowds of Egyptian wharfies and labourers jumping up and down and yelling themselves hoarse.

One of the storeships obviously had at least one Australian in her crew for as we came close the air was rent by a stentorian bellow of 'Aussies, you b_____ beauties!' But what pleased us more than anything else was the welcome given us by our Australian Flotilla. Each destroyer was flying seven Commonwealth flags. (Where they got them from heaven only knows.) From every halyard there fluttered one, and the cheering and whistling coming from their direction was even more vociferous than ever.[15]

Hec Waller, in *Stuart*, signalled 'Whacko *Sydney*'. John Collins, conning the ship to her assigned buoy, was so swept up in the welcome that he almost made a mess of it.

This was quite an experience, so much so in fact that I suddenly realised the engines were still going half speed ahead when we were only a couple of cables from our berth. Thus, unintentionally, I had to put a last test on men and material by ordering 'full speed astern'. As would be expected of that ship, she pulled up nicely between the buoys.

The Commander-in-Chief was lying off our berth in his barge, which came alongside as we secured. His first words were, 'Well done. I was very relieved when your enemy report showed you were on the spot, but how did you get there?' This seemed no occasion to go into details of my change of plan, so I replied, 'Providence guided me, sir.' With a smile, Sir Andrew replied, 'Well, in future you can continue to take your orders from Providence.'[16]

That afternoon the prisoners were unloaded from the destroyers wearing whatever scraps of clothing had been found for them and were marched in a long and forlorn column through the streets of the port to buses which took them to a temporary camp. For Gastone Tanzi, a war correspondent who had been on board *Colleoni*, it was a burning humiliation:

> Who would have thought of arriving here under these conditions? Naked, dirty, tired. Perhaps we are half as many as we were leaving Tobruk. Unfortunately they beat us and we must accept it. Look how they greet the arrival of the ships! The whole port is at the party. They had a nice day of hunting. If Admiral Casardi had been more versatile he would have launched the reconnaissance plane and would have discovered the ambush we were running into. It seems that he did not use it because there was a lot of wind and it would have been difficult to recover it afterwards. Among other things, he was sure of the air surveillance intervention from Rhodes.[17]

Most of the ship's company were given leave ashore that night and the celebrations continued, as Lorna Walsh wrote home to her mother:

> We eventually all went on to the Carlton to dine and dance. I felt in top form, and finished by a classical demonstration of boomps-a-daisy with the *Sydney*'s doctor – a very shy man, I was afterwards told. John Collins, the captain of the *Sydney*, had asked for a waltz, but as our steaks arrived with the first bars of the 'Blue Danube', the problem was a knotty one! However we managed both. We danced together and finished up en masse in the Palais Glide.[18]
> It was 3 am before the party broke up.[19]

The next day it was back to work, back to the endless round of readying the ship for sea again. Oiling, provisioning and ammunitioning came first. *Sydney* had spent 956 rounds of 6-inch ammunition at Cape Spada, with her for'ard magazine down to its last ten shells. In all, since her arrival in the Mediterranean, she had fired the impressive total of 2200 shells, a prodigious amount. There was some mending and patching to do here and there, once again repairing superficial but annoying damage done by the blast of her own guns. The gun barrels were scraped and repainted and the hole in the funnel was patched. An entire day was spent painting the ship in new camouflage colours, blocks of greys and charcoal which gave her hull and upper-works a strange, zig-zag look, and a new Seagull aircraft was found and hoisted aboard. There was time, though, for more socialising and the day after their return the officers of Nicolson's destroyers were invited over for drinks in *Sydney*'s wardroom to exchange war stories. They brought with them a ditty they had composed:

> And up jumped the *Sydney* and gripped them with glee
> And we cheered as we watched the Digger gunners shooting
> Crying 'Who'll come a-Waltzing Matilda with me' ...

Andrew Cunningham, still elated by the victory, had acted swiftly with a recommendation to the Admiralty in London that brought an even quicker response from on high:

CENTRAL CHANCERY OF THE ORDERS OF KNIGHTHOOD
St. James's Palace, S.W.1.
26th July, 1940
The KING has been graciously pleased to give orders for the following appointment to the Most Honourable Order of the Bath for distinguished service, in the gallant and successful action against two Italian Cruisers in which 'Bartolomeo Colleoni' was destroyed:—
To be an Additional Member of the Military Division of the Third Class, or Companion, of the said Most Honourable Order:
Captain John Augustine Collins, Royal Australian Navy,
H.M.A.S. *Sydney*[20]

The Order of the Bath, the CB, was a neat fit. The same decoration had been awarded to the captain of the first HMAS *Sydney*, John Glossop, an RN officer who had famously destroyed the German raider *Emden* in the Indian Ocean in 1914; symbolism not lost on *Sydney*'s officers or the wider navy. The *Emden* action had been the nascent RAN's first victory, celebrated ever since, and now here they were in the same exalted company. In the next few weeks there would be a silver shower of medals and mentions in despatches for twenty-two officers and sailors, including the DSO for the Commander, Tom Hilken, and the Chief Engineer, Commander (E) Lionel Dalton. In a bleak counterpoint, *Bartolomeo Colleoni*'s captain, Umberto Navaro, died of his wounds and was buried with naval honours in the Alexandria cemetery. John Collins and a handful of the destroyer officers were pallbearers at the funeral.

As the excitement was subsiding in Alexandria it was exploding in Australia. A couple of Australian war correspondents had been in Alexandria to see *Sydney* return, and they filed glowing accounts of the battle and the welcome home, which made a splash of bold headlines on the front pages of newspapers big and small across the country.

John Collins understood the value of publicity – unlike most of his brother officers, who thought it a bit vulgar and beneath them – and in his cabin he gave an interview to a correspondent from the Melbourne *Herald*, Jack Hetherington. It was syndicated around Australia.

From J. A. HETHERINGTON,
*Herald* Special Representative, with the A.I.F. in Palestine.
ALEXANDRIA, July 22. —
'The first half of the battle was won in the Design Department of the Admiralty and the shipbuilding yards of the Tyneside,' Captain J. A. Collins, captain of H.M.A.S. *Sydney*, told me in an exclusive interview on board the victorious Australian cruiser today.
'The second half of the battle was won with the reliable fighting weapon provided and handled by the ship's company of good Australians,' he said.

The news provoked an outpouring of patriotic pride and joy. The reports and feature articles, page after page, day after day, offer a poignant glimpse of a nation not yet fifty years old and its 7 million people in no doubt of their patriotism, courage and resolve but unsure of their place in a dangerous world. Australians thought of themselves as a part of a homogenous British race, and their membership of the Empire was both a comfort and a shield. Prime Minister Menzies, who could proclaim that he was 'British to the bootstraps', thought that:

The victory of the *Sydney* was a happy augury of what would happen to the Italian fleet if ever it came out. The exploits of the *Sydney* have indissolubly linked the name with the Empire.[21]

Never to be outdone where the map of the world was coloured red, Winston Churchill fired off a telegram to him:

Please accept and also convey to the Australian Naval Board my warmest congratulations upon the brilliant action fought by H.M. Australian ship *Sydney* in the Mediterranean which recalls most opportunely the exploits of her predecessor in sinking the *Emden* in the last war.[22]

Every detail and every angle, big and small, was picked over by the journalists and devoured by an eager public who expected victories, had been offered very few so far in this war, and wanted more. Civic worthies chimed in. Australian flags flew from every available flagpole. New South Wales state school principals were instructed to lecture their students on patriotic virtues, loyalty to King and Empire, and the grand achievements of the Royal Australian Navy in the Nelson tradition, and the kids were given a half holiday. Newspapers all over the country, dozens of them, scurried about to find local lads who had helped give 'Musso' a bloody nose:

'The success of the H.M.A.S. *Sydney* in sinking the Italian warship, *Bartolomeo Colleoni*, was of special interest to Narre Warren residents. Stoker Cyril Aumann, son of Mr and Mrs F. Aumann, of Narre Warren, is a member of the *Sydney*'s crew,' said the *Dandenong Journal*.

'Cyril was one of the local Boy Scouts Troop and took an active part in sporting and social activities in and around Narre Warren before joining the Navy. His many friends will follow his career with interest.'²³

The *Cumberland Argus and Fruitgrowers' Advocate*, of western Sydney, reported with heroic creativity that:

It is not beyond possibility that a Guildford sailor 'touched off' one of the torpedoes from the *Sydney* that sent the *Bartolomeo Colleoni* down to Davy Jones's Locker.

He is Torpedo Gunner Frederick Savage, second son of Mr and Mrs H. A. Savage, of Chetwynd Rd Guildford, and the only known sailor from the town serving on the *Sydney*.²⁴

There were scores more of these newspaper tributes, in the city and the bush. The *Courier-Mail* in Brisbane reported that:

The sinking of the Italian cruiser was acclaimed by 'Diggers' at the annual dinner of the Eastern Suburbs Returned Soldiers' Association last night. Lieutenant Commander Brewster R.A.N., representing the Commodore Superintendent of Naval Establishments, in replying to a prolonged demonstration, said: 'The *Sydney* had a job to do, and she did it, and that is all there is to be said about it.'

The gathering cheered for some minutes, sang the song, 'Sons of the Sea', and shouted 'Good old navy' and 'Well done *Sydney*!'²⁵

In Melbourne, *The Advocate* reported high excitement at John Collins's old primary school, the Christian Brothers College in Victoria Parade, East Melbourne.

On behalf of old boys of the college, the Old Paradians' Association sent the following cable to Captain Collins at Alexandria: 'Old boys of Parade College proud of your gallant achievement and merited distinction. Heartiest congratulations and good wishes.'

Last Monday, at morning assembly, the Principal of the college (Rev. Brother Garvey) delivered a short address on the *Sydney*'s exploit, and cheers for Captain Collins were given by the 450 boys present.[26]

If they actually knew it, everyone carefully ignored the fact that John Collins had converted to the Anglican faith at the naval college and had married his wife at that bastion of Anglican polite society in Sydney, St Mark's Darling Point. The Sydney *Sun* unearthed Phyllis Collins at their nearby flat, carefully informing its readers that she was 'small, chic, and dark-haired':

I'm so proud of my husband and the crew of the *Sydney*. I'm rather worried that there may be casualties, though. I know all the officers and their wives, as well as many of the crew.

As the Italian ship was sunk by gunfire, there must have been some damage to the *Sydney*. It'll be a miracle if there's not. Being a naval man's wife is worrying, especially in wartime, but I love the life.[27]

Inevitably, the *Australian Women's Weekly* found John Collins's mother Esther at home in Melbourne:

'I was in bed with influenza when someone knocked at my door in the early morning and shouted "Mrs Collins, your son has had a great victory". In these words Mrs M. J. Collins, mother of Captain Collins of H.M.A.S. *Sydney*, which sank the Italian cruiser *Bartolomeo Colleoni* in the Mediterranean, told how she heard the news which made her son a popular hero.

'Upon my word,' said Mrs Collins, 'it cured my influenza right away. Instead of spending a miserable day in bed I had a grand day in reading congratulatory telegrams and talking to friends.'[28]

Almost as satisfying was the web of invention spun from the fascist and Nazi propaganda mills. Casardi had reported he had been attacked by two cruisers, not one, and this was taken up and amplified in Rome and Berlin. *Sydney* became two heavily armoured cruisers, the Italians had put up an heroic fight against overwhelming odds, and two Allied destroyers were sunk by Italian 'super bombers', as Lord Haw-Haw himself was pleased to call them. Privately, Mussolini's son-in-law Count Galeazzo Ciano found Il Duce sunk in gloom.

'Today he was depressed on account of the loss of the *Colleoni*, not so much because of the sinking itself as because he feels the Italians did not fight very brilliantly,' he wrote in his diary.[29]

The last word on Spada can be left to Andrew Cunningham, from his report to the Admiralty:

The credit for this successful and gallant action belongs mainly to Captain J. A. Collins, C.B., R.A.N., who by his quick appreciation of the situation, offensive spirit and resolute handling of HMAS *Sydney*, achieved a victory over a superior force which has had important strategical effects. It is significant that, so far as is known, no Italian surface forces have returned into or near the Aegean since this action was fought.[30]

Cunningham's affection and respect for the Australian ships under his command was deepening. He was concerned, though, at the dangers of stopping to rescue survivors, and after Spada he issued a caution:

Difficult and distasteful as it is to leave survivors to their fate, Commanding Officers must be prepared to harden their hearts, for after all, the operations in hand and the security of their ships and ships' companies must take precedence in war.[31]

# CHAPTER 10

# A SUBMARINE KILL

August 1940, the last month of the northern summer, and September, the first month of autumn, saw the war grow more cruel and costly at an alarming rate, by land, air and sea. In just eight weeks the Germans sank 130 British merchant ships, more than 850,000 tons in total, mostly by U-boats but also by surface raiders, aircraft and mines. Only four U-boats were lost in that same period, a hideously unbalanced equation which suggested that Britain was losing the Battle of the Atlantic.

Hitler, triumphant, ordered his generals and admirals to step up preparations for *Unternehmen Seelöwe*, Operation Sealion, the invasion of Britain planned for mid-September. First, though, Hermann Göring's Luftwaffe would be given the opportunity to bomb the British into submission. The Blitz on London began on 7 September, with 400 civilians killed.

In the Mediterranean, each navy for a time turned its energies away from any grand fleet confrontation and towards individual, smaller actions and to gathering strength for the winter to come. In the first week of August the Regia Marina finally brought its brand-new battleships *Littorio* and *Vittorio Veneto* into service, handsome sister ships of 45,000 tons full load and carrying nine 15-inch guns. The Italians also redoubled their efforts to supply their army in Libya with convoys shuttling back and forth from Naples and Messina to Tripoli and Benghazi in pursuit of Mussolini's fantasy of invading Egypt and capturing the Suez Canal. Their submarines sowed minefields around both Malta and the Strait of Sicily, one of which claimed the destroyer HMS *Hostile* off Cape Bon on 23 August.

At Alexandria, Andrew Cunningham and his staff grappled with competing priorities, each as important as the other and offering no intersecting solutions. If you did this, you could not do that. Malta, where the bombing was getting heavier, had to be supplied with food, fuel and ammunition, and more aircraft for her defences; the Italian convoys had to be interdicted and broken up; Alexandria had to be sustained, too, for repair facilities there were stretched to the utmost and the admiral was in a perpetual lather about a shortage of 6-inch shells for his cruisers. The fleet was in urgent need of proper air cover for protection and reconnaissance – a modern carrier – and, apart from *Warspite*, its battleships were in poor shape with *Malaya* enduring constant condenser problems and the ancient *Ramillies* and *Royal Sovereign* reduced almost to the status of ornaments as their boilers slowly but steadily gave up the ghost. To add to the complexities, intelligence reports were indicating that the Italian army might soon begin its advance into Egypt.

Cunningham had a sympathetic ear back in London in the First Sea Lord, Admiral of the Fleet Sir Dudley Pound, a man much harassed but who had been Commander-in-Chief in the Mediterranean just before the war and understood the problems. In August, Pound sent reinforcements: the battleship HMS *Valiant*, a sister ship to *Warspite* and, like her, substantially modernised; the brand-new, armoured aircraft carrier *Illustrious*, carrying twenty-one Swordfish torpedo bombers and sixteen of the newly developed Fulmar fighters; and two modernised anti-aircraft cruisers, *Calcutta* and *Coventry*. The real prize, though, was radar. Both *Valiant* and *Illustrious* were equipped with it and, primitive though it was, it would transform Cunningham's view of the battle space. The four entered the Mediterranean from the Strait of Gibraltar in the last week of August, pausing at Malta to unload anti-aircraft guns and ammunition, and arrived at Alexandria on 5 September. The 8-inch heavy cruisers *York* and *Kent* arrived separately, and Pound promised Cunningham he would send the battleships *Queen Elizabeth* and *Barham* as soon as they became available. The tempo of the war at sea was about to rise again.

Finally, the Italians moved on land. On 9 September the Italian 10th Army, on Mussolini's direct order, began what would become known as the Western Desert Campaign, invading eastwards across the Libyan border into Egypt. There were elements of farce to it. The spearhead force, the *Raggruppamento Maletti*[1] of seven motorised infantry battalions, tanks and motorised artillery, managed to lose itself in the desert on the way to the border and had to be found and redirected by the Aeronautica. But the Italians had some 215,000 men in Libya while in Egypt Britain had only about 36,000 troops, and for the moment, anyway, weight of numbers told. The Italians advanced in some confusion along the coast road – the only paved road – while the British made an orderly strategic withdrawal.

As invasions go, it was a desultory affair. In a week, the 10th Army moved just 105 kilometres and on 16 September it slumped to a halt at Sidi Barrani, a sand-blasted Bedouin town on the Egyptian coast. There, evidently exhausted, it stayed to regroup. Estimates of the casualties vary, but the Italians lost perhaps 120 men and the British forty. The air forces of each side made constant bombing raids, and the Mediterranean Fleet bombarded enemy coastal positions every night, eventually forcing the Italians inland out of reach. Swordfish from *Illustrious* mined the harbour at Benghazi and sank a destroyer, but the newly arrived cruiser *Kent* was torpedoed in the stern while bombarding Bardia, had to be towed back to Alexandria and was out of action for a year.

—

Resplendent in her new warpaint, *Sydney* was at sea in early September, a part of the covering force that escorted *Valiant* and *Illustrious* through the Mediterranean. On 3 September – one year into the war – she was detached with the cruiser *Orion* and two destroyers to bombard the island of Scarpanto, where the Italians had an airfield that had become a base for bombing raids on Alexandria. Scarpanto* had been an Italian possession since 1912, a rocky and sparsely populated island of the Dodecanese in the south-eastern Aegean Sea, near Rhodes and about halfway between Crete and mainland Turkey.

---

\* Now Karpathos, a part of Greece.

*Orion* would strike the north of the island with the destroyer *Decoy*, while *Sydney* and the destroyer *Ilex* attacked the airfield on a coastal peninsula at Makri Yalo in the south. They parted company in the wee small hours.

With his customary meticulous preparation, John Collins put together a plan that would be part surprise and part ruse. The first thing would be to arrive at dawn when, hopefully, the defences would be asleep. Second, *Sydney* would be given a quick, makeshift disguise. Collins got his shipwrights to rig a frame of timber and canvas to shape her for'ard funnel like one of the Condottieri class cruisers, the same as the *Bartolomeo Colleoni*, a trick that just might confuse an untrained or drowsy eye in the half-light. It was worth a try. He would approach the little harbour at Makri Yalo at an easy 10 knots with *Ilex* astern, the speed an Italian ship might make on entering. With the target lined up she would come up to full speed, turn on a sixpence and open fire as she headed out again. Collins thought there might be the chance of meeting an E-Boat[2] on patrol, the small but very fast motor torpedo boats the Italians called a *Motoscafo Armato Silurante* or MAS. With two torpedoes, machine guns and a speed of 40 knots they could be a handful, but he would deal with that if it happened.

*Sydney* awoke at 0530 hours, about half an hour before dawn, to the piercing squawk of the alarms and the bosun's pipe for action stations. Men rolled from their hammocks on the mess decks and into their blue overalls, while the gunners donned their anti-flash gear. The morning was black and cold but clear, the two ships making their approach from out of the western horizon like phantoms from the dark into the sunrise. All was quiet on deck, save for the low drone of the fans sucking air to the boilers, a rush of wind through stays and halyards, the *swoosh* of the bow wave in a light sea and the occasional hum of the gun turrets fore and aft checking their training motors. Just before 0600 hours, with first light rising in the east, the peace was split by the splutter and bang of the Seagull reconnaissance plane warming up on the catapult, and within minutes it was up and away to spot the target and the fall of shot. Fifteen minutes later, with the rosy light growing, Scarpanto came in sight on the port beam, its forbidding grey crags and cliffs of volcanic rock rising to jagged peaks etched against the sunrise. Soon the air base itself emerged, the runway on the shore and its cluster of low buildings some 6 kilometres away, all quiet. Nothing stirred, no lights flicked on.

Then, against the shoreline, they saw a MAS boat patrolling slowly and quietly, unalarmed. It must surely have seen them, so it seemed *Sydney*'s disguise had worked. From astern, a signal lamp flickered from the destroyer, a tiny disc of light from the small beam of a hand-held Heather light.[3] 'From *Ilex*, sir,' said the Chief Yeoman on the bridge. 'E-boat port bow.' Collins felt that her captain, Lieutenant Commander Philip Saumarez,[4] would know exactly what to do when the moment came and he replied with just one word: 'Wait.'

Another couple of minutes and the Navigator, Clive Montgomery, told the captain they had reached the planned position. The MAS boat was even closer but still placidly unsuspecting. In a flurry of orders, *Sydney* put her helm hard over to starboard, at the jangle of telegraph bells the engine room opened the throttles and oil sprayers for full speed, and A- and B-turrets fired their first ranging shots to be spotted by the Seagull floatplane above the target. Without another order, Saumarez did exactly what Collins expected and *Ilex* opened fire with her 4.7-inch guns. Whether by good shooting or good luck she scored a direct hit on the MAS boat, which exploded in flame, sparks and smoke like a giant firework. Jack Ross in *Sydney*, with no particular part to play in the action, had climbed up to the after control position for a grandstand view and was watching the destroyer through his binoculars.

Suddenly, without any warning, she altered course about 30 degrees to port across our stern. At the same time her two after guns commenced firing astern straight down the line of our wake. I was puzzled for a moment and couldn't make out what she was engaging even though I could make out the distant splashes of her shells falling about three miles away. Then gradually I made out a cluster of tiny bow waves surmounted by black dots rapidly closing us. A flotilla of E-boats racing up to the attack!

... With her third or fourth salvo *Ilex* scored a direct hit on the group and two of the E-boats disintegrated in a sheet of vivid flame – hit in the fuel tanks. This twin explosion badly damaged at least one of the remaining three, all of whom immediately turned about and retired limping towards the shelter of the land.[5]

*Sydney* kept up her fire for twenty-five minutes, the Seagull reporting that the base was being 'well plastered'. With 135 of her 6-inch shells expended the job was done, executed exactly as planned, and she retired to the south with *Ilex*, leaving columns of greasy smoke rising above Makri Yalo and the wrecks of the burning MAS boats still glowing in the distance. She recovered the Seagull and rejoined the fleet, to be greeted by a signal from Andrew Cunningham: '*Sydney* from C-in-C. Well done. You are a Stormy Petrel.'

Later that afternoon they endured a sustained but fruitless bombing and the next day, 5 September, they were back in Alexandria. There *Sydney* went into dry dock again for another bottom clean and for some new bearings on her propellor shafts. The ship's company very much approved of the 'Stormy Petrel' compliment when they heard of it. After the war, Jack Ross made it the title of his book.

—

By September 1940, the strain of a year of war was telling on the destroyer men and their ships. For the ships' companies it was now twelve months away from family and home, a burden they all carried but the married men most of all. Mail from Australia was reasonably regular now, much better than it had been in the early months, and letters and parcels were eagerly sought as soon as a ship returned to Alexandria, but the news could still be weeks out of date. Mostly you were too busy to be homesick, but at night in the solitude of your hammock a longing for the comforts and pleasures of home could descend with a rush.

Added to that were the existential terrors of the war itself, chiefly the bombing, which was relentless and unending. It was worse in harbour, for the ships could not take evasive action as they did at sea. So far the Scrap Iron destroyers had come through largely unscathed, but there was always the fear that the very next bomb might have your name on it. It was frightening, heart-stopping, to be under attack from the air, yet most men faced it with a resigned, gritty courage, or a cheerful outward nonchalance and sometimes with black humour, which emerges occasionally in letters and diaries. At times it could even be entertaining. *Voyager* was refitting in Malta for most of September – the island's defences now strengthened by more anti-aircraft guns and a flight of Hurricane fighters. Her Gunner's Mate, Petty Officer Arthur Cooper, had a ringside seat:

Wednesday 4th. Quiet day except for air raid at 0800 hours but saw nothing except fighters go up. De-ammunitioned ship this morning. Duty tonight very quiet. All night leave.

Thursday 5th. Witnessed first spectacular air raid and dog fight. Sirens sounded at 10.30 am and everyone on upper deck to watch as usual. I was on bridge with movie camera and took photos of A.A. barrage overhead. Saw three Ity [sic] bombers up about 5000 ft. Our Hurricanes dived and we saw two bombers crashing down, we thought. Actually one was shot down and one damaged. Several minutes of thrilling battle were seen. The boys all cheered when one was shot down.[6]

Remarkably, discipline held, which speaks both to the character of the ships' companies, down to the greenest 'Rockies', and the qualities of leadership in their officers and senior sailors. There was the inevitable run of petty offences – late from leave, returning drunk, and so on – but that was it. Morale was high and it got the job done.

The destroyers, though, were more and more showing their age. This year of war had been the most intense of their lives, steaming further and faster than ever before. The old pre-war jokes about holding them together with string and chewing gum had a new currency and a more recent crack was that you could spin the rivets in the hull plates with a flick of the wrist. The Black Gang strove heroically to keep the turbines turning, working daily miracles, but then a steam pipe would rupture without warning or a boiler would lose pressure or a shaft bearing would run dangerously hot, and it would be an urgent scramble to patch up a repair that would get the ship moving again. One night in early September *Stuart* struck trouble as she was speeding home through the Antikythera Channel off Crete. For Ean McDonald, for everyone from the captain down, it induced a nerve-wracking tension:

We had to get clear of the danger area by daylight otherwise become yet again a sitting duck to bombers or torpedo boats ...

... on this clear, moonlit night the sea was still, torpid and glossy, and we were set for an admirably fast passage. Then, sounding like a pistol shot, followed by a great, piercing whistling, *Stuart* burst a main steam pipe. Slowing down over half a mile or so she gently came to a halt.

From below soon came the sharp, metallic hammering of the Black Gang. The clanging could have been heard by any enemy ship or submarine for miles around. As well, the shore of Crete was within hearing range. Hours it seemed the noises went on into the night, creating vulnerability more frightening than any action. For all those hours there was terror amidst the beauty of the night, as the Leader of the Crocks survived yet another impossible situation, born of her age and considering the sheer, urgent continuity of her service. She was revived once more by her dedicated machinery men.[7]

*Stuart* floated there motionless for two hours, as idle as that painted ship upon a painted ocean. Ean McDonald's fear of an enemy eavesdropper was real and rational: the sound of hammering below the waterline would travel far and could well be picked up by a submarine listening with hydrophones. If they spotted the telltale wake of a torpedo heading straight for them there was nothing they could do. The watch on deck tiptoed around as if Mussolini himself might be listening and in the mess decks they spoke in whispers. With steely self-control, Hec Waller resisted the temptation to go below to the engine room and remained seated on the bridge, confident that the engineers were working as quickly and quietly as they could and aware that his presence down there would only hinder, not help. It was a vote of confidence. Eventually the clanking and banging stopped and the word came up the voice pipe from Commander Rands that she was ready to go. The relief was palpable as the engines vibrated again and the ship got under way. They made it back to Alexandria later the next day.

*Stuart* got a quick patch-up job there, but with space at a premium and perhaps a month's more work to be done, it was decided she should go to the better dockyard facilities at Malta. Hec, as Captain (D) of the 10th Flotilla, would shift over to *Vampire* and *Stuart*'s First Lieutenant, the well-liked Rupert Robison, would take command when she sailed on 28 September.

That plan came unstuck when Robison reported some mystery illness and had to go ashore to hospital. It would now be the navigator, the tall and bearded buccaneer Lieutenant Norm 'Whiskers' Teacher, who would take over. They sailed as planned, with the full fleet – including *Warspite*, *Valiant* and *Illustrious* – escorting a troop convoy to Malta. That night was quiet, but the next morning, 29 September, the Aeronautica found them and the bombing began, in several waves. It was different this time and happily so. *Illustrious* sent her Fulmar fighters up to deal with the attackers and two were shot down. Then a Fulmar was shot down too, some 8 kilometres behind the fleet, and *Stuart* was sent off at full speed to rescue the two-man crew who had parachuted out. She picked them up safely and was heading back to her station when the exertion proved too much for her and another steam pipe burst: not enough to stop her, but it slowed her down, too slow to keep up with the fleet, and Cunningham in *Warspite* signalled: '*Stuart* is dying on us. I am sending him back to Alexandria.'[8] Norm Teacher turned her around and headed reluctantly for home.

The plan was to enter harbour the next morning in daylight so, with some hours on his hands, Teacher decided to run an anti-submarine search. Sunset came and went and then the change of the watch, with *Stuart* making an easy 10 knots and the Asdic *pinging* monotonously in the shack behind the bridge.

Late that night, all was quiet in the ship as she steamed slowly onwards when, as if a bomb had burst in their midst, the Asdic officer, Sub Lieutenant Tom Cree, reported: 'Echo bearing red one oh!'

'Stand by depth charges,' ordered Teacher.

Cree had donned his headphones and was tracking the course of the submarine. 'Range three hundred,' he reported.

'Full ahead both!' ordered the captain.[9]

———

The submarine *Gondar*, a modern boat of some 700 tons, had sailed from Messina in the dead of night on 25 September, carrying an unusual cargo. Bolted onto her casing were three large cylinders of strong, ribbed steel, two before the conning tower and one aft. Stowed inside them were three of the Regia Marina's most secret weapons: the human torpedo.

The Italians called it the *Siluro a Lenta Corsa* or SLC, the slow running torpedo. It was, in effect, a mini-submarine, manned by a crew of two *Gamma* frogmen, as they were known. Not quite 7 metres long, it was powered by a near silent electric motor which gave it a top speed of just over 4 knots at a maximum depth of 30 metres. Its range was about 28 kilometres. There was a detachable warhead on the bow packed with 250 kilograms of high explosive, more than enough to sink the biggest battleship.

The *Gamma* men sat astride it, their feet in metal stirrups as if on a horse, clad in protective rubber suits and masks, and carrying on their backs a six-hour supply of oxygen. The commander or pilot, seated forward, had a protective screen which contained a few instruments, including an illuminated magnetic compass, a depth gauge, and the controls for steering and diving. The man behind him had tools for handling the warhead.

The SLC was an Italian specialty, developed during the First World War and improved in the mid-1930s. Even then it was temperamental and difficult to steer, so much so that the crews nicknamed it the *Maiale*, or the Pig. The concept was simple enough: the Pigs would be released from a mother submarine and sent into an enemy harbour, where the warhead would be attached to the bottom of a target vessel by a rope slung between two magnets. A time fuse would give the *Gamma* men up to four hours to get away, if they could. Not many expected to do so. To ride a *Maiale* into the dark and muddy waters of a hostile port was an act of great courage.

*Gondar*'s captain, Tenente (Lieutenant) di Vascello Francesco Brunetti, set a course south-east at top speed on the surface while it was still dark, and then dived at dawn. The plan was to be off Alexandria on the night of 29 September, in position to send the three *Maiale* into the harbour before sunrise the next day to sink the biggest warships they could find. Among the *Gamma* men on board was Elios Toschi, a brilliant young naval engineer, one of the pioneers who had developed the SLC and who would lead the attack. Toschi understood the risks of success and the perils of failure better than most. He had been part of a first, disastrous attempt to deploy the Pigs just the month before, when another submarine, *Iride*, was surprised on the surface off the Libyan coast and torpedoed by three Swordfish from the carrier *Eagle*. Bold and resolute, Toschi did not expect to return to Italy from this mission. At best he might be captured. At worst he would be dead.

A few hours after sunset on 29 September, *Gondar* surfaced to receive a pre-arranged signal from Supermarina in Rome. Toschi went to the bridge atop the conning tower with the captain, Brunetti, expecting the latest air surveillance report to confirm that the British were in port. Instead, it was the opposite. 'British fleet all left harbour. Return to Tobruk.'

The game was up. Angry and disappointed, thwarted yet again, Toschi went back below to play a desultory game of cards with some of the *Gamma* men while the submarine set off on its new course. Half an hour later, all hell broke loose.

A piercing hiss, the signal for an emergency crash dive, suddenly sounded above the din of the engines, which at once stopped. The submarine, with all its air vents already open, rocked irresolutely for a few seconds, as if stunned by the mighty roar of water entering her false bottom in all directions. Then she shot swiftly down. Our cards were flung aside, we all jumped to our feet, making for the control room. Brunetti was in the act of springing down from the conning tower hatch. He explained, without waiting for our questions, that he had sighted the dark bulk of any enemy warship less than 800 metres away.

'Did they see us?'

'I don't think so,' he answered. 'But it's probably worse than that. They must have heard us, for they were coming straight for us.'[10]

---

In *Stuart*, the alarms shrilled and the men ran to their action stations.

'A-turret closed up!'

'Depth charge crew closed up!'

'Coxswain on the wheel, sir!'

The familiar reports came in. The Asdic operator, Leading Seaman Lionel Pike, a South Australian, worked the set to keep the sound pulse pinned onto the submarine.

*Ping ... bip.*

Over his shoulder, Tom Cree called the range as it came down. 'Range two hundred!'

At twenty-six years of age, Cree had the physique of the Olympic rower he had been before the war. He was born a Scot, in Glasgow. His father, a captain in the Cameronians Scottish Rifles, was killed in Palestine in 1917 when Tom was just three. His mother emigrated to Australia after the war, where she married a wealthy Queensland grazier. The boy went to Geelong Grammar and then to Jesus College, Cambridge, where he won a Rowing Blue. In 1936 he rowed for Britain at the Berlin Olympics, reaching the semi-finals of the coxless pairs with a Cambridge pal. He joined the RANVR as a provisional sub lieutenant in February 1939 and did the anti-submarine course at Rushcutters Bay in Sydney. Posted to *Stuart* at the outbreak of war, Cree had already made his mark in the ship by winning a Mention in Despatches for his part in the rescue of the tanker *Trocas*. Now was his chance for a submarine kill.

On the bridge, Norm Teacher waited his moment and then ordered the first pattern of depth charges. The bell rang at the racks and five canisters rolled over the stern, shaking the old ship as they exploded in her wake. Down in *Gondar*, in mounting tension, the Italian submariners could hear the menacing *choof-choof* of *Stuart*'s propellors as she came right over the top of them, and they braced for the onslaught:

Involuntarily my hands grasped, as if the better to withstand the coming shock, two metal handrails at my side. As I gripped them hard, five formidable explosions sounded one after the other. The lights went out. In utter darkness we heard thunderous crashes which the human ear, humming and throbbing, can hardly endure – thunder prolonged and repeated hundreds of times in cavernous echoes. From every side, immense waves, rising and falling under vast pressure, attacked our hull, which seemed, for all the weight of her 700 tons, like a feather in a hurricane.

In her interior the crash of broken glass and smashed instruments mingled with the ominous creaking of rivets and plates under almost intolerable strain.[11]

'I wonder if it's a spaghetti tin,' said Cree.

'I wouldn't be surprised,' said Teacher.

It was the beginning of a game of cat and mouse that would last all night, played by a very old cat to be sure, but still with teeth and claws. *Stuart* criss-crossed the position at her best speed, back and forth, the Asdic still clutching the barely moving *Gondar* in its grip.

*Ping ... bip.*

The first pattern had been fired at 2215 hours. The second came half an hour later. Lieutenant Brunetti had rigged for silent running, shutting down every possibly electric motor and running the lights on batteries as he sent the boat down, down, down to a depth of 120 metres, way beyond her tested depth of some 80 metres, and the hull creaked and groaned in protest. It must have been the captain's worst nightmare. He had been in command of *Iride* when she was sunk by the Swordfish, and now here he was in dire danger of losing his second boat. This next attack exploded a little further off, but still enough to cause leakages in the engine room and the stern torpedo compartment, seawater entering the boat, the submariner's deepest fear.

On the surface, 'Whiskers' Teacher had signalled the Rear Admiral Alexandria that he was attacking a submarine, and he was told that help would be on the way. He retired again to reload the depth-charge racks and begin his third approach, the bridge crew sustained as the night wore on by the inevitable cups of kye. The change of watch at midnight brought a new duo into the Asdic hut: another operator, Leading Seaman Ron MacDonald, a steady hand from Footscray in Melbourne who had trained at the Royal Navy's anti-submarine school in Britain, and another young RANVR officer, Sub Lieutenant Jim Griffin from Mosman in Sydney, who had also done the anti-submarine school at Rushcutters Bay. You could take only so long with the incessant electronic pulse of the Asdic drilling into your skull.

There would be another four depth-charge attacks that night and the next morning, 30 September, making six in all. Brunetti tried evasive action, but to no avail. Teacher's tactic of coming from a different direction each time led the Italians to believe that there was more than one ship above them, perhaps three, adding to the growing fear that they might be doomed. Each attack caused more damage and the air was turning thick and foul. The last pattern came at 0625 hours.

> ... the submarine was by this time practically out of control. It now began rising in a series of jerks from 120 metres to 20 and less. Such was the situation when, just before seven o'clock, as she was rising in a particularly abrupt jump that carried her only just below the surface, two charges much smaller than the others judging from the bursts, and which we thought might have come from an aircraft, fell right on top of the conning tower. From that moment until the end we executed the wildest manoeuvres, oscillating madly between death by crushing in the depths and being rammed on the surface.[12]

Those two explosions had indeed come from an aircraft, small bombs. Reckoning that *Stuart* might well be running out of depth charges, Alexandria had sent an RAF Sunderland flying boat to help out. Shortly afterwards, a stumpy little anti-submarine trawler, HMS *Sindonis*, turned up as well.

After the aircraft attack, *Gondar* plunged to the depths again, a nightmare descent which took her to 150 metres where, in theory, the water pressure should have crushed her like a tin can. Brunetti knew now that the only hope was to surface and surrender, and he ordered compressed air to be pumped into her ballast tanks. But would it work? In near blackness, in air so foul now it was barely breathable, in stark terror, the crew prayed for deliverance. When it seemed that all was lost, that death was inevitable, they felt the deck tilt slightly and, miraculously, the boat slowly began to rise, gathering speed as she went. She broke the surface and floated there, down by the stern, a little off *Stuart*'s starboard bow.

Teacher ordered the guns to open fire and a salvo of shells from the 4.7s streaked across the gap. Another destroyer arrived, sent by Alexandria, HMS *Diamond*. The Sunderland dropped a stick of bombs too, and men began to scramble from *Gondar*'s conning tower and jump into the water. The captain had planted scuttling charges which would sink her. Elios Toschi was among the last to leave:

> The weather was clear, with brilliant sunshine, and the pure, rich, salty sea air revived me. What a hell I had just left. What marvellous things are air and light!
>
> There were two enemy destroyers less than 300 yards away. On the stern of one I could distinctly read the name *Stuart*. There was a small corvette [*Sindonis*] rather closer, and all three vessels were directing heavy fire at us. I could hear the sound of the explosions and the whistle of the projectiles all around me ...
>
> ... Looking round to take stock of the situation, I saw the stern of the sinking *Gondar* standing up out of the water, against the blue sky, as if in a last struggle against her approaching death. There were small groups of swimmers some way off, near the *Stuart*. Opposite, a hundred yards away, lay the little corvette. I decided to make for the latter, though I was not sure whether, tired as I was, I would be able to reach her.
>
> I swam feebly, as best I could, with half-closed eyes, thinking only of the ruin of all my work, hopes and dreams. As I stretched out my hand to grasp the rope ladder hanging from the side of the corvette, I lifted my head and met the glance, as melancholy, shame-faced and tormented as my own, of my comrade Franzini. We both grasped the rope.
>
> For us the war was over.[13]

It was 0950 hours. On board *Stuart* there was jubilation as *Gondar* went down, although the elation was tempered by a slight worry that the RAF Sunderland might try to take credit for the sinking, and some mild regret that they had not been able to capture the submarine and tow her back to Alexandria as a very visible trophy. Some of the crew lined the rails, taking photographs. Teacher had scrambling nets dropped over the side and the Italians began to claw their way up them, including the captain. *Stuart* rescued twenty-eight men and *Sindonis* another nineteen. Only two men had been killed by the gunfire. Les Clifford reported that Brunetti broke down weeping

when he met Teacher, and that some of the rescued men were fearful
they might be shot out of hand. They had been told the British killed
their prisoners. Instead, they were offered hot drinks and cigarettes
and spare clothing.

*Stuart* returned to Alexandria in triumph late that afternoon,
a large Australian flag flying at her mainmast and most of the crew
on deck in the sun. The fleet was still at sea, but *Vampire*, *Vendetta*
and *Waterhen* were there, decked in Australian flags – the 'Wallaby
Jack' – and they turned on a rousing, cheering welcome. Hec Waller
was on *Vampire*'s bridge – how he must have wished he had been with
his old ship – and he signalled his congratulations: 'Whacko, you did
not waste much time.'

*Vendetta* put it more succinctly: 'Whacko Whiskers!'

Later, the Commander-in-Chief, in a general signal to the fleet,
hailed *Stuart*'s success as, 'An outstanding example of a result achieved
by patience and skill in operation of Asdic gear.'[14]

Certainly the RAF was not going to get away with taking the
credit. In due course, Norm Teacher was awarded the DSO and
Tom Cree and Jim Griffin the DSC. MacDonald and Pike, the Asdic
operators, were given the DSM. Elios Toschi was sent to a prison
camp in India, where he made several escape attempts and survived
the war. The *Maiale* finally came into their own in December 1941
when three of them penetrated Alexandria and badly damaged the
battleships *Queen Elizabeth* and *Valiant*, and a tanker.

—

All that exertion had been too much for *Stuart*'s old bones and, with
Rupert Robison back in command, she was sent to Malta for a long
refit. On the way, south of Crete, she broke down three times with
seawater leaking into her oil fuel. She would stay at the dockyard until
after Christmas, enduring the regular air raids day and night.

*Vendetta* was also feeling her age, limping into Malta that same
month at 14 knots on just one engine, and she went in for a refit too.
Her engines were patched up yet again and, to everyone's surprise,
her after torpedo tubes were removed and replaced by a platform
for a 12-pound anti-aircraft gun.[15] The gun itself would come later.
*Voyager* had been given her facelift in September, with her mainmast

lifted out and replaced and her after tubes also giving way for another 12-pounder. *Vampire* and *Waterhen* got their renovations in Alexandria, with *Vampire*'s entire ship's company sent ashore for a day while she was fumigated to get rid of a plague of cockroaches and rats. *Voyager* and *Vampire* were back at it again in the second week of October, for cameo roles in an explosive encounter that would become known as the Action off Cape Passero. *Sydney* was there too, with the 3rd Cruiser Squadron.

Cape Passero is at the southernmost tip of Sicily, meaning – inevitably – it has been the backdrop for the naval clashes of centuries. In 1718, in one England's sporadic wars with Spain, the British Mediterranean fleet inflicted a crushing defeat on the Spanish there, burning or sinking sixteen ships. This new fight would be shorter and sharper and fought almost entirely at night – and it was the Italians who brought it on.

Early in the morning of 12 October, the light cruiser HMS *Ajax*, a similar ship to *Sydney*, was 160 kilometres east of Malta and south of Cape Passero on a scouting mission, zigzagging at 17 knots towards Alexandria. Strung away to the south below her were more cruisers and destroyers and, further south still, Cunningham with the main battle fleet was providing distant cover for a convoy also steaming for Alexandria. The storms of the previous day had cleared to a bright night with a nearly full moon. All was peaceful until, at 0137 hours, *Ajax* was spotted by three patrolling Italian torpedo boats some 18 kilometres away on her port side. She should have seen them more or less at the same time but she did not. They moved in on her, fast mini-destroyers of some 800 tons, and they fired six torpedoes, all of which missed. *Ajax* woke up, returning fire with her main and secondary armament as she worked up to full speed, and she hit and disabled two of the torpedo boats, setting them aflame. One, though, hit her three times below the bridge and in the hull before escaping. Thirteen men were killed.

Next came three larger destroyers, which the embattled *Ajax* took on as well. In a twisting, turning duel they fired torpedoes which also missed, but they scored more hits with their guns, punching a gaping hole in the cruiser's side. Shooting back, *Ajax* sent one destroyer limping away; a second, the *Camicia Nera* ('black shirt') disappeared behind a smokescreen, and the third – *Artigliere* – was left dead in the water, heavily on fire.

Cunningham recalled the wounded *Ajax* to rejoin the fleet and sent more cruisers and destroyers to clean up. At eight the next morning, on a lovely autumn day, they found the *Camicia Nera* had returned and was towing *Artigliere* away. The shooting was one-sided now. *Camicia Nera* dropped the tow and fled, leaving *Artigliere* to be pounded to pieces by the 8-inch guns and then the torpedoes of the heavy cruiser *York*. Jack Ross saw the destruction from the deck of *Sydney*:

> It was an incredible and awe-inspiring sight. Both magazines exploded within half a second of each other, converting *Artigliere* into a huge ball of orange flame at least two or three hundred feet in diameter and equally as high, and when the flame had subsided a second or so later there was not a piece of wreckage of any description to be seen. Nothing remained except a tremendous column of mingled black and brown smoke which slowly billowed up until it was some two or three thousand feet high. We who were crowded on *Sydney*'s upper deck were completely dumbfounded by the spectacle and for several minutes after the explosion the only sound on board was an odd gasp or whistle of amazement.[16]

*Voyager* and *Vampire* were there too, steaming cautiously through the men in the water.

> We first sighted a Carley life raft full of survivors, and dozens of ratings swimming. *Vampire* picked them up. Dozens of others were seen in the water about 300 yards from us. We asked permission to pick them up but were told to remain with the fleet. One rating was drooped over a floating box. We all altered course and must have passed exactly over the spot where the destroyer sank, because we ploughed our way through pure oil on top of the water, about two acres of it.[17]

No longer willing to risk his ships in extended rescue operations, Cunningham radioed the Italians on a commercial wavelength to give the position of the survivors left behind and the fleet resumed course for Alexandria. After her early surprise, the skilful handling of *Ajax* – and the Italians' inexperience in night fighting – had delivered another British victory. The Aeronautica hit back, though, with wave after wave of bombing attacks over the next two days, and the heavy cruiser *Liverpool* had to be towed home after her bows were blown off by an aerial torpedo, with twelve men killed. Still in luck, the Australians made it safely back to port.

———

Towards the end of that month, Benito Mussolini committed what was perhaps his greatest act of folly in the war. Always the strutting braggart, anxious to emulate Hitler's conquests, he invaded Greece on 28 October. In three columns, 140,000 men of his divisions in occupied Albania struggled over the border passes of the Epirus mountains to meet a smaller and almost pathetically ill-equipped Greek army.

It was a disaster from the beginning. Two days of solid rain had swollen rivers and streams, washed away bridges and turned already primitive dirt roads into a morass of mud. The Greeks, fighting on the soil of their homeland, contemptuous of the *Macaronides*, put up an heroic resistance and brought the hesitant Italian advance to a stumbling and humiliating halt within a little over a week. On 14 November, the Greek army Commander-in-Chief, General Alexandros Papagos, launched a counter offensive which would force the Italians into a chaotic retreat to Albania.

The person least surprised by this rout was Hitler, who had cynically but accurately predicted the outcome when he first heard of the Italian plans. After meeting Mussolini in Florence on the day the invasion rolled, with the usual outward show of fascist *Kameradschaft*, the Führer privately concluded that he would eventually have to make war in the Mediterranean himself. He set about doing it.

# CHAPTER 11

# ENTER THE LUFTWAFFE

Epic battles that changed the flow of history are remembered by one familiar name, almost always the place where they were fought. Cannae, Agincourt, Trafalgar, Waterloo, Amiens, Midway, Kokoda …

Taranto is one of these. On the night of 11 November 1940, Swordfish aircraft of the Royal Navy's Fleet Air Arm dealt a devastating blow to the Regia Marina in its main base in Taranto Harbour on Italy's 'boot heel'. It was the first naval battle in history in which the enemy ships never saw each other, the attack coming entirely from the air.

Andrew Cunningham had long been dreaming of such a master stroke, and with the arrival of *Illustrious* he had both the ship and a new man to deliver it. A gunnery officer turned air enthusiast, Rear Admiral Lumley Lyster – officially titled Flag Officer Mediterranean Aircraft Carriers – had been planning an air attack on Taranto on and off since 1938. Operation Judgement was born.

At sunset on 11 November *Illustrious* and her escort of cruisers and destroyers were at the launch point some 275 kilometres southeast of Taranto for what promised to be a clear night with a nearly full moon – a 'bomber's moon'. For a week and more Lyster had been given detailed aerial reconnaissance photos of the harbour, the latest arriving just that afternoon showing five battleships in port and another about to join them. The Swordfish crews knew exactly what their targets would be and where to find them, and the defences of anti-aircraft batteries, torpedo nets and barrage balloons they would have to penetrate. Height would be critical and precision would be everything, for Taranto was a shallow harbour and the torpedoes would be set to run at a depth of 34 feet (10.36 metres). That would mean launching them at a height of 30 feet (9 metres), no more than 800 metres from the target.

The first wave of twelve aircraft left the flight deck of *Illustrious* at 2040 hours, with a second wave of nine following at 2130 hours. They were over the target from just before 2300 hours, one plane dropping flares to guide the way in. Caught at first by surprise, the Italians swiftly put up a veritable storm of light and steel, of brilliant orange gun flashes and red, white and green tracer bullets, described by Lieutenant Charles Lamb, the pilot of the plane that had placed the flares:

> The guns at the entrance were throwing long streaks of flame across the harbour, spitting venom out to sea, and the shells of these tracer bursts illuminated the first Swordfish so brightly that from above, instead of appearing a blue-grey, it seemed to be a gleaming white ... into that inferno, one hour apart, two waves of Swordfish, painted a dull bluey-grey for camouflage, danced a weaving arabesque of death and destruction with their torpedoes, flying into the harbour only a few feet above sea level – so low that one or two of them actually touched the water with their wheels as they sped through the harbour entrance.[1]

Courage and airmanship met in perfect union. Incredibly, only two of the Stringbags were shot down, with one crew of two killed and the other taken prisoner, an immense relief to Lyster and Cunningham, who had feared a higher toll. More aerial reconnaissance the next day revealed the scale of the destruction. Three battleships, half the Marina's battle fleet, had been knocked out. *Conte di Cavour* rested on the bottom with only her upper superstructure visible. She would never return to service. *Caio Duilio* and *Littorio* were holed and were saved only by being run aground, putting them out of the war for months. A cruiser and some destroyers and dockyard installations had also been damaged. Hurriedly, the Marina withdrew most of its intact ships to the relative safety of Naples. In Andrew Cunningham's own words:

> Taranto and the night of November 11th–12th should be remembered forever as having shown once and for all that in the Fleet Air Arm the Navy has its most devastating weapon. In a total flying time of about six and a half hours – carrier to carrier – twenty aircraft had inflicted more damage upon the Italian fleet than was inflicted upon the German High Seas Fleet in the daylight action at the Battle of Jutland.[2]

For the present, Cunningham had tightened his grip on the Eastern Mediterranean, but in the long view it was far more than that. Taranto emphatically marked the beginning of the end for the big gun line-of-battleship which had commanded the oceans for more than three centuries. Keen to learn from the battle, the Imperial Japanese Navy sent a small party of officers to Italy to study how it had been done, knowledge that would be put to good use a year later at Pearl Harbor. Like a rising sun, the era of the aircraft carrier had arrived.

—

On that same silvery night, *Sydney* penetrated deep into dangerous waters 'looking for trouble', as John Collins put it to the crew. With two other 6-inch cruisers, *Orion* and *Ajax*, and two of the modern Tribal class destroyers, *Nubian* and *Mohawk*, all designated Force X, she steamed north into the Adriatic through the Strait of Otranto, with the south-eastern coast of Italy to port and Italian-occupied Albania away to starboard, enemy territory if ever there was.

Jack Tovey had left the Med and returned to Britain to become Commander-in-Chief of the Home Fleet. His replacement as Vice Admiral Light Forces was Henry Pridham-Wippell who, as a lieutenant commander, had been the commanding officer of the destroyers at Gallipoli in 1915 and knew Australians well enough. A slender, reserved figure, he was flying his flag in *Orion*.

Steaming north-west past Corfu that afternoon, they prepared for action, not with any great urgency, but rigging towing gear fore and aft as a precaution and training the gun turrets more for something to do than anything else. Shells had already been sent up from the magazines and lay in the loading trays, ready to be rammed home. The sea was kind, the weather clear and sunny. Men with free time took the chance for a snooze in the sun on deck, to read or write letters or to play the inevitable game of cards or Uckers, a complicated form of Ludo that was a perennial navy favourite. In the engine and boiler rooms, the machinery was humming sweetly.

Only after nightfall did Collins tell them where they were going: the Adriatic, probably the one stretch of water that Mussolini could reasonably call *Mare Nostrum*. It caused a buzz of excitement and apprehension or, as Jack Ross put it:

> We were flabbergasted. Such a move had never occurred to even the wildest 'buzz-merchants' and we had no doubt we'd find plenty of trouble all right! It was easy enough to get into the Adriatic – the main problem was to get out again with a whole skin. However, to a man we had the greatest confidence in our Captain and our Commander-in-Chief.[3]

At its narrowest point at the southern end of the Adriatic, the Strait of Otranto is just 90 kilometres wide, easily patrolled by even one aircraft, and Taranto is tucked just around the corner to the west. Pridham-Wippell probably knew of the Swordfish raid planned for that evening but no one else did, including John Collins, who expected the undivided attention of the Italian fleet if their presence in the Adriatic was discovered. *Orion* led the line, followed by *Ajax* and then *Sydney* at a distance each of about four cables or 700 metres, with a destroyer out to port and starboard. The admiral ordered 25 knots and they passed through the narrows at midnight, closing up to action stations. So far so good. They had not seen the enemy and he had not seen them. At 0100 hours, some 100 kilometres into the Adriatic and at the latitude of the Italian port of Brindisi, the admiral put them into a sweeping turn to starboard and headed back south sou'east to begin the return run.

Out on the port wing, *Mohawk* made the first sighting at 0115 hours, off to the south-east. The alarm buzzers blared. A darkened convoy of four merchant ships, escorted by the small and elderly, three-funnelled destroyer *Nicola Fabrizi*, and an armed merchant cruiser, *Ramb III*, was plodding in ballast at 8 knots from the Albanian port of Valona* westwards towards Brindisi. *Mohawk* opened fire first, hitting *Fabrizi* with her fourth salvo at a range of 4000 metres, and from then it was on for all comers, virtually a night gunnery exercise conducted with methodical precision in the glare of star shells fired from the cruisers. *Sydney* hit one merchant ship at 7000 metres, setting her on fire, then shifted to a second. Ross watched in awe.

> All four merchant vessels are quickly smothered under a blanket of murderous fire and the night is filled with the roar of our guns and stabbed with savage flashes of vivid orange. The nearest merchant vessel is literally blown out of the water and sinks within a couple of minutes. Two others are ablaze from end to end and the fourth, damaged, manages to escape into the darkness down moon under the cover of a smokescreen.[4]

They did not know it at the time but in fact all four merchant vessels were sunk. The ancient *Fabrizi* and her captain, Tenente di Vascello Giovanni Barbini, put up a brave fight with guns and torpedoes, sending one torpedo uncomfortably close beneath *Sydney*'s stern, but the odds were impossible, weighed the more heavily against him because *Ramb III*, the armed merchant cruiser, fired off a few quick salvoes then turned tail and fled. Her captain, Francesco de Angelini, was relieved of his command and court-martialled for cowardice.[5] *Fabrizi* and a badly wounded Lieutenant Barbini survived.

The battle, such as it was, took less than half an hour. Job done, and with no wish to loiter for survivors in these waters, Pridham-Wippell signalled for a return to the main fleet cruising midway between Sicily and Greece. Cunningham, elated by success all round, signalled Collins: 'Did you have a wild Australian night?'[6]

Stunned by Taranto, the Regia Marina made no attempt to hit back. The Aeronautica sent out two Cant flying boats which found the fleet on its way back to Alexandria at noon on 12 September,

---

\*    Now known as Vlomë.

but both were shot down by Fulmars from the newly rejoined *Illustrious*. All in all, the night had been a crushing assertion of British sea power.

Yet for all the elation, all the success, all the quiet pride in a job well done, the strain was telling, the weariness never ending. It afflicted every man, even the young, but it fell most heavily upon those with the burden of command. In his memoir, Collins gives a telling account of bringing *Sydney* back home to Alexandria after long and perilous days and nights at sea:

> Ours was a difficult berth in which to secure, between two buoys closely flanked by *Orion* and *Medway*[7] with submarines alongside. It was necessary to pick up the forward buoy, kick ahead, drop an anchor, drop back to get a wire on the after buoy, and finally position the ship with cables to the buoys.
>
> I thought I was perfectly normal, despite having had little or no sleep for many days, but everyone else seemed clumsy and inept. The cutter's crew were like a lot of old women and appeared unable to get the picking rope on, there was an interminable pause after the order 'Let go' before the anchor went, and aft everything seemed to go wrong. At long last the final report 'All fast aft' came through and I gave the order 'finished with main engines' and turned to the Navigating Officer.
>
> 'Have I ever taken so long to secure this ruddy ship?' I asked in anger, and thought to myself, 'What can one expect when she is manned by a crowd of ham-fisted clots?'
>
> The imperturbable Montgomery calmly looked back through his Navigator's notebook.
>
> 'Your second fastest time, sir,' he reported.
>
> It then dawned on me that perhaps I was the one not quite normal. It was a lesson to remember.

—

Taranto had been a hard and demoralising blow to the Italians but it was by no means a knockout. The great part of the Regia Marina was still afloat and ready for action, although still constrained by the need to conserve precious fuel. There would be two more encounters with the British in the last weeks of November which began to shift the balance of the Mediterranean war further in the Allies' favour.

The first, however, was a disaster.

At dawn on 15 November, the commander of the Royal Navy's Force H, Admiral Sir James Somerville, launched Operation White, sailing a powerful convoy east from Gibraltar to deliver two much-needed flights of RAF Hurricane fighters to Malta. There were two carriers, *Argus* and *Ark Royal*, two cruisers, seven destroyers, and Somerville's flagship, the battlecruiser *Renown*.

An Italian agent on Gibraltar reported their departure and a fleet including the battleships *Vittorio Veneto* and *Giulio Cesare* left Naples and Messina under Vice Admiral Inigo Campioni to lie in wait a little south-west of the island of Sardinia. On 17 November Somerville learned that the Italians were at sea and he blinked, deciding to avoid the trap and to return home. Twelve Hurricanes and two Skua fighter bombers were flown off *Argus* to head for Malta at the extreme limit of their range, but they were buffeted by strong headwinds and confused by faulty navigation. Tragically, one Skua crash-landed in Sicily and eight of the invaluable Hurricanes ran out of fuel and fell into the sea. One of the Hurricane pilots was saved by a Coastal Command Sunderland but seven were lost.

Licking their wounds, the British passed another supply convoy from Gibraltar into the Mediterranean on 24 November, this time of three fast merchant ships – two of them bound for Malta and one for Alexandria, escorted by cruisers and destroyers. Somerville and Force H provided distant cover from the north and again Campioni, alerted by accurate intelligence, sailed to confront him. They met on the morning of 27 November off Cape Spartivento, the southernmost point of Sardinia, in a confused skirmish of big gun salvoes and smokescreens, cruiser and destroyer feints and sallies; the contest swinging this way and that, back and forth, and lasting less than an hour with surprisingly little damage done to either side. Seven British sailors were killed in the cruiser *Berwick*, but apparently no Italians.

Campioni's hands were tied by his orders from Supermarina, a masterly example of windy verbiage carefully designed to reflect glory on headquarters for any victory but sole blame for a loss on the admiral at sea.

Avoid action with the enemy if he enjoys an evident superiority. Favour any opportunity for naval guerrilla actions. Try to fight near base. Be animated by a highly aggressive spirit at all times and remember that the material difficulty of replacing our warship losses during the war dictates that we must coolly examine the effectiveness of any action.[8]

And once again, to Campioni's impotent fury, the Aeronautica failed to appear until the show was almost over, even though the fighting was just 60 kilometres south of land bases on Sardinia. Somerville, on the other hand, at least had *Ark Royal*'s aircraft working for him, although their reconnaissance reports were at times wildly inaccurate and their torpedo attacks scored not a hit. At one stage *Renown* very nearly blew out of the water two French passenger liners which had somehow wandered onto the scene.

The end of this depressing shambles came when Campioni decided, correctly, that he was indeed outnumbered and he headed for home in the mid-afternoon at a speed the British simply could not match. London would declare the Battle of Cape Spartivento a victory because the fast convoy did indeed get through, but privately Churchill was furious at what he believed to be Somerville's lack of aggression in not pursuing Campioni. The prime minister had conceived a spiteful dislike for the admiral since his reluctance to attack the French at Mers-el-Kebir, but Somerville had the backing of powerful friends in the navy including Andrew Cunningham, and to Churchill's displeasure a secret Admiralty board of enquiry found that he had behaved properly.

Inigo Campioni was not so fortunate. The Battle of Cape Teulada, as the Italians knew it, triggered an upheaval at Supermarina which saw the incompetent chief of naval staff, Admiral Domenico Cavagnari, fired and Campioni removed from command at sea and kicked upstairs to become deputy chief. He met a wretched end. When Italy abandoned the Axis and went over to the Allies in 1943, Campioni was arrested by the Germans on Rhodes, first imprisoned in Poland, then eventually handed over to Mussolini's puppet 'Social Republic' skulking in northern Italy. There they convicted him of high treason but with a reprieve if he publicly acknowledged Il Duce still to be Italy's rightful ruler. This he honourably refused to do and on 24 May 1944 he was shot by a firing squad of teenage conscripts in the central piazza in Parma.

—

December brought new disasters for Mussolini, this time on land. The British Commander-in-Chief Middle East, General Archibald Wavell, launched Operation Compass at dawn on 9 December, a carefully planned counter-attack from Egypt which sent the Italian 10th Army tumbling back westwards towards Libya in disarray. By nightfall the next day Indian troops had taken back Sidi Barrani near the Libyan border and the British were on the move again, the Italians collapsing like a pack of cards. In just two days the British were astonished to capture 38,300 prisoners, 237 guns and seventy-three tanks at a cost of some 600 casualties, a rout they had not planned for and which had barely begun. In the next week the Italians were forced back from Sollum and Fort Capuzzo to Bardia, the forlorn coastal fortification where *Sydney* had lost her 'Pusser's duck' back in June.

The harried Italians had no choice but to use the coastal road for their retreat, presenting an ideal target for bombardment from the sea. On 15 December Hec Waller was appointed to coordinate it as Senior Naval Officer Afloat of the Inshore Squadron. With *Stuart* still in Malta, he had the other four Scrap Iron destroyers – *Vampire*, *Vendetta*, *Voyager* and *Waterhen* – along with an old friend, the monitor *Terror*, and an assortment of small gunboats, minesweepers and anti-submarine trawlers. He set to the job with his customary zeal.

By 19 December, the Australian diggers had begun to arrive on stage. Major General Iven Mackay's 6th Division had completed its desert training outside Alexandria and was taking position to capture Bardia, sending out patrols to probe the defences, the first moves in what would enter history as one of the Australian army's great battles of story and legend.

Capricious as ever, the Med in winter turned on weather alternately fair and foul. Sailors never knew which to expect until the barometer soared or suddenly dived. A few delightful sunny days when a calm, azure sea shimmered in the light would be followed by icy gales hammering in from the north or, worse, by a choking Khamsin sandstorm out of the desert that left the ship and the watch on deck filthy with grit. On 13 December, at 0200 hours on a nasty morning, *Voyager* was screening *Illustrious* and the battle fleet on the way back to Alexandria, rolling and pitching violently, when she gave an almighty lurch that sent a man tumbling overboard. Able Seaman James West, a thirty-two-year-old regular from Grafton in New South Wales, had been working near the 3-inch gundeck wearing leather seaboots, his watch coat and a heavy oilskin. He should have been hooked to a lifeline but was not. Someone heard his cry as he disappeared into the vortex of wind and wave, and the Officer of the Watch sounded the alarm. Commander Morrow came to the bridge, slowed the ship, signalled the fleet, and put about to search for him, although not with any optimism in the dark of night and those heaving seas. Against all the odds, fate held. About half an hour later they heard a faint cry and sighted him swimming, a dim speck in the gloom. He had stripped down to just a singlet. They got a rope to him and hauled him back on board, exhausted and cold and weak with shock but unharmed. Married with a young wife, James West that night was reckoned by his messmates to be the luckiest man in the navy.

The bombardment itself was theatre, a spectacular directed by some invisible producer with a lavish hand. The ships ranged slowly back and forth offshore, orange flashes spurting from their gun muzzles, sometimes running in close enough to see surf on sandy beaches as the shells screamed inland at whatever targets presented themselves, occasionally dodging largely ineffectual return fire from the Italians ashore. More prosaically, they made anti-submarine sweeps and escorted supply ships and water carriers for Wavell's rapidly advancing divisions. Every so often the Aeronautica would appear for a bombing or torpedo attack, to be met by a barrage of anti-aircraft fire or, sometimes, a thrilling aerial dogfight as Gladiator fighters or even the occasional Hurricane of the out-numbered RAF pounced from above. By night the skies were alive with star shell, flares and the stabbing beams of searchlights. One night *Voyager* inserted a squad of commandos ashore behind the Italian lines, a cosmopolitan group of Poles, Arabs and Palestinians with British officers. Impressively violent men armed to the teeth with Thompson sub-machine guns, knives, hand grenades and even knuckledusters, they enthralled the stokers' mess with lurid tales of throats cut and heads severed.

—

In the closing months of 1940, as the northern winter approached, the Germans from the Führer on down increasingly despaired of their Italian ally. Nothing they did seemed to go well and often it went disastrously, as in their chaotic invasion of Greece. In the Mediterranean it seemed the British had their measure at every turn, not least of all psychologically. British admirals and captains expected to win any encounter; many Italians did not.

The chief of the Kriegsmarine, Großadmiral Erich Raeder, kept a clear focus on the Mediterranean, which he believed – rightly – to be the pivot of British imperial might and reach. Expel the Royal Navy and the Empire would totter and fall, he thought, handing a victorious Germany control of the Suez Canal and access to vast reserves of Middle East oil and such other staples as Egyptian cotton.

And the key to the Mediterranean – the *gateway* to the Mediterranean – was Gibraltar. Britain had captured that rocky bastion during the War of the Spanish Succession in 1704 and had controlled it ever since. Raeder and the naval staff dreamed of seizing Gibraltar and were constantly devising new schemes for doing so, impressing their importance upon Hitler.

In the afternoon of 23 October, the Führer arrived in his personal train at the French town of Hendaye near the border with Spain for a meeting with the Spanish dictator, Generalissimo Francisco Franco. Hitler's aim was to bring Spain into the war and to seize Gibraltar for the Reich, but things did not go well from the start. Spain was exhausted from its civil war and Franco had no wish to plunge his people and his stuttering economy into another conflict. Every bit as wily as Hitler, he deliberately arrived an hour late to knock the Germans off balance and then made impossibly extravagant demands for territory and treasure to reward his participation. After nine hours of talk a furious Hitler recognised that he had met his match and departed with only a meaningless 'memorandum of understanding' that Spain would enter the war at some future moment. 'I would rather have four of my teeth pulled out than deal with that man again,'[9] he told Mussolini a few days later.

With Spain out of the equation, an equally exasperated Raeder had largely given up on the Italians, writing in a scorching assessment for the Führer in mid-November that:

> The Italian armed forces have neither the leadership nor the military efficiency to carry the required operations in the Mediterranean area to a successful conclusion with the necessary speed and decision ... the Italian leadership is wretched. They have no understanding of the situation; above all, they have not yet perceived in what manner their offensive against Greece primarily damages Italy's power of endurance.[10]

Hitler had recognised for some months that he would eventually have to rescue his hapless Axis partner; certainly in Greece, probably in North Africa. For that the wheels were already turning, although it would take time to get German boots on the ground in any number. But there was an immediate move he could make, and on 20 November he wrote to Mussolini offering to send in the Luftwaffe, basing German bombers at Italian airfields to prey upon British warships and convoys. Il Duce accepted with alacrity. By December it was happening.

The Luftwaffe's Fliegerkorps X – the 10th Air Corps – had made its name in the Norway campaign, specialising in attacks on shipping. Its squadrons flew a conventional mix of Junkers Ju 88 and Heinkel He 111 bombers, reconnaissance planes and Messerschmitt Bf 110 fighters, but its spearpoint was forged from two squadrons each of forty Ju 87R-1 Stuka dive-bombers, the stubby but formidably lethal aircraft which had struck terror across Europe in the blitzkrieg.

The Stuka – the name was a contraction of *Sturzkampfflugzeug*, the German word for dive-bomber – was ponderously slow in level flight but it could dive almost vertically at speeds of up to 600 km/h to drop its load: usually one 250-kilogram bomb carried beneath the fuselage and two 50-kilogram bombs beneath each wing. There were two forward-mounted machine guns for strafing a target, and a system of air brakes which activated automatically to pull the aircraft up out of its dive if its two-man crew blacked out. Beneath its distinctive inverted gull wings, attached to its fixed undercarriage, were two sirens known as the 'Jericho-Trompete'. These emitted a carefully designed and truly terrifying banshee howl as the aircraft plummeted upon its target.

As Christmas approached, the Stuka squadrons began setting themselves up at the airfield at Trapani at the western end of Sicily, with the other bomber and fighter squadrons scattering elsewhere around the island at Catania, Comiso and Palermo. In the traditional manner of generals everywhere – and especially German ones – the Fliegerkorps X commander, General der Luftwaffe Hans-Ferdinand Geisler, installed himself and his headquarters in the most luxurious hotel to be found, the Hotel San Domenico in the picturesque coastal resort of Taormina.

The British were aware they were coming. Intelligence had sounded the warning, but there was nothing to be done about it. The RAF was still battling the Blitz at home and its resources in the Middle East were pitifully scant and stretched to the utmost. There was nothing to do but to wait to see what happened. It would not be long. Before the year turned, the Mediterranean Fleet and the Australian destroyers of the Scrap Iron Flotilla would be confronted by a skilled and resolute new enemy armed with weapons they had not met before.

—

Christmas Day 1940 found the Australians scattered across the eastern Mediterranean. For most it was their second Christmas away from family and friends. This meant at least that things were better organised than they had been in 1939, but it also sharpened the pangs of homesickness and the longing for peace.

*Stuart* was still undergoing her refit in Malta, in weather endlessly cold and wet, with the additional aggravation of regular although surprisingly ineffective Italian bombing. Many of the ship's company were comfortably billeted with local families, Les Clifford and two of his messmates finding a guest house in Senglea just a few minutes' walk from the ship and run by a Mr Theo Borg, who had done thirty years at sea as a canteen manager in the Royal Navy and well understood sailors and their wants and needs. There was a friendly pub, The Cruiser, a little further down Two Gates Street. Mr and Mrs Borg welcomed them like sons; they called him 'Pop'. The Borgs also made room for *Stuart*'s ship's mascot, a small and rascally monkey named Chico who had been smuggled on board in Alexandria a few months before by Tom Harsley, an old lag, three-badge able seaman from Melbourne who knew to a very fine point what you could and could not get away with in the navy. Chico normally had his hammock slung at the break of the fo'c'sle above the A-boiler room fan inlet. There had been an unfortunate incident recently in which some younger sailors had taken him on a bar crawl in The Gut and got him hopelessly drunk, but he was now in Les's more responsible care and was given lodgings in the attic.

On Christmas Day the Borgs turned on a slap-up lunch, the best that beleaguered Malta could offer.

'We could not have been made more welcome by these two kindly souls,' wrote Les. 'To say that we enjoyed that Christmas Day 1940 to the full would be superfluous. We certainly atoned for the disappointing anniversary of 1939.'[11]

A few weeks later the three would be dismayed to learn that the Luftwaffe – Fliegerkorps X – had blown to rubble much of Two Gates Street, including the Borgs' hospitable home and The Cruiser pub. The Borgs survived but lost all they owned. Everyone in the pub was killed.

*Sydney* was also in Malta for Christmas. On 23 December she steamed into Dockyard Creek for a refit where, to an eruption of surprise and joy, the crew found thirty or forty much hoped for but still unexpected bags of mail from Australia. A strange, unnatural silence fell on the ship as the men off watch settled into whatever quiet corners they could find to devour the news from home and to unwrap family presents. With the ammunition taken out of her, *Sydney* went into dry dock on Christmas Eve, her mastheads and yardarms garlanded in the traditional navy way with festive boughs of greenery which some enterprising soul had manage to hunt down ashore in record time.

Most of the crew got forty-eight hours' shore leave to do as they pleased: which was not as much as they had hoped for, because all the French and other foreign girls in The Gut had been deported to save precious food. The watch left on board made merry. Captain Collins joined his officers in the wardroom to enjoy a hot rum punch brewed to keep out the winter chills and the ship's band was summoned for a hearty round of Christmas carols, beginning with 'Good King Wenceslas'.

The day itself was again cold and wet, although Jack Ross noted appreciatively that:

> the Italians were also filled with the Christmas spirit and initiated no air raids to scatter us to the shelters ashore. At noon the Captain set off on his traditional tour of the mess decks to sample pieces of turkey and 'duff' and wish the ship's company good luck. It takes a good man to last the course, by the way, as courtesy demands that he accept a glass of beer here and there and a taste of this and that in every mess. The cooks had excelled themselves and the 'troops' sat down to plenty of steaming soup, turkey, potatoes, cabbage, cauliflower and a wonderful pudding with brandy sauce, the whole meal being topped off with fruit and nuts. As well, each man had a bottle of beer.[12]

*Vampire* also had a pleasantly quiet Christmas alongside the depot ship HMS *Woolwich* in Alexandria for three weeks of engine repairs. On the day itself, and just for the hell of it, one of her young signalmen, Laurie Packham, was dressed in a lieutenant's uniform and sent off to pay formal calls around the fleet, graciously accepting Royal Navy hospitality from wardroom bar to wardroom bar. He carried it off with aplomb, undiscovered, but practically had to be poured back on board some hours later.

The other Scrap Iron destroyers were not so fortunate. *Vendetta* steamed into Alexandria on Christmas afternoon, Gordon Hill and his mates hoping for a relaxed dinner on board or ashore, but she dashed out again after just two hours to join *Waterhen* and *Voyager* at Sollum, where the fighting went on unhindered by any notion of peace on earth.

Andy Nation's first Christmas at war began with an early morning air raid on *Waterhen*, a pair of Italian torpedo bombers appearing suddenly out of a glorious sunrise. A newly minted stoker from Geelong, just turned twenty, Andy had joined the ship only in November, part of a draft of new blood sent from Australia to the Mediterranean to replace old hands who had been promoted or posted to other ships. Unusually for a stoker – they were not a caste much given to literary effort – he kept a vivid diary throughout what would be a long naval career:

> We opened up with everything we had. They dropped their fish but missed us and roared away followed by bursting shells. It was a grand sight. The sun was just peeping up and the colour of the sky was really grand. We survived that attack all right and then at 10.30 am the alarm bell went. We raced up on deck, had a look at the sky, then I started to say my prayers. There flying towards us were five bombers and thirty fighters. Their first stick of bombs fell about 100 yards away on the port side, the next lot came screaming down about 50 yards on the starboard side, shrapnel flew everywhere and the decks were flooded with water from the explosions. Nobody got seriously hurt.[13]

There were two more attacks on *Waterhen* that Christmas Day, four in all, the ship writhing and twisting as the Irishman Jim Swain conned her through the explosions and the columns of filthy brown water they threw up. One raid, in the early afternoon, left Andy Nation rigid with fear:

> The first stick of bombs fell where we had been about thirty seconds before and lifted our stern out of the water. The rest fell further away. Then I had a real thrill. I was lying flat out on the deck and I rolled over to see where they were; and hurtling down on top of me was a bomb. I just lay there and stared at it. I can't tell you how I felt. It hit the deck about five feet from where I was and just lay there. It was a dud. I couldn't move for about ten minutes. I was sweating and just staring at it. Boy did I get a fright.[14]

In the final attack, at dusk, two torpedoes came at them from ahead, passing harmlessly one to port, one to starboard. The captain had called it well again, to the continued puzzlement of the ship's company, for he was something of a paradox. A nervous shiphandler in harbour, Lieutenant Commander Swain was notorious for taking an age to secure alongside a wharf or to come on to a buoy, dicking and dithering back and forth while the libertymen, eager to get ashore, waited on deck in mounting impatience. At sea, though, he handled *Waterhen* with flair. And that night he was to have a satisfying final say when the lookouts spotted a shadow creeping along the coast towards Bardia.

The alarm for action stations rang a little after midnight and the destroyer's searchlights revealed a three-masted timber schooner of perhaps 100 tons, under motor. The frustrations of the day spilled over and, after giving the enemy crew time to abandon ship, *Waterhen*'s gunners cheerfully and methodically blew her out of the water at point-blank range in quick time. She was identified as the *Tireremo Dirito* – one of Mussolini's favourite slogans, meaning 'We will forge ahead' – and her survivors, according to Swain's report, were 'twenty-four men and four officers, one fascist officer and one dog', who were made prisoner on board together with bags of mail for the Italian garrison at Bardia.

The next day, Boxing Day, it was back to being bombed again.

—

At home, Christmas for thousands of Australian families was tinged by thoughts of husbands, fathers, sons and brothers – and a few women, mostly nurses – serving far away in the Northern Hemisphere. The long casualty lists in the newspapers were still some months in the future, and very few families had known the heart-stopping fear of seeing the telegram boy from the post office cycle down the street and prop his bike at the front gate. The *Sydney Morning Herald* reported that Christmas shopping was brisk despite the wet weather, with the Commonwealth Bank increasing the note issue by £1,750,000[15] to keep the cash registers jingling. A handsome Christmas tree, 10 feet (3 metres) high, cost one pound and, as the *Herald* observed:[16]

Admiring crowds stood outside the poultry and provision shops and waited in long queues to be served. Chickens, which were plentiful, sold at from 3/3 to 6/9. Cockerels were scarce and dearer. Prices for ducks and drakes were on a par with those of last Christmas. Turkeys, mostly old birds, sold from 9/7 to 17/6, which was substantially cheaper than at last Christmas.[17]

Over it all there lay a gnawing sense that the worst was yet to come. Memories of the last war were raw and real and now the world seemed to be reprising the same folly and horror with much the same protagonists. To be sure, Führer had replaced Kaiser, but not much else had changed: it was still those same bloody Germans to be fought and beaten. And perhaps the evermore bellicose Japanese would come in eventually, White Australia's greatest fear. Like Italy, Japan had been an ally in the last war, even sending a cruiser to help escort the First AIF through the Indian Ocean to the Middle East in 1914. The world had changed much since then.

This was an era when every major city enjoyed a variety of daily newspapers, morning and afternoon, and even the smallest country towns boasted at least one paper, if only a weekly. The Christmas editorials they printed in 1940 were solemn, sombre, threaded with hope and foreboding in about equal measure. There is something especially poignant about the rural papers, published so far from the fighting and yet tied inexorably to it by the bonds of an Empire in which most Australians loyally and fervently believed.

In the central west of New South Wales, over the Blue Mountains from Sydney, the Bathurst *National Advocate* could offer no comfort to its readers:

Since last Christmas many more thousands of hearts and homes have been made desolate; the world has suffered to an extent hitherto unparalleled, even compared with the horrors of the 1914–18 savagery.

Death, destruction, and desolation have been substituted for progress and prosperity, and the world in general has been appalled at the additional ravages of the Molech of war. We face the Christmastide with no outlook for the brighter days to come.

There is no glimmer of light through the ferociousness of the struggle. When it will end no man can tell: few dare even attempt to forecast.

Civilisation stands aghast: not only at the tremendous sacrifices already made, but at those which must be made before the aims of Britain and her Allies are achieved.[18]

Across the continent, the *Mount Barker and Denmark Record* of Albany, on the rim of the Great Australian Bight, thought that:

It has been a year of heartbreak for many, of anxiety for millions, of grave responsibility for a few. It has produced deeds of epic heroism, so many that they cannot all be told. So many in fact that some of them will never be known. It has been a year of trial and testing, from which the Empire has emerged with many grievous wounds, but with its strength greater.[19]

In Queensland, the *Northern Miner* of Charters Towers waxed lyrical:

Whatever comes to pass, may those who have striven their utmost for the welfare of our land be spared to see the British Empire and its allies firmly re-established on the path of victory – the path that means security, freedom and happiness, and may the friends and relatives of those who have already made the supreme sacrifice in execution of their duty be comforted this Christmas by the stirring and immortal lines of Lord Byron: 'They never fail who die in a great cause.'

In the Mediterranean – on land, in the air, and at sea – the coming year, 1941, would see the great cause tested to the utmost, even to breaking point.

## CHAPTER 12

# HIS NAME IS WALLER

The last days of 1940 ended the year with a flick of the tail. Leaving Sollum Bay in a rough sea in the dead of night on 30 December, *Waterhen* collided with a small anti-submarine trawler, HMS *Bandolero*, which sank slowly in the dark. The details are lost to history, although it appears to have been the trawler's fault. *Waterhen* rescued all her crew, but the destroyer's bow was so badly damaged that she was sent for a month of repairs in Port Tewfik at the southern end of the Suez Canal. The ship's company was not at all displeased by this unexpected development. Tewfik was away from the bombing and the varied delights of Cairo were only a couple of hours distant. Andy Nation saw the Sphinx and the pyramids and ...

> I got into the best fight of my life. I collected three broken knuckles, a black eye and a big lump on my head. My cobber has gone to the hospital, while both our opponents are in hospital.
> We got back to the ship and sailed the next day for Port Said.[1]

That same pitch-black December night, about 12.30 am at the beginning of the middle watch, *Voyager* intercepted an Italian ketch, a two-masted sailing vessel hugging the coast as she motored stealthily away from Bardia. It was one of those long winter vigils on the bridge where the chief enemies are boredom and cold, fought off with occasional cups of kai and thoughts of home. Hugh McDonald, an eighteen-year-old midshipman from Port Lincoln in South Australia, saw it first, a vague black wraith perhaps a mile away inshore. Hugh had joined the ship back in August, gaining a reputation for having keen night vision.[2] Bill Cook, the first lieutenant, had the watch. Peering through his binoculars, he altered course towards the coast and rang the alarm gongs, which brought 'Copper' Morrow to the bridge as the blur became more distinct.

'Put a shot across her bow,' said the captain. A 4-inch shell from A-gun streaked across the gap and threw up a satisfying white splash in the dark. 'Searchlight ... open the shutter!'

A 10-inch projector sprang to life. A long cone of piercing white lit up their quarry and, better still, some stick figures on deck waving white sheets or shirts in surrender. Morrow's report picks up the story:

> The weather was too rough to go alongside or to lower a boat, but when hailed they replied they had English prisoners of war on board. At this moment a sergeant of The Queen's Own[3] shouted that he had the situation in hand, and he and eight of his regiment had one hundred Italian soldiers battened down below. I told him to collect all mail, correspondence and to tell the captain to follow me, whereupon he replied, 'We'll see to that' ...[4]

Their catch was the *Zingarella*, of 200 tons. *Voyager* turned her and her crew over to the monitor *Terror* in Sollum, and took the nine British soldiers – very relieved and happy men – back to Alexandria.

—

For the first two months of the New Year, three of the destroyers were with the Inshore Squadron, joining the bombardment of the retreating Italians ashore in Libya, carrying supplies from Alexandria to the army and bringing out wounded men and prisoners. *Vendetta* was escorting convoys in the Aegean. Back from her refit in Malta, *Stuart*'s ship's company had a couple of days leave in Alexandria where, to much excitement, they discovered the newly established Australian Forces Club set up by the Comforts Fund. It offered cold Australian beer, the nectar of the gods, the first they had tasted since leaving home. Hec Waller rejoined the ship and the bombardment.

It was dog-day work inshore, hard and unremitting for the shell handlers toiling below and the gunners on deck, all beneath constant bombing. In that first week of January the fleet joined them, the flagship *Warspite* and the battleships *Valiant* and *Barham* pounding Bardia with a storm of shells that sent some of the garrison deep into its bunkers never to re-emerge. Bardia fell to the onslaught of the Australian 6th Division on 5 January, for the loss of 130 diggers. In the words of the official army historian, Gavin Long, it was:

a victory for bold reconnaissance, for audacious yet careful planning, for an artillery scheme which subdued the enemy's fire at the vital time, and a rapid and continuing infantry assault which broke a gap in the enemy's line.[5]

Some 40,000 Italians were taken prisoner, along with a treasure trove of guns big and small, ammunition, and stores of food and alcohol. The 10th Army commander, Tenente Generale Annibale Bergonzoli – luxuriantly bearded and known therefore to his troops as '*Barba Elettrica*', 'Electric Whiskers' – escaped by the skin of his teeth, fleeing on foot across 120 kilometres of desert to reach Tobruk.

The victory was celebrated with justifiable elation at home and hailed throughout the English-speaking world, the *Times Herald* in Washington DC running the headline 'Hardy Wild-Eyed Aussies Called World's Finest Troops'.[6] Privately, the 6th Division commander, Iven Mackay, foresaw the storm to come, writing in his diary the next day that 'the Germans cannot possibly keep out of Africa now'.[7] He was right. Hitler was already making his next move. On 11 January, the German High Command began to put together the regiments, then the divisions of infantry, artillery and armour that would become the legendary Afrika Korps. Humiliated and apprehensive, on 19 January Mussolini travelled to the Berghof, Hitler's mountain retreat in the snows of the Obersalzburg, where – to his surprise and relief – a cordial Führer quickly assured him of German support in Africa and then launched into a long harangue about the evils of the Soviet Union.

—

*Sydney* sailed for home on 9 January, to the unconfined joy of her people but a certain amount of grumbling from the veterans of the Scrap Iron destroyers. The men felt, understandably, that she had snatched all the glory and been rewarded for it while they were being kept in the Mediterranean for more hard slog. A replacement, her sister ship HMAS *Perth*, had already arrived in Alexandria. *Sydney* carried with her a warm farewell from Andrew Cunningham:

> We part with you with great regret and the best wishes of the whole Mediterranean fleet go with you. I hope you will have a happy homecoming and that your countrymen will give you the reception you deserve.[8]

A month later to the day, 9 February, she was in her home port, where the welcome was indeed ecstatic. Hundreds of thousands of cheering, flag-waving Sydneysiders lined the streets to see the ship's company with Captain Collins at their head march to a civic reception at the Town Hall. Collins was feted as a bold national hero, the first of the war. In May, he handed *Sydney* to a new commanding officer, his college classmate, Captain Joseph Burnett, but the ship had only months to live. In the Indian Ocean off Western Australia on 19 November, in what remains to this day Australia's greatest naval disaster, she was lost with all hands – 645 men – in a battle with the disguised German raider *Kormoran*. Burnett, inexperienced in his first wartime sea command, had incautiously approached the German too closely and been taken by surprise. Most of those who died had been with the 'Stormy Petrel' in those brave days in the Med. Jack Ross, her diligent diarist, was not one of them. Just weeks before, on the last day of October, he had been posted out of her to join the cruiser *Canberra*. His grief at the loss of the ship, and so many shipmates, was wrenching:

> she died protecting our trade routes like the fighting ship she was, destroying a dangerous enemy raider even in her death throes. Truly it can be said of her and of all those fine chaps who passed on with her that 'they did their duty'.
>
> May we and our country always be worthy of them.[9]

Fortress Malta, with its great harbour, dockyards, skilled workforce and airfield, remained the keystone of British dominance in the Mediterranean. On 7 January, in a complex operation code named Excess, a supply convoy of four merchant ships sailed eastwards from Gibraltar towards Malta and Greece while another convoy carrying fuel headed for Malta from Alexandria.

All went to plan until 10 January. The Alexandria convoy arrived unharmed in Malta and the Mediterranean Fleet met the Gibraltar convoy and saw it safely through the Sicilian Narrows, a strait about 145 kilometres wide between Sicily and the African coast. Andrew Cunningham was at sea in *Warspite*, with the battleship *Valiant*, the usual prowling squadrons of cruisers and destroyers – including the newly arrived and still untested HMAS *Perth* – and the great carrier *Illustrious* at the very centre of it all. *Valiant* and *Illustrious* had radar.

The day started well enough when the patrolling cruiser HMS *Bonaventure* crippled and sank a wayward Italian torpedo boat at dawn. But from that moment everything began to go wrong, and badly so. With the fleet some 140 kilometres west of Malta, the destroyer *Gallant* struck a stray mine which blew off her bows and killed sixty-five of her crew; she had to be towed stern first into Grand Harbour. A Savoia bomber shadowing them was shot down by Fulmar fighters from *Illustrious*, but around 1220 hours another two came in fast and low below the radar, each launching a torpedo at the carrier's starboard side. Her captain, Denis Boyd, threw the ship into a violent turn to port and escaped unharmed, the torpedoes shooting past him and narrowly missing the stern of *Valiant*, while four Fulmars flying a combat air patrol (CAP) high above the fleet swooped down almost to sea level to chase the Savoias off over the horizon.

This was exactly what the enemy had planned. The Savoias had been a decoy to lure the fighters away. Just five minutes later, at 1225 hours, radar on both *Valiant* and *Illustrious* detected a massive formation of aircraft approaching from the north at about 12,000 feet, dropping quickly down to 7000 feet as they wheeled and formed to make their bombing runs. As the specks in the air drew closer and grew larger, from the bridge of *Warspite* a new and distinctive camouflage of black and grey blotches above the wings, grey and dirty white below, became starkly clear. Then they saw black swastikas on their tails. Germans! They were Stukas. Fliegerkorps X had joined the war in the Mediterranean. The fleet opened up with every available gun.

When he first touched down in Sicily in late December 1940, Walter Enneccarus was already one of the Luftwaffe's most skilful combat pilots. He had cut his teeth in the Heinkel 51 ground-attack biplane in the Spanish Civil War, graduating to the Stuka in time for the blitzkrieg on Poland in 1939, then flying in the Wehrmacht's conquest of Western Europe and, after that, the Battle of Britain. In the summer of 1940 he was one of the first Stuka pilots to win the singular honour of the red, white and black ribbon of the Ritterkreuz des Eisernen Kreuzes, the Knight's Cross of the Iron Cross.

At the age of twenty-nine, he was now an Oberst – a major – and the commanding officer of II/Sturzkampfgeschwader 2, Squadron Two of the Second Dive Bomber Wing based at Trapani under the umbrella of Fliegerkorps X. Most of his pilots were specialists in anti-ship operations and they had begun their training in Sicily with a slogan, or perhaps a war cry, drummed into them: 'Illustrious *muss versenkt werden.' Illustrious* must be sunk.

The carrier would be their prime target. To take her out of the war would radically shift the balance of sea power in the Mediterranean in favour of the Axis partners. Enneccarus had a rectangle of buoys the size of *Illustrious*'s flight deck floated in the waters off Trapani and for days his men honed their attack there. Just four or five bombs, accurately placed, should be enough to send her to the bottom, they thought.

Now was the moment. Enneccarus led his squadron into the storm of flame and bullets and shells and smoke in two carefully choreographed formations. The numbers vary from account to account, but some thirty Stukas with him at their head went straight for *Illustrious*, with another ten peeling off to attack the two battleships. They divided into several clover leaf formations to confuse the gunners and to strike from different directions, some releasing their bombs as low as 800 feet, their sirens howling to a shattering crescendo. In *Warspite*, the Commander-in-Chief looked on in fascination:

One was too interested in this new form of dive-bombing attack really to be frightened, and there was no doubt we were watching complete experts. Formed roughly in a large circle over the fleet they peeled off one by one when reaching the attacking position. We could not but admire the skill and precision of it all. The attacks were pressed home to point-blank range, and as they pulled out of their dives, some of them were seen to fly along the flight deck of the *Illustrious* below the level of her funnel.[10]

Captain Boyd was frantic to get more Fulmars into the air. To do that he had to turn the carrier into the wind. If he had been operating independently, off to one side and at his best speed of 30 knots, he could have turned and launched those fighters instantly. But Cunningham, inexperienced in carrier operations – and against the advice of those officers who were – had stubbornly insisted that *Illustrious* should remain in the centre of the fleet, ploughing along at 18 knots. Boyd, therefore, had to request permission to turn, Cunningham had to grant it, and then – and only then – could the entire mass of ships turn with him.

With signals back and forth this took an agonising ten minutes, and that delay was critical. Three Swordfish and four Fulmars struggled off the deck but they were barely airborne before the Stukas began methodically reducing *Illustrious* to a burning cripple. Six bombs hit the ship, some penetrating her deck armour and starting fierce fires. One knocked out her steering gear and another punched holes in her side, flooding several compartments. A Fulmar in the hangar deck exploded, its ammunition scything through the men there. Other men were killed by shrapnel or burned to death in fires raging out of control. Still more bombs were near misses. At one stage the mighty carrier disappeared behind rising walls of water. Lieutenant Charles Lamb was in a Swordfish about to land after a raid when the attack began:

The people in the hangar threw themselves on their faces on the steel deck to let everything pass over them. The bullets from the burning aircraft were whizzing around the hangar like hundreds of rubber balls being fired into an enclosed squash court, and nobody could stay in the hangar and live. The heat was quite unsupportable and noxious fumes were escaping from the exploding oxygen chambers, from the burning acid of batteries. The unfortunate men inside seized the first opportunity to rush out of the hangar through the airtight doors to the comparative safety of the battery space outside, but after the first bomb there were very few left alive to do so.[11]

Out of fuel, Lamb ditched his aircraft in the sea and was rescued by a destroyer. Still burning furiously, her buckled flight deck swept by billowing orange flames and clouds of oily black smoke, *Illustrious* began to struggle towards Malta at 17 knots, listing to starboard, Captain Boyd steering by her engines. Savoias bombed her again in the early afternoon from a high altitude but caused no damage, and another small flight of Stukas, about thirteen of them, appeared at around 1600 hours with one bomb detonating on the quarterdeck and killing more men. It was late evening when she reached the harbour, the merciful night bringing respite. In all, 126 men were killed and ninety-one wounded. The Germans lost just three aircraft.

The next day the Stukas returned, coming suddenly out of the sun to damage the cruiser *Gloucester* and hit the cruiser *Southampton* so heavily that she had to be abandoned and torpedoed. Bad weather over Malta saved *Illustrious* for a few days while teams of dockyard workers laboured to make her ready for sea again, but on 16 January the Stukas were back, with a fighter cover of Me 109s. It was hell revisited: the bombs, the bullets, more destruction, more death.

HMAS *Perth* was berthed nearby. In this, a baptism of fire for the ship and her crew, one stray bomb whistled down into the narrow gap between her hull and the wharf with an explosion that tossed her into the air like a bathtub toy. A direct hit might well have sunk her. When the raid ended, Jock Lawrance, a leading stoker, was in a party of *Perth* sailors sent over to *Illustrious* to give what help they could:

As we went on board, Maltese were carrying bags down the other gangway. I said to one of the Maltese: 'What's that?'
He said: 'This was a man.'

Blood was coming through the sacks. It was a bloodbath, right throughout the ship. There was a paymaster with his head blown off. He was sitting at his desk like he was reading, but dead, with his head blown off. A piece of shrapnel had come through and whipped his head off. He was still there with a pen in his hand. I just shut the door again.

The shrapnel went right though the bulkheads just like it was tissue paper.

And they had a Stuka in the lift. Dead. Shot down. It had a big swastika on its tail. But the *Illustrious* was a butcher's shop. There was a big engineer officer, a big bloke in his white overalls, still had his torch on, and a piece of shrapnel had taken out his stomach, just like that. That was the first time I'd seen bodies in war. It was shocking, blood everywhere.[12]

Eventually the carrier was patched together to make her seaworthy and she left the Mediterranean through Suez, around the Cape of Good Hope and on to the United States for a rebuild. HMS *Illustrious* would not rejoin the war until February 1942. The Luftwaffe had not sunk her, but they had taken her off the chessboard; a singular victory. As Andrew Cunningham wrote:

In a few minutes the whole situation had changed. At one blow the fleet had been deprived of its fighter aircraft, and its command of the Mediterranean was threatened by a weapon far more efficient and dangerous than any against which we had fought before. The efforts of the Regia Aeronautica were almost as nothing compared with the deadly Stukas of the Luftwaffe.[13]

—

The Libyan port of Tobruk entered the pages of Australian history on 22 January 1941 when General Iven Mackay's 6th Division captured the town and its harbour after a brilliantly directed assault of just two days. The young diggers had rolled west along the bitumen coastal road from Bardia in almost a holiday mood, with the starchy, humourless Mackay fretting over what he called a 'picnic spirit'. In an order to his units he warned that 'civilianism is beginning to break out'. He complained of 'promiscuous firing of rifles and exploding of bombs', of 'dressing in articles of Italian uniform like clowns and not like soldiers', of 'collecting of dogs and looking after dogs instead of men' and of 'fraternisation with prisoners'. 'We must keep our heads and maintain perspective and poise,' he concluded. 'If we do not we shall quickly lose efficiency and slip to the level of the foe we are hoping to defeat.'[14]

He need not have worried. The Italian collapse was swift and stunningly complete, humiliated generals and Tobruk's extravagantly bemedalled port admiral formally surrendering their swords or pistols with tears in their eyes. More startling still, the Australians captured 27,000 prisoners, 208 guns and twenty-three tanks, for the loss of just forty-nine of their own men. And the town of Tobruk itself was an eye-opener, its broad streets boasting stylish cafés and wine cellars and an elegant and fully equipped brothel. Soldiers wandering into the abandoned sleeping quarters of Italian officers found wardrobes of silk shirts and glittering uniforms, fancy toilet sets of Florentine leather, cases of champagne and all manner of other luxurious frills and trappings which – against Mackay's explicit orders – they cheerfully proceeded to loot.

*Stuart*, *Vampire* and *Voyager* had supported the army inshore, bombarding here and there as asked, along with the ever-present *Terror* and a 6-inch gunboat, HMS *Gnat*. They had orders, too, to prevent the escape from Tobruk of the ancient but still powerful Italian heavy cruiser *San Giorgio*, whose 10- and 7.5-inch guns might have given them a great deal of trouble if it had actually come to blows.

Early in the morning of the surrender the three destroyers crept into port, *Stuart* in the lead with Hec Waller on the bridge. The first sight that met them at the entrance was the partly sunk and still smoking wreck of *San Giorgio*, which had been heavily bombed by the RAF and finally destroyed by Italian army mortars. The harbour itself looked defeated, exhausted. Two large merchant ships lay aground at odd angles and there were other smaller wrecks strewn here and there, including a sunken submarine. But, surprisingly, the wharves were in reasonably good order and an electric power station was still operating with a nearby store of coal untouched. It would not take long to revive a working port for the supplies the army would need as it began the push further westward to its next objectives, the Italian strongholds of Derna and Benghazi. Tobruk would be held, come what may.

There was no going ashore that day, but *Stuart* returned a couple of days later and the captain allowed a few hours' leave to see the sights. Les Clifford went with two mates:

> Evidence of complete destruction met us at every turn as Jock, Ted and myself proceeded on a tour of inspection. Above the doorways of shops and houses the sign 'Looted' was chalked. The army had been in possession for three days! However, there were ample souvenirs left for 'Jack', who was soon observed staggering under the weight of blankets, rifles, bayonets, tin hats and other sundries.[15]

Ean McDonald also went for a look around:

> Obviously the Italians had vacated in one hell of a hurry. Houses had bedclothes only just turned back. Cafés had half meals still on tables, with half glasses of Chianti and the chairs pushed haphazardly back. We had a great time. We reheated and ate pasta. We drank lots of straw-covered Chianti that abounded for the taking. We looted unashamedly, taking what little there was of any value.[16]

Even the captain was not above a little selective pilfering. Hec somehow acquired a couple of sewing machines which he took back to Alexandria and presented to Cunningham's wife Nona for her sewing and knitting circle, a gesture which so impressed the admiral that he mentioned it in his memoirs.[17] That afternoon the Australians watched with a mixture of awe and amusement as long lines of Italian prisoners, hundreds of them in dishevelled green uniforms, wound their way onto a jetty and a ship that would take them to Alexandria. The spectacle was interrupted by another of those filthy sandstorms they hated so much and they were glad to put to sea again, the ship covered in grit.

*Stuart* and the other Scrap Iron ships would see Tobruk again and again, in very different and much more dangerous times. Weeks later, on 11 February, the advance guard of the newly formed Deutsches Afrikakorps and its commander, the aggressive and ambitious Generalleutnant Erwin Rommel, arrived in Tripoli.

—

To everyone's surprise – they had not been told he was coming – the Australian prime minister, Robert Menzies, turned up in Alexandria. Travelling in a Qantas flying boat, he stopped over in Egypt to assess the situation in the Middle East before going on to London for long weeks of meetings with Winston Churchill, the War Cabinet and the service chiefs, and to hobnob happily with the great and the good.

*Stuart*, in Tobruk, was suddenly ordered back to Alexandria to be there when Menzies arrived. On 7 February he met the crews of *Stuart*, *Vampire*, *Voyager* and *Perth*, to a somewhat patchy reception. Menzies was not then the colossus he became after the war. Suave and silver-tongued, radiating the patrician air of the successful Melbourne barrister he had once been – but widely viewed as devious and untrustworthy – he led his conservative United Australia Party in a fractious coalition with the Country Party, a minority government kept in office by the votes of two independent MPs. Labor voters – and that included a good many sailors – disliked him intensely. Cunningham took him to inspect the Australians. 'You are going to meet one of the greatest captains who ever sailed the seas – his name is Waller,' the admiral told him.[18]

As politicians will on these occasions, Menzies basked in what he took to be the approval of the troops, but not all were impressed. Brian Sheedy, a signalman in *Perth*, jotted in his diary that Menzies 'left us all with a bad impression ... he told us nothing of Australia and how things were back home'. Jim Nelson, another Perth sailor, wrote:

> Dutifully we stood there while he rambled on with a long, polit-
> ically inspired speech, telling us what good guys we were. We
> good guys were bored, and calls for liberty were interrupting the
> speech, which finally concluded with liberty being piped.[19]

Things went better that evening when the prime minister dropped into the Australian Forces Club with the Australian army commander in the Middle East, General Thomas Blamey. He shouted beers all round and, according to Les Clifford, there were cries of 'come along every day!'[20]

Political grandstanding aside, Menzies had urgent business crowding in. Every available intelligence source was predicting that the Italian rout in Greece would prompt the Germans to intervene there in force. Churchill was in a lather to get there first, avid to send in troops to support the Greeks, Britain's last remaining ally in Europe. It would be the honourable thing to do, he believed, and it would play well politically in the United States as yet more evidence of British resolve.

The nearest, most easily available troops for the job were the Australian 6th Division which was still rolling back the Italians in Libya. They could be accompanied by the Australian 7th Division and the New Zealand 2nd Division, both now forming up in Egypt but yet to enter the fighting. As usual, Churchill regarded Commonwealth troops as his to deploy around the chessboard wherever he saw fit, but Menzies had his doubts and, very properly, wanted to know more. On 10 February he flew to Cairo to meet the Commander-in-Chief Middle East, Archibald Wavell. This encounter was the opening act in a tragedy of error and folly that would lead to the bloody debacle of the Greece and Crete campaigns. Hundreds of Australians and Kiwis would die and thousands would end up in German captivity.

If Menzies was aloof, Wavell was glacial. Known to friends and enemies as 'Podgy', he was half soldier, half bookish intellectual, lugubrious and taciturn, with a deep-seated dislike of politicians. The prime minister sought to question him about his plans for Greece and the Australians but got little more than a frozen silence for his pains. Wavell, Menzies wrote later:

simply did not talk at all. He appeared to be blind in one eye, and this meant that when I sat next to him at table he would swivel his head right round, 90 degrees, fix me with the good eye and say either 'I see' or 'Maybe' or 'Um', or nothing. I wanted to put all sorts of things to him, and thought that I had some right to do so, since Australian troops were no small part of the forces under his command. For example, I asked him whether he thought that the

German forces might counter-attack to and through Benghazi, for this might have a bearing elsewhere. His only reply was to the effect that it was 'very difficult'. I left Egypt on my way to London with a depressing feeling that Wavell didn't trust me.[21]

The folly mounted. When Menzies arrived in London some days later, he quickly found that Churchill believed the deal was done. Wavell had told him that Menzies had agreed to send the Australians, Churchill said. This was at best a misunderstanding by Wavell, at worst a lie. Menzies had done no such thing and he was startled and perturbed to hear Churchill say otherwise. He had not even had the chance to put the proposal to the cabinet back in Canberra, which he was bound to do.

Meanwhile, in Cairo, Wavell called in General Blamey and the New Zealand commander, Major General Bernard Freyberg, to tell them their men would be off to Greece. There was no consultation, no request; it was simply a fait accompli. Wavell told Blamey that Menzies had given the green light – definitely a lie – leaving the Australian angry and much troubled. He had not heard that from Menzies and he had grave doubts a campaign in Greece could succeed. Freyberg said later he had not been asked for his opinion but had been 'given instructions to get ready to go'.[22] He felt he had no choice but to obey.

Blamey stewed for a few days, his anger swelling when he learned that although the majority of the troops would be Australian, command of the show would go to a British officer, the blimpish Lieutenant General Sir Henry 'Jumbo' Maitland Wilson. Preparations for Operation Lustre, for the navy to carry the Australians and New Zealanders to Greece, were rolling along. Eventually Blamey acted. On 10 March he sent a detailed document to the Australian cabinet in Canberra expressing his concerns. While the Allies could muster three divisions and an armoured brigade, he wrote, the Germans had 'as many divisions available as roads can carry' and 'within three to four months we must be prepared to meet overwhelming forces completely equipped and trained'. The military operation would be 'extremely hazardous in view of the disparity between opposing forces in numbers and training'.[23]

This warning landed like a thunderbolt in Canberra but it was too late. The Australians and the New Zealanders had already begun to embark upon the ships that would carry them to Piraeus. To his credit, Menzies questioned Churchill again but was assured that the operation had 'a reasonable chance of success'. Still uneasy but with nowhere to go, Menzies obtained a promise that if all went wrong, the Australians would be evacuated. Lamely putting the best possible gloss on it, he told his colleagues that Greece was a great risk in a good cause.

Others also had their doubts. At Alexandria, Andrew Cunningham feared that pulling the Australians out of Libya would undo their hard-fought achievements there, perhaps opening the way for the gathering German forces to counter-attack. As ever, he had more grasp of strategy in one fingernail than his prime minister could summon in his entire body, and he wrote later in his memoirs:

We were bound by treaty to help Greece if she were threatened, so there was no question at all that it was, politically, the right thing to do. On the other hand, we had serious misgivings if it was correct from the military point of view. We doubted very much if our naval, military and air resources were equal to it … We had no illusions that the help we could send the Greeks would enable them to stem a really serious German invasion. Indeed, when the decision to send the troops was finally taken, we started at once to think of how we should bring them out.[24]

———

Benghazi and Beda Fomm, two redoubts still further west along the Libyan coast, were taken by the 6th Division and British troops on 7 February in the now familiar, tragi-comic scenes of a chaotic Italian rout. Asked to report how many prisoners he had taken, a British lieutenant famously replied, 'Oh, several acres I would think'.[25] Even the elusive 10th Army commander, Annibale Bergonzoli, old 'Barba Elettrica', had been captured. It was an extraordinary feat of arms, masterminded not by Wavell but his subordinate, Lieutenant General Richard O'Connor. In two hectic months O'Connor's divisions – principally Australians – had advanced 800 kilometres, captured

130,000 prisoners, 400 tanks and 1290 guns, for the loss of 475 lives. Of the dead, 239 were Australians.

After the Menzies visit, *Stuart*, *Vampire* and *Voyager* returned again to the grind of patrol and bombardment along the barren and blasted Libyan coast, sometimes escorting supply ships, in the usual capricious weather that might throw up big seas or dust storms and sometimes both. It was monotonous work, although mines dropped by air posed a new and increasing danger. *Stuart*'s first lieutenant, Rupert Robison, offered a prize of two ounces of tobacco to any man who spotted one and the men – including Hec Waller – enjoyed despatching them by rifle fire.

Sometimes there was an event, a happening, that lifted the boredom and entered the ship's store of dits. Patrolling off Tobruk after nightfall on 11 February, *Stuart*'s bridge crew were startled to hear a voice crying out from the water on the port bow.

'Stop both,' said the captain. The ship glided to a halt; the voice cried feebly again.

Frank Watkins, the new Chief Yeoman, was the first to spot it. 'Raft bearing red one oh, sir.'

In the dark they could see a small shape off to port with a figure sprawled upon it. They brought the raft alongside with boathooks and a man was gingerly lifted on board, exhausted and in shock. He was taken below to be tended by the doctor, and as he revived he gave his name, C. J. Jones, and his story. A Royal Navy leading stoker, he had been on loan to an armed trawler of the South African Navy, HMSAS *Southern Floe*. He had just gone on watch at 0400 hours when there was an almighty explosion that flooded the engine room. Most likely a mine, he thought. As the little ship sank, in less than a minute it seemed, he squirmed his way out through a skylight and found a couple of other men struggling in the water. They had disappeared over the fourteen long hours since the sinking, he said. *Stuart* and *Voyager* searched the area for a while but there was no sign of any other survivor. From a crew of twenty-six, C. J. Jones was it.

Their loss of Benghazi aroused a new fury in the enemy, chiefly in the Germans who intensified their bombing along the coast. On 19 February, again off Tobruk, *Stuart* was dive-bombed and machine-gunned four times by Luftwaffe Heinkels, fortunately without any damage beyond frayed nerves that sometimes came close to breaking point. 'Hard Over' Hec's consummate shiphandling had saved them again.

Benghazi had a good port and the army hoped to use it as a major supply base but was unable to provide any adequate anti-aircraft defence to protect ships unloading there, which worried Cunningham. The redoubtable *Terror* was about all there was, but when she was narrowly missed by a bomb which started heavy leaks, her captain, Commander Henry Haynes, signalled Alexandria that, 'I consider it only a matter of time before the ship receives a direct hit'. Cunningham reluctantly ordered her to leave, but her number was up. Haynes had been all too prescient. As she steamed out of Benghazi on the evening of 22 February at her best speed of a mere 14 knots, she touched off two acoustic mines which caused more flooding. The next morning she was heavily bombed yet again and near misses broke her back and flooded her engine room. She had to be abandoned and sunk, her crew taken off by an escorting corvette, a dismal end to a doughty warrior that had served in both wars. Many of the Australians were saddened by her loss, for *Terror* had been a chummy ship, a mate, since their first meeting in Singapore back in 1939 and they had been through a lot together.

War, though, allowed little time for regrets. The carnage continued. On the same day *Terror* was scuttled, the destroyer HMS *Dainty* was set upon by no fewer than thirteen Junkers Ju 88 bombers off Tobruk. One bomb smashed directly through the captain's cabin, starting a fire which touched off an explosion in her after magazine and sank her with the loss of sixteen men. This, too, was a special blow, for *Dainty* was one of Hec's ships, one of his 10th Flotilla and the first of them to go.

—

Operation Lustre, the complex and hazardous convoying of troops to Greece, began in early March. The perennial shortage of transports meant that many had to be carried in the larger naval ships including *Perth*, whose people were less than amused when a bunch of British officers paraded airily up the gangway with wardrobe trunks, an array of heavy suitcases and four pet dogs which got explosively seasick on the trip to Piraeus.

After three days of boiler cleaning in Alexandria – always popular, because it meant a lot of leave for everyone but the unfortunate Black Gang doing the dirty work – *Stuart* sailed for Port Said to pick up two troopships on 4 March. At sea they were joined by two more merchant vessels full of soldiers, escorted by the destroyer HMS *Hereward* and the anti-aircraft cruiser HMS *Coventry*. For two days they were left in peace, steaming serenely beneath clear skies, but on 6 March, off the eastern coast of Crete, the enemy found them. They were bombed no fewer than seven times that afternoon, but with *Coventry* putting up a formidable barrage there were no hits. *Stuart* took a near miss in the last attack, which shook everyone up, as Hec Waller reported:

> This last aircraft seemed to be out for my blood and nursed his second bomb until I remained on a steady course. The bombs being so large, however, they could be followed all the way down and the requisite alteration could be made.[26]

*Waterhen*, the old Chook, had a still more lively time of it in Operation Lustre, attempting an exploit of daring seamanship and carrying it off triumphantly. On 18 March she sailed from Alexandria with *Coventry* and two other warships to escort a big convoy of thirteen ships carrying troops and supplies. They were routed west around Crete through the notorious Kythera Strait, that stretch of water known in the trade as 'Bomb Alley'.

After three sunny, uneventful days the weather turned on them in the strait with rising seas and sudden drifts of rain that blotted out the sky. It was 21 March 1941. At 1600 hours, seven Stuka dive-bombers swooped out of a squall and into the midst of the convoy.

'They almost took the masts off the ships, they came that low,' wrote Andy Nation. 'It was murder.'[27]

Zigzagging and dodging at speed, the ships of the escort were not hit, but one bomb smashed into a tanker in the centre of the convoy, the Danish-registered *Marie Maersk*, of 8271 tons, setting the bridge on fire and killing everyone there. *Coventry*, the senior ship, ordered *Waterhen* to do what she could. Commander Swain went in as close as he dared, rescued thirty-two survivors from the water, then called for volunteers to board the ship, still burning, to see if she could be saved. She was laden with fuel oil, perhaps the most precious cargo of all in the Mediterranean, worth more than diamonds.

Ten men put their hands up, including Lieutenant Colin Hill, an RANR officer from Sydney. A professional seaman since the age of seventeen, he had been second officer of the Canadian-Australia Line steamship *Niagara* on the Pacific route before the war, and knew his stuff. The *Marie Maersk*'s second engineer, a Mr Rasmussen, went with them, and Hill signalled back to *Waterhen* that they thought they could get the ship going again and into a port. It was a big call. The bridge island was still on fire, the deck plating had been buckled aft of the bridge and the oil in the tank was burning, giving off a pall of choking black smoke. The tanker could explode at any moment, blowing them all to kingdom come. But *Waterhen*'s men rigged firehoses, Rasmussen got the diesel engine working again and by 2100 hours they were heading for Suda Bay in Crete 150 kilometres away, the flames gradually being brought under control.

Then the steering broke down. Hill steered with the engines through the night while Able Seaman Ted Haydock of Maryborough in Victoria, a plumber in civilian life, battled with rope and wire to rig some hand-steering gear in the burned and buckled stern. It worked. Exhausted but elated, they brought the *Marie Maersk* into Suda at noon the next day with most of her cargo intact.

Colin Hill was awarded an MBE and Haydock and some of the others won a Mention in Despatches. 'I was only one of the party. Just as much credit must go to the lads who were with me,' Hill told the Sydney *Sun*.[28] In peacetime, their deed would have been plastered across the front pages. In wartime, the news made a couple of paragraphs in a few papers.

*Vendetta*, *Voyager* and *Vampire* did their share of the Greek convoys too, and met their share of the bombing. Remarkably, not a soldier was lost. When Operation Lustre ended in mid-April, some 68,000 men, including the Australian 6th Division, had been carried to Greece, where they were happily welcomed by the locals. The first units to arrive on the wharves in Piraeus were also greeted by a genial chap in pepper and salt tweeds who chatted affably with the officers in flawless English, enquiring politely who they were, what they were up to, and where they were going. It was the German military attaché, who had Scottish forbears.

As his divisions moved north, 'Jumbo' Wilson – 'tall, fat and cunning'[29] as Menzies described him – set himself up in Athens in the art nouveau splendour of the Acropole Hotel. The stage was set.

# CHAPTER 13

# DESTROYERS ATTACK!

Evermore frustrated by their Axis partner's failures, the Germans continued to prod the Italians to action. Hitler told a meeting of his service chiefs at the Berghof in the first week of January 1941 that it was vital for the outcome of the war that Italy should not collapse, and he was determined to do all in his power to prevent the loss of North Africa.

In mid-February Großadmiral Erich Raeder – not an ardent Nazi but certainly a German imperialist – met his Italian opposite number, Ammiraglio Arturo Riccardi, for two days at the picturesque alpine spa of Merano in the Italian Tyrol near the Austrian border. Leaving no room for misunderstanding, Raeder said he hoped to see aggressive operations from the Regia Marina very soon, stressing the importance of taking Malta. For his part, Riccardi was pessimistic and cautious. He argued that an Italian defeat would be disastrous for the Axis and advanced the strategy of a 'Fleet in Being' – that the mere existence of the Italian fleet, whether it put to sea or not, necessarily tied up a large part of Britain's naval resources. Moreover, the Regia Marina was critically short of fuel which, at the present rate of consumption, would run out in June. Perhaps the Germans could supply more.

Raeder's urgings had their intended effect. There was pressure too on Riccardi from his fleet commander, Iachino, who also favoured a more aggressive stance. After weeks of deliberation, on 16 March Riccardi – with some reluctance – gave orders for Operation Gaudo, a sweep by the fleet into the Mediterranean to interdict the British Operation Lustre convoys from Egypt to Greece. The force would be built around the fast and modern battleship *Vittorio Veneto*.

Supermarina then began the tortuous business of negotiating with the Regia Aeronautica and with Fliegerkorps X to provide air cover and reconnaissance. Unsurprisingly, the Germans were more efficient and more cooperative, with the Fliegerkorps commander, Hans Geisler, promising fighter cover above the fleet. The Aeronautica offered 'armed reconnaissance' from its Aegean Command, whatever that might mean.

The ships began to gather. As night fell on 26 March, *Vittorio Veneto* sailed south from the Bay of Naples, flying Iachino's flag and escorted by four destroyers. That same evening two light cruisers left Brindisi and three heavy cruisers, *Fiume*, *Pola* and *Zara*, sailed from Taranto. The next day, three more heavy cruisers, *Bolzano*, *Trento* and *Trieste*, headed from Messina to join the others. All told there were thirteen escorting destroyers. Operation Gaudo was underway. With luck and the element of surprise, they would wreak havoc upon the convoys.

—

A world away, other mills were grinding, and they were grinding exceeding small. Mavis Lever, the nineteen-year-old daughter of a London postal worker, had been at university studying the poets of the nineteenth-century German Romantic Movement when war broke out. The blitzkrieg violence of considerably less poetic Germans led her to quit her studies and volunteer for war work. In 1940 her language skills carried her to Bletchley Park, the spectacularly ugly Victorian mansion in the countryside north-west of London that was the top-secret headquarters of the Government Code and Cypher School, or GC&CS.

There, with other brilliant young women, Mavis worked as a codebreaker, trying to crack the Regia Marina 'Enigma' machine. On an evening shift in late March 1941, by random coincidence, curiosity and sheer intellectual firepower, she discovered a flaw in an Italian transmission which allowed her to penetrate its secrets and decipher a short, cryptic signal: 'Today is X-3.' This meant 'X minus 3'. It was dated 25 March. Intrigued, puzzled, she took it to her superiors who concluded it must be an advance notification of some major naval operation to come in three days' time, 28 March. But what operation, and where?

More of the bright young women of Bletchley were drafted in to work with Mavis around the clock, poring over every Italian Enigma signal, and in another couple of days they struck gold, platinum and diamonds. A long and detailed message from Commando Supremo to the Regia Aeronautica Aegean Air Command gave the order of battle of a fleet about to put to sea from three Italian harbours – the battleship *Vittorio Veneto*; six heavy cruisers; two light cruisers; and thirteen destroyers – under the command of Ammiraglio di Squadra Angelo Iachino. Better still, it gave the time and position for this fleet to rendezvous: at 0700 hours on 28 March, 30 kilometres south of the small island of Gaudo,[1] which itself lies about 50 kilometres south of Crete. Intelligence of this quality, accurate and immediate, was given the code name Ultra, for ultra-secret.

Only a handful of people got to see it – even Churchill's cabinet ministers had no idea it existed – but it did go to Commanders-in-Chief. The Admiralty swiftly conveyed this Ultra intelligence to Andrew Cunningham. Mavis Lever and Bletchley Park had delivered him a hand of aces.

—

At Alexandria, the Admiral laid his plans with care and a little theatrical subterfuge. He could not risk compromising Ultra. To take the fleet to sea and hotfoot it straight towards the Italian meeting point would be just too neat, too obvious, very likely arousing suspicion in the enemy that their codes had been cracked. There had to be a plausible discovery the Italians could recognise.

Cunningham requested air reconnaissance, and so it was that on the morning of 27 March a Sunderland flying boat from Malta just happened upon the heavy cruisers *Bolzano*, *Trento* and *Trieste* southeast of Sicily and heading towards Crete. The aircraft reported their course and speed back to Alexandria, although bad weather prevented it shadowing them. But it was enough: the Italians had seen the Sunderland and would know they had been found. Cunningham had his *casus belli*, a legitimate reason for putting to sea and heading in that direction. The ruse had worked, Ultra was safe. Iachino recognised that his hope for surprise was lost, but he decided to proceed anyway.

The British had some ships already waiting and available in the wings. The Vice Admiral Light Forces, Henry Pridham-Wippell, and his 7th Cruiser Squadron of *Orion*, *Ajax* and *Perth* were ordered to sail from Piraeus on the morning of 27 March to meet the cruiser *Gloucester* south of Crete the next day – X-day – and then to link up with the main fleet coming up from Alexandria. *Vendetta* was with the cruisers, one of the destroyer escorts.

In *Warspite*, Cunningham gave orders for his ships to sail that evening, enjoying himself in the afternoon with a neat little deception of which he was rather proud. Dressed in civvies and carrying a suitcase he went ashore as conspicuously as possible to let any onlookers – not least the ever-watchful Japanese consul – believe he was off to play golf and spend a quiet night out of his flagship. After dark, he slipped back on board and the fleet began the complex routine of putting to sea once more, to join with Pridham-Wippell's cruisers and to confront the Regia Marina. HMAS *Stuart* was among those to sail.

To Cunningham's displeasure, *Warspite* passed too close to a mudbank as she left, clogging her condensers and limiting her speed – and therefore the fleet – to 20 knots. But they steamed in good order to the north-west, relaxed at cruising stations, with two other battleships, *Barham* and *Valiant*, nine destroyers including *Stuart*, and a brand-new armoured aircraft carrier, HMS *Formidable*, which had just arrived in the Med via Suez to replace her sister ship, the damaged *Illustrious*. Both *Formidable* and *Valiant* had radar.

So it was, as X-Day dawned, the players were taking their places on the field for one of the great fleet actions of the Second World War, a bloody clash of men and steel that history would come to call the Battle of Matapan.[2]

—

It was a grand morning, with a glorious dawn of peach and pink heralding a sunlit day that set the calm sea sparkling. At 0600 hours both the Italians and the British launched reconnaissance aircraft.

HMAS *Waterhen* (RAN)

HMAS *Vendetta* (RAN)

HMAS *Vampire* (RAN)

HMAS *Voyager*
(AWM 065305)

Commanding Officer of HMAS *Stuart* Captain Hector Macdonald Laws 'Hec' Waller DSO RAN, on the bridge of the destroyer, December 1940. (AWM 005002/13)

Admiral Sir Andrew Cunningham GCB, KCB, DSO, the Royal Navy's Commander-in-Chief, Mediterranean (AWM P00433.001)

Signalman Ean McDonald
(private collection)

HMAS *Stuart* in
Grand Harbour,
Malta. The small
craft are *dghaisas*
or water taxis
(RAN)

HMS *Warspite*
entering Grand
Harbour, Malta
(Royal Navy)

Lieutenant Commander Rodney Rhoades (*left*), captain of *Vendetta*, with Hec Waller (RAN)

HMAS *Vendetta*, a heavy sea, with her gunnery officer secured by a lifeline (RAN)

The light cruiser HMAS *Sydney* (RAN)

Captain John Collins,
Commanding Officer of
*Sydney* (AWM 002447)

Able Seaman Terry Van Prooyen (*second from right*), one of the Danube
adventurers (family collection)

Captain Hec Waller on the
bridge. Note the typical Hec
touch of the non-uniform
sandals. (RAN)

Alexandria Harbour, circa 1939

HMAS *Vendetta* awaiting a convoy in Alexandria (RAN)

Commissioned Gunner John Endicott RN, the first man killed on an
Australian warship in the Second World War (AWM P02092.001)

Chief Petty Officer
(Gunners Mate)
Arthur Cooper (RAN)

Splinter damage to HMAS *Sydney*'s for'ard funnel after the battle of Cape Spada (RAN)

The Italian battleship *Vittorio Veneto*

Helping survivors from the Italian cruiser *Bartolomeo Colleoni* aboard following the battle off Cape Spada (AWM 002626)

HMAS *Stuart* at the Battle of Matapan (ART27623)

Admiral Angelo Iachino,
the Italian commander at the
Battle of Matapan (Alamy)

Gordon Hill (*right*) at
the Parthenon, Athens
(Naval Historical Society)

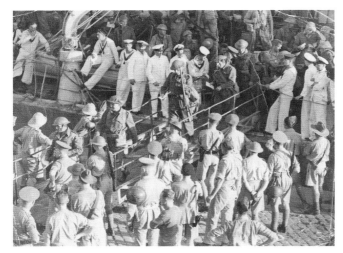

The evacuation from Crete (RAN)

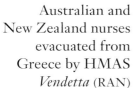

Australian and New Zealand nurses evacuated from Greece by HMAS *Vendetta* (RAN)

Mersa Matruh in Libya, 'a balm for body and soul' (AWM MEC1177)

HMAS *Parramatta* at Port Said (AWM ART26930)

Lieutenant Commander
Jefferson Walker, captain
of *Parramatta* (RAN)

Sister Street,
Alexandria, 1941
(Alamy)

A home from
home, the Fleet
Club (Royal Navy)

On leave in Cairo
(private collection)

*A Tribute to Ennio Tarantola*: Tarantola's Stuka wheels in to bomb
HMAS *Waterhen* (by kind permission of Ivan Berryman and Cranston Fine Arts)

Sergente Maggiore
Ennio Tarantola, the
Stuka pilot who sank
*Waterhen* (Alamy)

*Waterhen* takes water over her bow after being
crippled by German dive bombers off the
coast of Egypt, en route to Tobruk. She sank
the following day. (AWM P00034.001)

U-559, which sank HMAS *Parramatta*

Able Seaman Fred Tysoe,
a survivor of HMAS *Parramatta*
(Denmark WA Historical Society)

HMAS *Stuart* being used as a troop transport towards the end of the war,
with its A-gun removed (RAN)

Floatplanes catapulted from *Veneto* and a cruiser; Swordfish and the newer Albacore torpedo bombers lifted off from *Formidable*'s flight deck. The Fairey Albacore – inevitably christened the 'Apple Core' – had been designed to replace the old Stringbags, but it was not much of an improvement. Still a single-engined biplane, it carried a crew of three – pilot, observer and air gunner – in an enclosed cockpit, in which the heater notoriously toasted the pilot but left the gunner freezing in the rear. Its top speed was 259 km/h at a stretch, about 40 km/h faster than the Swordfish, but its controls were heavier which, to the discontent of the pilots, made it harder to fling around the sky. It was phased out in 1943, the Stringbag outlasting it.

Almost from this moment, early morning and long before a shot was fired, confusion and mischance began to play their inevitable part, bedevilling admirals and their staff on both sides trying to form a picture of the forces that opposed them.

The Italians had the better luck to start with. At 0630 hours their aircraft found Pridham-Wippell's cruisers heading south-east about 60 kilometres away. Iachino ordered three of his heavy cruisers to chase after them and followed on in his flagship.

*Formidable*'s aircraft spotted that cruiser trio – *Trieste*, *Trento* and *Bolzano* – not quite an hour later and reported their position, course and speed. But the position they gave was so close to the British cruisers' location that Pridham-Wippell assumed they had merely discovered him. He carried on unconcerned at a leisurely 18 knots, still heading towards the south of Crete to link up with Cunningham and the fleet later that morning as planned.

All hell broke loose at 0800 hours with sudden, shocking clarity. Each side spotted the other. A lookout on the bridge of *Orion*, Pridham-Wippell's flagship, reported the three Italians astern to the nor'east and closing fast. The flag hoist 'enemy in sight' whipped up *Orion*'s halyards. *Trieste* discovered the British at the same moment and the chase was on. Recognising that the Italian cruisers outgunned his own ships – 8-inch guns to his 6-inch – all Pridham-Wippell could do was to clap on full speed and run south-east, hoping to draw the enemy towards Cunningham and the battlefleet.

In *Perth*, in all four cruisers, the duty buglers blared action stations and the alarms rattled. Below in the engine rooms the telegraphs jangled and the stokers threw open the sprayers, feeding oil to the furnaces. *Perth* vibrated and shuddered as she worked up to 30 knots, her 72,000-shaft horsepower driving her four great bronze propellors deep, her stern almost lost in a curving, tumbling white wake. An enormous Australian flag broke out on her mainmast. Though the war was more than a year old it was the first time her people had sighted an enemy surface vessel, a thrilling, heart-stopping vision. *Orion* and *Ajax* bounded along in line ahead of her pell-mell, *Gloucester* – which had suffered some engine trouble – bringing up the rear. *Vendetta* and the other escorting destroyers raced to the fore like greyhounds unleashed.

The Italians opened fire at 0812 hours, at a range of about 20,000 metres. Up in *Perth*'s high angle director tower above the bridge, Bill Bracht, a young gunner's mate from Kurri Kurri in the New South Wales coalfields, heard the first shells:

> like a steam locomotive thundering past, and suddenly tall gouts
> of dirty yellow water shot skywards as shells landed in the sea only
> a few metres away.[3]

Yet the shooting was lamentable. The Italians' 8-inch guns had a theoretical range of 31,000 metres, but their rangefinders were old and not up to the task, and although they hammered away for three quarters of an hour they scored not a hit nor even a near miss. *Gloucester* was the only British ship to return fire, getting off three salvoes from her two after triple turrets, but they all fell short. Eventually Iachino suspected – correctly – that the British were trying to lead him into a trap, and at 0900 hours he called off the chase. The Italian cruisers turned back on their tracks, to the north-west. Pridham-Wippell then turned as well, to keep them in sight, shadowing them out of range. At about this time the exertion proved too much for *Vendetta*; she struck engine trouble and was sent back to Alexandria.

Well beyond the southern horizon, some 140 kilometres away, Cunningham in *Warspite* was in a fever to come to Pridham-Wippell's aid and get into the action, pacing the admiral's bridge. Though the flagship still had her condenser problems he ordered the fleet up to 22 knots, the best possible speed to be squeezed out of the elderly

*Barham.* He knew both from Ultra and by instinct and experience that an Italian battle fleet was at sea, but he did not yet know where. He ordered aircraft from *Formidable* to start searching and at 1000 hours six Albacores and two Fulmar fighters took to the air.

The picture was suddenly resolved just before 1100 hours, in a way so absurdly comical that it became part of the folklore of the fleet. On the bridge of *Orion*, Commander Ralph Fisher, the cruiser Squadron Operations Officer, was relaxing after the excitement of the first chase:

> It was sunny and the sea was void of enemy; the turret crews were sitting on the roof of their turrets, and action bully beef sandwiches arrived on the bridge. The Commander (T. C. Wynne) came on the bridge and, with his mouth full of sandwich, nudged me and said, 'What battleship is that over there on the starboard beam? I thought ours were miles to the east of us.'
>
> As I took my binoculars to examine a vessel hull down to the northward there was a whistling noise and the first salvo of 15-inch from the *Vittorio Veneto* landed somewhere around. We made a very hurried turn to the south ...[4]

Pridham-Wippell had sailed into Iachino's trap. He radioed three emergency signals:

'Make smoke by all available means.'

'Turn together to 180 degrees.'

'Proceed at your utmost speed.'

The four cruisers and the destroyers put their helms hard over and swung around, the engineers sending clouds of filthy black oil smoke roiling from the funnels. On *Perth*'s flag deck, Signalman Brian Sheedy – a baker's apprentice in Melbourne just two years before – held his binoculars at the ready:

> From the ship ahead of *Perth* – *Ajax* – I read the flag signal DB. As a signalman, many signals are committed to memory. This group was easy. The signal decoded was 'proceed independently'. In the vernacular, this meant 'Get to buggery out of it', or 'Every ship for itself'.

The four ships broke line ahead formation and each strove to out sprint the other. *Perth* pulled out of line to starboard and strove to overtake *Ajax*, drawing level with her. The destroyers were finding it hard to keep up with the cruisers. Speed and more speed. We were doing 34 knots with the quarterdeck sunk almost from sight as the ship's four propellors dug deep into the sea.

There was order here, too. For four ships in a straight line presented an Aunt Sally shooting gallery target. Proceeding independently presented four different ranges for the enemy range finders. *Perth*'s engines were actually making speed for 36 knots; the making of black smoke absorbed two knots of speed. It was a glorious sight all round: the colour, the noise, the flags streaming bar taut with the speed of our passage.

And so the race went on, the enemy trying to hit us, and we trying to escape. *Gloucester*, who was nearest the enemy, unhidden by smokescreen, received the full brunt, the three enemy cruisers bringing their concentrated fire to bear on her. Salvo after salvo of heavy shells crashed into the sea around her but she went on, not deviating from her course, it seemed to us observing her plight.[5]

Pridham-Wippell's ships were now in dire peril. A battleship was after them and the three big cruisers, *Trieste*, *Trento* and *Bolzano*, were coming back for them as well. They 'snaked the line', zigzagging rapidly and randomly to confuse the Italian gunners. Still well out of the action, Cunningham had heard *Orion*'s signals and realised that a battleship must have joined the chase. Seething with frustration, he ordered *Valiant* to go ahead to Pridham-Wippell's aid at her best speed.

A little after 1100 hours the balance changed decisively in favour of the British. The Albacores from *Formidable* found *Vittorio Veneto* and turned to attack. It was a struggle. The battleship was doing 30 knots away from them and the aircraft were battling into a 30-knot headwind and a ferocious anti-aircraft barrage, the air about them alive with tracer and thick with smoke. Straining to the utmost, it took more than 20 minutes for them to lumber into a position to launch their torpedoes. Out of nowhere two Luftwaffe Ju 88s jumped them as they wheeled in, but one was shot down in flames by a Fulmar and the other fled.

Not one of the six torpedoes struck *Veneto*, although they passed close astern. But it was enough for Admiral Iachino. He had not landed one hit on the British cruisers behind their smokescreen. Now, unmistakably, a British aircraft carrier was nearby and that very likely meant battleships as well. His prime objective of attacking the Operation Lustre convoys had been lost. Gathering up his skirts, dispirited, at 1140 hours he turned north-west and headed for home at top speed.

For Andrew Cunningham, endlessly pacing his bridge, this would not be good news. He was still some 130 kilometres away to the south, the fleet hauling on every bone and sinew in the chase, but he knew the Italian was faster and feared he could very well forge ahead, off and away from him by nightfall. His best hope – his only hope – was in the air. Shortly after midday, *Formidable* turned into the wind once more to fly off another torpedo strike force of three Albacores and two of the ever-reliable Swordfish, with another two Fulmars to watch over them. Throughout the afternoon, land-based Swordfish from Crete attacked Iachino's cruisers and two waves of RAF Blenheim bombers from Greece went for the flagship, all without luck.

As ever, the Regia Aeronautica was notable for its absence, although two Savoia M79 bombers did make an unsuccessful torpedo attack on *Formidable* in the early afternoon. Their action report, crawling up the long and tangled Italian chain of communications, took two hours to reach Iachino, by which time it was useless. It was the same old story.

'I felt pretty well deceived by the lack of cooperation,' the Admiral wrote after the war. 'We continued to remain for the rest of the day without any fighter cover.'[6]

The second strike force from the carrier sighted *Veneto* at 1510 hours, swooping out of the sun with the squadron commander, thirty-one-year-old Lieutenant Commander John Dalyell-Stead, in the lead. The two Fulmar fighters machine-gunned the battleship's upperworks to distract her gunners while the torpedo bombers made their run.

Determined, undaunted, Dalyell-Stead gallantly flew his Albacore low and dropped his torpedo ahead of *Veneto* at almost point-blank range, just as she began to heel over in an emergency turn to starboard.

Then he jinked off to the left and into a blizzard of machine-gun fire. The little aircraft shuddered, stalled, then plunged into the sea about 1000 metres away from his target. Dalyell-Stead, his observer and gunner were killed.

Their torpedo, though, ran straight and true. On *Veneto*, still turning to starboard, they watched in helpless horror as it streaked towards them. It exploded in the battleship's stern well below the waterline, damaging her two port screws and blasting open a hole that sent 4000 tons of water flooding in. She slumped to a halt, immobile for what must have seemed like an age but was in fact about ten minutes. Finally, her engineers managed to get her going again, gradually and gingerly working up to 19 knots, listing slightly to port. Iachino plugged along, flanked by his cruisers and destroyers, still heading for Taranto some 600 kilometres away.

As the afternoon drew on and with dusk approaching, Andrew Cunningham was struggling to gain a reliable plot of the action. Where exactly were the Italians, and where were they heading? The picture was fragmentary, contradictory. Reports from pilots and observers claimed hits that had never been made; others evidently confused destroyers for cruisers, cruisers for battleships, in positions widely varying. At 1735 hours he ordered another air strike. Six Albacores and two Swordfish left *Formidable*, to be joined by another two Swordfish from Crete. At 1745 hours the Commander-in-Chief catapulted his own observer from *Warspite*, an experienced lieutenant commander who knew his stuff. He reported, accurately, that *Vittorio Veneto* was 70 kilometres ahead of *Warspite* and making some 15 knots westward. A little later, the radar in Pridham-Wippell's flagship, *Orion*, – further ahead of the main fleet – detected the ships bringing up the Italian rear about 15 kilometres away. Slowly, surely, the British were closing in.

—

The sunset that evening was as brilliant as the dawn had been, an orange fireball settling over the port bow, night slowly drawing on in lovely shades of lilac and violet, then grey and finally a moonless black. The Albacores and Swordfish reached the Italians in the last rays of light, at about 1930 hours, flying through a withering anti-aircraft barrage into vast shrouds of funnel smoke and a new nocturnal addition – searchlights probing and piercing to blind the pilots. They pressed the attack home and, by some miracle, not one was harmed.

The last to go in was an Albacore flown by Sub Lieutenant Patrick Williams, a man of twenty-four who had been a police constable, a helmeted London Bobby, before the war. His torpedo was the only one that struck home, but it was the shot that turned the battle and for which he would be awarded the Distinguished Service Cross.

Back in *Warspite*, the Commander-in-Chief now had to decide how he would prosecute the battle that night. His instinct was to go after *Vittorio Veneto* come what may but some of his staff officers counselled caution, fearing an attack by the enemy's cruisers and destroyers might cripple some of the British ships in a confused night action and leave them helplessly exposed to dive-bombers in the morning. Cunningham was scornful, as the Fleet Gunnery Officer, Commander Geoffrey Barnard, related later:

> ABC took one look at his supposed helpers and said, 'You're a pack of yellow-livered skunks. I'll go and have my supper now and see after supper if my morale isn't higher than yours.'[7]

At around this time they received a report from *Formidable*'s Albacores that a ship had been torpedoed, but it was vague and nobody paid much attention to it. When Cunningham returned from dinner his course was clear, his mind resolved. He would continue the pursuit at night, come what may. At 2037 hours he ordered eight of his newest and fastest destroyers under Captain Philip Mack to go on ahead and attack the enemy with torpedoes. Mack hared off into the night, working up to 30 knots, leaving just four destroyers to screen the fleet. Jokingly referred to as 'the old, the halt, the maimed and the blind', they included *Stuart*. Fearing he would miss out on the action, Hec Waller watched, disappointed, as Mack vanished.

The torpedo dropped by Sub Lieutenant Williams had struck the heavy cruiser *Pola*, one of three stationed on *Vittorio Veneto*'s starboard flank, at 1945 hours. It hit amidships with devastating effect, flooding five boilers, damaging the main steam line and cutting off all electrical power. *Pola* slumped to a halt, never to move again. Inexplicably – astounding to this day – this news took half an hour to reach Admiral Iachino, still heading away at 19 knots, and when it did he dithered for another three quarters of an hour with a flurry of signals back and forth to the cruiser admiral, Carlo Cattaneo. Believing the pursuers were some 150 kilometres behind him, it was not until a little after 2100 hours that he ordered Cattaneo to take the cruisers *Fiume* and *Zara* and four destroyers to head back south-east to *Pola*'s aid. They set off at a leisurely 16 knots, to conserve fuel.

Now it was the turn of the British to succumb to some confusion. At 2014 hours, radar in Pridham-Wippell's *Orion* detected a large, unknown ship stopped dead in the water some 9 kilometres ahead. They had found the stricken *Pola*. But the admiral assumed that it was *Veneto* and, aware that Mack's destroyers had been tasked to handle her, he steamed on at full speed to tackle the rest of the Italian fleet as he been ordered to do. The error was understandable but unfortunate, for it would take him and his ships – including *Perth* – out of the battle. They played no further part.

Hoping that it might indeed be the Italian flagship, Cunningham shifted course a little to the west and at 2210 hours *Valiant*'s radar found their quarry. It was an Australian who got the first visual sighting: on *Stuart*'s bridge, out on the starboard wing and some distance ahead of *Warspite*, the Chief Yeoman, Frank Watkins, picked out an apparition in the night:

> I was keeping a very good lookout peering through the darkness, when suddenly right ahead of us loomed a shape which I reported to the Captain. I was ordered to make the night alarm which I lost no time in doing by W/T [wireless telegraphy]. I ran back to my position and this time picked up one – two, three – seven ships. There may have been more but I never had the time to count them. They were coming down fast from a position ahead to pass a mile or so on the port beam of the battleships.[8]

Watkins had spotted first the helpless *Pola*, then her sister ships *Fiume* and *Zara* and the four Italian destroyers crossing the bows of the fleet from starboard to port. Receiving *Stuart*'s report – startling, electrifying – Cunningham ordered *Formidable* out of the way and turned to starboard to put his battleships into line ahead on a parallel but opposing course to the enemy, opening up the 'A' arcs to bring all their guns to bear.

> I shall never forget the next few minutes. In the dead silence, a silence that could almost be felt, one heard only the voices of the gun control personnel putting the guns onto the new target. One heard the orders repeated in the director tower behind and above the bridge. Looking forward, one saw the turrets swing and steady when the 15-inch guns pointed at the enemy cruisers. Never in the whole of my life have I experienced a more thrilling moment than when I heard a calm voice from the director tower – 'Director Layer sees the target'; a sure sign that the guns were ready and that his finger was itching on the trigger. The enemy was at a range of no more than 3800 yards – point-blank.[9]

It was 2228 hours. The Gunnery Officer, Commander Barnard, gave the order to open fire. *Warspite*'s guns belched smoke and flame. High above *Valiant*'s bridge, nineteen-year-old Midshipman Philip Mountbatten, Prince of Greece, was operating the port searchlight:

> I reported that I had a target in sight, and was ordered to 'open shutter'. The beam lit up a stationary cruiser, but we were so close by then that the beam only lit up half the ship. At this point all hell broke loose, as all our eight 15-inch guns, plus those of the flagship and *Barham*'s started firing at the stationary cruiser, which disappeared in an explosion and a cloud of smoke. I was then ordered to 'train left' and lit up another Italian cruiser, which was given the same treatment.[10]

*Pola* had spotted the British in the night and, mistaking them for her rescuing cruisers, had actually fired a welcoming red flare. The searchlights and *Warspite*'s first salvo took the Italians utterly by surprise. In yet another baffling error of judgement, Admiral Cattaneo had kept his ships steaming placidly in line ahead – first *Zara*, then *Fiume*, then the destroyers in the rear – all with their guns unmanned and trained fore and aft, all as unwary and unsuspecting as if they were entering a friendly harbour. Elementary prudence would have had the destroyers scouting ahead and the crews closed up at action stations. But no one had seen a thing.

Frank Watkins had a grandstand view from *Stuart*'s bridge:

> The sky opened up, at least it seemed so, when first the *Warspite* and then *Valiant* followed by *Barham* fired with both their main armament of 15-inch and secondary armament of 6-inch guns. A moment after the *Warspite* fired, the leading cruiser burst into a mass of flames right from one end of the ship to the other.
>
> Then the second cruiser burst into flames as a salvo from either the *Barham* or *Valiant* caught her. By this time, a matter of seconds after the first gun, the air was full of noise, searchlights, tracers and spray. The destroyers *Greyhound* and *Griffin* who had been on their way to join us from the port side, and who would have been right in the way of the enemy had they remained in their old position, had opened up on the destroyers.
>
> Star shell were hovering in the sky and the tracers from Breda bullets twined a vivid line across the dark background …

Cunningham noted that five of *Warspite*'s first six shells hit home on *Fiume*.

> The plight of the Italian cruisers was indescribable. One saw whole turrets and masses of other heavy debris whirling through the air and splashing into the sea, and in a short time the ships themselves were nothing but glowing torches and on fire from stem to stern. The whole action lasted no more than a few minutes.

The devastation was complete, absolute, reminiscent of the days of fighting sail when wooden battleships battered each other to pieces at the range of a pistol shot. This, though, was one-sided. The Italians had no chance to man their own guns, no chance to hit back, no chance to escape. The cruisers were doomed. *Fiume* sank rapidly. *Zara* lived a little longer, burning fiercely, but she too would be gone before midnight. *Pola* endured a more protracted agony.

—

For most of that long, sunny day, *Stuart* had steamed placidly along with the battle fleet, one cog in a great and complex machine. All that changed with Frank Watkins's first sighting. The alarms shrilled for action stations, as the guns elevated and trained, as the torpedo tubes were swung through their arcs.

'Coxswain on the wheel, sir.'

'Torpedo tubes closed up and cleared away.'

'All boilers connected.'

'All guns closed up.'

*Stuart* was as ready as she could ever be and her men as keen, although for some it would be their first test in action. Most of the gun crews, some sixty of them, were reserve ordinary seamen fresh from Australia who had been in the ship just five weeks and had never seen a gun fired at night. The crew of B-gun had five new men who had come on board just two days before. They would have to measure up.

Midshipman Tony Synnot was one of the novices. The son of a Queensland grazier and a former student of Victoria's Geelong Grammar, he had followed his elder brother into the navy in March 1939 as a special entry cadet. The navy packed him off to the Royal Naval College in Britain for a nine-month crash course in how to become an officer, where one of his fellow cadets was the young Prince Philip.

Tony had joined *Stuart* in January, a few weeks after his nineteenth birthday. Now, a world away from the farm in Queensland, here was the marvel of a great fleet deployed before him: three great battleships splendid in their charcoal, grey and off-white camouflage; the mighty bulk of *Formidable* with her aircraft coming and going like bees at a hive; the bustling destroyers; and everywhere the splash of the White Ensign and the almost carnival gaiety of signal flags whipping up and down foremasts with every change of course or speed.

A mere midshipman – a 'snotty' – was about as likely to encounter a knighted admiral and Commander-in-Chief as he was to meet God. Tony Synnot was the lowest form of officer life, but in the coming months he would make his mark at the beginning of a long, glittering career.

The battleships' job done, Cunningham turned away to avert any possible torpedo assault from the Italian destroyers and ordered his own screening four – *Stuart*, *Havock*, *Greyhound* and *Griffin* – off the leash and into the fray with a simple, two-word signal: 'Destroyers attack.'

It was Hec Waller's moment. His entire career had been spent in preparation for this night, as if all the long years of honing his skills in times of slogging tedium or furious action had been but an overture to the main act. It would be fleet destroyer warfare in its purest form of cut and thrust and parry, improvised on the run, and he was the man for it, in his element. As Captain (D) of the 10th Flotilla he had the other three destroyers nominally under his orders but for now that was irrelevant. Their captains also knew the job at hand and would do it without any prompting.

'Starboard thirty.'

'Full ahead both.'

'Steer course two one oh.'

'Stand by to fire torpedoes!'

'Hard Over' Hec had the burning *Zara* in his sights. Back aft at the tubes, the Commissioned Torpedo Gunner, Frank 'Shorty' Ley, and his men waited as tense and taut as coiled springs.

'Turning to fire,' said the captain.

'Thirty degrees to go, sir.'

'Twenty degrees to go, sir.'

'Ten degrees to go, sir.'

'Fire one! Fire two! Fire three!'

The three torpedoes plunged into the sea, the men on the bridge watching their ruffling wakes heading away in the dark, 'Shorty' Ley counting the seconds before they should hit. Two struck their target, in distant muffled explosions. At the same time the Gunnery Officer, Rupert Robison, had lined up his five 4.7s and they began pumping salvoes into *Zara*, which fitfully but fruitlessly fired a few shells back.

*Stuart* wheeled again, this time to attack *Fiume* off to starboard.

'Shift target to cruiser bearing green six five!'

Three more torpedoes entered the water, the last they had, and more shells arced over the gap to strike with sharp yellow explosions. *Stuart*'s chronicle describes the fire and fury:

The snarl and snap, bark, bristle and rapid yap of a dog fight would be the best way to draw a parallel of the next fifteen minutes. Faint splashes in the darkness indicated enemy shells falling unpleasantly close; the flame and roar of our guns; a searchlight suddenly switched on to circle a moment and then, shut off, to leave the night blacker than before. (For one awful moment *Stuart* was centred in *Warspite*'s searchlight. 'Would *Stuart* be recognised?' She was.) The pallid light of slowly falling star shell, brief silhouette of an enemy frantically firing streams of coloured tracer bullets, phosphorescent wake, the *ting ting* of the fire goings and the shouts of the supply party sweating as they sent up ammunition for the insatiable guns ...[11]

Below in the steaming heat and roar of engine and boiler rooms, the stokers and artificers struggled to keep their feet as the ship lurched and twisted, their boots sliding on the greasy deck plates, hands clutching at hot oily rails, sometimes half-blinded by sweat.

'All sprayers!'

'More air!'

The pressure gauge needles hit their tops – 220, 230. The drainpipes shone copper red in the glow of the furnaces. Air from the fans pummelled the men's eardrums. Telegraphs kept up a constant jangle. Flakes of asbestos fluttered down from the lagged steampipes as the ship recoiled from the thump of her guns above.

At the chart table behind the bridge, the navigator, 'Whiskers' Teacher, juggled parallel rulers, dividers and pencils to keep track of every twist and turn.

Lieutenant Richard Chenevix-Trench, a Royal Navy officer who had joined *Stuart* a few weeks before also recorded what he had witnessed:

A shadow rose up and grew as it approached. Two voices said simultaneously, 'Enemy destroyer!' The shifting of the guns to this more urgent threat seemed intolerably slow. As the shadow loomed bigger, the leader [*Stuart*] turned to present her full broadside and to avoid a collision at a mutual speed of perhaps 50 knots.

For a few seconds, a man could be seen walking along the Italian's deck, guiding himself with a torch. Then, when she was right abeam, the momentary picture disappeared in a blinding orange flash as the leader's guns at last spoke. Armour piercing shell, bursting inside the enemy's bridge, silhouetted its disintegrating fragments and her stern began to burn fiercely. There was time for only one more broadside as the ships raced past each other, but the destroyer astern finished the work.[12]

That enemy ship was the destroyer *Giosuè Carducci*. Out of torpedoes, *Stuart* swept on, ordering *Havock* to sink her. On fire and foundering, her decks awash, *Giosuè Carducci* blew up and went down at 2330 hours.

From here, the battle became more confused, its moves more difficult to piece together, for in the aftermath everyone's account differed. What is certain is that the action waxed faster and more furious although at times it is very likely that foe was mistaken for friend and vice versa. Late in the night, *Stuart* believed she had been chased by an enemy cruiser – which could not have happened, because they had all been immobilised. Certainly, she found the wallowing *Pola* away from the main battle and fired more shells into her before turning to take on yet another destroyer, *Vittorio Alfieri*, which she hit several times as well. *Vittorio Alfieri*, badly wounded, fired a couple of torpedoes back at *Stuart* but missed and eventually rolled over to sink a little before midnight. Two of the four Italian destroyers managed to get away.

Just after 2300 hours, Andrew Cunningham decided to regroup and made a general signal: all forces not engaged in sinking the enemy withdraw north-east. He conceded later that this was a mistake, for it had the effect of calling Pridham-Wippell off his chase for the Italian main force. Hec Waller's four destroyers reluctantly obeyed, each of them still unscathed by the fight. When he went off watch that night, Ean McDonald, the signalman from Perth, tired but elated, wrote his mother a letter which was eventually published in the *West Australian* newspaper:

The time is somewhere around 2 am ... I've just come down from the bridge ... The night is now still, we might be on a Sunday night river trip.

An hour or so ago it was different, so terribly, gloriously different. Even now in the distance we see specks of light, mute witnesses to the fact that men over there are fighting for their lives, fighting flames.

For over that last hour or so we have taken part in one of those glorious spectacles that only occur once or twice in a lifetime and are only viewed by the chosen few – a night action between two fleets at sea ...[13]

Well after midnight, Captain Mack's eight destroyers came dashing back from the north-west and *Jervis* went to finish off the wretched *Pola*.

It was a miserable, squalid business. In the glare of the searchlights they could see panic-stricken men jumping off *Pola*'s stern. Someone had hung out what looked like a white sheet as a flag of surrender and an unsecured turret door was banging open and closed in the slight swell. When *Jervis* went alongside and put some men aboard, they found a tableau of horror: a fire still burning on the quarterdeck, some of the cruiser's crew lying about drunk and insensible amid a litter of empty bottles and rubbish, others naked and weeping, scores wounded in varying degrees. The destroyers took on board as many survivors as they could, some from the water, some from the ship herself, 237 men in all. *Jervis* put two torpedoes into her and *Pola* exploded and sank just after 0400 hours.

The battle was over.

—

That next morning, 29 March, dawned fine and clear and calm. With the fleet together again, Cunningham steamed back to the scene of the action to find the sea thick with stinking fuel oil and littered with bodies, rafts, boats and wreckage; the detritus of death. The living floated among hundreds of corpses already bloated and disfigured; the wounded crying for help.

The destroyers set about rescuing them but were interrupted by a pair of Luftwaffe Ju 88s who flew low to bomb *Formidable* but succeeded only in killing more Italians in the water. That was enough for the Commander-in-Chief. His ships had rescued 905 men. That would do. He ordered a course for Alexandria, taking time to signal Supermarina, in clear English, the position of the battle and a guarantee that any rescue ships would have free passage. They thanked him for it. An Italian hospital ship reached the scene two days later but could find only another 160 men.

It was a stunning British victory and Italy's worst ever defeat at sea, although not the Nelsonian annihilation Cunningham had hoped for. *Vittorio Veneto* had gotten away, which Cunningham lamented, but three cruisers and two destroyers had been sunk with 2300 Italians killed, including the cruiser admiral, Carlo Cattaneo. The British fleet was unscathed and had lost but three men, the crew of Dalyell-Stead's *Albacore*.

The effect on Italian morale was profound, pervading. *Zara*, *Fiume* and *Pola* had been the pride of the fleet, of the nation. As Italian car designers had created the world's most beautiful automobiles pre-war – Alfa-Romeo, Bugatti, Lancia, Isotta Fraschini – so the naval architects had built ships that were a unique fusion of power and elegance and famed for it. There was grief in cities and towns and villages throughout Italy at their destruction and the loss of the men who had served in them. And never again would Mussolini's navy put to sea in any strength to challenge the British hold on the Mediterranean.

Eleven years later, in 1952, a man walking on a beach at Cagliari in Sardinia found a bottle lying in the sand, encrusted with weed and barnacles but sealed. Curious, he broke it open and discovered inside a torn and faded piece of canvas on which someone had scrawled a crude message:

*R. Nave Fiume – Prego signori date mie notizie alla mia cara mamma io muoio per la Patria. Marinaio Chirico Francesco da Futani, via Eremiti 1, Salerno. Grazie signori – Italia!*
Royal Ship Fiume. Please gentlemen give my dear mother the news that I am dying for the homeland. Seaman Chirico Francesco from Futani, Via Eremiti 1, Salerno. Thank you gentlemen – Italy!

The bottle had floated 1500 kilometres westwards from the battle. Its discovery caused a national sensation. The naval authorities indeed found Francesco's widowed mother at Futani, a hilltop country hamlet in southern Italy, and presented her with a posthumous bronze medal for military valour. And they named the main street after him, Via Chirico.

—

Hec Waller had good reason to be pleased with his ship's company and the old lady herself. They had stood the test, not least the new arrivals who amused the old lags by asking if every night in the Mediterranean was like that one.

There was no time, though, to rest on the oars. On the day after the battle, in the forenoon, *Stuart* was despatched to Piraeus with *Hereward* and *Griffin* to escort a convoy back to Alexandria. They were joined on the journey home by the smart new light cruiser HMS *Bonaventure*. On yet another of those dark and moonless nights, 31 March, about halfway between Crete and Alexandria, the watch on *Stuart*'s bridge heard two heavy explosions. *Bonaventure* had taken two torpedoes from an Italian submarine, full square amidships, and she began sinking immediately.

Hec Waller ordered *Hereward* to pick up survivors and *Griffin* to continue with the convoy while he put *Stuart* into an Asdic search for the sub. It was a feisty battle. They got a quick contact and depth-charged it seven times, narrowly avoiding – by sheer luck – a torpedo from the submarine which exploded 50 yards astern. At one stage the boat surfaced, to be met by a quick blast of gunfire, but she crash-dived again and, although Hec thought he had a kill, the post-war records show she escaped. The destroyers rescued 310 survivors but 139 were lost. *Bonaventure* had been in the Med not quite three months.

It was a heavy loss of a valuable ship. In the coming months, there would be many more.

# CHAPTER 14

# ONLY THE NAVY COULD SUSTAIN THEM

Victors write the history. It was Cunningham who named the battle Matapan, and it was big news back in Australia, a pleasing naval accompaniment to the diggers' victories in the Libyan desert. Newspapers offered their readers elaborate and sometimes highly creative accounts and charts of the battle. Hec Waller was briefly interviewed by a correspondent from the Australian Associated Press:

> 'The behaviour of all concerned was excellent. They were absolutely marvellous,' said Captain Waller today. 'A large proportion of the ship's company were reserve ratings who had only recently joined the ship; indeed, some of them only joined on the day of sailing.'[1]

After a couple of weeks, reassuring letters home from some of *Stuart*'s sailors made their way into print. Bernard Davis, a telegraphist, wrote to his mother at Carlisle in Perth:

> What an action it was. It was plain hell while it lasted. We were right in the thick of it. There were shells flying about all over the place. You could see the shells boring their way through the steel like an emery wheel in a shower of sparks, before they exploded inside.

Our captain was splendid, and thank God for guiding his hand that night for we certainly were in a hot spot.

I was going to cable to tell you that I was all right but I thought perhaps the sight of the telegraph boy at the door might be a shock knowing that we were in action.[2]

Twenty-year-old Ordinary Seaman Les Eldridge of Henley in South Australia was one of *Stuart*'s new boys, fresh from his training at Cerberus.

A Dago destroyer loomed up suddenly across our bows. It was point-blank range, and our guns opened fire without sighting through their telescopes. The result was as before: in fact, Bradman had nothing on this, for the upper structure and bridge just went for a six clean over the fence, putting its guns out of action before she could fire on us …

The boys are now highly delighted and satisfied at having done something to better *Sydney*'s results, and at last, having been recognised for having done distinguished service in the war.[3]

Privately, Andrew Cunningham disagreed with some of *Stuart*'s account of her exploits, believing she had indeed mistaken a friendly destroyer for an enemy cruiser at one stage. But there was no doubting the result and he wrote later, with dry good humour, of '*Stuart*'s wild night'. It was certainly that.

—

Others were also putting pen to paper. Every night when he was away, unfailingly, Generalleutnant Erwin Rommel wrote to his wife Lucie at their home in Wiener Neustadt, south of Vienna. On 3 April 1941, from his caravan headquarters in Libya, he had good news:

Dearest Lu,
We have been attacking since the 31st with dazzling success. The staff people in Tripoli, Rome and possibly Berlin will be astonished. I have dared to proceed against earlier orders and instructions because I saw an opportunity. In the end they will

give their approval and I am sure that anyone would have done the same in my place. The first objective, planned for the end of May, has been reached. The British are on the run.

... our losses are unusually light. It has so far been quite impossible to take stock of the material we have captured. As you may imagine, I cannot sleep for joy.[4]

Rommel was not exaggerating. The withdrawal of the Australian army's battle-hardened 6th Division and other troops from North Africa for the campaign in Greece had all the makings of a strategic disaster for the Allies, which he had recognised and seized upon. Ambitious and energetic, as eager for the laurels of victory as any general of ancient Rome, he saw that the way back east lay open for him, as far as Egypt if he dared. Nominally under the command of the Italian governor-general in Libya, Italo Gariboldi, Rommel had ignored his orders counselling caution and begun a drive that in a few months would see his Afrika Korps recapture almost all the territory gained by the Allies since Christmas.

On that night of 3 April his first reconnaissance units entered and took back Benghazi from where, despite a shortage of fuel, they headed further east both along the coast and inland towards Tobruk. The British and the newly arrived, ill-equipped and barely trained Australian 9th Division retreated – 'retired' was the word – before the German advance. They had been almost entirely unprepared, for General Wavell had German Ultra intelligence telling him the Afrika Korps would not move until at least May. He could not have guessed that Rommel would jump the gun. Berlin was equally surprised.

Each day brought a new German advance, a new Allied reverse. On 6 April the two senior British commanders in the field, Lieutenant Generals Sir Philip Neame and Sir Richard O'Connor, were captured in their car when first Neame and then his driver got lost and took a wrong turn during an inspection tour at the front near Derna. Two days later, the ineffectual Major General Michael Gambier-Parry surrendered the remnants of his 2nd Armoured Division to the Italians and was also taken prisoner with 3000 of his men, 100 Australians among them. When Rommel arrived at the scene he souvenired a pair of big British desert goggles and fixed them above the visor of his cap. The image of *der Wüstenfuchs*, the Desert Fox, would be care-fully cultivated.

Exultant at these early successes, the Afrika Korps rolled on down the highway the troops had begun calling the Rommelbahn, a blitzkrieg in the desert. Hoping to stem the rout, Wavell flew from Cairo into Tobruk where the 9th Division was digging in to take a stand, along with tanks, armoured cars and field guns of the British 3rd Armoured Brigade, some 25,000 men in all. There he met the two Australian commanders, both lieutenant generals: the volatile John Lavarack and the newly promoted Leslie Morshead, known to his diggers of the 9th Division as 'Ming the Merciless'. Tobruk must be held at all costs, Wavell told them. The port was critical. Without it, Rommel could not land the supplies of men, munitions and fuel he needed to sustain his advance towards Egypt. On 10 April, Morshead issued an order to his men:

> There will be no Dunkirk here. If we have to get out we will fight our way out. There is to be no surrender and no retreat.[5]

That same day, Rommel made his first attempt to take Tobruk, ordering his 15th Panzer Division under the aristocratic General Heinrich von Prittwitz und Gaffron to attack from the west. It failed and Prittwitz was killed in a direct hit on his car by an anti-tank gunner of the Australian 2/28th Battalion. Unexpectedly repulsed, Rommel returned to the attack again the next day, 11 April, Good Friday. Three times the German wave broke upon the rock of Tobruk that day and three times the rock held. And it continued to hold. The long, long siege had begun, the defenders with their backs to the sea. Only the navy could sustain them. Andrew Cunningham assured the army it could be done and would be done.

———

If North Africa was building to an Allied disaster, Greece in those first weeks of April was descending into catastrophe. Whatever might be the political imperative for Britain to send an army to support the Greeks against the Axis, as military strategy it was an act of culpable folly. The blame lay entirely with Winston Churchill. His heroic

reputation in history as the inspirational saviour of the Free World
conceals the uncomfortable truth that his strategic judgement was
often fatally flawed and foolish. As it had been in 1915 at Gallipoli.

In the Balkans, Churchill hoped that a victorious British presence
in Greece would be the springboard for a grand alliance of Greece,
Yugoslavia and Turkey to make war on Germany, a fantasy so prepos-
terous that it now seems laughable. The Turks and Greeks had loathed
each other for centuries and the Yugoslavs – Serbs and Croats – were
chiefly intent on fighting each other. Few, though, had the courage to
challenge Churchill. Andrew Cunningham frequently did, privately
confiding to his diary:

> What a drag on the wheel of war this man is. Everything is cen-
> tralised in him with consequent indecision and waste of time
> before anything can be done.[6]

But the military decision to go to Greece belonged to Wavell and
the army and, for all his patrician aloofness and often against his
better judgement, Wavell bent to Churchill's will.

Hitler's urge to fight in the Mediterranean, in both Greece
and Africa, had been inflamed by – of all things – a coup d'état in
Yugoslavia in late March that ousted the pro-Nazi government of
the Regent, Prince Paul. The next morning Belgrade had been hung
with British flags, there was rejoicing in the streets and crowds spat
upon the car of the German ambassador. Furious at this perfidy, the
Führer ordered Hermann Göring to send in the Luftwaffe. At OKW,
the Oberkommando der Wehrmacht, they burned the midnight oil
to recast Operation Marita, the invasion of Greece, to encompass
Yugoslavia as well. Belgrade would be obliterated. On 6 April, the
Luftwaffe unleashed three days of airborne savagery that would kill
some 17,000 civilians there; that same day the German ambassador in
Athens informed the government of the Hellenes that the Reich had
declared war, even as the Wehrmacht was rolling across the Greek
border from Bulgaria. It was Palm Sunday of the Greek Orthodox
calendar.

And so the rout began. The British and Commonwealth commanders admired the undoubted courage of the Greeks but were

staggered by the state of their army; its soldiers sparsely equipped with ancient weapons and tattered uniforms, often reliant on wheelbarrows, ox carts and donkeys for transport. One Greek battalion's only tactic was to roll boulders onto German tanks as they passed through a valley below. The language barrier made cooperation difficult at best, impossible at worst, and the Greek 2nd Army, near the important port of Salonika, surrendered in three days. Australia's General Blamey had been correct: the Germans did indeed have as many divisions as the Greek roads could carry and they employed them with implacable efficiency.

In the air, the Luftwaffe had 800 aircraft it could hurl into the battle, the RAF just eighty. On the night of the invasion, 6 April, a Ju 88 bomber, piloted by Hauptmann Hans-Joachim 'Hajo' Hermann, an ardent Nazi and a protégé of Hermann Göring, dropped a single bomb over Piraeus Harbour and changed the face of the campaign. It hit a fully laden ammunition ship, the *Clan Fraser*, touching off first a fire and then an explosion that literally wrecked the port, rendering it useless. Twelve other ships either caught fire or blew up as well. The blast was so immense that the Parthenon, 24 kilometres away, was silhouetted by the flames. Hundreds of civilians were killed. HMAS *Perth* might have been destroyed too, for she had been berthed next to the *Clan Fraser* until the day before, when her captain prudently decided he'd be safer moored to a buoy in the outer harbour and moved the ship away.

On the ground, the German divisions surged south, ever onwards, making light of the primitive roads, making prisoners of units that had been cut off or somehow left behind. Fresh from the sun and sandstorms of the African desert, the Australians and New Zealanders found themselves in northern Greece defending narrow, winding tracks on snowy razored mountains and deep defiles. There was no warm clothing, not enough blankets. Most of the Australian boys from the cities or the bush had never seen snow before and they shivered in the cold. The conditions would have tested even seasoned alpine troops.

The only course for the Allies was withdrawal, retreat. 'Jumbo' Wilson and his subordinate generals drew lines on maps here and there and commanded that stands be made and positions held and rearguard actions fought. It was largely in vain, although there was the occasional Allied success. On one night of sometimes hand-to-hand fighting in a snowstorm, the Australians captured troops who turned out to be from the Leibstandarte SS Adolf Hitler, the supposedly Aryan supermen of the Führer's elite SS bodyguard regiment.

In London, at Easter, the Australian prime minister had been enjoying himself immensely, accepting honorary doctorates, making speeches, lunching and wining and dining with the famous and the fabulous. Sunday, the Duke and Duchess of Kent; Monday, Lord Astor; Tuesday, Noël Coward. After Matapan everything had seemed so promising, but as the news came in from both Libya and Greece, Menzies was confronted by the awful fact that the cream of the Australian army was in deep peril on two fronts. He attended a meeting of Churchill's War Cabinet in its underground Whitehall bunker on 14 April, Easter Monday, and came away deeply disturbed, noting acidly in his diary:

> Wavell and the Admiralty have failed us. The Cabinet is deplorable – dumb men most of whom disagree with Winston but none of whom dare to say so. This state of affairs is most dangerous. The Chiefs of Staff are without exception Yes Men, and a politician runs the services. Winston is a dictator: he cannot be overruled, and his colleagues fear him. The people have set him up as something little less than God, and his power is therefore terrific.[7]

Despite growing disquiet at home over his absence, Menzies resolved to stay on in Britain to insist on preparations to evacuate the 6th Division from Greece if the worst came to the worst. The next day, 15 April, Wavell, Cunningham and the RAF Air Officer Commanding in the Middle East, Air Chief Marshal Sir Arthur Longmore,[8] met on board *Warspite* in Alexandria. It must have been a grim occasion, for that day they decided that Greece was lost. The Allied forces would have to be brought out, the Greeks abandoned to their fate. Ever the realist, Cunningham was ready. His staff had been planning an evacuation even as the troops were still arriving in Greece in the Lustre convoys. Without waiting for approval from London he sent one of his flag officers and a personal friend,

Rear Admiral Tom Baillie-Grohman, to Athens to get things started on the ground. It was a fortunate choice, not least for the Australians. As a commander in the lean times of the mid-1920s, Baillie-Grohman had spent two years in Melbourne as Assistant Chief of the Australian Naval Staff.

The evacuation was code named Operation Demon, to begin on 28 April.

—

There was no mistaking the hospital ships. *Vita* and *Devonshire*, both converted passenger liners, were painted white with bold red crosses on their hulls and upperworks. At Tobruk they were a welcome sight. On the Easter Monday morning they made their way through the gate and into the harbour to secure alongside a wharf, where khaki-clad clumps of men, some of them walking wounded, some on stretchers, were waiting with grumbling resignation, as soldiers do, to be loaded on board for the journey back to Alexandria.

Inevitably there was an air raid – Luftwaffe dive-bombers screaming in from the horizon – but there were no hits. The harbour was still littered with wrecks, including the hulk of *San Giorgio* and the bomb-blasted Italian troopship *Liguria*, and the masts or funnels of smaller vessels protruded from the slop. The town itself, or what you could see from the harbour, had a forlorn and defeated air to it, pockmarked with ruined buildings and bomb craters. Dark plumes of oily smoke rose on the horizon; the irregular thump of the guns of the British Royal Horse Artillery firing at the enemy. That very day, Corporal John Edmondson of the army's 2/17th Battalion died of wounds he had received in a bloody bayonet action out on the perimeter wire. He would be awarded the first Australian Victoria Cross of the war.

*Waterhen* and *Vendetta* were already in port, their crews nervy and close to exhaustion. They had been based at Tobruk for ten days to bolster the harbour's anti-aircraft defences with the Breda machine guns souvenired back when the Italians had been on the run, and the men had nearly had it. The two ships spent the daylight hours with steam on their engines, swinging on their buoys to fire on swarms of bombers in raid after raid, both Stukas and the bigger Ju 88s. It never seemed to end, a seamless torment of fire and fury. There would be a brief lull to snatch a cigarette, a hasty bully beef sandwich or a quick kip if you could, and then the air raid red alarm would sound and it would be on once more, the gunners and the watch on the bridge struggling again into their tin helmets and the sweaty anti-flash hoods. On the best day, the quietest day, there were six separate attacks. On the worst they counted sixteen from dawn until dusk, some aimed at the harbour, some at the airfield. Sometimes RAF Hurricane fighters would appear out of the blue and an enemy bomber or two would be shot down. There should have been rest and relief at night for the men, some calm for aching minds and bodies, but there was none of it, no letting up; as evening fell both destroyers would leave the harbour and patrol out to sea until sunrise the next morning.

Her human cargo embarked, *Vita* put to sea at 1630 hours. She was barely out of the swept channel and only a few kilometres off the coast when she was jumped by dive-bombers, perhaps eight or ten of them, an attack that can only have been in deliberate defiance of the Geneva Convention. The day was clear and the white paint and the red crosses of a hospital ship must have been obvious to any pilot or bomb aimer.

'The bastards just kept diving and dropping their bombs,' wrote Alan Whetton, an able seaman in *Vendetta*. 'This is the lowest thing I have ever witnessed.'[9]

Hurricanes arrived and destroyed three of the attackers and no bomb struck *Vita* herself, but she was an old ship and one near miss was enough. She lurched onto her beam like a piece of driftwood in surf, opening hull plates below the waterline, flooding her engine room and bringing her, powerless, to a dangerous, listing halt.

Both *Vendetta* and *Waterhen* went to her aid, *Vendetta* circling with her Asdic *pinging* on a submarine search while Commander Swain manoeuvred the old Chook to take *Vita* in tow to a nearby coastal anchorage. Night was beginning to fall. For a few hours the little destroyer hauled the bigger ship in her wake at walking pace, but eventually the line snapped a couple of times and *Vita* was wallowing ever lower in the water. After midnight Swain decided to abandon the tow and to take her people off. He ordered the hospital ship to anchor and then, with consummate seamanship on a black night, he eased *Waterhen* alongside and began the extraordinary task of transferring

her patients and crew onto his decks. Happily the sea was calm but it
was still a daunting exercise for, disabled though she was, *Vita* towered
over the destroyer like a cliff. Many of the patients could move unaided,
but there were also men heavily bandaged, some of them amputees in
pain, who had to be lifted and lowered with the most tender care.
Their cries in the night were piteous. With no electric power in the
hospital ship much of the transfer was done by the flickering light
of candles and the beams of *Waterhen*'s signal projectors and main
searchlight aft. It took almost two hours but by 0150 hours on 15 April
*Waterhen* had embarked 432 wounded soldiers, six doctors, six nurses
and thirty sick berth attendants, in effect trebling the size of her crew.
The worst cases were gingerly taken below to the seamen's messes but
most were simply crammed into every available space on the upper
decks. Stoker Andy Nation wrote:

> They were stacked about two high all over the ship. It was the most
> murderous thing I have seen, they are proper swines, those Huns.
> We left immediately for Alex and got there twenty hours later.
> The ship was a shambles, they were nearly all sick and half were
> three parts dead. They were all mostly Aussies. We had nothing
> to feed them on other than bully beef and biscuits. As soon as they
> chewed that they brought it up again. I have never been so glad to
> see Alex in all my life … it was two o'clock in the morning by the
> time we had got them all off.[10]

*Vita* was saved and refitted once more as a hospital ship. She would
encounter the RAN again a year later.

Off Derna the next day, *Vendetta* stalked and then fired on a big,
three-masted Italian schooner full of ammunition, touching off an
explosion so tremendous that the onlookers on deck were knocked
flat by the blast, much to everyone's amusement. Two days later, after
she had been cleaned, *Waterhen* was back at sea again with *Stuart* and
*Voyager* to support a commando landing at Bardia.[11] For the Scrap
Iron Flotilla, the war in North Africa would loom ever larger in the
weeks to come.

—

In Athens, Admiral Baillie-Grohman hit the ground running. With Piraeus Harbour destroyed he had to find beaches, coves, bays – anywhere – that the troops could be assembled for evacuation, and he despatched search parties to discover them. He signalled Cunningham asking him to send a core of officers, sailors and signalmen who could manage the operation on the beaches, which was done. The Germans continued to sweep south, the situation becoming more desperate for the Allies with each passing hour: the Greek government was preparing to surrender and the prime minister, Alexandros Koryzis, had left a cabinet meeting, put a pistol to his head and blown his brains out.

With 'Jumbo' Wilson, Baillie-Grohman drove north from Athens to Thebes, an inland city in central Greece, to confer with Blamey. Thebes was already besieged by the enemy, the sky glowing red from the light of burning buildings. At a midnight meeting beneath a group of plane trees, with maps and charts spread out before them, the three agreed that the start of the evacuation would have to be moved forward from 28 to 24 April. Blamey would somehow have to get his divisions south over the single road and railway bridge across the Corinth Canal to the Peloponnese, the peninsula which hangs off mainland Greece like an apple from a branch.

This was fraught with peril. The Luftwaffe had seized mastery of the air. The aerial spearpoint of its bombers and fighters was Fliegerkorps VIII, commanded by the extravagantly named General der Flieger Wolfram Karl Ludwig Moritz Hermann Freiherr von Richthofen, a cousin of the famed First World War fighter ace Manfred von Richthofen, the Red Baron. This new Richthofen, a man regarded even by his own officers as ice-cold and ruthless, had led the infamous attack on Guernica in the Spanish Civil War in 1937. He knew his business. On Easter Sunday over Greece, a squadron of his Me 109s shot down six RAF Blenheim bombers, one by one. Two days later, they destroyed sixteen more Blenheims and fourteen priceless Hurricanes caught on the ground. His Fliegerkorps swept on, bombing and strafing all in its path.

Tom Blamey brought the Australians and New Zealanders together under his command, renaming them the Anzac Corps with what he hoped would be an inspiring message:

the reunion of the Australian and New Zealand divisions gives all ranks the greatest uplift. The task ahead, though difficult, is not nearly so desperate as that which our fathers faced in April twenty-six years ago. We go to it together with stout hearts and certainty of success.[12]

It was an odd moment to remind everyone of the defeat at Gallipoli, but the retreat continued. At last out of the mountain snows, thousands of weary men wound south along narrow, dusty roads lined by olive groves and cypresses, some marching, others in trucks, jeeps and Bren-gun carriers, the Luftwaffe harrying them endlessly. At times they would stop to fight a rearguard action, or to blow up bridges in their rear. Panic-stricken Greek refugees frequently blocked the way. With luck, the soldiers could conceal themselves beneath the olive trees by day to snatch some sleep and food and move on again in the dark of night.

Others had to stay put. Doctors and fifty female nurses of the 2/5th Australian General Hospital had arrived in Greece from Palestine on 12 April. Molly Nalder, a nurse from Greenwich in Sydney, aged twenty-six and with the army rank of lieutenant, was among the brave:

Our hospital had been hastily set up within two days in a pine forest in Ekali, a holiday resort north of Athens. We had tents, mostly with palliasses [straw mattresses] on the floor and our equipment was very scarce. Badly wounded arrived day and night, starting two days after we landed, and although we displayed red crosses on our tents we were constantly buzzed by German aircraft.

I had a ward of wounded men, 'minimal' equipment, a phial of morphine tablets and a hypodermic syringe. I was told to do the dressings, give morphia as required, and mark on the patient's head what they had, and when, and then – when possible – they were to be evacuated.[13]

At Alexandria, with the euphoria of Matapan long faded, Andrew Cunningham faced a near impossible dilemma of meeting three urgent, competing duties. He had to attack Rommel's supply lines across the Mediterranean; he had to sustain the beleaguered garrison at Tobruk; and he had to find the ships to bring back the army from Greece – with the evacuation suddenly brought forward by four days. For the moment, Greece took priority. His staff began rounding up whatever vessels they could find, from landing craft to troopships, cargo vessels and converted liners, to the cruisers and destroyers of the fleet itself. Operation Demon would pick the men off the beaches in Greece and carry them the 200 kilometres across open sea to Suda Bay on Crete's northern shore, where the fleet had established a fuelling base. The Vice Admiral Light Forces, Henry Pridham-Wippell, would be in charge of despatching the ships to Greece when and where Baillie-Grohman required them. It sounded simple, straightforward. In fact it was tortuously complex, with infinite possibilities for error and disaster. And what if the Italian fleet recovered from its humiliation at Matapan and entered the fray again? That was the stuff of nightmares. *Warspite* and the battlefleet, including the carrier *Formidable*, could not leave Alexandria without their anti-submarine screen of destroyers, all of which would be engaged in the rescue. To his chagrin, the Commander-in-Chief would have to remain ashore.

—

By 23 April, the RAF had ceased to exist in Greece. That afternoon the Luftwaffe destroyed another thirteen Hurricanes on the ground. The remaining few were ordered away to Crete. In very much less than their finest hour, the senior RAF commanders quietly flew themselves to safety as well, leaving their mechanics and other ground staff behind to fend for themselves under the command of junior officers who were engineers or administrators with no military experience. Some could barely load a rifle.

Again, Baillie-Grohman had to reshape his plans. The sky belonged to the Germans. With no hope of Allied air cover over the beaches, the embarkation would have to be done under cover of darkness. He and Pridham-Wippell decided that the rescue ships should arrive at the beaches one hour after dark and leave again no later than three the next morning, to give them time to get away from the Greek coast unobserved.

Still the retreat went on. On that same day, 23 April, the doctors and nurses of the 2/5th hospital were at last ordered to leave in a convoy of trucks that would take them through Athens and then across the Corinth Canal to the Peloponnese and the small port of Nafplion. A good many of them – including the nurses – refused to go, protesting that they would stay with their patients, but the women were told that General Blamey had specifically ordered them to leave. A group of British and Kiwi nurses joined the group, 160 women in all, Molly Nalder among them. She was horrified at the thought of abandoning the men:

> Having to leave wounded men, knowing they were to be taken prisoner, and not knowing how they would be treated was one of the most dreadful moments of my life.¹⁴

Nobly, eight doctors did stay behind, led by Major Brooke Moore, a surgeon from Bathurst in New South Wales; they would spend four years in German prisoner of war camps.¹⁵

The trucks were under the command of a senior doctor, Charles McDonald, a surgeon from Sydney who, after the war, would build a stellar medical career, become Chancellor of the University of Sydney and a knight of the realm. In 1941, a mere lieutenant colonel with no combat experience, he shepherded his charges on a perilous journey to the coast:

> Again and again we were blocked on this dreadful road. Dead horses and mules machine-gunned by the Hun during the day, upturned trucks and large bomb craters made our passage slow and hazardous ...
>
> ... a lorry behind us containing NZ nurses overturned and some were injured. No sooner had this happened than Boche bombers came over and machine-gunned behind them. It was during this raid that our nurses got out of their trucks and hid in a field of barley. At 9 am on the 24th there was a violent air raid on the aerodrome near us and on bodies of escaping soldiers who were around us. Later I ordered the nurses into a cemetery, and each time the bombers came over they crouched

behind the tombstones and in the ditches beside the grave mounds ...

... I did my best to keep the nurses cheerful, but they were wonderful. I think they can stand up to bombs and shrapnel better than the men.[16]

Exhausted, they reached Nafplion in the eastern Peloponnese at 2130 hours that night. Told to bring only what they could carry, they left the trucks and were guided to the docks by a young army officer who led them to a battered caique, a local fishing boat. Surely this ancient tub could not be their transport across the Mediterranean.

—

*Voyager* crept into Nafplion that night like a cautious cat in a dark alley. It was eerie, the glow of two big fires ashore lighting the faces of the men on deck and streaking the black waters of the little harbour a bloody red. Able Seaman Terry Harris, a Tasmanian, stood on the bow – in the chains, it was called – heaving a line and lead to gauge the depth beneath the ship, a skill as old as sailing itself but rarely employed in the twentieth century. The charts of Nafplion – of all the evacuation points, in fact – were primitive at best and Commander Morrow was taking no chances.

'By the mark, three!'

That meant a depth of three fathoms or about 5.5 metres. Getting uncomfortably shallow.

'Full astern both!'

The ship backed away, but a strong current swept her stern around to the shore again, and it took smart work with rudder and engines to bring her out into deeper water where it was safe to anchor. One ship had already run aground there that evening. HMS *Ulster Prince*, a former Irish Sea ferry, touched the bottom alongside the little dock and remained wedged there.

It had been a tough journey from Suda, in company with *Ulster Prince*, *Stuart*, the corvette *Hyacinth*, the cruiser *Phoebe*, and one of the big new infantry landing ships, HMS *Glenearn*. That afternoon *Voyager* had an Asdic contact and dropped three patterns of depth charges, but with no luck. Later, one of two attacking dive-bombers hit *Glenearn*, starting a fire on her fo'c'sle and stopping her for a while until she regathered and battled on.

At Nafplion there was no time to waste. Landing craft, ships' boats, Greek caiques – anything that floated – began ferrying troops back and forth from the beach. An old caique pulled alongside *Voyager*, the moment described by Ordinary Seaman Cyril 'Spider' Webb, aged twenty-six from North Richmond in Melbourne:

> When the big Greek boat came alongside we saw it was packed with troops, still encumbered with their packs, respirators and steel helmets. Willing hands leaned over to help the tired troops aboard. As each stepped onto *Voyager* there was a quiet 'thank you'. I got a bit puzzled. I took a closer look at these troops and was amazed to see the face of one of our beloved Aussie girls. I turned to our gunner [Mr Edmonstone] standing nearby and whispered: 'Look, sir. They're women!'[17]

With a light swell running and the caique lurching uncertainly, a British nurse lost her footing and fell with a scream into the dark water. It was 'Spider' Webb who dived in after her, a brave move, for if the two hulls had bumped together the pair could have been crushed. Other *Voyager* sailors did their best to fend the caique off with their legs and feet while a line was thrown to them and they were hauled on board.

*Voyager* took on all 160 nurses that night, with another 141 Australian soldiers. The First Lieutenant, Bill Cook, did his best to cram them all in:

> It was an amazing night – girls were everywhere, in the wardroom and the officers' cabins, and the overflow in the chiefs' and P/O's messes. After seeing they had been fed and settled down, I went into the wardroom to find a NZ nurse still awake. She said she couldn't sleep, so I reminded her what day it was. At 1 am on the 25th of April, Anzac Day, I opened the wine cupboard and gave her a small nip of whisky in celebration.[18]

The ships were well clear of the coast by daybreak, heading back to Suda. On his inspection round in the morning, Cook was amused to find the crew freshly bathed and shaved, hair carefully slicked down, smartly turned out in clean, pressed overalls or uniforms with best white caps, all chatting up the nurses. There was a party atmosphere on the upper deck, with the cooks outdoing themselves to turn on a buffet breakfast, the fun hardly spoiled when a pair of Ju 88s came over:

> The nurses and soldiers scattered from under the gun muzzles as we opened fire. Steel-helmeted womenfolk urged the gun crews on: 'A little lower! That nearly got him!' The soldiers who had mounted two Bren guns on the deck also opened fire. The Brens and other weapons on the other ships also opened fire as the planes dived into the attack. Some hits must have been scored as the planes wobbled and dodged, let go eight bombs and sped off. The bombs missed ahead.[19]

There were no more alarms, and the convoy reached Suda safely that afternoon. By Pridham-Wippell's count, more than 6600 men and women were rescued from Nafplion that Anzac Day, an astonishing total. The *Ulster Prince*, though, could not be moved and she was bombed to a flaming hulk the next day.

—

Low on fuel and with little available at Suda, *Voyager* was sent back to Alexandria and assigned to join *Vampire* on the Tobruk run again, leaving *Stuart*, *Waterhen* and *Vendetta* to their roles in Operation Demon. There would be four more days of an existential battle on the sea against a rampant enemy in the air.

On the night of 25 April, *Waterhen* and *Vendetta* were among ships collecting more men from the beach and boats at Megara to the west of Athens. On their way back they endured three heavy dive-bombing attacks but no hits, and another 6000 troops were duly delivered to safety. The next evening *Stuart* took on board 600 men she happened upon in a landing craft at Tolon and delivered them a few kilometres up the coast to *Orion* at Nafplion, before going back for more. The young midshipman, Tony Synnot, a long way from Geelong Grammar, made trip after trip in *Stuart*'s motorboat from ship to beach to pick up men wading into the water. *Stuart* then returned safely to Suda in company with *Perth*, which was also loaded with men.

By day, the soldiers were dispersed into hillsides or villages or groves of trees to conceal them from the air. It worked surprisingly well. Behind them lay the detritus of a beaten army, dumps of abandoned equipment. Trucks had their tyres slashed with bayonets and the radiators bashed in with rifle butts, the sumps drained of oil, engines left to run red hot. Most men behaved well. Some did not. An RNVR lieutenant commanding a landing craft saw some panicky Australians trampling wounded men into the water in their haste to get on board. When he shouted at them through a megaphone to stop he was abused and threatened and a rifle bullet whistled past his ear.[20]

But for all the apparent confusion, the two admirals, Baillie-Grohman onshore and Pridham-Wippell at sea in *Orion*, had got the evacuation down to a fine art, a masterpiece of tactical coordination and cooperation in which the left hand knew exactly what the right hand was doing. The beachmasters – naval officers – directed the embarkations with the help of a couple of petty officers and a signalman or two.

Yet fate and folly would play havoc with the plans of admirals. That same night at Nafplion, a big Dutch liner, the SS *Slamat*, was at anchor loading Australians, more and more of them arriving by boat and landing craft. The clear instructions to her master, Captain Tjalling Luidinga, were to sail at the safety hour of 0300 hours come what may. But despite increasingly testy signals from the cruiser *Calcutta*, he refused to move and kept taking on more troops. Eventually, *Calcutta* and another troopship, the *Khedive Ismail*, left without him, with a destroyer escort of *Isis*, *Hotspur* and *Diamond* also filled with soldiers.

The *Slamat* eventually got away at 0415 hours, with perhaps 500 men on board, sailing at her best speed. It was too late, fatally too late. As she neared the *Calcutta* convoy just before 0700 hours, the Stukas came diving in, followed by Me 109s and Me 110s to strafe with machine gun and cannon fire. Two bombs struck the *Slamat*, destroying her bridge and wheelhouse and all who were there and starting fires which flamed out of control from stem to stern. A few boats got away and men were seen jumping into the sea from her upper deck, some with their clothes burning.

From this moment, chaos and disaster piled upon each other, the sea strewn with ships, the skies swarming with the enemy. *Vendetta*, *Waterhen* and the destroyer HMS *Wryneck*, one of their chummy ships from the 10th Flotilla, had been sent from Suda early that morning to do what they could. The two Australians collected another convoy in the vicinity and headed back home, to be bombed twice in raids which set another troopship, the *Costa Rica*, slowly foundering. Her passengers from the 2/1st Australian Machine Gun Battalion were picked from the water by the destroyers.

*Diamond* torpedoed and sank the burning *Slamat* and then, with *Wryneck*, began to collect survivors, hundreds of them. But the Stukas found them that afternoon and both destroyers were bombed and sunk, with more than a thousand men killed, including some 500 Australians, the two destroyer captains, and the *Slamat*'s master.

—

Confusion, incompetence and tragic bad judgement brought on another failure at Kalamata in the southern Peloponnese on the last night of the evacuation, 28 April. There were about 7000 men waiting there, mostly New Zealanders, Australians and British but with some Yugoslav refugees and Palestinian Jews, all under the command of a British artillery officer, Brigadier Leonard Parrington. A small advance force of Germans – a company from the 5th Panzer Division – was pressing towards them.

Parrington – starchy, pessimistic and incompetent – bungled his outer defences and, despite some spirited fighting from the Kiwis, the naval beachmaster, Captain Clark-Hall, and his signalman were captured. This was a bad blow. There was now no experienced naval officer ashore to contact ships arriving for an evacuation and to supervise the embarkation, an accident of war that would contribute directly to the coming failure.

That night, a strong force of two cruisers and six destroyers from Suda approached Kalamata under the command of Captain Sir Philip Bowyer-Smith in *Perth*. An RN officer and hereditary baronet, Bowyer-Smith was well liked by his Australian crew and judged by them to be a good and competent captain, but on this night he called it badly wrong.

When he was about 15 kilometres offshore he sent the destroyer *Hero* to assess the situation. Amid a tangle of confused signals – some of which were delayed by wireless trouble in *Hero* – and with some big explosions seen on shore, Bowyer-Smith eventually decided that the Germans had taken control of the beach and that the evacuation could not go ahead. He ordered his force to turn around and withdraw at 28 knots. They sped away into the night, back towards Suda. Later, in his defence, he would say he was concerned that his ships would be silhouetted by the fires on shore in a hazardous tactical position if there was an attack by the Italian fleet: Taranto was just twelve hours away. This made no sense and Andrew Cunningham, with arch understatement, would later call it 'unfortunate'.

Brigadier Parrington announced to his officers that he would surrender to the Germans the next day, 29 April. They protested, convinced that they could hold out and wait for another evacuation attempt, but he was adamant. A fool to the end, Parrington paraded his troops on the Kalamata beach in the morning, where the Luftwaffe – unaware of the surrender – bombed and killed 200 of them. The rest of the 7000 were taken captive, save for a couple of hundred who escaped along the coast and were picked up over the next two nights by searching destroyers.

—

Tom Baillie-Grohman left Greece early in the morning of 29 April from a little jetty at Monemvasia in the south-eastern Peloponnese where four destroyers and the cruiser *Ajax* had come to collect him and 4000 men of the 6th New Zealand Brigade. A man of considerable style, while he waited he cracked a bottle of champagne he had carried all the way from Athens and shared it with his officers. It was 0300 hours when he climbed up *Ajax*'s scrambling nets with the Kiwi Major General Bernard Freyberg, the last senior army officer in Greece. They were safely back in Suda in time for lunch.

Baillie-Grohman had reason to be satisfied. He and Pridham-Wippell had done what they had been asked to do, to conjure order out of chaos, and they had done it magnificently. For all its flaws and failures, Operation Demon had brought 50,000 men out of Greece, far more than anyone had expected or even hoped for. The price, though, had been high. Some 10,000 men had been captured by the Germans, 2030 of them Australians, and the loss in ships and sailors had been grievous.

A merciful grace had been the failure of the Regia Marina to come out. Evidently the Italians were still binding their wounds after Matapan, but if their battlefleet had crossed the Aegean and descended on the Demon convoys there would have been precious little Andrew Cunningham could have done to stop them.

# CHAPTER 15

# THE DISASTER OF CRETE

The tiredness was the worst thing, that gnawing lack of sleep that sapped both mind and body for days and nights on end. The bombing was certainly more frightening but at least you could do something about that by conning the ship out of harm's way, by shooting back and even, occasionally, by bringing one of the enemy plummeting into the sea. Tiredness, weariness, exhaustion were unrelenting, though, and the only remedy, a long undisturbed sleep, was rarely available. Men off watch who had curled up in the heat and fug of the mess decks to snatch some rest would be lucky if they managed to steal a couple of hours before the alarms woke them again.

It afflicted the captains most heavily, for they carried the ship. Their standing orders invariably required them to be called, day or night, to deal with anything sudden or unexpected or even a little out of the ordinary, from an air attack to a smudge of smoke on the horizon. When they were getting some time in their bunks most had a sixth sense of the passage and the conduct of the ship. The smallest change, like a sudden rumble of the steering gear or a surge in the engine revolutions, would snap them awake even before the inevitable call down the voice pipe of 'Captain to the bridge'.

The Tobruk run was the most enervating of all for there was rarely an hour free of the enemy's attention, night or day. The course from Alexandria to Tobruk, 570 kilometres, ran in a more or less straight line westwards along the coast, the second half of it well within the range of the Fliegerkorps X squadrons that had been transferred to

North Africa. With the withdrawal from Greece completed and the month of May beginning, the five Scrap Iron destroyers were assigned again to the Inshore Squadron to carry supplies to the garrison and to bring away their wounded, a shuttle service back and forth. It had to be done at best speed, with the unloading at Tobruk well after dark and often into the next morning. The sailors called it the 'Spud Run', or sometimes the 'Tobruk Ferry'.

At first they sailed singly. *Voyager* and then *Waterhen* made the first trips, on 5 and 6 May. Long lines of Egyptian labourers would load the ship in Alexandria under the searching eye of the 'Jimmy', the First Lieutenant, who would somehow find space on the upper deck for cases of ammunition and detonators; medical supplies; bags of potatoes, onions, cabbages and bananas; boxes of tinned meat and fruit and sacks of mail; anything else that a besieged garrison might require. It had to be done systematically so as not to disturb the ship's trim, to leave room for the gunners and torpedomen and depth charge hands to operate their weapons, and to make unloading as swift as possible at the other end. Often there would be soldiers to carry as well, men going into Tobruk as replacements, who would be brought on last with their kitbags and rifles and told to squat where they could.

Loading done, the routine was to be 'out the gate' before 0800 hours, slipping west into the Mediterranean at 25 knots or so. The first couple of hours would be relatively quiet save, perhaps, for the occasional appearance of the annoyingly well-informed Lord Haw-Haw on Berlin Radio:

> Calling HMAS *Voyager*. We know you'll be off Bardia at 1600 and in Tobruk at midnight. If our bombers don't get you this afternoon then our gunners will get you tonight.[1]

Ean McDonald, one of *Stuart*'s signalmen, succinctly described the outward journey:

> There was little danger till late afternoon but then we would come within range of the German Stuka dive-bomber airfields in Libya. From about 1600 until dark we could expect to be under attack

from masses of Stukas that would be almost right on schedule. From that moment we would clap on all speed and dash for Tobruk.

For an hour or two we played a game of dodging the Stukas in their terrifying dives towards us, whilst shooting them down if we could. Darkness would relieve us to complete our dash to Tobruk. Almost as we arrived the long-range German guns beyond the perimeter could open up. Over would come their shells with high whines and frightening explosions ... they had intricate maps of Tobruk and knew of our whereabouts to a few yards. They knew of our time of arrival within a few minutes, even on pitch-dark nights. We were sitting shots on moonlight nights ...[2]

They came to call the last leg of the run 'Bomb Alley'. It was ever a relief to get through it shaken but unscratched for the entrance to Tobruk itself, just before midnight. The captain and the navigator would be on the bridge, peering through their night glasses, searching for a faint and distant pinprick of blue light that would be their only welcome to the harbour.

'There it is, sir.'

'Very well, pilot. Take her in ...'

This too was hazardous, for there was always the chance of a new and uncharted wreck lying in the harbour, unseen in the dark. There was a naval staff on shore to plot all that and to deal with the berthing and unloading and scheduling, in charge of the Senior Naval Officer Inshore Squadron, an RN captain named Albert Poland, and a good job they did, but nothing was ever certain, ever foolproof.

The ship would secure alongside a wharf if one was available, but more often it would be dropping an anchor to wait for a stream of tugs and lighters to come alongside in the dark. Mess tables would be rigged as makeshift chutes for the boxes and bundles to slide down to the waiting soldiers, again with the Jimmy in charge. With practice they got it down to a fine art, done very quickly, although with no little shouting and swearing.

Next would come loading whatever had to be taken out. There would be bags of mail from the garrison to go home, some soldiers going out on leave and the wounded – always the wounded – to be loaded on with infinite care. It varied, but there might be 200 soldiers and more. The smell could be overpowering: the sour stench of men in filthy, torn or bloody uniforms, of men who had not had a bath for weeks, of men whose wounds and dressings had an eye-watering hospital odour. The stretcher cases would be taken down to the mess decks for the ship's doctor and the sick berth attendants to do what they could. On the upper deck the diggers – the 'Swotties', the sailors called them – would at last relax, grateful for the mugs of kye and biscuits passed around from the galley. Some were cheerful, others silent and brooding. 'Thank God for the Navy,' they would say sometimes.

'Ship ready for sea, sir.'

'Main engines ready.'

'Very good. Cox'n ring on the engines. Fo'c'sle heave in …'

It was essential to be away well before first light while, hopefully, the Luftwaffe was still asleep. Out of the channel and into the Med proper and it was up to 27 knots again for the run back down Bomb Alley, heading towards the hint of a glow rising in the east.

'Course oh-nine-five. Officer of the Watch, all yours …'

'Aye aye, sir.'

With luck there would be a couple of hours' kip for the captain before dawn action stations and the return of the bombers. The next stop would be not Alexandria but the small anchorage of Mersa Matruh, about halfway down the coast across the Libyan border into Egypt, still in Allied hands. There was a rail terminal there where the soldiers could be put on trains for Alexandria and still more supplies taken on for another trip back to Tobruk.

Mersa Matruh was balm for body and soul; almost paradise. It had been a holiday resort before the war, renowned for its beaches of gleaming white sand, and with the unloading done there was an eager wait for that most welcome pipe of all – hands to bathe! The men would be overboard in the water in a flash, frolicking like kids, among them Les Clifford from *Stuart*:

We were berthed only a few feet from the sandy foreshore and the water was crystal clear. We could see some soldiers bathing from the white sandy beach a few yards astern of us. The June day was terrifically hot and very soon most of the ship's companies were bathing …

... During the afternoon shore leave was granted and we took a stroll through the 'town'. Wrecked buildings greeted us everywhere, in fact there was not one structure undamaged ...

... We had been informed by the soldiers – Australian and British – that it was customary at about 4 am for a few Nazi planes to carry out a nuisance raid on Mersa Matruh. We saw one of these raids the following morning. Almost on the hour we heard the humming of aircraft engines and bombs whistled down a few seconds later. AA guns went into action but the target for the Nazis was not in our vicinity and they were just wasting their bombs on unimportant wrecked buildings.[3]

Then it would be back to business, loading more supplies for a return to Tobruk to repeat the process, and the next day back to Alexandria for an all-night leave.

When the ferry began the ships did it singly, but *Vendetta*'s CO, Rodney 'Dusty' Rhoades, had a better idea:

After a number of these 'solo' runs, it appeared to me that it was time we did the run in pairs, so as to be able to give one another support when attacked and in the event of one ship being hit, her consort could pick up survivors.

I pondered this idea for a while and one morning I went to see the Chief Staff Officer to the Rear Admiral (Alexandria), who ran the port and gave us our sailing orders for work on the coast. I explained the situation to him and then heard a voice from over a partition say, 'When you have finished tearing up my Chief of Staff, come in and see me.' 'Who is that?' I said sotto voce. 'The Admiral,' the Chief of Staff replied.

Well, in I went and he asked me who I was. I told him and repeated my plea to work the run in pairs. He said, 'Are you frightened?' and I said, 'My bloody oath I am at times, sir.' He laughed heartily, shook hands and said, 'I will go and see the Commander-in-Chief.' This he did forthwith and from that day on we worked in pairs.[4]

In another of his sneering broadcasts, Lord Haw-Haw proclaimed that the diggers of Tobruk had been 'caught like rats in a trap'. They would live like rats and die like rats, he scoffed. The Australians rather enjoyed that and so the 'Rats of Tobruk' entered the nation's history. They were sustained in their ordeal by courage, by the leadership of General Morshead and by the ships which brought them succour.

—

For the Royal Navy, that month of May 1941 would be one of the most bitter in its long history. In the Atlantic, the battlecruiser HMS *Hood* was sunk by the German battleship *Bismarck*, with only three men surviving from the 1418 on board. Vengeance came when the *Bismarck* was destroyed three days later, but *Hood* had been the pride of the fleet and the nation, and the speed of her loss – she sank in just three minutes – was almost inconceivable.

It was the Mediterranean where disaster fell most heavily. Flushed by his victory in Greece, Hitler determined that he would take Crete and the Allied forces that had regrouped there. On 25 April, at his headquarters in Berlin, he issued Führer Directive No. 28 for Operation Merkur, built around an airborne invasion.

The Luftwaffe would employ Richthofen's Fliegerkorps VIII in air cover and attack; Generaloberst Kurt Student's Fliegerkorps XI of some 600 transport aircraft, gliders and paratroops would land on the airfield at Maleme in the north of Crete. Student was keen to prove the worth of his paratroops, the Fallschirmjäger. There would then be a seaborne assault by some 6000 infantry troops carried in fleets of caiques. D-Day was set for 17 May, but later changed to 20 May.

There were some 40,000 Commonwealth troops on Crete, under the command of Bernard Freyberg.[5] The British knew the plans for Merkur down to the last syllable. Bletchley Park was reading the Luftwaffe Enigma messages almost in real time and on 13 May first Cunningham in Alexandria and then Freyberg were sent Ultra intelligence laying it out in detail: dates, times, units engaged, targets, the lot. The Commander-in-Chief sent his ships to sea, uncomfortably aware that they were low on anti-aircraft ammunition and that they would be almost entirely without air cover. Constant pleas for more RAF aircraft in the Middle East had continued to fall on unreceptive ears in London, where they were concentrating on the bombing campaign over Germany. On Crete there were exactly three RAF Hurricanes, their pilots overworked and exhausted, and the carrier *Formidable* had only four serviceable aircraft.

There was one glimmer of light. The Mediterranean Fleet had at last been reinforced by another battleship, HMS *Queen Elizabeth* – a sister ship to *Warspite* – and two cruisers, *Naiad* and *Fiji*. More destroyers had joined as well, including HMAS *Nizam* and HMAS *Napier*, modern ships owned by the British but commissioned into the RAN and crewed by Australians, handsome vessels so new that their paint was still fresh. At 2500 tons full load, armed with six 4.7-inch guns and no fewer than twelve torpedo tubes, with a top speed of 36 knots and a crew of 225, they could lord it over the old crocks. Many of their people who had previously served in the Scrap Iron destroyers found these new ships almost luxurious.

Merkur began exactly as planned on 20 May, the skies over the Maleme airfield dark and thunderous with Student's Ju 52 transports dropping his paratroopers in their hundreds upon hundreds. It was a bloody massacre, the New Zealand defenders shooting them as they floated to earth or struggled to untangle themselves from their parachutes on the ground. Cretan peasants attacked them too, with shotguns, pitchforks and shovels. One battalion lost 400 of its 600 men, and for most of that day and into the night the Germans were facing a crushing defeat, until the Kiwis made a small but disastrous mistake. Inexplicably, they abandoned a strategic hill overlooking the Maleme runway. The Germans seized it and thereby gained control of the airfield, allowing their troop transport aircraft to land in swelling numbers. From that moment the tide of battle turned against the Allies.

Initially, there was some success at sea. Cunningham had again decided, reluctantly, that he should command from ashore. He deployed the fleet with his customary skill, in four separate groups, and on the night of 21 May, to the north of Crete, a force of cruisers and destroyers massacred a German troop convoy of small steamships and caiques. Contemporary estimates assumed that some 4000 men were killed or drowned, although post-war records suggest the total was probably less than half that. The next morning HMAS *Perth* destroyed another caique filled with troops, only to be set upon by aircraft that bombed her and strafed her with machine guns. The attack punched a few holes in her hull and brought down the wireless aerials and signal halliards in a tangle of cables and ropes but caused no casualties.

Inevitably the strength of the Luftwaffe prevailed, wreaking havoc. At sea, ship after ship succumbed to what seemed to be an unending onslaught of Stukas and Ju 88s. The toll was appalling. Within twelve hours the cruisers *Gloucester* and *Fiji* and the destroyers *Greyhound* and *Juno* were sunk, with nearly 1000 sailors killed. *Greyhound* alone lost seventy-six men, with another dozen more killed when two Me 109s strafed them in the water. Three more cruisers, *Ajax*, *Naiad* and *Carlisle*, and the battleships *Warspite* and *Valiant* were damaged by bomb blasts or hits. *Carlisle*'s captain died too. The body of *Gloucester*'s captain, Henry Rowley, was washed ashore at Mersa Matruh a month later, identifiable only by his uniform jacket.

More was to come. On the morning of 23 May, the destroyers *Kelly*, *Kashmir* and *Kipling* were attacked by twenty-four dive-bombers south of Crete. *Kashmir* sank within two minutes and *Kelly*, steaming at 30 knots under full helm, was hit by a single bomb so devastating that she capsized while still moving. She floated upside down for half an hour while the survivors clustered around her with their captain, Lord Louis Mountbatten, were machine-gunned by fighters. *Kipling* rescued 279 men, including Mountbatten, in the teeth of still more bombing attacks. She ran out of fuel before she reached Alexandria and had to be towed into the harbour. On 26 May, the carrier *Formidable* was badly hit by two Stukas, one bomb passing right through her flight deck and killing twelve men. Another bomb blew the stern off the accompanying destroyer *Nubian*, with fifteen dead.

—

Ashore on Crete, the end was nigh. In days of bloody fighting, the Germans had seized mastery of the island. That same day, 26 May, just six days after the German landings, General Freyberg signalled that his men had reached the limit of their endurance. Winston Churchill, evidently ignoring the reports from his commanders in the field, fired off another of his stirring exhortations to General Wavell: 'Victory in Crete essential at this turning point of the war. Keep hurling in all you can.'

At Alexandria, the loss of men and ships weighed heavily. It was evermore clear that the battle for Crete was yet another disaster, a word Cunningham himself used in his despatches. Events were moving quickly. Again that same day the Admiral met Wavell, Blamey, the new RAF Commander-in-Chief, Air Chief Marshal Arthur Tedder, and the visiting New Zealand prime minister, Peter Fraser, on board *Warspite*. They had before them a unanimous recommendation from the joint planning staff in Cairo that the army on Crete should surrender: if the battle had been a disaster, a retreat from the island could be worse, far worse. Wavell, gloomily pessimistic, feared any attempt to evacuate the soldiers would mean the loss of the fleet, prompting from Cunningham the remark that would echo in history:

> It has always been the duty of the Navy to take the Army overseas to battle and, if the Army fail, to bring them back again. If we now break with that tradition, ever afterwards when soldiers go overseas they will tend to look over their shoulders instead of relying on the Navy. You have said, General, that it will take three years to build a new fleet. I will tell you that it will take three hundred years to build a new tradition. If, gentlemen, you now order the Army in Crete to surrender, the fleet will still go there to bring off the Marines.[6]

His staff began to allocate the ships for the evacuation as best they could, unsure of how many men would be where and when. Wavell sent a message to Churchill that the end was near and the Chiefs of Staff in London replied that, 'You should evacuate Crete forthwith.' Freyberg's forces began a bloody, fighting retreat over the mountainous spine of the island to the iron-bound southern coast.

It began on 28 May, first from the little harbour at Heraklion on the north coast of Crete where some 4000 soldiers were waiting in the night, including the Australian 2/4th Battalion, whose medical officer, Captain Paul Tomlinson, described the wreck of war:

Heraklion was one large stench of decomposing dead, debris from destroyed dwelling places, roads were wet and running from burst water pipes, hungry dogs were scavenging among the dead. There was a stench of sulphur, smouldering fires and pollution of broken sewers ...[7]

Six destroyers nosed one by one into the jetty to bring the men out to the cruisers *Dido* and *Orion* and by 0320 hours the next morning they had begun the return to Alexandria. They were heavily attacked on the way home not long after dawn and the carnage began. Two destroyers were lost. *Dido* suffered a direct hit on B-turret with forty-seven sailors dead and 103 out of 240 soldiers of the Black Watch killed. *Orion* was battered into little more than a floating wreck by successive waves of Stukas that set her on fire and killed her captain and 261 men, 155 of them soldiers she had embarked. Her bridge wrecked, conned from the after control position, *Orion* hobbled on and made it back to Alexandria almost out of fuel, blackened and still smouldering, her decks strewn with corpses. The Commander-in-Chief was there to greet them:

I shall never forget the sight of those ships coming up harbour, the guns of their fore-turrets awry, one or two broken off and pointing forlornly skyward, the upper decks crowded with troops and the marks of their ordeal only too plainly visible ... [*Orion*] was a terrible sight and the mess decks a ghastly shambles.[8]

*Stuart* and the two new Australian destroyers, *Nizam* and *Napier*, took part in the evacuation trips. Ever the lucky ship, *Stuart* survived unscathed, but the other two were damaged, *Nizam* only lightly. *Napier*, on her way back to Alexandria, was attacked by twelve planes on the morning of 31 May, two sticks each of eight bombs falling along her port side and close astern. Her engines and boiler rooms were roughed up by near misses, but she shot down one Ju 88 in return and limped home on one engine, with no one hurt.

*Perth* did not escape so lightly. On 30 May, her upper deck crowded with soldiers, she was caught halfway between Crete and Alexandria. A stick of ten bombs passed over her, dropped from a bright blue sky by an aircraft so high that no one saw it. Nine bombs landed harmlessly in the sea. One struck her. It grazed the foremast and plummeted below decks into one of her boiler rooms, where it exploded with the infernal power of a ton of TNT. *Perth* staggered like an animal shot on a hunt and wallowed to a halt. Signalman Brian Sheedy thought she was finished:

> There is a dreadful feeling when you feel a ship die beneath your feet. The thrumming vibrations of a ship's engines always permeate all that live in her; the low roaring sound of the engine room fans forcing air to the boilers, the sound of the ventilation fans through the mess decks, are an always present background hum. All cease. A silence falls. Good God! Is this the end ...?9

It was not the end, but it easily could have been. The blast should have blown the bottom out of her but by some miracle it did not, for the shock waves were deflected upwards, killing thirteen men in the galley and on the upper deck, most of them soldiers. The starboard side where they had been sitting was choked with dismembered bodies and running with blood, men screaming in agony. After half an hour or so the cruiser got under way again, slowly on two engines, heading home in the noonday sun. Sheedy came off watch:

> I clambered down the ladders to the upper deck and went for'ard along the port side. The escaping steam was under control and the ship was moving to catch up with the group ahead. I came upon an Australian soldier in the port waist. He was shivering violently from shock, his hands were trembling and he was close to tears.
> 'Are you all right, mate?'
> 'It's my mate,' he replied. 'I was standing with him round the other side and had just come around to this side for a few minutes when the bomb hit us.'
> His mate was one of the nine soldiers who had been killed, blown to pieces ...10

They buried the dead at sea that afternoon, a proper naval funeral with the crack of rifles in farewell and the plangent notes of

'The Last Post'. Four more enemy bombers swooped towards them as the shrouded bodies were committed to the sea but were chased off by Fulmars which had turned up from Alexandria. *Perth* made it safely back to harbour before sunset.[11]

—

The Admiralty in London kept pestering Cunningham with supposedly helpful suggestions and, at least once, countermanding a direct order he had given. That infuriated him but he ignored them and carried on. The Commander-in-Chief remained outwardly imperturbable, but alone in his office he began to dread a knock on the door or the ring of the telephone, fearing it would be yet more bad news. His despatches to the Admiralty regularly spoke of high morale and the fighting spirit of his sailors but, intentionally or not, he was gilding the lily. Cracks had begun to show among men driven to the bitter end. Cunningham's barge was booed in the harbour as it passed one anchored warship. Whether he was aware of it or not, some men began to call him 'the Butcher'.

A story ran around the fleet of a near mutiny in a battered cruiser that Cunningham had visited where, with an attempt at jocularity, he told the crew mustered before him on the quarterdeck that, 'I see you've been peppered a bit.' Some of the men broke ranks and surged forward as if to throw him into the harbour; they had to be restrained by their officers.

COs were not immune to the fear and the horror. Returning from sea on the second last day of the evacuation, the captain of the cruiser *Calcutta*, Dennis Lees, was looking forward to a couple of nights' rest in harbour. Visiting the operations room the next morning, he was furious to learn that he would be sailing again that night, and he exploded:

I must have been fairly near the end of my tether because I'm afraid I let fly a torrent of vituperation and abuse at the staff. A.B.C. whose office adjoined the operations room must have heard as the door opened and, without saying a word, he beckoned me to come into his room. Having sat me down he said, 'Now, what's the matter?'

I replied, 'I know tonight is the final evacuation. My ship's company is tired out. I'm tired out. And now I hear we have to go to sea again at 2300 tonight.'

Most Commanders-in-Chief would have given a very severe ticking-off to a very junior post captain for such an outburst; not so A.B.C. He understood the strain we had been under for long weeks. He talked to me quietly, like a father, explaining everything, including his own misery at being shore-bound whilst the ships of his fleet were being decimated. After about a quarter of an hour he asked, 'Now are you happy to go out tonight?'

Of course I was.

His method of dealing with me increased my loyalty and affection so that I returned to my ship thinking, 'What a very great man!'[12]

When *Calcutta* sailed, four of her crew jumped over the side, preferring to face the inevitable court martial rather than go to sea again.[13] She left in company with her sister ship *Coventry*, two cruisers of the First World War modernised as anti-aircraft ships, to provide protection for a small convoy returning from Crete. At 0900 hours the next morning, 1 June, about 100 kilometres north of Alexandria, *Coventry*'s radar detected approaching aircraft. Twenty minutes later two Ju 88s dived out of the sun.

A stick from the first aircraft just missed her, landing harmlessly in the sea, but two bombs from the second plane scored a direct hit on *Calcutta*. Captain Lees barely had time to give the order to abandon ship before she sank beneath him, 118 of her crew dying with her. *Coventry* picked up 255 men from the water, including Lees, and returned to Alexandria.

Andrew Cunningham was on the wharf to meet them, only too aware that he had sent *Calcutta* to her death. The blow was the heavier because he had commanded her himself in the 1920s, and she had been his flagship as a rear admiral in the Med in the 1930s. He greeted Lees with tears in his eyes.

So ended the retreat from Crete, with three cruisers and six destroyers sunk. Some sixteen more ships were put out of action in

need of repairs, some of them for a very long time, including the battleships *Warspite* and *Barham*. And more than 2000 sailors had been
killed, with many hundreds more wounded.

The culpable folly and failure of Winston Churchill's strategic
gamble in the Balkans can be measured simply. The official figures
count 1742 Allied soldiers killed on Crete or in the retreat – 274 of
them Australian – and 11,370 men taken prisoner there, including
3102 Australians. The navy recovered 16,500 Allied troops from the
island. Some men stayed on, hiding out in caves to conduct a guerrilla
war with the help of local people.

The toll is more devastating still when the losses in Greece are
added to the count, a total of 594 Australians killed from the army's
6th Division and 5132 taken prisoner.

Germany too had paid a high price. The Luftwaffe alone had lost
more than 3000 men on Crete, many of them the paratroopers who
had landed in the slaughter at Maleme. But Hitler had achieved his
chief aims: to aid his fascist partner Mussolini; to defeat the British;
to secure his oil supply from Romania; and to protect his southern
flank for his next great move.

On 22 June 1941 he launched Operation Barbarossa, the invasion
of the Soviet Union.

—

*Vampire* was the first to leave the field. In May she made two runs
to Tobruk, carrying out 180 wounded men on the first trip. On her
second run on 21 May, Lieutenant Commander Walsh and the ship's
company were not sure her old grey bones would make it back to
Alexandria again. Defects, big and small, had been mounting for
months and she had begun a bone-shaking vibration at any speed
above 18 knots, a problem her engineers could do nothing to fix.
After a patch-up job in Alexandria, John Walsh said his goodbyes:

Admiral Cunningham sent his barge for me – my motorboat
having been sunk in a collision some twelve months before – and
said a warm farewell to me and the ship's company. He thanked
us for a good job well done and expressed his regrets at having
to lose us. I remember saying rather facetiously that I hoped the

Japs would let us get to Singapore and his remark that there was 'no worry about that, they are our friends'. It was remarkable how many VIPs at the time held that opinion.[14]

She sailed on 28 May for Port Said and then Suez and the Indian Ocean. Many if not most of her ship's company had been with her in the Mediterranean from the very beginning. There would be a thorough refit in Singapore, at the big British naval base. It was not home, but it was a long way from the bombing.

—

Tobruk remained an intense and persistent irritant to Rommel for he had to hold substantial forces there to maintain the siege, troops he would rather have used to push on towards Egypt. The best efforts of the Afrika Korps and the Italians had failed to dislodge the Australians and for all the ferocity of the Luftwaffe bombing, supplies were still getting through to sustain the garrison. In May the British and German armies tussled back and forth to the east of Tobruk, each gaining ground and losing ground for no decisive result. On 15 May, Wavell mounted Operation Brevity, a limited offensive in the border area of Egypt and Libya that initially took the Germans off guard but which sputtered out in a day after Rommel rushed in reinforcements. Brevity indeed.

Further to the south – much further – another war was being waged for possession of Africa Orientale Italiana, Italy's East African colonies in what are now modern-day Ethiopia, Eritrea and Somalia. The few people who were aware of it at all called it the East African War, or sometimes the Abyssinian War. In the grand scheme of things it was a sideshow to the great conflicts in Western Europe, the Mediterranean and the Atlantic, but it was nonetheless a vital theatre for Britain: the Italian colonial coastline there dominated the Horn of Africa, the Gulf of Aden and the Red Sea highway to and from the Suez Canal, the main artery of the Empire.

That made it also critical for Australia as the supply route for our troops and our ships in the Middle East and the Balkans. The cruiser *Hobart*, a sister to *Sydney* and *Perth*, had been operating in the Red Sea when the Italians declared war in 1940. She was joined there by the sloops HMAS *Yarra* and *Parramatta* to support the British forces on land, sea and air.

Navies no longer use the term 'sloop', but in the twentieth century it meant a ship that, to an untrained eye, looked like a small destroyer or perhaps a large gunboat. Lightly armed and manned, sloops were maids of all work: escorting convoys, minesweeping, and occasionally turning up in some distant colonial port to fly the flag or, if needs be, to subdue troublesome natives. *Yarra* and *Parramatta* were a British design known as the Grimsby class, but they had both been built at the Cockatoo Island dockyard in Sydney Harbour and launched in the late 1930s.[15] At 1500 tons full load they were smaller than the Scrap Iron destroyers, perhaps two-thirds the size, with a single upright funnel and the customary compass platform open to the sea and sky. Fine sea-keeping vessels, the sloops could turn out 2000 shaft horsepower to push them through the water at a very best speed of 16.5 knots – slower than the destroyers' 30 knots – but more than enough for convoy escort. They had a principal armament of three 4-inch high-angle guns, designed for anti-aircraft work, and depth charge racks at the stern, but they carried no torpedoes. The wartime crew was 160 men.

Lieutenant Commander Jefferson Hirst Walker, a Victorian, commissioned *Parramatta* in Sydney in April 1940, two months before Italy declared war. She was his first command in a long career. Walker had been born for the sea and the navy. As an infant he had played in his bath with little wooden ships made by his father, an electrician of Yorkshire origins. His boyhood summer holidays were idylls of swimming and messing about in a sailing dinghy at Mordialloc on the eastern shore of Port Phillip Bay. It was only natural for young Jefferson to apply to the Naval College at the age of thirteen, and discerning of its grandees to accept this slight, shy, straw-haired kid as one of thirty-one cadet midshipmen in the January 1915 intake on the shores of Jervis Bay.

In 1919, too young for the First World War, the newly appointed Midshipman Walker and five others of his term joined the gunroom of the British battleship HMS *Revenge*. He was there on that extraordinary day of 21 June when fifty-two of the interned ships of the Kaiser's beaten High Seas Fleet scuttled themselves in a watery

Götterdämmerung at the Royal Navy's anchorage at Scapa Flow in the Orkney Islands. Walker was in a party hurriedly sent to board the battlecruiser *Derfflinger* to close her sea cocks and stop her going down, unsuccessfully as it turned out.

His career flowed along the conventional lines of a battleship here, a cruiser there, destroyers and shore postings, and the Royal Navy's Long Navigational Course at Portsmouth in 1924. That done, in 1929 he married a South Australian society beauty, Mary Cheadle, a vivacious and independently minded young woman who shocked her relatives by abandoning the traditional white wedding dress to wear 'a beautifully cut gown of gold lamé with flared skirt and long sleeves'.[16]

As a lieutenant commander in 1935 Walker was navigator in the heavy cruiser HMAS *Australia*, the fleet flagship, when she carried His Royal Highness Prince Henry, Duke of Gloucester, the third son of King George V, home to Britain from a royal tour. All went swimmingly until, at the last moment, a navigator's nightmare descended: a pea soup fog in the teeming English Channel as they approached Portsmouth. Walker carried them through it and was among the ship's officers rewarded with an MVO, a gong in the Royal Victorian Order.

*Parramatta* arrived in the Red Sea in July 1940 as the war there was gathering speed. She was to be based at the port of Aden. There was bombing from the Italians, a constant threat of submarines and the drudgery of convoy escort, but the chief enemy was the vicious climate – the scorching, roasting, sickening, draining heat that never left you, day or night. In the engine and boiler rooms men collapsed in temperatures that could reach 60° Celsius or more. One of *Parramatta*'s lieutenants, Percy Forwood, described it in a letter to his son:

> Conditions now are very far removed from comfort. Men stripped to the waist, bleary-eyed from the incessant sand and dust that blows right out to sea; men baked almost black, unshaven, breaking out in sores for want of fresh provisions; water restrictions, no laundry for three weeks, a temperature that never drops beneath about 88 [31° Celsius] and even at night, when relief is expected, none forthcoming as the seawater is warmer than the atmosphere.

Conditions for living are impossible below decks and everyone sleeps fully clothed on deck anywhere, sometimes being called to action stations seven times during the night and then having to carry on again as usual next day, and day after day the same.[17]

Sickness and sometimes hunger stalked them. Sunstroke and prickly heat were common, sometimes with tormenting rashes in the groin, or raging diarrhoea, or rampant, chronic tinea, despite the best efforts of the doctor, Surgeon Lieutenant Charlie Harrington.[18] The supply of food was uneven at best, occasionally supplemented by goat and camel meat bought in local markets. Fresh fruit was almost unheard of, milk an inconceivable luxury, and when the flour was finished there was no bread. Swimming over the side was out for fear of sharks.

The war did keep them busy. On land, two British armies with stirring imperial names – the 5th Mahratta Light Infantry. The Kings African Rifles – were slowly but firmly crushing the Italians in the jaws of a pincer, one army advancing south from the Sudan into Ethiopia and another driving northwards from Britain's East African Colonies led by Lieutenant General Alan Cunningham, the younger brother of the admiral. On water, the Regia Marina's curiously inert Flottiglia del Mar Rosso, the Red Sea Flotilla of seven destroyers, eight submarines and five of the MAS torpedo boats, was gradually ground down. Destroyers ran themselves aground, two were bombed and sunk by the RAF and at least two submarines were lost to poisoned gas from faulty air-conditioning. Four submarines escaped and made their way south around Africa and on to Bordeaux in occupied France. Italian and German merchant ships trying to make a run for it were rounded up by the RN and the RAN in the Indian Ocean. Like Tobruk, the main Italian port of Massawa in Ethiopia was strewn with wrecks.

*Parramatta* worked her fingers raw, shepherding convoys and minesweeping, searching for submarines, carrying troops, evading the occasional air attack from the apathetic Regia Aeronautica. When the cruiser *Capetown* was torpedoed by an Italian MAS boat in the Red Sea, *Parramatta* towed her, with enormous effort and consummate seamanship, 500 kilometres to Port Sudan. Occasionally, for light relief, Walker might be in diplomatic negotiations for food and provisions with some local sheikh who was treated with elaborate courtesy.

Through it all, he wrote almost daily to Mary back home: long, literate letters that were informative, witty and tender, sometimes dark, sometimes light, always warm and candid. In the lofty loneliness of command he could unburden himself only to the wife he loved.

At 7.15 after a bath, I dined on tinned soup, very tiny boiled potatoes and dear old bully beef (the same as lunch). This, with a glass of tomato juice, was the issue, but I played several lovely Bach records on the gramophone.

Don't worry about me. I feel tonight as I thought I were a very lucky man. I have a ship under my feet which has demonstrated the honest workmanship put into her building and which has already proved herself. My officers and men have been adequate and admirable beyond my wildest hopes. I know I'm competent at my job and I know the ship's company have no doubts about the matter. Under the harshest conditions we have been what is called 'a happy ship'.

Moments of anxiety and periods of strain are inevitable, but they have not hurt me, nor do I suffer any fear. In these lonely, monotonous, strenuous months I have experienced a serenity I have never known before. It seems that my life has been a preparation for this task now set me. It's good to feel men respect you and are happy to serve with you; and in a straight-forward job like this I feel I am able to compete with whatever the fates may bring. I am healthy and to my knowledge owe no man anything. I believe in the cause and am now certain of the eventual result.

And in God's good time there is home to return to – perhaps. If not, my dear, do not mourn for me if it occurs. Just be thankful for what we have had together.[19]

On 16 April 1941, General Cunningham's army entered the Ethiopian capital Addis Ababa to see the Emperor Haile Selassie, the 'Lion of Judah' returned from exile and re-installed on his throne. A month later, on 19 May, after hard fighting in the mountains to the north, the Italian Commander-in-Chief – the English-educated, seamlessly bilingual, fox-hunting and polo-playing, immensely tall, stunningly handsome and impossibly named Prince Amedeo Umberto Isabella Luigi Filippo Maria Giuseppe Giovanni di Savoia-Aosta, Duke of Aosta – surrendered his forces. Some isolated fighting went on but the campaign was effectively over, the first complete British victory in any theatre of the war. For a couple of weeks *Parramatta* stayed on for the mopping-up and life returned to something a little more peaceful. At the end of May Walker was told that he would be going to the Mediterranean.

> My last evening at Aden was, as it happened, one of the pleasant-est I had there. We went swimming in the evening and I found myself immersed in surprising magic. The sea was infused with phosphorus and, as we swam, we were literally ablaze with silver light and swimming in a silver mist. When we emerged we were clothed from head to foot in silver pearls. It was a strangely lovely note to end on and it was equalled by the sunset as we left harbour the next day. Aden seemed to bathe itself in glorious colour for our benefit, and a glowing sky of red and pale green silhouetted Little Aden to the east. The sea took some of the magic of the sky and the whole effect brought us to silence on the bridge ...[20]

On the way north the little sloop met the battle worn *Voyager* coming south and exchanged greetings, and then *Barham* and the wounded cruiser *Dido* on their way for repairs. Since her commissioning just over a year earlier, *Parramatta* had steamed nearly 85,000 kilometres. On 3 June she secured to a buoy in Alexandria where, to much pleasure all round, she found *Perth*, *Stuart*, *Vampire* and *Vendetta* there to welcome her, and *Waterhen* arriving the next day. *Waterhen*'s captain, John Swain, threw a wardroom party for the commanding officers and first lieutenants, where the *Parramatta* men were introduced to a 'Tobruk Cognac' made from fiery Italian raw spirit souvenired in Tobruk itself and broken down with condensed milk and beaten eggs. It was, thought Walker, 'enough to kill a Wesleyan bishop'.

Another surprise awaited them too, and one even more deadly. That night there was an air raid by the Luftwaffe. It was the first time *Parramatta* encountered the deadly menace of the Stuka dive-bomber.

# CHAPTER 16

# FAREWELL
# TO THE CHOOK

After the torments of the Red Sea, *Parramatta*'s ship's company revelled in the milder climate of the Mediterranean and the fleshpots of Alexandria. Praise be, they found cold Australian beer at the Forces Club and music and sex in the bars of Sister Street. The food on board improved immeasurably, as did health and morale, a relief for both the captain and the doctor.

Sometimes the officers would join friends from other ships in harbour to feast on seafood at the Monseigneur restaurant by the waterfront, or to munch the pastries and drink cocktails at the marble-topped bar of the elegant Pastroudis café on Fouad Street. The hospitable patron, Athanash Pastroudis, was Greek with a Swiss wife, Gabrielle. Splendid with its glass front doors monogrammed in gilt initials, its rich mahogany panelling, its high, pillared ceiling, and its obsequious waiters, Pastroudis billed itself as *le rendezvous de l'elite Alexandrine*. The expatriate English writer Lawrence Durrell passed long evenings there, dreaming of the novels that would become his *Alexandria Quartet*.[1] The boy King Farouk occasionally entertained a mistress in a back room. Athanash's famous *canard à l'orange* was a stretch for the pay of a naval lieutenant but a distinct improvement on bully beef fritters, and there were times when it was worth it.

On a higher plane, after Greece and Crete the Mediterranean Fleet was binding up its wounds, now a shadow of what it had been at Matapan. There were just two battleships left, *Queen Elizabeth* and *Valiant*; four cruisers, including *Perth*; and seventeen destroyers, among them the Scrap Iron ships. Admiral Cunningham could still use submarines based on Malta to attack Rommel's supply lines from Italy to Tripoli, and they did it well, but Malta itself had to be supplied in the face of the ferocity of the Luftwaffe bombing. And then there was the Tobruk Ferry to be maintained.

With no aircraft carrier to replace *Formidable*, Cunningham again pleaded with London for more RAF aircraft to provide air cover for his ships, but in vain. Things were made worse by the attitude of the new RAF Commander-in-Chief in Cairo, Arthur Tedder, who, unlike his predecessor Longmore, had no grasp of the need to cooperate with the fleet and who indulged in the old games of inter-service rivalry – fun enough in peacetime, folly in wartime. From Cunningham's memoirs it is evident that he came to dislike and distrust Tedder a great deal. The Luftwaffe, with the on-again off-again support of the Regia Aeronautica, maintained complete superiority in the skies over the Mediterranean.

One bright spot was the inertia of the Italian battle fleet. Despite the evermore insistent entreaties of the Germans it remained in port, its admirals pleading a shortage of fuel. At a naval conference at the Berghof on 6 June 1941, after complaints again from Großadmiral Erich Raeder, Hitler promised to write to Mussolini himself to get things moving. If he did, nothing came of it. It was a lost opportunity for the Axis. Boldly handled and with Luftwaffe air cover, the battle-ships of the Regia Marina could have wrought more havoc during Greece and Crete, and after.

At Cairo, Archibald Wavell was planning yet another offensive against Rommel, this one code named Battleaxe. On 12 May, a big convoy from Britain arrived in Alexandria carrying 238 tanks for the British army's 7th Armoured Division and forty-three crated Hurricanes for the RAF. When they were landed it was found – incredibly – that they had not been adapted for desert conditions. It took two weeks to equip the engines of both the tanks and aircraft with sand filters, which meant postponing Battleaxe for a month. And the recalcitrant Tedder told Cunningham that, anyway, the new Hurricanes would be used only to support the army, not the navy.

The ships of the Tobruk Ferry would just have to battle through on their own.

—

The *Pass of Balmaha* was a squat little tanker of just 760 tons. Balmaha is a pretty Scottish village on the bonnie banks of Loch Lomond, and the Pass carries the country high road winding north between the hills, but there was no music to the ship herself. Glasgow-built in 1933, with a black hull and white upper works, the *Pass of Balmaha* was the sort of workaday coastal steamer that would have gone unremarked in any port of the Empire before the war.[2]

But in the Mediterranean in 1941 she and her cargoes – 700 tons of petrol – were crucial to the survival of Tobruk. Back and forth she went. Her English master, Stanley Hardy, was only twenty-eight but had been in the merchant service since the age of thirteen and knew his trade. Most of the crew were in their twenties as well, including two of the three RN able seamen who manned the *Pass of Balmaha*'s only defensive weapon, a largely useless Bofors anti-aircraft gun mounted in the bow. The third gunner was nineteen. The oldest of the twenty men on board was the cook, Mohamed Hassan Ibrahim, a venerable figure of thirty-eight. The merchant seamen of the Second World War were a special breed but tanker men more so than most, for they were perfectly aware that they were sailing on a floating bomb.

As night was falling on Sunday, 22 June, Captain Hardy took the *Balmaha* down the main swept channel out of Alexandria, past the tall pillar of the Ras el-Tin lighthouse and out to sea, where he met the escort waiting to accompany him to Tobruk, *Parramatta* and another sloop, HMS *Auckland*. They formed into line, *Auckland* leading, the little tanker in the middle and *Parramatta* stationed astern.

Renowned for her lurid camouflage in greens and greys and creams, *Auckland* had been one of *Parramatta*'s chummy ships in the Red Sea where they had worked and fought together, and the crews knew each other well. She was bigger, faster and better armed, at 1200 tons with a top speed of 19.5 knots and eight of the 4-inch high-angle guns in two turrets fore and aft, against *Parramatta*'s meagre three. Her captain, Commander Mervyn Thomas, was an old Mediterranean hand who'd suffered the destroyer *Dainty*, one of Hec Waller's 10th

Flotilla ships, bombed and sunk beneath him off Tobruk back in February. Senior to Jeff Walker, he was in charge of the trio as they headed west, the two darkened warships zigzagging with their Asdics pinging, the tanker slowly ploughing a straight furrow in the calm sea at her best speed of around 6 knots.

That night passed quietly and so did the next day and night, the watches changing calmly without incident. Tuesday 24 June dawned fine and clear with a smooth sea and the promise of a hot day to come. The first sign of trouble appeared in the forenoon watch at 0840 hours when the lookouts on *Auckland* sighted a single aircraft ahead and out to the west, an Italian Savoia S.79. It was evidently just a reconnaissance plane, for it made no attempt to attack and it flew off when *Auckland* rather optimistically opened fire. But everyone knew now that they had been discovered and that there must be more to come.

It did not take long. Jeff Walker was doing some minor job back aft on the upper deck when another S.79 came out of the sun from astern. The alarms rang. As he raced to the bridge a stick of bombs fell just ahead of the ship, the spray drenching him and his clean white shirt in dirty water. It also, by chance, put the ship's rangefinder temporarily out of action so *Parramatta* could not open fire. *Auckland* did, though, and again the enemy flew off, no harm done.

By now they were almost 80 kilometres due east of Tobruk and still hours away, closed up at action stations. All they could do was to trudge on, waiting and watching. The next attack came at midday, three S.79s now, one of them acting as a decoy for the gunners while the other two lined up a torpedo run from ahead. Both warships opened fire this time, possibly putting the aircraft off their stride. They dropped two fish, one which apparently passed beneath the *Pass of Balmaha* and another aimed at *Parramatta*. The lookouts spotted that in good time and the captain ordered the helm hard over to see it streak harmlessly past out to starboard. Another single S.79 approached at 1345 hours, relatively high at around 6000 feet, dropping four bombs that straddled *Parramatta* but again without result.

So far so good. The afternoon wore on in a long, nervous wait, everyone scanning the clear blue, treacherous skies, everyone acutely aware that they were well into Bomb Alley with every likelihood that the attacks so far had been merely a rehearsal for the main act to come. It had been only the Regia Aeronautica until now. Surely the Luftwaffe would eventually put in an appearance.

—

Major Walter Enneccerus, the Stuka pilot who had commanded the devastating attack on the carrier *Illustrious* back in January, had taken his squadron II/StG 23 from Sicily to North Africa in support of the Afrika Korps. There his fame had grown. He was credited with dropping the bomb that had smashed through the flight deck of *Formidable* in May.

This June afternoon Enneccerus was biding his time at the airfield at Derna, further along the Libyan coast west of Tobruk. From the Italian reports he was getting he knew the exact position, course and speed of the British tanker and its two escorting warships, and their destination was obvious. There was no hurry. The later his squadron took off the less fuel it would use, a critical consideration. Waiting with him was one of his youngsters and another Stuka ace, Leutnant Hubert Polz, a flamboyant and experienced twenty-three-year-old lauded for both his skill in the air and the enormous red and white, fiercely fanged snake painted along each side of the fuselage of his plane. They called him die Wüstenschlange, the Desert Snake.

*Zeit für uns zu gehen, Polz. Zwei Englische Kriegsschiffe. Viel Glück!*
*Jawohl, Herr Major!*
Time for us to go, Polz. Two English warships. Good luck!
Yes, Major!

They took off a little after 1600 hours, forming up and then flying south-east. By 1730 hours they could see the enemy ahead. Enneccerus worked around towards the sun and chivvied his charges into their well-practised attack formations.

*Auckland* saw them first, specks in the distance, and Commander Thomas ordered the air raid red alarm, which was picked up in *Parramatta*. Both sloops were already closed up at action stations, guns loaded, their turrets training. Weeks later, when it was over, Jefferson Hirst Walker wrote a long and candid letter to his beloved Mary at home in Melbourne, describing the action:

The expected attack occurred as late as 5.35 pm and was in full force by about (estimated) three formations of sixteen aircraft each moving in at about 14,000 feet, and then dive-bombing. This is pretty heavy weight for two small ships. We both opened fire at the formations when they were at long range and they worked round to the sun, then overhead, and then down in numbers.

When they started to come down things happened at pace. About two thirds of them attacked *Auckland*, one or two the *Pass of Balmaha* and the rest at me. I don't know whether I can convey the intensity of this sort of thing, with the sky above alive with aircraft whistling down (or rather, roaring down at one), pulling out at the last moment, and bombs crashing into the sea continuously, the whole being added to by the continuous crash of one's own guns.

The effect is terrific as the sky seems to rain death at one. I have a vivid memory of seeing aircraft apparently just missing the masts of the *Pass of Balmaha*, fairly spitting bombs at her. On the bridge I was continuously nearly blinded and wet through with spray from the bombs around me.

At 5.50, when this particular hell had been going on for about ten minutes, disaster overtook us. I suddenly saw *Auckland* become covered with brown smoke with bits of wreckage jumping into the air, and realised she had been hit. For about a minute as I approached the smoke head on I couldn't see her. Then she emerged heading straight for me.

I got the ship turning just in time and avoided her, passing between the two ships. As she went down my starboard side I saw she was heavily on fire and listing, and her stern was a wreck from the mainmast aft. In fact little was visible above the waterline. She swung away to port and gradually came to a standstill, burning aft and with a heavy list.[4]

The Stuka pilots had taken *Auckland* to be not a sloop but a much larger cruiser, so they directed the weight of their attack on her. There were a couple of near misses which roughed her up a little, but shortly before 1800 hours a large bomb scored a direct hit on Y-turret aft, blowing her stern above the water to pieces and starting the fire they could see from *Parramatta*. It is likely that bomb was dropped by the Desert Snake, Hubert Polz. To her captain's surprise, *Auckland* kept moving at about 10 knots and her for'ard guns kept firing, but her steering was wrecked. Though the wheel was jammed hard over to port she somehow made a 180 degree turn to starboard, slumping and listing lower in the water.

Almost immediately she was hit by another three bombs, one smashing through the sick bay skylight, a second plunging at an angle through the bridge and exploding as it burst out through the ship's port side, the third landing somewhere amidships. Still her for'ard turrets kept banging away, but she was now listing so heavily that her port gunwale was awash. There was nothing for it: she was dying, gone.

For the second time in his war, Commander Thomas gave the order to abandon ship. Some men rushed to the boats and rafts. Others did what they could to tend to the wounded strewn about the canting upper deck, coughing and choking in the smoke. There was fear but discipline prevailed and there was no panic. Methodically, the First Lieutenant and the telegraphists set about destroying the confidential books, heaving the lead-weighted bags of codes and *Fleet Orders* overboard.

Remarkably, impossibly, *Parramatta* was still unscathed and still weaving and shooting as the planes began to depart. Three guns, only three guns against this air armada. The Commissioned Gunner, Arthur Brown, was beside himself. Brass shell cases piled up on the deck. Out on a bridge wing the Chief Yeoman, Bill Allsop, was firing a machine gun, shouting and swearing like a man possessed. The tanker had taken a few splinters, but no real damage. Walker could see men had begun to leave *Auckland*, jumping into the water, so he circled her and then stopped to windward to drift gently down upon them. As the enemy left and the guns ceased fire, something like a calm descended, broken by the cries of the men in the sea and the dull roar of the flames from the burning wreck. *Auckland* had managed to get only one boat and a couple of rafts away; the rest were burned or wrecked or jammed. Walker ordered all his boats to be lowered, whalers and skiffs, lifebelts and Carley floats, and a few men who managed to swim to him were hauled aboard.

In the midst of all this, another six planes appeared and began to line up. As they came in, a mighty internal explosion lifted the burning wreck of *Auckland* literally out of the water. Perhaps her depth charges detonated, perhaps it was her boilers. It was astounding, incredible. To the awe of the men watching she rose a metre or more into the air, almost clean out of the sea, like a breaching whale. That broke her back and she snapped in half and slumped back and sank. The bold and brave red, white and blue of the big battle ensign on her mainmast was the last glimpse they had of her. Walker signalled Alexandria that she was gone – position 32°15′N, 24°30′E – but there was not time to ponder this horrible spectacle, not time to mourn. *Parramatta* was under the hammer again.

> For some moments I was unable to get under weigh as there were men in the water around my screws, and the attack caught me when the ship was gathering speed. Most of the bombs fell clear of the men in the water, and I sincerely hope none of them were hurt by them. It is obviously impossible to tell. The first salvoes fell very close but short of me, some of them seeming to lift the ship a foot or two out of the water.
>
> The enemy passed overhead, turned and came back again, whilst we went on slamming at them. They again altered course when nearly over me again, and passed, bombing, over the *Pass of Balmaha* but missed her over.
>
> Then the swine went low over the men in the water and machine-gunned them. What damage they did I do not know but I have never felt so angry in all my life. It was a satisfaction to see that one of them was out of formation and flying low making smoke. What happened to him I do not know.
>
> There were about thirty fighters and bombers. I knew there was more to come and that it would be pretty fierce when it did come as there had been time for the bombers to get back, re-fuel and re-load. The sun was a beastly distance still above the horizon. There was little point in steaming away from the place, and I wanted to pick up the 'Aucklands' after darkness about nine o'clock. So I went a little distance, away but near enough to cover the tanker and the survivors, but far enough to keep the

bombs away from the latter, and just steamed about waiting and, I may say, not liking it one little bit. I have never felt so lonely, or known the sun sink so slowly in the sky.

I cannot now look at a blood red sun just above the horizon without feeling my back tickling.[5]

At about this point the crew of the *Pass of Balmaha* began to lower boats and leave their ship. The tanker had not been hit yet but her people reasonably feared that it must happen soon enough, blowing them to kingdom come, and they sought what illusion of safety they could.

The last attack came at 1955 hours, the sun almost gone, the sea crimson and gold in its fading rays. This time it was both German and Italian Stukas, weaving and diving in concert and, if anything, more ferocious than all that had gone before. It lasted for nearly half an hour, the little *Parramatta* snaking and dodging about the ocean to the blast of her guns, the howl of the Stuka sirens, the roar of aero engines, the thunder of bombs in the sea exploding sometimes close enough to send waves of filthy water over the ship. But they fought back like madmen, the gun barrels red hot, and they had the satisfaction, the inspiring, handsome joy, of seeing two Stukas and then a third fall smoking into the sea. At 2035 hours the attack ended, the enemy flew off. The burning rim of the sun slipped below the horizon and it was over.

Almost. Drawn and haggard, wet through, Jeff Walker walked by himself to the back of the bridge and stood there alone, looking down on his ship, almost unable to comprehend that she was unharmed and still afloat and his men still alive. But that moment could not last either, for there were decisions to make, orders to give. He turned back to the compass platform. There were the *Auckland* survivors to be rescued and something still had to be done about the tanker. Slowly, things began to resolve themselves in the way they often do in the navy. Some of his men dived overboard to help those struggling in the water – Stoker Henry Fox, Able Seaman Chris Goldie, Chief Petty Officer Writer Ted Purtell, who'd joined the navy as a boy in the old training ship *Tingira* in 1921. *Auckland*'s captain, Mervyn Thomas, was helped aboard, filthy, drenched and bloody, but still alive and otherwise unharmed, and ushered up to the bridge.

And suddenly deliverance arrived in the stirring sight, the vision splendid, of *Waterhen* and then *Vendetta* steaming to them out of the western horizon like the cavalry coming over the hill. Alexandria had despatched them to the rescue. The men from the *Pass of Balmaha* returned to their ship but discovered some near-miss damage to their bunkers and couldn't start the fires, so *Waterhen* took her in tow to Tobruk and they made it safely. And that sealed the victory. They had won. The tanker's precious cargo made it through.

With 162 of *Auckland*'s survivors on board and the night now thickly fallen, *Parramatta* began the long return to Alexandria, enduring another, different agony: the misery of the wounded below decks crammed into the tiny sick bay, into the wardroom, into the seamen's messes, in passageways; anywhere a space could be found. Twenty of them were cot cases. These were the pathetic human flotsam and jetsam of war: men burned by the fire, men coughing and retching and vomiting with lungs and stomach clogged by fuel oil, men with broken limbs, men with their guts torn open by shrapnel, men crying in pain, men shocked into staring, quivering silence. The doctor, Charles Harrington, and the stewards and sick bay attendants moved among them with swabs and bandages and morphine, slipping on wet decks slimed with blood and vomit. The cooks found them food and drinks. Two men died overnight and were buried at sea.

*Parramatta* secured alongside at Alexandria at 1945 hours the next day, 24 June, to the cheers of a handful of onlookers. The news had gone before. But still there was no rest, for the wounded had to be put ashore, the ship cleaned and readied again, and some slashed wireless aerials replaced. There was some good news: two new Oerlikon guns were fitted amidships.

A few weeks later, they were surprised and gratified to get a pat on the back from no less than the First Sea Lord in London, Admiral of the Fleet Sir Dudley Pound. That did not happen a lot.

Personal from First Sea Lord.
The ship-handling and shooting of HMAS *Parramatta* must have been very good when picking up survivors of HMS *Auckland* as all attacks were avoided, and three aircraft shot down.[6]

Jeff Walker's letter to Mary, written a week after the battle, is moving and poignant, revealing his strength of character as a man and a captain commanding men:

Of course I was terror-stricken throughout. I don't think it would be possible not to be. But I was much too busy at the time to think about it. The following days, however, when imagination set in, were very nasty ...

... This letter is not so much a 'news' letter as a 'Battle' story, is it? I will therefore not intrude other matter but leave it as it is – the simple story of a frightened child.

—

Operation Battleaxe was a costly failure. Wavell had planned a grand sweep from Egypt westwards into Libya to relieve Tobruk and push Rommel back towards Tripoli, but he underestimated his enemy's strengths and agility. It was launched on 15 June. By midday the next day three-quarters of the 200 British tanks deployed had been destroyed or put out of action, and a German counter-offensive by the newly arrived 15th Panzer Division forced the British back. By 17 June it was all over. Winston Churchill had expected a triumph and was livid when he did not get one. On 20 June he told Wavell he would be replaced by General Sir Claude Auchinleck, a man more to Churchill's liking. There was, though, one light in the gloom: Tobruk was continuing to hold out.

—

*Waterhen*, the old Chook, left Alexandria on 28 June for a ferry run to Tobruk, in company with another destroyer from the 10th Flotilla, HMS *Defender*. Her upper deck was crammed with ammunition boxes and crates of food and around seventy soldiers sprawling where they could. Unusually, there were several big jars of some sort of acid stowed on the port side but, apart from that, it was just another run, the same old route, with a stop at Mersa Matruh on the way back. Before they sailed, Ean McDonald, the young signalman, visited a patisserie in Alexandria and bought a tray of pastries, four dozen of this and that, as a surprise for a bunch of old school mates he had run into at Mersa, army gunners in the garrison there. Lord Haw-Haw farewelled them the next morning. 'Calling HMAS *Waterhen* ... our bombers will get you'.

The next day was quiet, but the bombers did indeed find them in the evening at 1945 hours, to the north of Sollum. Nineteen Ju 87s appeared in the dusk, twelve of them German from I/StG 1 and seven Italian from 239a Squadriglie Autonoma Bombardamento a Tuffo, the 239th Autonomous Dive-Bombing Squadron specially formed to fly Stukas in the Regia Aeronautica.

There were two crack pilots in the 239, the squadron commander, Maggiore Giuseppe Cenni, and Sergente Maggiore Ennio Tarantola, both veterans of the Spanish Civil War. When the Germans made Stukas available to the Italians, these two were in a select group of fifteen chosen to train at the Luftwaffe's elite Stukaschule at Graz in Austria, where they graduated with honours. The Italians nicknamed their Stukas 'Picchiatelli', from a type of pasta found in Puglia.[7] Cenni, twenty-six years old, pioneered a new form of attack with the Stuka, impressive even to the German pilots and named after him: the *Picchiata Cenni*, the Cenni Swoop. He would dive vertically as usual, then pull out and fly level at a height of just 50 metres, releasing his bomb at a speed of around 450 km/h. That sent it skipping along the surface of the sea like a pebble skimmed on a lake, to smash into a ship's side. It was very dangerous and very effective. Cenni had taken part in the attacks on *Auckland* and may have dropped one of the bombs that hit her. His fellow pilots called him *il Piccolo Ballerino*, the Little Dancer.

Also twenty-six and a renowned extrovert, Ennio Tarantola had made pocket money as a kid selling bananas in the piazza at Como in northern Italy, and the nickname 'Banana' stuck with him for life. He preferred flying fighters but had made dive-bombing his art form for the present. On this summer evening, with two British warships in sight below, the Picchiatelli circled in a holding pattern while the Germans went in first at *Defender*, which was already twisting and turning like a fox on the run. She disappeared a couple of times in the giant splashes and explosions, but they missed her. Then, to Cenni's customary war cry of *'Valzer, ragazzi!'* – 'Waltz, boys!' – the Italians made their dives on *Waterhen*.

Andy Nation, the stoker from Victoria, had been relaxing with a book on the upper deck when the alarm rattles went:

The sea just seemed to erupt all round us but we came through okay. They were not very discouraged though, they started to come at us from all angles. The ship was turning and dodging all over the ocean. We were firing with everything we had, for'ard, aft and both sides. I was sprawled out on the deck amidships and watched this Stuka coming down almost perpendicular. He let his bomb drop; it was a dirty big 1000-pounder. It dropped alongside up for'ard and almost blew the ship wrong side up. The next instant a great shower of water enveloped the ship and I was bloody near drowned.[8]

That first bomb, probably dropped by Cenni, sprang a leak in a for'ard fuel tank and some shrapnel cut through the wireless aerials. The next bomb from the next aircraft splashed close astern. Petty Officer Reg Raymond watched, transfixed, as it fell towards them:

It looked like the side of a house as it screamed down, and it was a bright yellow. It exploded just behind us, and the whole ship was literally covered with sooty water. The huge hissing spouts surged over us and the whole sky went black.[9]

That bomb apparently damaged the rudder. In the wheelhouse the coxswain, Chief Petty Officer Maurie Cole, shouted up the voice pipe to the bridge that the ship was not answering the helm. Lieutenant Commander Swain would have to steer with the engines if he could.

Ennio Tarantola dropped the third bomb. He howled in low, very low, and left it until the last minute before releasing on the destroyer's port side. Andy Nation, sprawled on the deck, thought he had had it:

He came screaming down on us; I could see every detail on the plane. The bomb dropped from the plane and I knew it was a moral to hit us. The skipper swung the ship to port but it was no good. It was another 1000-pounder. I could see the big metal nose on it and another blue band around the middle. It hit us as we were on the turn and smacked us just below the waterline on the side. The deck shook and shuddered and she took on a hell of a list. I was laying on my belly and the deck came up and hit me in the nose and made it bleed. The bomb blew the dynamo to pieces, flooded both the engine room and the after boiler room and blew the side of the ship wide open for about 15 yards. White smoke was pouring out of the funnels and the sea was full of oil. They ran up the Aussie flag and gave it a cheer.[10]

*Waterhen* staggered to a halt, listing first to port but then, as more water rushed in, slowly heeling over to starboard. Men on deck, sailors and soldiers, tried to lighten her by heaving the ammunition cases and the boxes of supplies over the side but it made no difference. She was getting lower. But at least the attackers had flown off. On the bridge, Commander Swain turned to the Yeoman.

'Make to *Defender*: abandoning ship. Request spare bunk.'

The Aldis clattered out the signal.

'Abandon ship, sir?' asked the First Lieutenant.

'Not yet, Number One.'

At moments like this, in harm's way, men can do strange things. Reg Raymond had just acquired a new uniform, complete with real gold buttons that were usually impossible to get in wartime. He dived below to the petty officer's mess to find it and bundle it up to take with him. Ean McDonald's first thought was for his lovingly compiled photo collection and then – madly – for the pastries he had brought from Alexandria. Obsessed, he clambered down the ladders below to his mess to find it pitch-black and a jumble of upturned furniture and lockers, the water slopping and swilling knee-deep. Suddenly scared, he groped around for his things and, with extraordinary luck, found the case with his films. There was no sign of the pastries. He fled back to the upper deck.

Amazingly, *Waterhen* was still afloat, her crew in life jackets calmly lining up on the fo'c'sle. *Defender*'s captain, Lieutenant Commander Gilbert Farnfield, nosed his ship alongside and *Waterhen*'s men and their soldier passengers stepped on board their rescuer, one by one, as easily as if they were catching a ferry. The ship's dog, Stuka, lovingly described as a cross between a mongrel and a doormat, was carried across. No one got a foot wet. No one was killed.

The only man injured was the Gunner's Mate, Sid Prowd, who for ever after would tell the story of how his nose had been broken by a flying tin of peaches which burst from a case of supplies when the bomb hit. If the jars of acid stowed on the port side had exploded it might have been a very different story.

Jim Swain was the last to leave, as a captain should be. *Defender* withdrew and stood off, and the question now was what to do next. Swain and Farnfield talked it over and, after an hour or so, decided it might be possible to tow *Waterhen* back to Alexandria or at least to Mersa Matruh. Farnfield was turning his ship back towards the stricken ship when, in the light of the rising moon, one of the lookouts spotted the dark block of a conning tower and the upper hull of a submarine on the surface, very near *Waterhen*, about 200 metres away.

Each was as startled as the other. *Defender* opened fire with her machine guns, raggedly at first, then with concerted fury as the sub crash dived in a lather of foam and splashes. The boat was Italian, the *Tembien*, and her captain had been intending to deliver *Waterhen* the coup de grâce. As he dived he haphazardly fired two torpedoes from his stern tubes but they vanished into the night. Asdic searching, *Defender* ran down the sub's track but lost contact, and after a fruitless hour or so she called it quits and returned to attempt the tow. A party of ten volunteers was waiting to go on board, led by *Waterhen*'s Commissioned Engineer, Reg Oram, and Lieutenant Colin Hill, the RANR officer who had shown his mettle at the rescue of the tanker *Marie Maersk* back in March. As they approached *Waterhen*, someone noticed a light flickering fitfully on her deck. Perhaps the enemy sub had left a boarding party there. Pistols were handed out. Hill and his men jumped across the gap onto *Waterhen*'s fo'c'sle, guns at the ready, crept warily towards the light, then rushed it. They found a torch someone had left turned on, rolling with the motion of the ship.

The tow was set with a cable from *Waterhen*'s bow to *Defender*'s stern – fine seamanship in the dark – and gingerly both got under way, slowly, slowly. *Waterhen* yawed and wallowed, and the motion was too much for her. One or two of her bulkheads collapsed, sending more water surging through her, and Hill's men returned to *Defender*.

They cast off the tow and that was that. They had tried everything. There was nothing more they could do.

At 0150 hours on 30 June, the Chook reared up, bow in the air, and then sank back again, as if with a sigh of relief that at last it was all over. Within minutes she was gone in a gentle swirl of water, the first ship of the RAN to be lost to enemy action in this war. It had been her thirteenth run to Tobruk, unlucky thirteen. They noted the position – 32°15′N, 25°20′E – about 80 kilometres north of Sollum. A few days later, in a signal to Commander Swain, Andrew Cunningham wrote her epitaph in stiff naval prose:

> His Majesty's Australian Ship *Waterhen* having been sunk by enemy action it is my direction that she is to be regarded as having been formally paid off on Monday the 30th of June 1941.[11]

—

They have their exits and their entrances, and one man in his time plays many parts. That same day, 30 June, yet another little convoy of two storeships was winding its way at 6 knots from Mersa Matruh towards Tobruk, escorted by a sloop, an ancient gunboat, and one of the converted South African whalers. Not far from Tobruk, at 1340 hours that afternoon, they were jumped by German Stukas and fighters which attacked them in waves over the next few hours. Towards evening, four Stukas of 239 Squadriglia joined the battle – one of them flown by Ennio Tarantola – with an air cover of Messerschmitt Bf 109s and Bf 110s.

This time the result was very different. Finally and at last, the RAF came to the party. At 1730 hours the attackers were themselves attacked by the RAF's 250 Squadron flying the brand-new American-built Tomahawk P40 fighters. Several of the pilots were Australians on loan to the RAF, including a thirty-year-old pilot officer who would later become the RAAF's most celebrated fighter ace, Clive 'Killer' Caldwell. It was a ferocious dogfight. Caldwell had been in the Middle East only a few weeks, but he had already shot down his first Stuka and this day he claimed two more and shared one of the 110s with another pilot, part of a spirited British victory in the air.[12]

'Banana' evaded the fighters and dived for his bombing run but was hit by anti-aircraft fire from the sloop HMS *Flamingo*. He struggled for height but his engine spluttered and died and his gunner, Ruggero Pittini, released their emergency dinghy. They both parachuted from the plane. Pittini disappeared, but Tarantola reached the dinghy and drifted in it for eighteen hours until he was discovered and rescued by an Italian seaplane. The two supply ships made it through, shaken but unharmed.

—

The loss of *Waterhen* cast a shadow of gloom over the Australians for a week or so, but there was no time to grieve. The show had to go on. With 38 tons of ammunition stacked on her upper deck and thirty-six fresh troops for the garrison, *Vendetta* arrived at Tobruk late on the night of 10 July in company with *Defender*. They threaded their way into the harbour, securing at the oiling wharf to unload their supplies and collect wounded soldiers and German and Italian prisoners, all swiftly done through long practice. *Vendetta* had an extra 175 men crammed on her upper deck and *Defender* about the same. The Italians were left together, but the Germans were divided into groups of six men each, with two armed guards. They sailed again just after 0100 hours, zigzagging and varying their speed to make life difficult for any prowling submarine as they settled on a course of 95 degrees back to Alexandria, in line abreast about a mile apart.

The moon was full, a bomber's moon. Everyone on deck was uncomfortably aware that their wakes were leaving a glittering, silvery trail glaringly obvious from the air, and *Vendetta*'s captain, 'Dusty' Rhoades, posted extra lookouts to scan the skies. Not that you could see much at night, they knew. All was quiet until about 0300 hours when ...

a large number of explosions were heard and blue splashes observed very close to *Defender* and on *Vendetta*'s port quarter. At first these were taken to be cannon shots from an aircraft but later it was decided they were more probably incendiary or anti-personnel bombs. No aircraft were seen or heard.[13]

It was eerie and unsettling but no harm was done and there was nothing to do but keep going. They were travelling at full speed when, a little after 0500 hours they were discovered. It was just one aircraft on a coastal reconnaissance flight, a Ju 88 of I/LG 1 flown by Leutnant Gerd Stamp, one of the pilots who had sunk the cruiser *Gloucester* in the battle for Crete. Ordinary Seaman Lester Brien, a nineteen-year-old kid from Granville in Sydney, was on watch:

we didn't see the aircraft coming until it was low overhead. The bomb load was intended for us but the pilot coming in from ahead released his bombs late. *Defender*, which was about 800 yards off our starboard beam and slightly astern, disappeared behind a giant eruption of seawater.

From my position on the 12-pounder amidships I could see great mountains of water rising hideously. The blast effect cracked along the whole length of our old warrior. We saw no target and not a round was fired.

I could vaguely make out *Defender* almost stopped and swinging stern to us.[14]

Rhoades was watching from his bridge as pinpoints of light began to blink from *Defender*'s signal platform. 'I think I have been hit. Come alongside and take off military personnel.'[15]

The bomb was a near miss, but it had exploded so lethally close that it burst open her engine room and virtually broke her in half. *Vendetta* swung to starboard at speed towards her, then slowed to pick up a man they spotted floating in the water who had been blown overboard from *Defender*. Lester Brien continued:

*Defender* slowly adopted the appearance of a giant V. Her iron deck amidships was a few feet under water. As we approached I heard the hissing of her tubes as the water reached them. Her torpedomen trained the tubes away from us and fired their 'fish' harmlessly.

Dawn was now breaking and in the first light we began to take off survivors. Scramble nets were over both sides, and as the seas were the usual Mediterranean calm a gangplank was rattled across *Defender*'s port waist.[16]

*Vendetta* opened fire on a Savoia that flew near them just after 0600 hours but it made no attempt to attack and flew off. She had taken 175 soldiers and prisoners on board from *Defender*, including some wounded in stretchers and now she began the long, arduous business of taking her stricken consort in tow. For all their best efforts, it was not a success. One of *Vendetta*'s wires snapped with a crack like a gunshot, then a manilla line parted, and another, and it wasn't until 0900 hours that they began to make any headway, at an agonising 4 knots. There was one blessing: RAF fighters appeared overhead in the sunshine and kept watch over them.

By 1030 hours *Defender* had taken enough. It was obvious she was beginning to go, so they cast off the tow for the final time and Commander Rhoades sent over his whaler to pick up her captain and the few hands left on board. At 1100 hours he fired a torpedo into her to hasten the end and when her fo'c'sle reared up he pumped two shells into her from the 4-inch. Watching their ship go down, the British crew gave three cheers and the officers saluted.

With 760 souls on board, *Vendetta* made her best speed back to Alexandria and at 2030 hours that night she secured at the No. 15 Quay. In the chaos and carnage of war there had been a certain symmetry to it, if not exactly pleasing then at least unusually neat. As *Defender* had saved *Waterhen*'s crew without a life lost, so *Vendetta* had performed the same service for her.

When some of *Vendetta*'s men dropped into the Fleet Club for a drink a day later, the British sailors there gave them a standing ovation.

# CHAPTER 17

# THANK GOD FOR THE NAVY

By that northern summer of 1941, the three remaining ships of the Scrap Iron Flotilla – *Stuart*, *Voyager*, and *Vendetta* – had been in the Mediterranean for eighteen months. There was no denying they were tired and worn, both by the stress of battle and the sheer effort of just staying afloat and keeping moving. Defects big and small were occurring more often, always with the prickling worry that something truly grave might happen at just the wrong moment. An engine breakdown that stopped the ship beneath a Stuka attack would almost certainly be fatal. Sometimes it seemed the old crocks were kept going more by willpower than anything else, exerted in the unflagging, unfailing work of the engineers nursing the old machinery in their charge.

The men too were feeling the strain. Some of those who arrived before that Christmas of 1939 had moved on, posted to other ships or returned home, but most had not. In particular, the men in critical jobs – the captains, the engineers, the senior petty officers – had been left in place to keep the show going. They stuck it out because there was no alternative, really; there was a war on and it had to be fought. That is what they had signed up for.

Yet the burden was heavy and the personal cost was high. The fear of death or wounding lingered always in the background, surging sharply to the fore after the bombers had been and gone. At other times it might be the imagination running riot as you lay awake and sweating in your hammock off watch, wondering if a torpedo with your name on it might be speeding towards you at that very moment.

And for even the most stoic mind there was the absence from home, tough enough for single youngsters to bear but tougher for married men. Some had not seen children born after they left, kids who were now more than a year old but a presence only in photographs and letters. At home, family lives went on. Children fell sick or started school, a brother or sister got married, nieces and nephews were born, the farm had a bad season or perhaps a good one, a much-loved grandparent died: the sailor far away on the other side of the world would learn of these things only weeks later when the mail arrived, with never a chance to shape events or to take part in them. If it was good news you could rejoice, but even then only belatedly. Bad news might drive a man to despair, to be solaced by his mates as best they could.

Those at home knew the other side of the coin. In a society and era where it was the natural order of things for men to make the family decisions, wives and mothers were inevitably thrust into the role. They too bore it because there was a war on and nothing to be done but to rise to the occasion. If the roof leaked or a child was misbehaving, if the bills were piling up or the drains became blocked, there was no man to make the decisions, fix the problem or mete out discipline. The woman had to deal with it. There was another strain for them as well; the worry of wondering if son, brother, husband or sweetheart were still alive. After a big happening made the newspapers – Matapan, the retreat from Greece and Crete – sailors would often send a cable from Alexandria to let their loved ones know they were okay, but even that could be fraught: the mere sight of the telegram boy cycling down the street towards the front gate struck fear in many a heart.

Three things made it work for the sailors: naval discipline, which was there whether you liked it or not; a genuine conviction that the war was a just cause and that King, Empire and Country were worth fighting for; and, underpinning it all, the concept of mateship. You kept going, you kept turning up, you kept doing your job so as not to let your mates down. This was perhaps the most powerful impulse of all.

The evidence suggests that naval law and order was enforced with a pragmatic light touch. Norm King, a feisty young stoker from South Australia, struck trouble in *Perth* when an officer pushed him aside in a passageway and he shoved back. Striking an officer could mean real trouble, even jail, but Norm was only busted back a rate from leading stoker to stoker, stripped of his good conduct badge and transferred out of *Perth* to *Stuart*, where he found himself under the discerning eye of Hec Waller.

> His ideas of good order and discipline bore little resemblance to that of a traditional naval captain, as I discovered when I was told to report to the bridge. We were at sea, with *Stuart* in its usual role of leading the destroyer screen. Captain Waller was dressed in shorts, sandals and an old floppy hat. He shook hands and welcomed me aboard. His conversation went as follows, interspersed with 'yessirs' from me:
>
> 'The chief tells me you have just dipped your rate, he tells me you can run a boiler room or engine room, we are short of killicks.[1] If you are prepared to behave yourself you can sew your badges back on.'
>
> As I was leaving the bridge, totally bemused, he called after me, 'You try that caper on any of my officers and you will lose more than your rate.'[2]

The punishment returns rarely showed much more than the usual humdrum naval misdemeanours – 'did return late from leave drunk', and the like – and the officers evidently behaved properly as well. In the Mediterranean there was nothing to match the explosive affair on board the new destroyer HMAS *Nestor* working up at Scapa Flow in May 1941, when the crew quite rightly refused to put to sea with a drunken captain and first lieutenant.[3]

As for King, Empire and Country, they were a given. Australians believed their place in the world was defined by their role as a dominion in the greatest empire the world had seen, a view widely shared across the political divide where politicians could speak of 'the British Race' with unaffected pride. Loyalty to the Crown and its current monarch, George VI, was unquestioned, of the natural order of things. Naval people knew that George had been a sailor himself, an acting sub lieutenant serving as a turret officer in a battleship at Jutland in 1916.[4] The sailors of the RAN jokingly called their British cousins 'kippers' – they said they were two-faced, no guts and smelled a lot – but it was not meant maliciously beyond the usual Anglo-Australian rivalries. Each side might enjoy a street brawl in Alexandria if the need arose, but when it mattered they were there for each other, as the misfortunes of *Waterhen* and *Defender* had shown.

There were medals enough to go round too. The *London Gazette*, the official weekly which announced these things, recorded in one issue in November 1940 the award of the red and blue ribbon of the Distinguished Service Order to Hec Waller and 'Copper' Morrow, a Distinguished Service Cross to Lieutenant Geoff Corlett of *Stuart*, and the Distinguished Service Medal to Leading Seaman George Cooper of *Voyager* and Able Seaman Harry Warr of *Stuart*. Norm 'Whiskers' Teacher, *Stuart*'s navigator, also won a DSO for sinking the *Gondar*. Mentions in Despatches were unremarkably common. These were all British medals, recommended by the Commander-in-Chief, approved by the Admiralty in Whitehall and conferred by the King. The Naval Board in Melbourne, the government in Canberra, and the Governor-General did not get a look in. That was the way it was done and nobody thought it unusual.

A shared loathing of the enemy kept things on an even keel, too, although there was perhaps a hint of grudging sympathy for the Italians, however detestable the fascist braggart at their head. There was none for the Germans, not when they machine-gunned survivors in the water. After Matapan, a German naval officer pulled from the sea by the British destroyer *Mohawk* was unwise enough to greet his rescuers with a Nazi salute and a crisp 'Heil Hitler!' An Australian on exchange in the ship, Ordinary Seaman Frank McAuliffe from Randwick in Sydney, promptly threw him overboard again with the command to 'salute properly when you board a British ship'. If called on, the Australians could bawl 'Rule Britannia' as lustily as any likely lad from Chatham, Portsmouth or Plymouth Hoe.

———

Over the months, the evermore months, there were things or moments or events that lodged in the memory. Some were light-hearted or humorous. Others could arouse a chill of fear or horror in recollection. Some were intensely personal, to be nursed privately. More were shared by your mates, or the rest of the ship's company who saw them happen or perhaps were involved. Often they became yarns to be retold – dits.

There was the dit about the little bloke in the grey civilian suit who approached the coxswain of *Waterhen*'s motorboat at the wharf in Alexandria and asked for a lift out to *Warspite*. The coxswain assumed he was the battleship's canteen manager or some such. 'Sure, mate, hop in,' he said. 'But you'll have to jump for it when we get there because the clutch is buggered and I can't go astern.' When the boat reached *Warspite*'s gangway ladder the coxswain shouted 'jump', the civilian made a practised leap, gave a farewell wave, and bounded up and on board. They only realised who their nondescript passenger had been when the Commander-in-Chief sent a signal to *Waterhen*'s captain thanking him for the ride.

The British usually called Cunningham by his initials, ABC. The Australians, a little more laconic, had taken to calling him Andy.

———

For some, when they were in harbour in Alexandria the nightly bombing raids became a spectacle you could almost enjoy. Bernard Morris, a sick-berth attendant in *Voyager* described one exhilarating night in a letter to his brother at home in Fremantle.

> Well, we have been in among the excitement again. Everything seems to be lively. The dive-bombers have a try at getting through the barrage at Alexandria, but what a barrage we put up!
>
> A week ago we were returning from shore when the sirens sounded. We scattered as arranged, but nothing happened, so a few of us boarded our motorboat to go out to the ship. We had gone only a few yards when all hell was let loose.
>
> I've never seen such a Guy Fawkes Night. Did we push the old motorboat to the nearest wharf? Shinned up the wall and made

a hundred yards dash for a nice big verandah. We knew what to expect in the way of shrapnel from our own shells.

No bombs were dropped; the barrage beat the Jerries. Three times they tried. We had a good view of the effect of nice big lumps of shell shrapnel hitting the cobblestones, sparks flying everywhere. The gun flashes and red tracer bullets made a wonderful show, but after an hour it got monotonous and I and a few others sat on a pillar and went to sleep.

It was quiet when we awoke but just as we got back to the ship they opened up again. The blast of all these guns together on a calm night makes quite a decent draught and it is quite a fascinating noise to hear the shells whistling through the air.[5]

—

Sensual, sultry Alexandria had its esoteric pleasures if you knew how and where to look for them and how to indulge when they appeared. Ean McDonald, the good-looking and personable signalman from *Stuart*, had come a long way from home in Perth:

I had found two havens. One was with a French family who ran a Pension, a friendly, small private hotel. They accepted me with my schoolboy French and took me into their private quarters and dining room for some lovely meals. I really felt at home in the bosom of that family.

The other haven was with a very wealthy lady named Alice Rofe. High born and genteel living, she was older, but not quite as my mother. Alice took me and two friends into her home as free entry guests. She introduced us to dinners in elegant French style and company. We would arrive by taxi through her great iron gates and drive up the long circular driveway to the Porte Cochere. A maid would greet us with directions that we were to join Madame in her boudoir. There she would entertain in pink satins and feathers surrounded by admirers, lady friends already decorated, gentlemen in spats, mirrors and dozens of perfumes. Occasional sweetmeats or titbits were served by the maid.

Before her audience she would complete her final makeup touches, like the glitter to already beautifully shaded eyelids, or the little lines around her gorgeously shaped red lips. Dining at home would be in full style with whole settings of silver and ranges of glasses doing justice to sumptuous meals and wines.

We were also treated out at dinner parties. Through Alice I met General Wavell and his daughter, as well as Monsieur Zavvy who made diamond bracelets for King Farouk's favourites. We swam on secluded beaches with Egypt's hierarchy and attended ambassadors' garden parties meeting Counts and Barons and engaging in glittering 'conversaziones' during extended dinner.

But by 0800 next morning we would be off once again to Tobruk.[6]

Other young men resisted the lure of the fleshpots. Able Seaman Chris Goldie, from Manly in Sydney, was one of those who had dived overboard from *Parramatta* to rescue survivors from *Auckland*. A devout Catholic, he kept a promise to his mother and visited a Franciscan church in Alexandria for Mass on his twenty-seventh birthday in June 1941. An amateur poet, he sent some lines home to her.

Bright flowers about an altar small
Scented the summer air.
Deep silence stretched from wall to wall
Like one long prayer.
The chapel clock it struck the hours
And the chimes rang out from the chapel tower
Ringing out the hour of three
Ringing out the Blessed Trinity.
Lord, in a month where shall I be?
And what, O Lord, in a year?
Where a lamp burned red
A soft voice said:
Draw near my son, draw near
For I am the Way, by land and sea,
I am the Truth and the Life
And if ye believe, my son, in Me
Ye shall live, though ye die in strife

I am He of whose Flesh thou art
And to thee is My promise given
For I am the Son and the Holy Ghost
And thy Father, who is in Heaven.[7]

Chris Goldie was killed a few months later. His mother sent the verses to be published in Sydney's *Catholic Weekly*.

Sometimes the moment was of unspeakable horror, lodged in the mind and never to be erased. Stoker Andy Nation was in *Waterhen* on a trip back from Tobruk, the ship crowded with soldiers as usual, when they were machine-gunned by three German aircraft. The men dived for what little cover they could find as the bullets zipped across the upper deck. One soldier hurled himself into one of the big fan chutes that sucked air down to the boilers, the intake normally covered by a grating of heavy wire mesh.

The grating gave way and he went headfirst down into the fan, he didn't even have time to scream. I had just arrived down below when all this clothing and stuff came flying out of the fan kicking up a hell of a din. I thought we had collected one.

The next thing I knew the petty officer and I were covered in blood and gore from head to foot. The guns were roaring and the machine guns chattering. I nearly passed out. We shut the fan down and the petty officer had a look in the fan with his torch and then perked all over the place. I had a look and my knees gave way. We did not know what to expect but when in the torchlight you see a head it gives you a hell of a shock. He was cut to ribbons. They pulled his body up on a rope, then went down for his arms, legs and head.[8]

Luck could have its way, too, a stroke of great good fortune that warmed them all. One night south of Crete *Stuart* was at sea with the fleet as the rearguard destroyer, zigzagging at speed in the wakes of the great ships. It was dark, with no moon. One of the lookouts saw a light ahead, the tiniest pinpoint so faint and flickering that it was there, and then it wasn't, and then it was again; a strange orange glow, like a candle.

Could it be a submarine on the surface? Unlikely, but Captain Waller brought the ship to action stations and ordered an Asdic search. The light grew a little bigger as they closed in on it, not by much, but enough to tell that it was not a submarine. Waller stopped the ship and the light passed down the starboard side, where the Bosun's Mate and a party of seamen were waiting with a boathook and heaving line. And there they saw a sailor and the light flickering on his lifebelt.

They hauled him on board. He was British and a teenager, grey with shock. They helped him down to the galley to warm him and dry him in spare clothing, to give him a reviving tot of officers' rum, and to listen to his story.

He had been the bridge messenger on the leading destroyer in the van of the fleet. The Officer of the Watch had sent him down to the galley to collect some kye but coming back he had tripped on the deck. The guard rails were down and he went overboard. Nobody heard his cry. And there he was alone in the Mediterranean as the cruisers and battleships swept past him one after the other. Miraculously, someone on the last ship heard his scream for help and tossed over one of the standby lifebelts. These had a ripcord device on them which ignited a small carbide flame when the belt hit seawater. It was this that saved him; that and the extraordinary good luck that *Stuart* had spotted him on that zigzag leg. That was very much a dit worth the retelling.

And then there could be something that brought a special meaning; a small, even fleeting happening which made sense of all the fear and the horror, all the boredom and the longing for home. Bill Reeve, an engine room artificer from Tasmania, put it in his own words:

I think one incident will always remain in my mind. *Vendetta* had just completed a rather torrid run from Tobruk and we had tied up alongside the pontoon at Mersa Matruh. The wounded were being carried ashore to the waiting ambulances. I came up on deck from the engine room just as a badly wounded digger was passing on a stretcher.

He looked a tough customer, covered with bloody bandages and with a week's growth of beard on his face. As he passed, he grabbed my arm with his good hand and I saw the tears well up in his eyes. He pulled me down to him and just said 'Thank God for the Navy.' Then he was gone. When you hear such sentiments it makes you feel that your efforts have been worthwhile.[9]

—

By the middle of 1941, *Voyager* was on her last legs, making heavy weather of it, her defects and breakdowns evermore frequent, evermore frustrating, evermore worrying. Even with everything working her best speed was now about 22 knots, a far cry from her death'n'glory days of 32 and more.

For the entire month of June she barely stopped, shuttling back and forth from Alexandria to Mersa Matruh and Tobruk with not a pause for breath, let alone leave ashore for the ship's company. A snapshot of *Voyager*'s war diary for one week of that month is a log of unending grind and monotony, with much of the hard work done in the midnight hours.

| | | |
|---|---|---|
| 5th | 0600 | Embarked military stores and personnel for Tobruk. |
| | 0700 | Left for Tobruk in company with HMAS *Vendetta*. |
| | 2342 | Anchored in Tobruk Harbour. |
| 6th | 0120 | All military equipment and personnel were disembarked and 200 Senoussi[10] were embarked. |
| | 0122 | Slipped and proceeded with *Vendetta* for Mersa Matruh. |
| | 0930 | Secured alongside in Mersa Matruh. |
| | 1832 | Proceeded in company with *Vendetta* to search for survivors from an RAF bomber shot down at sea. |
| 7th | 0756 | The search being unsuccessful, re-entered Mersa Matruh and secured alongside oiler *Zahra*. |
| 8th | 1259 | Embarkation of military equipment and personnel complete *Voyager* and *Vendetta* left Mersa Matruh for Tobruk. |
| | 2322 | Secured alongside jetty in Tobruk Harbour and commenced unloading passengers and stores. Fuel was also taken from tanks ashore. |
| 9th | 0027 | Embarked British wounded and Senoussi and proceeded with *Vendetta* for Alexandria. |

|        | 1540 | Secured alongside in Alexandria, all wounded and Senoussi being disembarked. |
|--------|------|------|
| 10th   | 2122 | Left Alexandria in company with HMAS *Waterhen* for Mersa Matruh. |
| 11th   | 0620 | Secured alongside in Mersa Matruh and commenced loading with military stores and personnel. |
|        | 1302 | Loading completed, proceeded with *Waterhen* for Tobruk. |
|        | 2259 | Came to anchor in Tobruk Harbour and commenced disembarkation of passengers and cargo. |
| 12th   | 0015 | Disembarkation completed, 220 Senoussi personnel were loaded and both left Tobruk for Mersa Matruh. |
|        | 0930 | Secured alongside in Mersa Matruh to disembark Senoussi.[11] |

*Voyager*'s Chief Engineer, Lieutenant (E) Albert Eric Edwards, was old navy, born in 1895 and at forty-six years of age the father of the ship, older than Commander Morrow himself. He had begun life in the RAN in 1923 as a warrant mechanician, serving in pretty much everything afloat at one time or another. Dedicated and dependable like most of his trade, he knew the innermost whims and workings of Brown-Curtis steam turbines and Yarrow boilers as well as any man alive. He and his right-hand man, Chief Engine Room Artificer John Picken, another old salt, had kept the ship going through thick and thin since their arrival in the Mediterranean.

But that exceptionally hot summer of 1941 and the constant strain of long hours and breakdowns pushed the Black Gang beyond the limit. Picken and several of the senior ERAs and stoker petty officers succumbed to exhaustion and had to be put ashore at Alexandria to recuperate in hospital. In early July, at their wits' end, Morrow and Edwards visited the port admiral to plead for replacements. A few were scraped together from around the fleet and sent over, as Edwards recorded:

By this time things had reached such a condition with the old ship's works that I never knew what was going to break up next. Our engine room now had an average temperature of 135° Fahrenheit [57° Celsius] with nearly 100 per cent humidity due to worn shafts and steam leaks. Even to perfectly fit people this would be almost unbearable. But I had to keep working my men day and night to keep things going. The inexperience of the new ratings made our job all the more difficult. Very soon they too were feeling the strain. But we had to stand up to it as long as we could get those vital supplies to our cobbers in Tobruk.[12]

They spent the first week of July alongside a wharf in Alexandria repairing defects, with a spell in dry dock, enduring air raids in the light of a full moon. On the evening of 10 July they loaded 40 tons of ammunition and thirty-two British troops and the next morning, at 0715 hours, they sailed for Tobruk once more. They lasted an hour and a half before a breakdown forced them back into harbour.

After yet another hurried patch-up job they tried again the next day, leaving in company with the destroyer HMS *Hero* on a voyage into a nightmare, compellingly described by Edwards:

On pins and needles we steamed across that fateful sea until within our last hundred miles of Tobruk. It wanted three hours to sunset when bang went something below. A boiler-room fan had broken, something which effectively put it out of action. This forced us to reduce speed still more, otherwise lack of an air supply to the oil-fuel burners would have caused heavy smoke that would have brought bombers like vultures to a dying beast.

Half an hour later there came a crack like a pistol shot as a steam valve support on one of the turbines snapped off. We managed to tie this down with wire, however. We crawled into Tobruk at last, wearily unloaded, and started back with the very best we could get out of the engines. Just at daylight a vital lubricating oil pipe to one of the turbine bearings snapped off, putting one of the turbines out of action. This gave me fearful worry. It meant that one hundred and fifty men were depending on me and worn-out machinery and an exhausted engine-room staff to get them out of

this. And the only thing that could keep us afloat and take us to
safety was speed.

Not daring to look, but with an ear miserably cocked for the
enemy's dawn patrol, I climbed to the bridge and reported to
the captain.

He patted me on the back and smiled. 'Never mind, chief. Do
your best and we might be lucky.'[13]

They were lucky. One aircraft flew over but it gave the recognition
signal and turned out to be an RAF fighter which – very welcome –
stuck with them for a while. Down below, Edwards' men were near
the end of their rope:

> We toiled like galley slaves, got her going on the one engine, and
> actually managed to work her up to 18 knots. It was done only
> by 'blood, sweat and tears' on the part of my men and myself.
> Because of the breakages and leaks, heat was escaping everywhere
> and turning the engine and boiler rooms into a near furnace. The
> men could only last ten minutes at a time. I had to call up all
> hands; as fast as a man collapsed he was hauled up top to recover.
> The man who relieved him would then toil until he too tumbled
> over. Just after daylight a submarine had a go at us but missed, and
> was chased away by our escort.[14]

With *Hero* shepherding her all the way, *Voyager* re-entered
Alexandria the next evening, at 1900 hours on 13 July. Once again
she secured alongside the big destroyer tender HMS *Woolwich* with
its well-equipped workshops, and once again they began the job of
binding up the wounds. A buzz began doing the rounds that they
might have done their last run to Tobruk, that they might even be
going home to Australia.

Men not needed on the work got a decent run ashore at last, with
overnight leave, and it was there that the trouble started. Just how and
why it happened and who was at fault is lost to history, but there was
evidently a violent fight that involved *Voyager* sailors and local Greeks
and Egyptians. Four sailors were arrested by the Egyptian police and
later another two – rather more inventively – were nabbed dressed in

civvies as they tried to sign on as merchant seamen on an outward-bound South African freighter. When they were returned to the ship over the next few days the mills of naval discipline began to grind: First Lieutenant's report, Captain's table and, finally, the reading of punishment warrants.

This was a serious business much dreaded. Punishment warrants were for severe offences attracting condign penalties that had to be approved by the higher powers ashore, and the process was formal and fearsome, little changed since the eighteenth century. The offenders were paraded on deck before the entire ship's company for their crimes to be read out and the punishment proclaimed. In this case it was a sentence of 'ninety days cells' for each man, which meant three months in a British military prison in Jerusalem notorious for its brutal regime. It must have come as a heavy blow, and all the heavier within a few days when the buzz turned out to be true: no more Tobruk Ferry, no more Spud Run. *Voyager* was indeed going home. The prisoners would be left behind to serve their sentences.

The first exciting sign that the rumours were correct came a couple of days later when the Italian Breda anti-aircraft guns souvenired from Bardia so long ago were unbolted from their mountings and sent ashore, along with their ammunition. The 3-inch anti-aircraft gun went too, another good sign. After that, things moved at a run. On 24 July, not quite an hour into the second dog watch, HMAS *Voyager* sailed from Alexandria for the last time, the sun sinking astern as she headed east to Port Said to take on a pilot for the Suez Canal. Away at last.

—

After the evacuation of Crete, *Stuart* enjoyed a brief respite in mid-June, joining the 15th Cruiser Squadron in the eastern Mediterranean bombarding the Vichy French in Syria. The Allies had invaded Syria on 8 June to forestall a German push there that might have threatened Britain's oil supplies from Persia and Iraq. Syria[15] was nominally a French protectorate, actually a colony, and the governor-general there had cast his lot with the Axis. The fighting on land was hot, with the Australian army's 7th Division advancing on Beirut and the RAAF's 3 Squadron flying its brand-new Tomahawk fighters in support.

At sea there was little to do. The weather was travel-poster perfect. Well away from the Luftwaffe, *Stuart*'s ship's company basked in the sun on calm seas for six days until, on 16 June, they returned to Alexandria to join the notorious Spud Run again. It was back to the war proper. Week after week they made the journey beneath air raid after air raid. One day they sighted an Italian submarine on the surface, which Hec Waller went for with his usual ferocity, but they lost contact after it dived.

A couple of days later they nudged a shoal on the approach to Tobruk, badly damaging the starboard propellor, and on the leg back to Alexandria the next day there were, as Hec's Report of Proceedings coolly put it, 'Heavy moonlight and dawn attacks by enemy bombers at 0508, 0509, 0512, 0520, 0521, 0535, 0538, 0607, 0616'.

She was not hit and the propellor was replaced, but the tortuous twisting and turning at high speed may well have brought her undone. On 26 July her port engine packed it in, and when they opened it up in Alexandria they found an engineer's nightmare of four rows of stripped blades and ground metal. It would have taken months to repair there, consuming valuable time and resources needed for other ships. And the faults and breakdowns were becoming all too frequent. There was nothing else for it: *Stuart* should go home too, back to Australia on one engine.

If there was any sense of anti-climax, of going out with a whimper rather than a bang, it was more than well-tempered by the delicious prospect of leaving that blasted, seething Mediterranean and the sheer joy of seeing home and family again. Not everybody struck it lucky. Some of *Stuart*'s crew, including her faithful diarist, Signalman Les Clifford, were transferred to *Perth*, but most would be heading south. Ashore there was a feverish buying of souvenirs, or 'rabbits' as the navy oddly called them for some long-forgotten reason.

There were the proper goodbyes to be said. Hec Waller was the senior Australian in the Mediterranean Fleet and it is possible, even likely, that Cunningham gave him a farewell dinner at the Commander-in-Chief's residence, something he and his wife Nona enjoyed doing regularly for his officers. If it did happen, neither man left a record of it and we can only speculate. Horatio Nelson, the

extrovert with his heart on his sleeve, borrowed from Shakespeare's
*Henry V* to laud his Mediterranean captains as a 'band of brothers'.
Cunningham, imperturbable and collected, certainly no seeker of the
eighteenth-century notion of glory that inspired Nelson, was nonetheless cut from the same steel as his predecessor and he made it plain
that he liked, admired and respected Waller immensely, a view shared
around the fleet. Hec's final 'flimsy' in the Med, a report on an officer
by his superior, was as good as it gets. The Rear Admiral (Destroyers)
Irvine Glennie wrote that he was:

A much-valued officer whose services I am very sorry to lose.
A first-class fighting leader whose cheery, buoyant and resolute
outlook brushes difficulty aside and gets the best out of those
serving with him.[16]

He recommended Waller for promotion to flag rank. Andrew
Cunningham signed it and added the word 'concur'. Rather more
practically, the Naval Board in Melbourne decided that Hec could
come home by air instead of spending a month or more limping
south through the Indian Ocean on one engine, an offer gratefully
accepted. Nancy and the two boys, Michael and John, would travel
from Melbourne to Sydney by train to meet him at the Qantas flying
boat base at Rose Bay. Father and warrior, he was still only forty-one
years old.

Then there was the old crock herself to be handsomely sent off.
Her long-serving and loyal first lieutenant, Rupert Robison, by
now a lieutenant commander, would be taking her home, his first
command. On the afternoon of 22 August, the day of her sailing, the
Commander-in-Chief's barge cut a furrow in the harbour waters and
came alongside *Stuart* on her buoy. All dazzling white uniform, gold
braid and medal ribbons, Andy bounded on board to be received with
due ceremony and to address the ship's company. One of the men
there that day, Arthur Collins, then an acting leading seaman, made
a careful note of Cunningham's words:

Well, you're off home. And I didn't think I could allow your ship
to leave without coming on board to say a few words of goodbye to

you. You have been here nearly two years. You came in the piping days of peace.

*Stuart* and the four other Australian destroyers formed the most substantial part of the Mediterranean Fleet, and I kept you fairly busy. I think I said to your Captain at the time, 'You needn't worry, no great war ever took place without spreading to the Mediterranean' and sure enough it did.

You have done splendidly. If I were to enumerate all the operations you have taken part in and all you have done, you would never leave Alexandria, it would take so long. One or two, however, I would like to mention. I seem to remember that time off the coast of Italy, when I ordered the *Stuart* and the remaining Australian destroyers to go and look after the *Eagle*. The next thing I saw was *Stuart* leading the van of the destroyers after the Italian fleet. I said, 'That damn fellow ought to be court martialled.' But you see, he wasn't.

If ever there was a submarine reported, I always said, 'Send out the *Stuart*'. Later on, I remember, you had a wild night at Matapan. I always wondered, when the other destroyers were sent off and *Stuart* was left behind to look after the battle wagon – I always wondered what you were saying! However, you had a night to make up for it.

I am very grateful to you for what you have done and for the example you have undoubtedly set. A special word for the Black Squad – the engine room department. They have done magnificently to keep these ships going and I am grateful to them too. Every destroyer was most valuable and had to be kept running.

We shall miss you here. The whole fleet will part with you with great regret. We are very proud to have had you with us, and I hope you are proud to have been in the Mediterranean Fleet.

I hope you will have a very happy homecoming, and that the folk Down Under will give you the welcome you deserve. Goodbye to you all.[17]

When the Admiral left they saw him standing in the stern of his barge, waving his cap at them. The next day he sent a formal signal to the Naval Board in Melbourne:

It is with great regret that we part with HMAS *Stuart* from the Mediterranean Station. Under the distinguished command of Captain Waller she has an unsurpassed record of gallant achievement. She has taken a leading part in all the principal operations of the Mediterranean Fleet and has never been called up in vain for any difficult job. The work of her engine room department in keeping this old ship efficient and in good running order has been beyond all praise. The Mediterranean Fleet is poorer by the departure of this fine little ship and her gallant ship's company.[18]

Rupert Robison took her to sea that evening, farewell messages from other ships in the harbour keeping the signalmen on the jump. From the Vice Admiral First Battle Squadron, from *Queen Elizabeth*, from *Valiant*, from cruisers and destroyers, it seemed they came from every ship they passed. It was fine, it was fitting.

The next day they were in the Suez Canal, leaving forever that ancient Mediterranean battlefield and its graveyard of ships and men. Remarkably, for all the enemy had thrown at them in twenty tumultuous months, not one life had been lost.

—

*Vendetta* was the last of the Scrap Iron ships to leave, sticking to it on the Tobruk convoys longer than any, for a record thirty-nine runs in and out between May and 3 August. The official figures credited her with taking 1532 troops into Tobruk and bringing 2951 away, and transporting 616 tons of supplies. After that she was doing mostly convoy work between Egypt, Syria and Cyprus, still under frequent air attack but with not nearly the intensity of the Spud Run. She sailed for Singapore on 20 October.

Other Australians stayed on. The light cruiser *Hobart* arrived in Alexandria on 18 July to replace her sister ship *Perth*, which left for home the next day. Another of the new N class destroyers, HMAS *Nestor*, turned up to join *Napier* and *Nizam*, and the little sloop *Parramatta* kept plugging away, mostly escorting those slow and dangerous convoys of the Tobruk Ferry.

*Parramatta*'s captain, Jeff Walker, had a taxi accident in Alexandria which put him in hospital for a spell and left him with a nagging

back pain, but he was back in his ship by the end of August and on
1 September he was promoted to acting commander. The horrors
of the war bore in on him and his crew. At sea off Tobruk on one
hideous day they passed a Carley float and later a rubber raft, both
containing the bodies of RAF aircrew sprawled in death. There was
no way of knowing how long they had been floating, and stopping to
recover them would have been too dangerous and simply pointless.
There was nothing to do but salute them and keep going.

The unceasing bombing at sea and in harbour played on their
minds, ground on their nerves. Walker wrote of it constantly to Mary
at home in Adelaide:

Harbour brings little relief from the strain because of the
incessant air raids. Night-time in harbour on board is no
longer a relief to one's nerves ... my ship's company and most
of the officers no longer turn in between decks. They sleep in
their clothes (even those not on duty) at their guns and action
stations, ready to spring up at a moment's warning. They wake
up instantly, stand about for minutes or hours, fire the guns
madly, and finally fling themselves down again and are asleep
almost at once ...

... A few nights ago in the crowded fleet anchorage a bomber
nearly took out both masts from this ship, and dropped a bomb
which nearly sank the buoy of the large warship moored a few feet
away from us. It holed a destroyer in a number of places along her
waterline and killed a man in the fo'c'sle of the larger ship. I was in
the Director and tried to shrink through the floor of it when I felt
the wind of the plane, and hid my head in my hands as the bomb
came down. One large piece of bomb passed two feet from us and
tore a large hole in the funnel ...

... We have to face up to realities, my dear. We are really up
against it here, and I am very tired and so are we all. God knows
there's little encouragement, but you hold in your dear hands
peace for me in a wild, chaotic world ...

... We haven't had any mail for some time, and I hope to find
some in port. Darling, if you can, make sure someone tells us when
this war is over, so that we will know to come home ...[19]

There was a change of scene for the little sloop in October when she went back to the searing heat of the Gulf of Suez again. It was mainly a humdrum surveying job, but everyone's spirits were lifted briefly when Berlin Radio, with its customary creativity, proclaimed them to be searching for a new base for the fleet when it was driven from the Mediterranean, as it surely soon would be. One hectic day and night, though, of consummate seamanship from Walker and daring boatwork in heavy surf by his executive officer, Lieutenant Commander Percy Forwood, saw *Parramatta* rescue the crew of a bombed freighter driven onto a coral reef.

After that it was back to the Tobruk Ferry again, where she was joined by her sister ship *Yarra*, newly arrived from the Red Sea.

—

Towards the end of the year a new menace was emerging in the Mediterranean, slowly at first but with a quickening drumbeat. In the early hours of 17 October, a convoy of two merchant ships, escorted by an armed trawler, sailed from Alexandria for Tobruk. One ship was *Parramatta*'s old charge, the plucky little tanker *Pass of Balmaha*. The other was a Greek freighter, the *Samos*, carrying general supplies to the garrison.

About 80 kilometres west of Alexandria, well before dawn, both ships were torpedoed and sunk. Fully laden with petrol, the *Pass of Balmaha* exploded in a fireball that killed her young master, Stanley Hardy, and all twenty of her crew.

The successful attacker was a German submarine, *U-97*. Kapitän-leutnant Ugo Heilmann, *U-97*'s captain and a renowned ace from the Battle of the Atlantic, noted in his war diary that the flames from the tanker rose 300 metres in the air.

U-boats had finally arrived in *das Mittelmeer*.

# CHAPTER 18

# SCARED STIFF
# AND ANXIOUS

The Kriegsmarine had been reluctant to send U-boats to the Mediterranean again. Großadmiral Raeder and his Befehlshaber der Unterseeboote, Vizeadmiral Karl Dönitz, recalled all too well the fiasco of the three boats which never made it in 1939 and had no wish to repeat the experience. The Strait of Gibraltar would always be a narrow and dangerous choke point, well patrolled by the British, they thought.

Dönitz, in particular, wanted to keep his force in the Atlantic where he was successfully developing his *Rudeltaktik*, the 'wolf pack' attacks on convoys micro-managed from his mansion headquarters at Kernével in France. For that he needed all the boats he could lay his hands on. In the Führer's naval conferences of 1941 he and Raeder resisted the Mediterranean idea as best they could. At the Wolfsschanze, Hitler's redoubt in East Prussia, Raeder explained in July that:

> It is not possible to send submarines into the Mediterranean as this would handicap operations in the Atlantic. Moreover, British submarines and aircraft are the forces used in the Mediterranean to attack transports, and these cannot be combatted with submarines. Italian anti-submarine defence must be properly organised for this purpose.[1]

The army, though, kept up the pressure. The supply lines for the Afrika Korps from Italy to Tripoli and Benghazi were tenuous at best, Erwin Rommel never being comfortable that he would have the fuel, men, food, ammunition and tanks he needed to keep the Allied armies at bay, let alone to roll them back east. Evermore impressed with Rommel's energy and aggression, Hitler agreed. At another naval conference on 22 August, Raeder made one last attempt to keep his boats in the Atlantic but he was overruled, with the Führer pronouncing that:

> The surrender of North Africa would mean a great loss both to us and the Italians. The British are very dependent on supplies by sea in the Eastern Mediterranean. The Italians have achieved nothing with their submarines. It is very desirable to relieve the Afrika Korps with a few German submarines. Six should be sent.[2]

The Kriegsmarine reluctantly gave in. At the next naval conference, on 17 September, Dönitz reported that two boats were on the way and another four would leave later in the month. The first, *U-371*, passed east through the Strait of Gibraltar on 21 September and *U-559* followed on the 26 September. These two would form the nucleus of the 23 Unterseebootsflottille, the 23rd Submarine Flotilla based on the captured Greek navy port at Salamis, west of Piraeus.

Eventually, sixty-two U-boats attempted the passage into the Med. At first they used the logical approach and passed Gibraltar submerged, rigged for silent running and drifting in with the easterly current, a process which took a long and nerve-wracking five hours. Experience taught the captains it was actually better and much quicker to do it on the surface by night, on moonless nights if possible when the tide was flowing in from the Atlantic at some 5 knots, relying on the boat's low silhouette to remain undetected. Nine were caught and sunk on the way in and another twenty or so were forced to abort the passage for one reason or another, but most made it. The crews came to call the Mediterranean *die Mausefalle*, the Mousetrap, for not one of the boats that entered the sea returned home to Germany; they were either sunk or scuttled. But that lay in the future. For the rest of 1941 and 1942 they set about creating havoc. The loss of the *Pass of Balmaha* was but the beginning of a very long line of destruction. There would be no *Rudeltaktik* here, though. That was for the grey wastes of the Atlantic. In the shallower, smaller Mediterranean, they would be lone wolves.

—

By July 1941, both General Blamey in Cairo and the Menzies government in Canberra were beginning to press for the withdrawal of the Australians holding out at Tobruk. Broadly, there were two reasons: the declining physical stamina of the men there, with a growing fear that they could not take it much longer; and increasing disquiet at the British habit of employing Australian divisions here, there and everywhere, piecemeal instead of as one consolidated national force. After a meeting that month with General Morshead, the garrison commander, and with the approval of the Australian government, Blamey wrote a formal letter to the Commander-in-Chief and his nominal superior, Auchinleck:

> It is recommended that action be taken forthwith for the relief of the garrison at Tobruk. These troops have been engaged continuously in operations since March and are therefore well into their fourth month. The strain of continuous operations is showing signs of affecting the troops. The commander of the garrison informs me the average loss of weight to be approximately a stone per man ...[3]
> ... With reference to the Australian portion of the garrison: the agreed policy for the employment of Australian troops between the British and Australian governments is that the Australian troops should operate as a single force ...[4]

The British were unimpressed, to say the least. Churchill and Auchinleck were both planning yet another offensive in North Africa and, understandably, they wanted none of what they regarded as unnecessary Commonwealth distractions. There was bad blood. Auchinleck thought 'Old Blamey' to be mired in the trench warfare of 1918 and the two had an angry row, which Auchinleck began with the customary, tedious British barbs about ill-disciplined diggers failing to salute. The British general threatened to fire the Australian general who in turn called his bluff and bluntly dared him to do it. Auchinleck backed off.

From London, Churchill quickly weighed in with his usual wiles of bullying and bombast, seeking to browbeat the Menzies government into keeping the 9th Division in place. In fairness, he carried the weight of the wider war on his shoulders; the RAF bombing campaign over Germany was getting into high gear, and in September alone U-boats sank fifty-six merchant ships in the Atlantic convoys, nearly a quarter of a million tons. But he never shook the belief that the troops of the Empire's independent dominions were his to deploy, with their governments and peoples stepping obediently into line.

Matters were not helped by the ongoing political crisis in Australia, in which Menzies was stabbed in the back by his own party and replaced on 29 August by his deputy, the National Party leader Arthur Fadden. Churchill sought to exploit the political differences, probing for any chink, but Fadden was just as anxious to get the Australians out. The British prime minister had no choice but to back down, agreeing eventually and reluctantly that the withdrawal could happen, but adding a little velvety blackmail:

> I trust, however, that you will weigh very carefully the immense responsibility which you would assume before history by depriving Australia of the glory of holding Tobruk until Victory was won, which otherwise, by God's help, will be theirs forever.[5]

It cut no ice. And when the Fadden government also collapsed a month later the new prime minister, Labor's John Curtin, was equally adamant that the Australians should be relieved. Curtin, more than most, had an eye on the rising menace of Japan, a concern the British chose to diminish. The withdrawal began.

—

As ever, the men actually doing the fighting had no inkling of the schemes and ructions of statesmen and generals, of great matters decided far above their heads. If anyone had suggested it to them, it seems unlikely the Rats of Tobruk would have embraced the historical grandeur of staying on to final victory. At sea, the Ferry remained in business, as harried as ever. Andrew Cunningham had no liking for the Australian evacuation either and he pointedly met Blamey to show him the long list of men and ships already lost from the Inshore Squadron, but that done he dutifully set about making it happen in four separate operations. Fast ships would go into Tobruk on the moonless nights of August, September, October and early November, taking out the Australians and bringing in their replacements.

With the Scrap Iron ships gone, the N class destroyers *Nizam* and *Napier* replaced them on the fast runs, while *Parramatta* took her turn escorting the slow supply convoys. Eventually, *Yarra* came up from the Red Sea as well and *Hobart* both carried troops and joined the bombardment of the Germans and Italians ashore. The British put their backs into it, too, adding more cruisers and destroyers to the Inshore Squadron and the swift minelayers HMS *Abdiel* and *Latona*, brand-new ships which could turn on an impressive 38 knots.

The bombing continued, the attrition continued. On a dark night entering Tobruk on 14 August, *Nizam* struck a hidden wreck in that treacherous harbour, damaging her bow. A month later, on 17 September, this time leaving Tobruk, a near miss stopped her oil fuel pumps. She had to be towed clear by the destroyer HMS *Kingston* to make some running repairs at sea that got her going again and back to Alexandria.

On 20 October, the Australian 2/24th Infantry Battalion was ready to leave Tobruk, more than ready. Raised in Victoria and proudly calling themselves 'Wangaratta's Own', they had been in the garrison from the beginning in April, in and out of the thick of the fighting – the Easter Battle, the Battle of the Salient, Hill 209 – with many dozens killed and wounded and some captured. In their last week they packed their weapons and all the bags and baggage of a battalion, making way for the men of the incoming Sussex Regiment. They published their final Tobruk edition of their newspaper, the *Furphy Flyer*; they held a sing-song and, most solemnly of all, they tended the graves of their mates for the last time, men buried in a small dirt cemetery beneath a monument with the inscription: *This is hallowed ground, for those who lie here have died for their country.*

That night the 2/24th was divided in two: the 'North' group of 289 men, who trooped with their kit on board the minelayer *Latona*, and the 'South' group of 298 men who were crowded shoulder to shoulder on the upper deck of *Nizam*. It was reckless, almost impossible overcrowding, but there it was. The ships sailed just before midnight on a fast passage to Alexandria, together with the destroyer *Kingston*, cleaving through a disturbed sea which brought on the miseries of seasickness for men who only recently had been enduring North Africa's punishing dust storms. The night was uneventful, those diggers not vomiting over the guard rails snatching what sleep they could curled up on their kitbags. Shortly before dawn the two destroyers were diverted to go to the aid of the gunboat *Gnat* which had been torpedoed north-east of Bardia and both ships hared off, only to be diverted a couple of hours later and ordered back eastwards to avoid a flight of enemy bombers reported in the area.

It was 0940 hours. As *Nizam* heeled into the turn onto the new course, disaster struck. A rogue wave, bigger than all the rest, hit them green on the bow, tons of water surging the length of the ship and washing twenty soldiers overboard. Others clung on, buffeted and bruised. The captain, Lieutenant Commander Max Clark, brought the ship around and stopped her upwind of the khaki-clad figures thrashing in the waves. The bosun's mates struggled through the milling, horrified throng of soldiers on deck to get a scrambling net over the side. There was no way to lower a boat, not in that crowd. All the men in the water were wearing heavy boots and webbing. Some sailors dived overboard to help, dragging the soldiers to the net and the willing arms waiting to heave them back to safety.

Six of the twenty did not make it. In the confusion, in the turmoil of the troubled seas, they vanished. Privates Leo Considine, Reg Fidge, Alf James, Alf Salixs and Eric Willis – all Victorians and all in their twenties – and Jim Nash, a Tasmanian the same age, were washed away, the wretched irony of soldiers meeting a sailor's lonely end, the sea their grave. One more man, Corporal Denis Horan, died of his wounds on board.

*Nizam* made it back to Alexandria that evening.[6] There should not have been so many souls crammed on board. Commander Clark should not have made the turn at speed. But that is hindsight.

—

Sir Claude Auchinleck launched his long-planned offensive, Operation Crusader, on 18 November. The commander in the field would be General Sir Alan Cunningham, the admiral's brother and the man who had beaten the Italians in East Africa. Before dawn that morning, the Western Desert Force of British, Indian, New Zealand, South African and Australian troops – now renamed the Eighth Army – sprang forward from its base at Mersa Matruh and surged across the border into Libya. The object was to relieve Tobruk and to hurl the Germans and Italians back westwards, to ultimate defeat if possible.

It was a day of driving rain which kept the Luftwaffe reconnaissance and bomber aircraft largely grounded, and Rommel made the mistake of assuming that the British were just probing, not making a full-scale attack. By nightfall the British 7th Armoured Brigade was halfway to Tobruk.

But as the Axis forces regrouped there were fierce tank and infantry battles with heavy losses on both sides, their fortunes swaying back and forth. It was the essence of the elder von Moltke's dictum that 'no plan of operations reaches with any certainty beyond the first encounter with the enemy's main force'.[7] The British narrowly retained the upper hand and kept pushing west.

At sea, November would be a hard and bitter month. The great carrier HMS *Ark Royal* was sunk by a U-boat, *U-81*, near Gibraltar on 13 November although, miraculously, with the loss of only one life. And on 19 November, far away in the Indian Ocean, the RAN suffered its greatest ever disaster with the tragic destruction of the cruiser *Sydney*.

It began late that afternoon, some 200 kilometres off Dirk Hartog Island, the most westerly point of Western Australia. *Sydney*'s new captain, Joseph Burnett – inexperienced, in his first wartime command – incautiously took his ship in close to inspect what appeared to be a Dutch merchant steamer, the *Straat Malakka*. She was in fact the disguised and well-armed German raider *Kormoran*, whose captain, Fregattenkapitän Theodor Detmers, slowly and methodically lured *Sydney* towards him with a flurry of deliberately confused responses to Burnett's signals. The two were about

1300 metres apart, point-blank range, when the Dutch flag came down, the Kriegsmarine ensign soared up *Kormoran*'s mast, and her concealed guns and torpedo tubes opened fire. Burnett was taken by surprise, entrapped. *Sydney* fought back gamely but she was reduced to a burning wreck, drifting off into the night and vanishing with her entire ship's company, every one of them, 645 men.

*Kormoran* was also hit hard and she sank when mines in her hold exploded, but her crew had already abandoned ship and of 399 men on board there were 318 saved,[8] including Detmers. Interrogated when they were taken ashore, the Germans gave what details they knew of the battle and *Sydney*'s end, evidently truthfully.

Most of the Australians killed, officers and men, had been with the cruiser in her glory days with John Collins in the Mediterranean, and the nation and the RAN were plunged into shock, disbelief and anguish when the disaster was announced eleven days later on 30 November. Australians had proudly regarded *Sydney* as emblematic of everything their navy should be: the hero of Cape Spada, strong and victorious. The defeat was inexplicable, incalculable. John Curtin, in office less than two months, expressed the national mood.

### CURTIN URGES AUSTRALIA TO FOLLOW *SYDNEY*'S LEAD

'I have no doubt that the Royal Australian Navy will always include an HMAS *Sydney*,' the Prime Minister (Mr Curtin) said in Canberra yesterday in urging the nation, with the example of the cruiser before it, to an iron resolve to face the facts of the war.

'Every fact and portent demand that Australians should put the war in the forefront of all our thinking and of all our acts.

'What we call the Australian station is a station of war. What we call Australian security is a security which is being attacked.

'It was in resisting and overcoming enemy action against Australia that the gallant men of HMAS *Sydney* rendered to this nation their full measure of devotion. Our gratitude can have no limit.

'The call on us, however, goes far beyond sentiment. War is a grim thing. Deeds and conduct are what count. Today, with the example of HMAS *Sydney* before us, let this nation make its tribute an iron resolve to use every effort of which it is capable to face the facts of war, not only with proud courage but also with all our might and all our strength.

'Whoever we be, and whatever we are, there is a place of high service for each of us.'[9]

The naval toll mounted around the globe. On 24 November, the cruiser HMS *Dunedin* was sunk by a U-boat off Brazil, with 419 killed. The very next day, the Mediterranean Fleet suffered its heaviest blow when the grand old battleship *Barham* was torpedoed about 100 kilometres north of Sollum. Andrew Cunningham was among the hundreds who witnessed it:

I was sitting in my bridge cabin in the *Queen Elizabeth* having tea. I suddenly heard and half-felt the door give three distinct rattles and thought we had opened fire with our anti-aircraft guns. I went quickly up one ladder to the bridge and then I saw the *Barham*, immediately astern of us, stopped and listing heavily over to port. The thuds I had heard were three torpedoes striking her. She had been torpedoed by a U-boat.

The poor ship rolled nearly over on to her beam ends and we saw the men massed on her upturned side. A minute later there came the dull rumble of a terrific explosion as one of her main magazines blew up. The ship became hidden in a great cloud of yellow-ish black smoke, which went wreathing and eddying high into the sky. When it cleared away the *Barham* had disappeared. There was nothing but a bubbling, oily-looking patch on the calm surface of the sea, dotted with wreckage and the heads of swimmers. It was ghastly to look at, a horrible and awe-inspiring spectacle.[10]

On board *U-331*, Oberleutnant zur See Hans-Diedrich von Tiesenhausen had boldly penetrated the destroyer screen at periscope depth and fired four torpedoes at a range of just 700 metres, three of which hit. An RAN officer, Ian McDonald was flag lieutenant to the Vice Admiral First Battle Squadron, Pridham-Wippell. After helping his boss into a life jacket he fled the bridge. The battleship was rolling over but still moving as he clambered onto her emerging bottom.

It was probably only about four minutes since the ship had been hit. I estimate she then had a list of about 60 degrees.

Those of us who were scrambling over the barnacles, which were pretty sharp, were close to the swirling sea when there was a tremendous shudder throughout the ship which turned out to be a major explosion in one of the 15-inch magazines aft. One sailor near me said 'Christ, another torpedo', and another said 'Nah, the bastard's blowin' up'. That was enough for me to hurl myself at the sea and hope for the best.

When I hit the sea, the ship was rapidly disintegrating by the force of the tremendous explosion. Gun turrets and pieces of superstructure were being hurled hundreds of feet into the air, and I was immediately engulfed in the vortex of a 33,000-ton battleship which was sinking rapidly. I had no control of my limbs which were at the mercy of the swirling water, but I had the presence of mind to hold my breath as long as I could. I think my first attempt lasted about three-quarters of a minute. The second wasn't so good because I breathed in some water, but when I tried again I was apparently in the middle of a God-sent bubble until I surfaced – on the point of giving up the ghost and barely conscious. Nearer my God to thee!

I could see nothing because of the pall of black smoke covering the sea. I think I can owe my miraculous survival to the efficiency of my inflated 'Gieves Waistcoat' as I have never been able to swim more than about 50 yards at the best of times.

When I could see where I was, the ship had gone, and there were no signs of life nearby. The surface of the sea was covered with oil fuel and so was I. When I was submerged I had time to think of my mother and my wife, but my over-riding thought was to survive – and I was lucky.[11]

Ian McDonald was rescued by the destroyer *Hotspur*, as was the admiral. Legend later had it that Pridham-Wippell gave his life jacket to a young sailor and then, to keep up the survivors' morale, floated in the sea singing 'There'll Always Be an England'. *Nizam*, which was with the fleet, picked up 150 survivors, but 862 men were killed. The bereaved families were informed but told to keep their loss secret, and

*Barham*'s destruction was not revealed by the Admiralty until January the next year.[12] Only then did von Tiesenhausen find out what ship he had sunk. He was awarded the Knight's Cross.

—

Too small and too slow to sail with the battlefleet or a destroyer flotilla, *Parramatta* plugged on with her humble yet arduous task of escorting the supply vessels to and from Tobruk, day after day, night after night, week after week.

On 18 November 1941, the day of Auchinleck's advance, she and *Yarra* and three of the little anti-submarine whalers, *Falk*, *Soika* and *Klo*, ushered two merchant ships out of Alexandria in dirty weather of gales and rain. Visibility was bad, the coastline often vanishing in sudden squalls, although that at least had the benefit of keeping the Stukas on the ground. Aware of the army operation ashore, Jeff Walker wrote another of his long and candid letters to his family:

> Ten a.m., and we are taking part in an historic event. The sky is almost entirely covered with massed white and grey cloud, and the sea is leaden and sluggish below … I don't feel warlike one bit. I feel tired and harassed and scared stiff and anxious, and oh, I would like a little peace of mind. I flatter myself that my face manages to look calm and confident …
>
> … Ashore, not far from us, our army fights what will be undoubtedly one of the greatest battles in history. Also ashore, and not far from us, the enemy holds certain points and particularly, probably, the aerodromes from which come the fearful Stukas. Below, the sea may produce an enemy torpedo at any moment. Torpedo attack from the air or high or medium level bombing may develop without much warning. And we three, in a flexible formation, surround a tiny ship loaded with hundreds of tons of the most fearful high explosive, badly needed by a hard-pressed garrison. It must get through the cordon tonight.
>
> This voyage, although of course like all the others hereabouts, has been particularly one long headache.[13]

That tiny, loaded ship was the *Toneline*, of 811 tons, another tramp petrol tanker. Not long after nightfall she broke down and began drifting ashore in the murk towards a rocky coast. *Parramatta* went to take her in tow, attempting to send over a line in the ship's whaler, but that effort was defeated by the heavy sea. Exasperated, Walker told *Toneline* to anchor while he recovered his boat in the dark, not daring to show a light that might attract an enemy aircraft.

> I manoeuvred off again into the blackness and thankfully hoisted the whaler and its exhausted crew. Then once more I carefully approached the anchored, broken-down ship and with strained precision anchored *Parramatta* ahead. It wasn't quite where I wanted her as she fell off at the right moment. This proved rather lucky as, on the yaws of the wind, the two ships swung together, just not touching. By jockeying the cable I got 'em just right and we passed over a line with surprising ease.
>
> At this moment the night was lit by flares not far away. One of our own aircraft had discovered an enemy submarine on the surface. It dived at once of course. Well! There we were, a gift for him if he spotted us, both of us anchored and helpless. I just decided not to think about it and to get on with the job.
>
> After a long delay and infinite precautions, I had both ships underway and set off at a crawl through the night for the nearest intermediate port. Obviously the submarine did not attack us, I thank God. The rest of that night I spent on the bridge smoking nervous cigarette after cigarette and feeling seasick, mostly with worry I think.[14]

One false move and *Parramatta* might well have lost her whaler or ended up on the rocks in the dark. She managed to get the *Toneline* into Mersa Matruh, where engineers got her going again and, after an intensive air raid that evening, they set off once more for Tobruk. The ship and her cargo were delivered safely that night, another win against the odds. It had been a remarkable trial of seamanship, fraught with real risk. Joining up with *Yarra* again, *Parramatta* returned to Alexandria early in the morning of 23 November, happy to have a fighter escort for part of the way; aircraft with the cheering sight of the RAF red, white and blue roundels on their wings rather than the hated swastika.

Andrew Cunningham had heard of their feat. The little sloop had barely secured at the wharf and not yet lowered her gangway when, without ceremony, the admiral appeared from nowhere and vaulted over the guard rail and onto the deck to offer his congratulations. Not expecting any such visitation, Jeff Walker had gone to take a bath. Andy burst in on him. The Commanding Officer of His Majesty's Australian Ship *Parramatta* greeted the Commander-in-Chief of His Majesty's Mediterranean Fleet clad only in a hurriedly gathered towel.

But at last there was some rest. The sloop was due for a boiler clean, which took up a couple of days and gave the hands some long-awaited leave and Walker a chance to take a reluctant crack at the mountain of paperwork the navy demanded of its captains. In that he would be helped by the worthy Chief Petty Officer Writer Ted Purtell, a rock of industrious common sense who had joined the navy as a *Tingira* boy in 1921. Done with the bumph, Walker could look forward to the relaxation he enjoyed most: a few games of tennis and squash. More time, too, to write to Mary about the house she had just bought for them in Adelaide, their first house, real ownership, something that excited him very much. All his letters were threaded with a longing for peace and home, together with confessions of what he believed to be human frailty but which were, in fact, a demonstration of high moral courage and leadership.

In Libya, the fighting had reached a new pitch of ferocity. That same Sunday 23 November, a day that Protestant Germans called *Totensonntag*, Death Sunday, an annual religious festival for honouring the dead, the 15th Panzer and Italian Ariete Divisions encircled and annihilated the 5th South African Infantry Brigade at Sidi Rezegh in the desert south-east of Tobruk. In a day of bloody combat, more than 3000 of the brigade's 5000 men were killed or captured. It would turn out to be something of a pyrrhic victory for Rommel, though, for he lost seventy valuable tanks which he could not replace.

And still Tobruk defied him.

—

U-boats usually received a cheering farewell from dockyard workers and other crews when they sailed, sometimes with a band playing and perhaps with Dönitz himself turning up for a special occasion. Their captains had become Nazi propaganda celebrities ever since Kapitänleutnant Günther Prien had boldly penetrated Scapa Flow to sink the battleship *Royal Oak* in October 1939. *U-559* sailed from the great concrete U-boat pens at St Nazaire in Brittany on the night of 20 September 1941 and turned into the Bay of Biscay on a course south-west. She was the second of the six boats Hitler had ordered to the Mediterranean, all collectively designated *Wolfsrudel* (Wolfpack) *Goeben*, a symbolic naming. In 1914 the Kaiser's battlecruiser *Goeben* had famously thumbed her nose at the Royal Navy and steamed through the Mediterranean to Constantinople to bring Ottoman Turkey into the First World War.

Kapitänleutnant Hans Heidtmann, newly promoted, had orders that would take *U-559* south down the Atlantic around Spain, through the Strait of Gibraltar and on to Salamis in Greece. Now twenty-seven years old, Heidtmann had joined the old Reichsmarine as a cadet in 1934, the year before the Nazis renamed it the Kriegsmarine. He had been in training boats in the Baltic in the early months of the war, his career solid but unspectacular. *U-559* was his first real command when he commissioned her at Kiel in January 1941 and went operational in the Atlantic that June. So far he had sunk just one ship, a small British freighter off Ushant on his second patrol in August.

*U-559* was a Type VIIC boat, the workhorse of the submarine fleet, one of 568 built throughout the war. Sixty-seven metres long, 857 tons submerged, she carried fourteen torpedoes which could be fired from four bow tubes or one stern tube. On her for'ard casing there was one of the Kriegsmarine's commonplace 8.8-centimetre quick-loading guns. With a crew of four officers and about fifty men, she had a top speed on the surface of 17.7 knots from her Germaniawerft twin diesels and 7.6 knots submerged on electric motors. It would take about a month to reach Greece, depending upon how much time was spent on the surface and how much underwater.

The passage was uneventful, on the surface by night in the Atlantic, well beyond the range of any Allied aircraft, and mostly on the surface by day as well. On 25 September Heidtmann dived off the southern tip of neutral Spain and shaped a course to glide past Gibraltar into the Med, keeping as close as he dared to Cape Spartel and Tangier on the African shore. This was the most dangerous part, for the British patrolled the Strait with ships and aircraft day and night. But he was well past unnoticed and untouched the next day, north-east through the Med to pass through the Strait of Messina between Sicily and mainland Italy and then to head south towards Tobruk to see what might be seen. He found nothing there and on 20 October, exactly a month after leaving France, he arrived at Salamis. The emblem of the 23rd Flotilla, a white donkey, was painted on *U-559*'s conning tower.

—

Towards the end of November 1941, the great battles of North Africa, with Tobruk at the epicentre, were growing evermore confused and shot through with error on each side. Both Auchinleck and Rommel made their mistakes, thrusting here and there but neither able to land the crushing blow. Flushed with the *Totensonntag* victory over the South Africans and perhaps committing the fatal mistake of believing his own publicity, Rommel personally led his 21st Panzer Division in a race to the Egyptian border on 24 November, convinced he could come up behind the British rear and encircle the bulk of the Eighth Army.

It became known as 'the dash to the wire' and it was a failure. There was almost nobody to attack beyond some headquarters units, for the bulk of the Eighth Army was elsewhere. The Germans unknowingly by-passed two vast British supply dumps whose destruction might have ended everything and, to top it off, Rommel's car broke down behind the British lines that night, leaving him almost alone in the desert. It was only by chance that he was rescued by a passing sub-ordinate who helped him back across the wire the next morning.

Yet the British were having their own troubles. Also with the intoxicating scent of victory in his nostrils, Auchinleck visited General Cunningham at his forward headquarters and issued a ringing message to the troops:

His position is desperate and he [Rommel] is trying by lashing out in all directions to distract us from our object, which is to destroy him utterly. We will not be distracted and he will be destroyed.

You have got your teeth into him. Hang on and bite deeper and deeper and hang on until he is finished. Give him no rest. The general situation in North Africa is excellent. There is only one order: ATTACK AND PURSUE. ALL OUT EVERYONE.[15]

That done, Auchinleck then decided that Cunningham was exhausted and too cautious. The next day, 26 November, he sacked him and replaced him with his deputy chief of staff, General Sir Neil Ritchie, another in what would become a conga line of fired or failed British generals in North Africa. Rommel, meanwhile, racing back towards Tobruk, was startled to find the advancing New Zealanders had captured a key Luftwaffe airfield and forty-one destroyed aircraft. That same day, the Tobruk garrison broke out towards the south, topped off with a spirited bayonet charge by the Australian 2/13th Battalion, which had not been evacuated. They linked up with the Kiwis at a spot on the map named El Duda, and the siege had been broken. For a while, anyway. The fighting raged on.

—

In a far corner of Alexandria Harbour, the SS *Hanne* spent 24 November loading ammunition for Tobruk, where the renewed fighting had left supplies dangerously low. At 1360 tons, launched in 1903 as the *City of Bradford*, the shabby little *Hanne* had been through several name changes and any number of owners in her longish but entirely uneventful life. Part passenger vessel, part freighter, with a Greek master and a mixed crew, her last job before the war had been ferrying Jewish emigrants from Romania to Haifa in Palestine.

Now she was that most dangerous floating bomb, an ammunition ship in the Tobruk Ferry service. HMAS *Parramatta* was assigned to get her there, in company with one of the new Hunt class escort destroyers, HMS *Avon Vale*. After the welcome rest of the boiler clean – welcome for all but the engine room staff – *Parramatta*'s people were making ready to go to sea again, nerves and fears keying up once more. It would be the usual hard slog with a sluggish merchant vessel. The *Hanne* could supposedly make 12 knots but it had probably been many a long year since she had managed that. *Avon Vale* would be a welcome companion, though. Less than a year old, she had arrived

in the Med only a few weeks before. With a best speed of about
25 knots, these escort destroyers were smaller and slower than a fleet
destroyer but they were well-armed against aircraft with six 4-inch
guns, machine guns and depth charges.

*Parramatta*'s First Lieutenant, Bill 'Scrub' Langford, was hoping
this next trip would be his last. He had married his wife Marjorie just
six months before the ship left Australia in June 1940, with a honey-
moon of only a couple of days at Sydney's Manly Beach before he was
back to work again. He was aching to get back to see her and their
baby daughter Jill, born in his absence. A few days before they sailed
he received the great news that he was to be promoted to lieutenant
commander and posted back to HMAS Penguin, then the name for
the navy's main shore base on Garden Island in Sydney. Overjoyed,
he wrote a quick letter home:

> My darling,
> This will only be a scribble of a few words but very good news!
> I have been appointed to 'Penguin' additional – which means some
> job starting off in Sydney anyway.
>
> I was having an afternoon sleep when they brought me the
> signal and couldn't believe it! Everyone else is to be stepped up
> one and a sub [sub lieutenant] to join. I went ashore for a bit of a
> party that night!
>
> Trouble is I don't know when I can get away – I should like to
> leave the ship straight away but the trouble is we are so terribly
> busy just now. However I'm coming sometime, darling, which is
> the great thing and perhaps you might know more about that than
> I do.
>
> Am much too incoherent to write much but you should know
> how I feel – I can't register very well!
>
> Am going to hop ashore this morning and see what I can find
> out. Wish I could wait ashore and get some shopping done – we
> are never in harbour long enough lately.
>
> Must close – Lord I'm longing to see you both. Will write
> more as soon as I get a chance.
>
> All my love,
> Scrub[16]

The letter went ashore with the rest of the ship's mail the morning she sailed, part of the job of getting away: raising steam, testing engines and telegraphs, checking the libertymen had all returned; all the familiar routine. Reg Oram, the Commissioned Engineer, had joined *Parramatta* after his old ship *Waterhen* was sunk.

'Engines ready, sir.'

Then 'Scrub' Langford's final okay to the captain, 'Ship ready to proceed, sir.'

They got away at 1100 hours, *Parramatta* in the van, followed by the *Hanne* beneath her unhelpfully conspicuous clouds of black funnel smoke, and then *Avon Vale* in the rear, the two warships zigzagging as usual as they turned west to leave the Ras el-Tin lighthouse and Alexandria astern. The weather was bad again, rainy and cold with a rising sea, the watch on deck huddled on the bridge and around the guns in oilskins and seaboots. It worsened as they headed along the distant blur of the coast away to port, beneath a heavy cloud cover with more sharp showers, which at least would have the benefit of keeping the Stukas away as they neared Tobruk. They settled into their usual routine, as Jeff Walker described it to Mary:

The ship is at full battle stations and will be all day and possibly most of the coming night. The only person not at his station is myself, and I am at the end of a voice pipe to the Navigator and Officer of the Watch just above my head. A ring would bring me to the bridge in a few seconds, and the officers up there know their job. It is better for me to keep away until something starts ...

... I have just been to the bridge and looked around the decks. I looked at the chart and studied our position and calculated distances and speeds, looked at the formation of the convoy and the escort, watched the zigzags, studied the far-off coast and searched the skies. At the back of the old brain are the constant thoughts: 'Where's the sun and how about clouds, and what does the sea look like? What do I do in the event of a dive from that direction, and what about a periscope from this, etc?'[17]

That first night was quiet, blessedly so. The men off watch got some sleep, undisturbed by anything more annoying than the rolling and pitching of the ship in the heavy seas. One enemy aircraft did fly over them the next morning, 26 November, and both *Parramatta* and *Avon Vale* fired at it although with no result. It made no attempt to attack and disappeared into the murk and no more appeared. Things were looking up. As the long day wore on and the second night drew in, hopes rose cautiously: it seemed they might make it unmolested.

At around midnight, when they were approaching Tobruk from the north-east, perhaps three hours away, something went wrong with the *Hanne*. In the dark and the rain, on a surging sea, she slowed almost to a stop. To the constant exasperation of the navy, one trouble with these small tramp merchant vessels was that there was never anybody on the bridge who could receive or send a signal, by light or flag. It could drive escort commanders and Officers of the Watch to despair. The only way to talk to them, to work out what on earth was going on, was to go in close and shout back and forth with megaphones. *Parramatta* was the senior of the two ships, so it was her job to do it while *Avon Vale* stood off in the distance. The Officer of the Watch called Jeff Walker to the bridge and he took her carefully in. The two ships wallowed along together, port to starboard at about 3 knots, Walker shouting through his megaphone to the *Hanne*'s captain, who was apparently nervous about entering Tobruk Harbour.

The torpedo struck just before half past one.

## CHAPTER 19

# THE DESTROYER
# BREAKS UP AND SINKS

*U-559* left Salamis on her fourth war patrol on 24 November 1941, skirting western Crete and heading due south again for the waters off Tobruk. A day out of port the starboard diesel had begun playing up, which was a worry, but Kapitänleutnant Heidtmann decided to press on anyway, even at the slower speed. Two days later he was off the Libyan coast quite literally waiting to see what might turn up.

On the night of 26 November the boat was on the surface, rolling in the swell and lit occasionally by flashes of lightning darting from the clouds. Sometimes the moon would appear, leaving the men atop the conning tower feeling nervously exposed against the brighter horizon.

At 2245 hours they spotted a shadow to the north-east and turned towards it. On the bridge, peering through the *U-boot-Zieloptik*, an optical targeting sight, the First Watch Officer, Oberleutnant zur See Herbert Engel, determined it was a small enemy convoy of perhaps three or four ships, moving slowly, the escorts zigzagging, and heading for Tobruk. *U-559* began to follow in its wake, cautiously but deliberately. An attack on the surface – by far the most common U-boat tactic at night – required practised teamwork. The First Watch Officer would remain on the bridge with the lookouts, feeding information to the control room below. There the captain would be at the attack periscope to call the target's speed, range and the target angle on the bow. These numbers would be fed into the *Torpedo-Vorhalterechner*, an analogue computer of dials and knobs which would calculate the proper settings for the torpedo. When he was in position and everything was ready, the captain would give the order to fire.

Heidtmann had four of the Kriegsmarine's standard G7e(TII) 21-inch torpedoes in his bow tubes, carrying a warhead of 280 kilograms of high explosive and capable of a speed of 30 knots. There was silence in the boat, broken only by the rumble of the port diesel as he lined up his first shots. Just before midnight he gave his orders:

> '*Gegner Bug links, Lage 80.*'
> '*Eingestellt!*'
> '*Entfernung 2000.*'
> '*Steht!*'
> '*Gegnerfahrt 8, Torpedotiefe 4 meter …*'
> '*Eingestellt!*'
> '*Fächerschuss aus Rohr 1 bis 3, Streuwinkel 3.*'
> '*Schaltung Rohr 1 bis 3, Streuwinkel 3!*'
> '*Mündungsklappen öffnen!*'
> '*Fächer Rohr 1 bis 3 … los!*'
> ('Bow left, angle of the bow 80.'
> 'Locked on!'
> 'Range 2000.'
> 'Locked on!'
> 'Enemy speed 8, torpedo depth 4 metres.'
> 'Locked on!'
> 'Fan shot from tubes 1 to 3, spread angle 3.'
> 'Open bow caps!'
> 'Fire tubes 1 to 3!')

At that speed and range it should take perhaps two minutes for the torpedoes to reach the target. Tense, expectant, they counted down the seconds. Nothing. The torpedoes vanished into the night, not a hit. Perhaps it was what the U-boat crews had come to call *die Torpedokrise*, the torpedo crisis, the notorious unreliability of these weapons that had infuriated Dönitz and the U-boat captains at the beginning of the war. All too often they ran off course, or sometimes plunged to the sea floor, or simply did not detonate. It was a closely guarded secret, but in October 1939 off the Orkney Islands, *U-56* hit the battleship HMS *Nelson* with two torpedoes at a range of just 800 metres; they bounced harmlessly off her side. In the Norwegian campaign of 1940 all ten torpedoes fired on one patrol by the ace Gunther Prien of *U-47* had failed to explode or just disappeared.

Heidtmann had one torpedo left in his bow tubes. One more try, better luck this time. He carefully conned the submarine into position again:

> Again we approach to attack. The destroyers make a tempting target but I cannot afford to take my time – the convoy must be nearing the approaches to Tobruk. I fire a single torpedo from a range of 1500 metres with the same coordinates as before, at a destroyer with just a single funnel. A hit followed by two detonations in quick succession.
>
> Destroyer breaks up and sinks under the pall of the explosion. Shortly after there is another powerful detonation, presumably her depth charges going up.
>
> I withdraw to the south-east because I want to use all the time available to put some distance between myself and the scene of the sinking, using our one good diesel.[1]

———

The torpedo hit *Parramatta* amidships on her starboard side at 0125 hours, detonating right in her guts. The engine room crew would have died instantly, including Reg Oram, the Chief Engineer who had survived the *Waterhen* sinking. The second explosion, which Heidtmann thought might be depth charges, was more likely to have been the after magazine going up below her quarterdeck. That would have killed more men below. The lights went out and all power was lost.

Almost instantly the little sloop began to roll over to starboard, so suddenly and so swiftly that, on the bridge, Commander Walker recognised that nothing could save her. He gave the order to abandon ship and that was the last that anybody heard or saw of him. We cannot know if he tried to save himself. We do know from his letters that Jefferson Hirst Walker lived his life dutifully and well, with a quiet pride in the navy's traditions, the ship he commanded, and the men he led. Among the bravest of the brave, shouldering the burden of leadership, he had the courage to overcome his fears. We can honour his memory by believing that he would have remained with the ship and his people until he was sure that the last soul had left. As a captain does.

Those still alive – mostly men who had been on the upper deck – were jumping or diving into the sea. A few managed to make it up from below decks. Harold Moss was a fresh-faced, eighteen-year-old ordinary seaman from Sydney who had been in the ship just six months. Normally he would have slept on deck but when he came off watch at midnight the rain sent him back to his mess in the fo'c'sle, where he curled up on the port side using his Mae West life jacket as a pillow.

> When the ship was hit, it blew me over the mess table into the ship's side. I somehow knew it was a torpedo and had to get out. Near that mess was a ladder going up behind the funnel and I was up there like a flash. Right opposite me, as I got on the deck was the whaler and I thought: 'I will get into that', and as the ship went down I would float off.
>
> Silly me forgot that it was all tied down and as the ship turned over I was washed out. I was not a strong swimmer, but a good dog paddler and luck again was with me. There was a Carley raft right next to me, I got in and helped the other guys in.[2]

Harold was lucky to have been on the port side. Those on the starboard side of the mess were trapped beneath falling lockers, tables and other furniture as the ship listed. There was chaos on the tilting, wallowing upper deck as men tried to heave Carley rafts overboard. A few managed to wrestle one of the heavy Oropesa minesweeping floats over the side and jumped after it. All of them could hear the screams of men trapped below. With groans of rending steel the little sloop broke in half, the bow section plunging beneath the water in a suction whirlpool, carrying with it men who would meet a protracted drowning death as the remaining bubbles of air left their mess decks.

The stern floated for a while, a grotesque hulk, and some men sought refuge on it. They perched there for half an hour or so until, with a shudder, that too sank beneath them and she was gone. A little way off, around thirty men were clinging to the Oropesa float, including Percy Forwood and the Supply Officer, Lieutenant Vic Johnston, and they could hear other men calling in the darkness. When an indistinct black shape appeared in the gloom some distance away, a few thought it might be the U-boat and others hoped it might be *Avon Vale* come to their rescue. Two men, twenty-year-old Signalman Harvey Stewart and twenty-five-year-old Stoker Fred Greenfield, decided to take their chances and abandoned the Oropesa, swimming off to whatever it was.

In *Avon Vale*, Lieutenant Commander Peter Withers was doing his best to collect *Parramatta*'s survivors, always with the possibility that the U-boat might turn on him next. Asdic pinging, he took the risk, a sitting duck, for he could not know that the attacker had already left the scene. With scrambling nets over the side, he picked up nineteen men who swam or floated to him, including Harold Moss:

> I was sitting on top of the raft on the rope handles and it was mighty uncomfortable. Also, I had my hands gripped around that rope because it was a bit rough, and cold too. When the *Avon Vale* came alongside they yelled out: 'You have two minutes to get up the net!'
>
> Everybody went except me. I couldn't get my hands off the rope, they were clenched tight around it, so I yelled out 'I need help' and someone came down the net, undid my hands and threw me over his shoulder and took me up on the deck. I was covered in fuel oil and had a couple of scratches on me. The doc cleaned me up, gave me a tot of something and they wrapped a blanket around me and took me away.[3]

After a swim of about a kilometre through those heaving seas, the surface strewn with wreckage and filthy with oil, Harvey Stewart and Fred Greenfield reached *Avon Vale* too, the last men she saved. No one else from the Oropesa float made it. They disappeared without trace. Commander Withers waited until about 0300 hours, moving slowly back and forth. When it appeared that there were no more survivors he resumed the task of escorting the *Hanne* to Tobruk and the two ships arrived there safely that morning. Kapitänleutnant Heidtmann and *U-559* had taken one opportunity and succeeded, but missed what surely would have been two more easy targets. The ammunition supplies got through.

—

Coming on 3 December, just days after Australians learned of the tragedy of *Sydney* in the Indian Ocean, the announcement of *Parramatta*'s loss was another grievous blow. Again it fell to John Curtin to break the news:

> The Australian Naval Board has received information that HMAS *Parramatta* has been torpedoed and sunk while on escort duties.
>
> It is with deep regret that I announce that the sinking was attended with considerable loss of life of Royal Australian Navy personnel. Of the total complement of 161 of HMAS *Parramatta*, 141 officers and men are reported missing, believed killed.
>
> The next of kin, to whom the Government and the Naval Board extend deepest sympathy, have been informed.
>
> Following so closely on the loss of ship and men in the case of HMAS *Sydney*, the loss of HMAS *Parramatta* and so many of her gallant complement represents a heavy blow.
>
> But the nation, and the Service to which the men belong, will be stiffened in determination and inspired to emulation by the example of self-sacrifice and devotion to duty which the recent losses have afforded.
>
> In the words of the Commander-in-Chief under whom HMAS *Parramatta* was serving when lost: 'The record of achievement established by his Majesty's Australian ships has been fully upheld by this fine little vessel.'
>
> There could be no higher praise. In deploring the loss of HMAS *Parramatta*, the Commander-in-Chief expressed his sympathy and that of the fleet in his command, to the Royal Australian Navy, and to the next of kin of the men.[4]

There were few details given: simply that *Parramatta* had been torpedoed, but no information of how or where. Bereaved families were told only that their loved one was missing, presumed killed. All the officers were lost. Scrub Langford's baby daughter, Jill, would never know her father. Over the next few days poignant little paragraphs began to appear in newspapers big and small around the country, in the cities and in the bush, each recording the death of a young man from a local community and often some aspect of his pre-war life: 'a highly admired wicketkeeper ... respected family ... well known in the Boy Scouts ... a popular student ...'.

The sorrow was profound. A national 'Jacks' Day' fund was set up to raise money for the families of men lost in both *Sydney* and *Parramatta*, and in Sydney and Melbourne naval wives organised the collection of Christmas toys for children who no longer had sailor fathers. Memorial services were held in cathedrals and churches around the country on Sunday, 7 December 1941.

Then it all changed. The very next day, the afternoon newspapers in the capital cities were reporting a surprise Japanese air attack on Hawaii and an attempted Japanese landing in the Federated Malay States close to the Thailand border, which had been 'repulsed by small arms fire and air action'.[5] That evening, speaking from Melbourne in an ABC radio broadcast that began with the playing of 'Advance Australia Fair', Prime Minister Curtin told the people that a nightmare had become reality:

Men and women of Australia, we are at war with Japan. That has happened because, in the first instance, Japanese naval and air forces launched an unprovoked attack on British and United States territory; because our vital interests are imperilled and because the rights of free people in the whole Pacific are assailed. As a result, the Australian Government this afternoon took the necessary steps which will mean that a state of war exists between Australia and Japan. Tomorrow, in common with the United Kingdom, the United States of America and the Netherlands East Indies Governments, the Australian Government will formally and solemnly declare the state of war it has striven so sincerely and strenuously to avoid.[6]

Over the next tumultuous days, as Christmas drew nearer, the front-page headlines grew ever bolder and blacker and the news evermore grave. The first pictures of the attack on Pearl Harbor with its sunken and burning battleships were seen in the cinema news-reels, together with President Roosevelt's 'day of infamy' speech to Congress in Washington. Hong Kong had been attacked too. And the Philippines. They had bombed Singapore. Britain had declared war on Japan. And the Imperial Japanese Army, far from being repulsed, was firmly lodged on the Malay Peninsula, where tens of thousands of Australians were fighting. It was an encouraging thought that Fortress Singapore would hold out, the rock against which the Japanese wave would break, and there was much bold talk of 'hurling back the little yellow man'. But it was starkly clear in every Australian home that the war was no longer an affair of the faraway northern hemisphere. It had widened to the Pacific, to our part of the world. The loss of HMAS *Parramatta* faded into the dark background until, just a few days before Christmas, there was a startling shaft of light.

Listeners to the BBC radio news at breakfast time on the morning of Friday, 19 December, heard a brief item reporting that three Australian sailors from *Parramatta* had been found alive and well in the Libyan Desert. Their names were given as Able Seaman G. S. A. Ladhams, Able Seaman W. F. Tysoe, and Signalman A. N. Miller.

At her small cottage in Olive Street, Enfield, a suburb of Adelaide, Mrs May Ladhams had not been listening. She was first startled, then burst into tears when a neighbour's daughter ran in to tell her the news: her son Alec was safe. Much the same happened further across the continent at a quiet family farm outside the coastal village of Denmark, in southern Western Australia, where Roger and Martha Tysoe also heard from friends that Fred, the youngest of their eight boys, had made it okay. That was one crushing burden banished, although there was still worry about their fourth boy, Harry, who had farewelled his wife and four children and gone off with the army's 2/4th Machine Gun Battalion. They knew he was in the fighting in Malaya but the news from there was not encouraging and they had not heard from him.

The families crowded around their wireless sets to hear the news repeated an hour later, they hoped, but the names were not mentioned again. Gnawing anxiety turned to ecstasy later that morning when the telegrams from Navy Office in Melbourne arrived, quickly followed by reporters from the newspapers.

### BEST XMAS BOX, SAYS MOTHER

'Thank God. That's the best Christmas box that any mother could have,' exclaimed Mrs M. M. Ladhams, when she heard of her son's safety from a representative of the *News*. Turning to members of her family, she said, 'You need not give me any presents now. That's all I want.'

Never had she given up hope since she was first informed that her son was missing from the *Parramatta*, Mrs Ladhams said.

'On the day that the *Parramatta* was lost I knew something had happened. Alec's eyes forced me to keep looking at his photograph on the piano. They followed me wherever I went.

'A few days ago I heard violent sobbing while asleep. It woke me, but there was not a noise in the house. I dropped off again, and the sob rang clear, waking me a second time.

'I thought then that it was Alec trying to give a message. It must have been a premonition,' she said.

The three rescued boys were firm friends aboard ship, said Mrs Ladhams as she sobbed with joy.

'When the *Parramatta* called at Port Adelaide on her way to the Mediterranean Alec brought young Tysoe home to dinner, as he had nowhere to go in Adelaide.

'This is the best news I have ever heard. I always told friends that Alec was a strong swimmer, and would save himself if he had the slightest chance.

'He was always able to battle on his own. He went round Queensland "jumping the rattler" and told me not to worry, as it would not be hard on his stomach if he went without meals for a day or two.

'I hope he did not have to put that into practice in the desert,' she added.[7]


At Glenelg, on the beach in Adelaide, Mrs Thelma McIvor, Al Miller's sister, confirmed that he too was safe. It was front-page news around the country. They were still boys: Fred was twenty-two, Alec was twenty, Al just nineteen, mates who had trained together at Cerberus in Victoria and joined *Parramatta* on the same day back in June 1940. A story filed by the Australian war correspondent in Cairo, John Hetherington, had a brief description of how they had been found by South African troops in the desert near Tobruk.[8]

The three were brought back home by a returning troop ship in March the next year, 1942, a sea voyage in which – it was hard to believe – they were not required to stand a watch, load a gun, scrub a deck, send a signal or endure a bombing. Fred Tysoe went home, straight home. Denmark is at the very bottom of Western Australia some 400 kilometres south-east of Perth, today a picture-perfect tourist oasis where a pristine river flows into the Wilson Inlet, past beaches of brilliant white sand and out to the Southern Ocean. In 1942 it was a timber town, battling along after the rich jarrah forests had been logged almost bare. Roger and Martha Tysoe had emigrated from England before the First World War, brought out by a state government scheme to populate the west with staunch, hard-working British stock willing to make a go of it. From nothing they had cleared their acres and pioneered a humble farm in the bush to become a respected local family.

One evening early in April, the Denmark Public Hall was festooned with Australian and British flags and lots of bush greenery, and there were tables of good country food, all to welcome the sailor boy home. Denmark was as far from the war as it was possible to be in mainland Australia but Roger and Martha still had their fears for Harry. There had been no word from him since the fall of Singapore and the Allied surrender, and they could only hope that he was still alive as a prisoner of war. Still, tonight was for celebration. Young Fred was formally welcomed by the neighbours and local dignitaries and showered with gifts, and he made a speech of thanks in return.

Later he sat down for a long chat with a local journalist who took notes and then wrote the story of his deliverance for the *Western Mail* newspaper.[9] It bears repeating here:

> It was raining at nightfall and there was a choppy sea. About 1 am we were hit by two torpedoes from a submarine whose presence

was unsuspected. One of these exploded by the wardroom under the aft gun blowing the turret to blazes and causing some casualties. The sloop of 1060 tons reeled like a drunken man with the impacts and then broke in halves and capsized.

Our position at this time was about 25 miles from shore, 120 miles north of Bardia. Her bow and stern were projecting. There was no time to launch boats and some of the crew were trapped below. Discipline was however excellent despite the pitch blackness of the night and a rough sea.

I had just come off watch at midnight and was asleep in a motorboat on the upper deck. The impact jolted me off my slumber and I secured a cork lifebelt which I just draped under my arms, not having time to don it. I had to climb the upper deck midships and then walked down the sloping side, and entered the water which was coated with oil.

I swam about for some time, and contacted two mates, but later lost touch with them. I then swam back to the ship and was pulled onto the stern by another man to join nine others. One chap near the water slipped, but we stayed there about half an hour. The stern part then tilted and put us back in the water. This would be about 1.45 am. One of the convoy was standing by, about a quarter of a mile away and we swam towards her, but she did not remain, fearing the submarine might also get her. She did pick up nineteen of our chaps.

I then swam with a mate to a Carley float about 4 foot 6 inches long and 3 foot wide. There was another chap – Signalman Miller of Glenelg, South Australia on the float and my mate was another 'crow' Alec Ladhams of North Walkerville, Adelaide, SA. It was now 3 am and pretty cold. I was fully clothed except shoes, and Miller was pretty right also, but poor Ladhams only had a pair of shorts on. The float had no provisions and only one paddle. We drifted until daylight, and often heard calls but could do nothing for those less fortunate than ourselves.

'That's the end of it; we'll try and make shore,' said Miller next morning, when a ship about 10 miles off failed to see us. About midday we saw a whale boat, dropped from one of our ships. It was about a mile closer to shore, which was just discernible.

Miller, with one paddle managed to get our float close to it, and we boarded only to find it half full of water – somebody had forgotten to put in the plug. We found plenty of bully beef, biscuits and water on her and also a tin hat, with which we baled. Poor old pal Ladhams was feeling – and looking – pretty blue owing to lack of clothes and we used to snuggle him between us at night and let the whaler drift closer to shore. At times two of us would row and the other steer.

About 5 pm on the day after we had lost our ship we landed on a little beach between two reefs about 20 miles north of Bardia. We beached our craft high and removed the provisions and plenty of water. On an adjacent ridge we could see trucks passing occasionally and thought they were some of ours. We were making towards them when we ran across an Arab camp of about thirty tents. They first took us for Italians, our bodies being discoloured through swimming in the oily water when the ship went down. Believe me the fumes were pretty crook.

We were taken before the chief who spoke broken English, having been a native policeman. We were allowed to wash and given clothes. I had an issue of a pair of British Army trousers, and the rest was of Italian make. We were not given footwear, as they thought we might run away. Our feet were too sore for that however having been cut by barnacles, and we had no desire to do so. Our first meal comprised a boiled egg each, coffee and Arab bread, which isn't the best in the world. We were given a tent and had dropped off to sleep about 6.15 pm.

We stayed with the Arab camp about a fortnight. The Arabs had some women in their party, and the old chief seemed to have about ten wives. One of these gave Ladhams the 'Glad Eye', and we told him he was in the boom. The weather was still bad, and we were flooded out one night having only grass mats for bedding. We just sat like shags on a rock and awaited daylight – pretty wretched and miserable. One day the chief got word of a likely move from a big German camp about 2 miles away, so he removed us to a big cave for the day. We came back at night.

About 3 miles off, a big tank battle was in progress and at night planes could be seen dropping bombs. Our ration was now mainly bully beef from the whaler. When this gave out we went back to Arab fare. We tried to get a letter through to the English lines by an Arab messenger, but we never saw or heard of him again. Frequently Italian and German soldiers came to the camp and had a meal before going on. We were hidden in a nearby tent under blankets and could hear their conversation very plainly. Luckily the old chief never gave us away. He was a great diplomat and maintained neutrality, at least outwardly.

A South African force broke through the enemy lines one day and the Arabs welcomed them with open arms – so did we. The scouts at first took us as Italians; owing to our colour and a sentry challenged as we advanced towards him.

I said, 'You're a sight for sore eyes' and he lowered his rifle and grinned. They took us to trucks and fed us with tinned sausages, biscuits and coffee. I was given cut-away sandshoes and the other two received books. We then went to headquarters off Bardia and were given fine treatment. Our next move was a field hospital. We had been dressing our cuts and abrasions with a compound called 'Razorquick' found in the Arab camp and this turned out to be shaving cream. Anyhow it was effective, having healing ingredients.

It took us a week of travel with many stoppages to reach Alexandria. Our first move was to send cables to our folks telling of our safety. We spent two very happy months in that city, doing the sights in great style with a new issue of white shorts and singlets.

We sailed from Alexandria on 20 January for Bombay and arrived in Melbourne on 28 March. A Tasmanian lad named Smith had also been picked up in the desert after getting ashore from the *Parramatta*. He had a rougher spin than we did before the Arabs found him. He came home from with us and is now well.[10]

Miller, Ladhams and I were all good pals in the Flinders depot being in the same class and we were drafted to the *Parramatta* together. Miller is nineteen and full of courage, while Ladhams is twenty and a great scout also. I guess we will all enjoy our leave before reporting for duty again.

I know the old bed at home felt good to me after nearly three years absence from it. Still when one goes to sea, he cannot look for a luxury existence. My experiences to date have well fitted me for anything the future might hold. But it is sure great to see the parents and brothers at home rejoicing that I have returned safely. I have a brother somewhere in Singapore, I hope his luck will equal mine.[11]

For some families, the pain of loss was lifelong and all the sharper for not knowing the manner of your sailor's death. Was it quick or prolonged? Gentle or agony? They were at least spared the cold, bureaucratic note jotted on the individual service records, the letters 'D.D.' for Discharged Dead. In July 1942, after he had been posted to the destroyer *Napier*, Harold Moss wrote to the mother of a shipmate, Ordinary Seaman Lyall Smith, of Plympton in Adelaide. Aged eighteen when he died, Lyall had been in *Parramatta*, his first and only ship, for three months:

Dear Mrs Smith,
I have been asked by my mother to write to you and to tell you what I know about Lyall. I would like you to understand that I would have written to you months ago, only for the fact I felt that to write then would be to induce more grief to you than you were already suffering; so I thought I would drop in and see you when I return home.

But now as you have asked I will say what I would have said before. First my really deep sympathy to you for his loss. The last four or five months before he died I was one of his real cobbers. He joined up the same time as I did and we both travelled to Melbourne together. That ten days' leave in August 1940 we were together. I saw him several times in Adelaide. Then back we went and finally overseas together. Of course, he had his own particular cobbers and stuck to them. We also incidentally used to go out and to the same place to see our girls and his girl knew mine and we sometimes used to go to the theatre together.

Anyhow we arrived in England and were sent to depot where we were sent on leave. I went to Scotland (Glasgow) and he went to Edinburgh. I never saw him until we were back on leave. Then we were drafted to the *Aurora*, we were nearly nine months on her and then paid off. After some more leave we were split up and eight of us were drafted to the *Parramatta*.

He was then separated from his cobbers, one of whom was Alan Roberts. Anyhow we used to get together and talk about the different things we were going to do after we got out of the Service and he was telling me he didn't think he would marry until after finishing his twelve years. We went ashore together in Durban and Suez. In Suez we had our photos taken in Arab dress. I went back there when I was there last to try and get the photo again but the negative was destroyed. I really was looking forward to getting that photo.

We picked up our ship there and later on was to see our first bit of action. A German plane attacked us in the Red Sea but his bombs fell over us. We caught him as he went away and was later credited with shooting it down. I reckon we were all rather nervous but none of us new hands said anything and then after that we felt like old hands. Shortly after that we went through the canal to the Med. We went ashore together in Alexandria. After that we had several air attacks and once went to Tobruk at night. Coming back we anchored in Mersa Matruh and had hardly dropped anchor when they started to bomb the shore. They kept us awake for hours. We came back and two days later we left Alex for Tobruk. These were the days of the siege and supplies just had to get through. We took a convoy of small supply ships with us.

Anyhow to get to the night on which we were sunk, we were off Tobruk and this night was rather heavy seas, moon was generally hidden by dark clouds and rain. This rain by the way caused the greater majority of deaths. Everyone used to sleep on deck and through the rain they all had to go below. Lyall was my opposite watch then and at midnight when I went below he came on deck to keep his watch on the forward gun. It was raining and just before I went down I had a funny feeling. I thought that it would be pretty awful to be adrift in that sea. I went right forward to try to get a place to sleep but there was no room so I came back amidships and lay on a stool in a little spare mess we had. My lifebelt was blown up and near my feet.

At 12.20 I looked at my watch and then I was just dozing off when she was hit. I never want to hear that noise again ever. I was thrown to the deck and the lights were out. I grabbed my life jacket and was up the ladder and on deck in ten seconds. I just got on deck when she lurched over and immediately began to sink. I couldn't tie my belt on and it was swept away.

I was then in the water and swam to where I saw a float. I got on and began helping other fellows on. We floated away and soon lost sight of the ship. We were picked up in about 2½ hours. Although the chaps below who were forward wouldn't have had a chance to get away there was those on deck who should have been all right.

A large party of men were on a big float and the last chap to be picked up said they were still okay when he left. I can't possibly help you in definitely saying Lyall went. Because no one I know who knew him ever saw him. There were lots of men clinging to rafts and pieces of wood. The next morning there was no survivors in sight. The night was bitterly cold and I couldn't have lasted much longer myself. For myself I can't believe that everyone who is missing is dead and I feel that there may be some who are in POW camps in Germany. It was hard for me to realise that my friends, chaps who I had known as brothers were gone and it affected me for a long time. I'm not of an emotional character myself but have found myself close to tears whenever I remember that night.

I'm afraid that is all I can tell you. I can give you Ian Roberts's address but of course he wasn't on the ship. I do sincerely hope I haven't told you anything which may cause you more grief but rather may help you.

Anything more I can do I shall only be so pleased.

Yours sincerely,

Harold Moss[12]

—

The mistakes of British and American policy and strategy and, worse, the absence of plain common sense which led to the disasters at Pearl Harbor, Hong Kong, the Philippines and Singapore are obvious in hindsight and well known now.

Many of them should have been obvious at the time, but states-men, admirals and generals were all too often blinkered by wishful optimism and an obstinate refusal to ascertain the facts or to believe such facts as were put before them. Racism certainly played a part. Everyone knew that Imperial Japan had a large army, navy and air force – they had brutally and effectively subjugated China – but it was assumed that they would not much trouble the physically, mentally and scientifically superior White Man.

In August 1941, just four months before Pearl Harbor, the popular *Smith's Weekly* magazine in Sydney could write reassuringly:

> Japanese are bad pilots. All Asiatics are poor in the air. Their physical make-up is against them.
>
> For instance, they black-out very easily pulling out of power dives. This makes them poor at aerial combat. Resistance to black-out of Anglo-Saxons, in particular, is high because of their physical characteristics. In dog-fights, they would have every advantage over the Japs ...
>
> ... In addition, Japanese have the worst eyes in the world, which makes their judgment in the air extremely faulty, particularly in such operations as landing and taking off ...[13]

This was not mere journalistic froth. It was an official opinion as well, held on high in London, Washington and Canberra. Strategic policy was equally delusional. Winston Churchill clung tenaciously to the chimera of Fortress Singapore, which he boasted as an impregn-able British bastion of Empire that Japan would not be so foolish as to attack. At any sign of trouble the fortress would be reinforced by despatching great capital ships to the Far East, a very public demon-stration that Britain meant business. 'Main fleet to Singapore' was the pre-war catchphrase.

As the Japanese menace became undeniable and impossible to ignore, the British energetically tried to convince the Americans to send part of their Pacific Fleet to Singapore. President Roosevelt, though, was not interested in deploying American lives, ships and money to defend British colonies. Against all the best naval advice and opposition from the First Sea Lord, Churchill and the War Cabinet then resolved to despatch the new battleship *Prince of Wales* and the old battlecruiser *Repulse* to station themselves on the island.

This was folly of a high order, comparable to the decision to send an army to Greece. One bitter, hard-learned lesson of the Mediterranean was that air power was a potent and all too successful menace to ships at sea. Yet these two would have no carrier with them and no assurance of shore-based cover from the RAF or the RAAF. To be fair, London was caught in a bind not all of its own making. Not to have sent the ships would have provoked fierce private protest from the Australian and New Zealand governments and widespread public perceptions of Britain abandoning its most loyal dominions. It was yet another case of a political imperative trumping military sense.

*Prince of Wales* sailed from the Clyde with three destroyers on 24 November. When they stopped at Cape Town on their way to Singapore there was much flag-waving publicity deliberately intended to disconcert the Japanese, to deter them from any aggression. It had entirely the opposite effect. Forewarned is forearmed. Japanese air force and navy squadrons based in Thailand were strengthened with more aircraft, and knowing now exactly what they would be looking for, they began to practise tactics for the low-level torpedo bombing of capital ships at sea. *Repulse* was already in the Indian Ocean. She met *Prince of Wales* at sea south of Ceylon on 30 November and on 2 December they and four destroyers arrived at the Sembawang naval base on the north of Singapore island.

On 5 December, *Repulse* and two destroyers, *Tenedos* and the old *Vampire*, were sent off south to Darwin to show the flag in an Australian port, but the next day they were hurriedly recalled after an RAAF Hudson aircraft on reconnaissance reported two large convoys of Japanese transports and warships off southern Indo-China and heading towards Malaya.

When the Japanese made their landings in northern Malaya on 8 December, *Prince of Wales*, *Repulse* and a screen of four destroyers including *Vampire* – all now designated Force Z – put to sea from Singapore on a rainy, misty evening to oppose them. Their Commander-in-Chief, Admiral Sir Tom Phillips, had been one of the feisty Whitehall desk warriors constantly urging Andrew

Cunningham to greater activity in the Mediterranean. He had not been to sea in this war, had never commanded a battle squadron and had never seen an air attack, but he was a Churchill favourite and was jumped up two steps in rank for the job. To compound the folly, Phillips had evidently learned little from a year of disasters in the Med and believed, as a matter of dogma, that the battleship would always beat off attack from the air. Cunningham, on learning of his appointment, commented scathingly that Phillips hardly knew one end of a ship from the other.

Two days later, on 10 December, both *Prince of Wales* and *Repulse* lay on the bottom of the Gulf of Siam, clinically despatched in less than two hours by wave after wave of Japanese high-level and torpedo bombers. Inexplicably maintaining wireless silence even though the enemy knew exactly where he was, the hapless Phillips never once radioed Singapore to ask for fighter air support that was just half an hour away. He and *Prince of Wales*'s captain, John Leach, went down with the flagship and another 838 men lost their lives. One of them was an eighteen-year-old Australian midshipman, Bob Davies, who was last seen firing an Oerlikon gun at the Japanese as *Repulse* sank beneath him. Four other Australian midshipmen survived. *Vampire*, unscathed, picked up 225 survivors including the captain of *Repulse*, Bill Tennant.

It was not a great season for British capital ships. After the loss of *Ark Royal* and *Barham*, *Repulse* and *Prince of Wales*, there were two more blows to come. On 19 December six intrepid Italian frogmen made a daring raid on Alexandria Harbour on their *Maiale* human torpedoes, placing limpet mines beneath the battleships *Valiant* and *Queen Elizabeth*. Neither ship was sunk but they were holed and disabled, immovable for months. The six Italians were captured.

The Alexandria raid was kept secret but the destruction of Force Z was trumpeted by Japanese propaganda and had to be conceded by the Admiralty. There was consternation in Australia. Triumphant and seemingly unstoppable, Imperial Japan forged onwards, south to Fortress Singapore and beyond, to the riches of the Netherlands East Indies. Two days after Christmas, the Melbourne *Herald* published a New Year message from John Curtin shaping a new course in Australian defence and foreign policy that endures to this day:

we refuse to accept the dictum that the Pacific struggle must be treated as a subordinate segment of the general conflict. By that it is not meant that any one of the other theatres of war is of less importance than the Pacific, but that Australia asks for a concerted plan evoking the greatest strength at the democracies' disposal, determined upon hurling Japan back.

The Australian Government, therefore, regards the Pacific struggle as primarily one in which the United States and Australia must have the fullest say in the direction of the democracies' fighting plan.

Without any inhibitions of any kind, I make it quite clear that Australia looks to America, free of any pangs as to our traditional links or kinship with the United Kingdom.

We know the problems that the United Kingdom faces. We know the constant threat of invasion. We know the dangers of dispersal of strength, but we know too, that Australia can go and Britain can still hold on.

We are, therefore, determined that Australia shall not go, and we shall exert all our energies towards the shaping of a plan, with the United States as its keystone, which will give to our country some confidence of being able to hold out until the tide of battle swings against the enemy.[14]

For Australia, the sternest tests were yet to come.

# CHAPTER 20

# SHIPS THAT PASS ...

By early 1942 the Scrap Iron Flotilla had receded into memory, a touchstone for courage and resolve that would, in time, become the stuff of legend. The war had moved on, and so had the surviving ships. *Vampire* still had life in her. The refit in Singapore had taken five months but it had been thorough and, if she was not exactly as good as new, she was once again in reasonable fighting trim. At last, her bone-shaking engine vibrations had been sorted out. She had a new captain, too, Commander Bill Moran, a West Australian whose last job had been as the Executive Officer of the heavy cruiser HMAS *Canberra*. A lot of the ship's company were new as well, some fresh from the naval depot.

After the disaster of *Repulse* and *Prince of Wales* they spent some weeks in December and January convoying merchant and troop ships here and there, in and out of Singapore and Batavia without any particular excitement. Then, on 26 January 1942, Australia Day, there were reports of a new Japanese troop landing at the fishing port of Endau, on the Malayan east coast about 120 kilometres north of Singapore. It was a formidable force: two transports, a light cruiser, six destroyers and five minesweepers, and at first the RAF's Far East Command attempted to deal with it by bombs. This, too, was a disaster. Some minor hits were scored on enemy ships, but the obsolescent bombers and fighters scraped together were no match for the Japanese Zero fighters and even Allied aircraft were shot down.

That afternoon, *Vampire* and a Royal Navy destroyer, HMS *Thanet*, were sent off to see what could be seen. *Thanet* was also of First World War vintage, so ancient that her five sister ships in the RAN – *Tattoo*, *Tasmania*, *Stalwart*, *Success* and *Swordsman* – had been scrapped in the late 1930s. Bill Moran, the senior officer, decided on a night approach, so the two ships took their time going north and arrived off Endau around 0200 hours. *Vampire* led as they headed in towards the coast at 15 knots. After about half an hour they saw a dark shape in the distance, perhaps a Japanese destroyer, but it did not notice them so they kept going.

A few minutes later they sighted another vessel dead ahead and close. *Vampire* swung around to port and fired two torpedoes from a range of about 600 metres, but both missed. That was a small minesweeper, it turned out, and the two destroyers gave her the slip in the darkness and continued in towards Endau, still in the hope of finding some troop transports. They drew a blank. By 0315 hours, with nothing seen, Moran decided to return to Singapore and *Vampire* and *Thanet* turned back south-east at full speed.

Five minutes later the Japanese found them. *Vampire* spotted a destroyer on the port bow and she and *Thanet* fired more four more torpedoes, but again they missed. Now it got serious. The cruiser *Sendai* and three more Japanese destroyers appeared and a hot pursuit ensued for some forty minutes, *Vampire* in the lead and *Thanet* astern, both racing for safety, each side firing at the other. Sheer weight of numbers told. At around 0400 hours *Thanet* was hit in the engine room, fracturing the main steam pipe until she stopped altogether in a large explosion that threw up clouds of steam and smoke and sent her listing sharply to starboard. *Vampire* swung around and tried to conceal her behind a smokescreen but *Thanet* sank at around 0420 hours. Some of the Japanese destroyers started shooting at each other and, with no chance of rescuing survivors, *Vampire* escaped in the confusion and returned safely to Singapore. It was the first Australian confrontation with the Imperial Japanese Navy at sea, and it became known as the Action off Endau.

Of *Thanet*'s ship's company, twelve died in the battle. Her captain, Lieutenant Commander Bernard Davies, and another sixty-four men swam ashore and made their way down the coast to Singapore.

But thirty-one were plucked from the water by one of the Japanese destroyers and handed over to the army at Endau the next day. It is almost certain they were executed.

With the fall of Singapore, still *Vampire* could not make it home to Australia. She was assigned to join the British Far Eastern Fleet, based on Ceylon.[1] In early April, British codebreakers got wind of Japanese plans for a massive bombing raid by carrier aircraft on Trincomalee, the great naval base in northern Ceylon, set for the early morning of 9 April. The Japanese had sailed into the Indian Ocean in force, with five fast carriers, four battleships, three cruisers and eleven destroyers. Ships in Trincomalee were sailed the night before, including the carrier HMS *Hermes* and *Vampire*, to get them out of the way to safety at sea. The raid duly happened, causing massive damage to the dockyard. When it was over, at around 0900 hours, *Hermes* and *Vampire* were ordered to return to Trincomalee.

They were quickly spotted by a Japanese reconnaissance aircraft and at 1045 hours were attacked by swarms of dive-bombers, eighty-five of them in all, coming out of the sun in wave after wave. *Hermes* was the first target. She was hit by no fewer than forty bombs and within a shocking ten minutes she rolled over and sank. Three hundred and seven men lost their lives, including her captain, Richard Onslow. *Hermes* had been Britain's first purpose-built carrier but she had no aircraft on board that day; they had all been landed ashore. Not that it would have made any difference: the Zeros would have picked off RN's Fulmar fighters like hawks at sparrows.

The remaining Japanese bombers then turned their attention to *Vampire* as she twisted and turned beneath them, putting up ? of anti-aircraft fire. One bomber was shot down, but it The attackers came from every angle. At first, two near her up, and then a direct hit in the boiler room b halt, followed by four more direct hits. She was fi nothing to do but abandon ship. Commander M from the bridge. Men began launching floa were away when yet another bomb broke h quickly; her stern floated for perhaps an another explosion sent it to the bottom and borne so much in the Mediterra direct encounter with overwhelming Japanese air power at sea in the Indian Ocean, the second of the Scrap Iron Flotilla to go.

It is remarkable that only eight men were lost that day, including Bill Moran, who was not seen again after giving the order to leave. The survivors from *Hermes* and *Vampire* were rescued by the hospital ship *Vita* which was in the area but not attacked, the very same *Vita* which had been towed to safety by *Waterhen* and *Vendetta* when she was bombed off Tobruk the year before.

With *Waterhen* and now *Vampire* gone, there were only three Scrap Iron destroyers left.

—

When the Japanese found her on that fateful morning of 8 December, *Vendetta* was an empty hulk, lying immoveable at King's Dock in Keppel Harbour on the southern shore of Singapore. She had been there for a month, her vitals removed for a complete refit: engines and boilers stripped down, her big guns, ammunition, torpedo tubes, everything that made her a fighting warship sent ashore to stores and workshops.

A skeleton crew was with her: a new standby captain, Bill Whitting, an RANR lieutenant who had been in the ship for all her Mediterranean days; two other officers; six petty officers and twelve junior sailors. Their first, shocking indication of war with Japan was a pre-dawn air raid, the roar of engines dragging them from their sleep and a stick of bombs landing in the water just 200 metres away.

At age twenty-six, Whitting was a resourceful officer and a professional seaman. Born in Cardiff in Wales, he had been a midshipman in the RN before switching to the merchant marine and emigrating to Australia; his last job before the war was aboard ships of the mining and steel company BHP. Keppel Harbour had no anti-aircraft defences at all. Whitting went to the Singapore Harbour Board to what he could do to help but, in the chaos, he received little more despairing shrug of the shoulders. On his own initiative, he commissioned Torpedo Gunner, John Lace, mounted their and high-angle gun on the wharf astern of the ship and the eight Lewis machine guns. The crew manned t as the raids grew bigger and more frequent. On noted in the ship's diary:

On this day Singapore had its worst blitz, being attacked by 125 bombers in all. This was a good day for *Vendetta*. A squadron of twenty-seven planes flying low over Keppel Harbour suddenly appeared astern ... Our 12-pounder went immediately into action and to our great delight a 12-pounder H.E. shell hit one of the bombers in the bomb rack and she instantly blew up, damaging the planes (2 in No.) on either side with flying debris ... the whole of the gun's crew acting worthy of the tradition of the RAN.[2]

Two days later, Whitting was ordered by the Rear Admiral Malaya to prepare the ship to be towed out of Singapore to Tanjung Priok, the harbour for Batavia on the north-west coast of the Netherlands East Indies island of Java. Beneath raid after raid, lashed by drenching monsoonal downpours, through exhausting, frightening days and sleepless nights, the captain and the crew toiled to recover as much of the ship's equipment from various sheds and stores as they could find in the chaos. Entries in the ship's diary describe this last frantic scramble:

All hands preparing for the coming tow. Everything being hurriedly replaced back in the ship. Air raids continuous throughout the day. The native labour being almost at a standstill, all work has to be done by the ship's company.

The Gunner (T) Mr J. C. Lace RAN, accompanied by his Yeoman of Stores Able Seaman [William] Robertson, proceeded to the naval base in an endeavour to recover the ship's main 4-inch armament and as much stores as they possibly could before leaving Singapore. On arrival at the naval base they found the Gun Mounting Shed and workshops had already been bombed and badly damaged. The native labour had completely stopped, as most of them had deserted after the heavy air attacks. Mr Lace located our guns in various stages of assembly, the barrels and mountings being left in a state of complete chao

... Ship's company filling up ship with all na be saved, work proceeding very slowly due to co when men must drop everything and man their A native labour is now practically at a standstill. M to the naval base in an endeavour to rescue all the armament and torpedo stores he could. Unfortunately, due to constant raids over the naval base this was not possible, although he successfully saved all the ship's charts, chronometer and Confidential Books.[3]

On 28 January *Vendetta* was dry docked – beneath more air raids and more driving rain – and her bottom cleaned and painted. She was back afloat three days later and on 1 February she was ready to be taken in tow by the coal-burning RN tug *St Just*, with the destroyer HMS *Stronghold* to escort them out to sea. Again the diary gives the flavour of these desperate days:

H.M. tug *St Just* berths alongside *Vendetta* to tow us, along with HMS *Stronghold*. Owing to desertions among crew of *St Just* and lack of coolie labour, *Vendetta*'s ship's company had to coal this tug. As the master was afraid of still more desertions, we gave him a .45 pistol and ammunition while he mounted guard over the gangway. Air raids have been continuous throughout the day and night. Japanese artillery can be distinctly heard bombarding the north of the island across the Straits of Johore. Hands secured and lashed all stores and gun barrels on the upper deck preparatory to going to sea next day.[4]

They slipped and left the harbour at 0700 hours on 2 February, the scarlet flames and thick black smoke of bombed and burning Singapore slowly fading astern. It was the beginning of a voyage unmatched in the history of the navy before or since, a long, slow and perilous odyssey in which the fury of the enemy and the rage of sea and weather would test their ship and their seamanship, their courage and character beyond imagination.

For the first four days heading south-east from Singapore they were bombed and bombed, in wave after wave of attacks that seemed to have no beginning or end. Wallowing along at no better than 4 or 5 knots, their immediate destination was Palembang, a river port on the east coast of Sumatra well within range of the enemy squadrons. The weather mocked them, the clear blue skies thick with aircraft and soaring with the Japanese red rising sun on their wings.

They passed a burning tanker, victim of a direct hit, but miraculously received not a hit themselves. There were frightening near
misses, though, and plenty of them: two for'ard off the port bow,
one to starboard amidships and one off the port quarter, splattering
the ship with shrapnel that drilled holes in her sides and upper deck
and both funnels, and smashed the guard rails on the fo'c'sle. One
bomb splinter narrowly missed Bill Whitting on the bridge before
shattering windows and severing the electric cables to the Asdic set.
Whitting noted in his report that in just one day, 3 February, between
100 and 120 bombs were dropped close around the three ships. The
crew fought back with the 12-pounder and the machine guns, 'a very
fine performance', the captain wrote. A couple of times the tow line
parted, to be laboriously reset.

They wound their way up the Palembang River, 80 kilometres of
it, to the town itself, hoping to find a faster and stronger ship to tow
them on to Tanjung Priok. Again there were air raids but no damage
this time, and after four days the *St Just* took them back down the
river and turned the tow over to the sloop HMAS *Yarra*, which had
been sent for them. They reached Tanjung Priok without any further
incident on 10 February and there they made ready for the next leg
of their journey – a daunting 3000 kilometres south down the Indian
Ocean to Fremantle and home.

The towing vessel this time would be one of the oddest ships ever
commissioned into the Royal Navy. In fact 'ship' was too grand a
word. HMS *Ping Wo* was a Chinese river steamer of 1912 vintage that
had plied the Yangtze River before the war. She escaped south before
the fall of Hong Kong and was taken up by the navy in Singapore.
The name roughly translates as 'equitable harmony', but *Ping Wo*
was a squat and ugly, single-funnelled, flat-bottomed rust bucket of
3000 tons with blunt, bluff bows descending to a low freeboard amidships that gave her a most inharmonious look, like a cross between
a garbage truck and a coal barge. With a supposed best speed of
14 knots her crew was a mix of Royal Navy re
seamen from a British merchant ship which had
sunk in Singapore.

Unknown to almost everybody, *Ping Wo* was
extraordinary cargo. Stowed in her hold were tw

gold bullion belonging to the Straits Settlement Bank of Singapore, worth some £85,000,[5] being sent for safe keeping in Australia. If Bill Whitting's heart sank at the sight of the *Ping Wo* – and it surely must have, if only for a moment – he made no mention of it and got on with his business.

With the best luck in the world, the long haul to Fremantle would be taxing and testing, even if the weather and the sea were benign. *Ping Wo* had been built for river work, not any stretch of water so vast as the Indian Ocean. *Vendetta* was still an empty hulk, with no boilers, no electrical power and therefore no lighting; no refrigeration, no tap water, no working toilets in the heads; none of even the sparse amenities of her regular existence. The only food she had was canned, a disgusting monotony of bully beef and vegetables or a glutinous stew day in and day out, warmed up on a coal-burning stove. And with no power to her winches the anchor had to be weighed by hand and the heavy manilla or wire tow lines managed by brute strength, men tramping her fo'c'sle and heaving on capstan bars. John Lace, the hard-working Torpedo Gunner, was now officially First Lieutenant. The very backbone of the ship, though, was the senior sailor, Chief Petty Officer Alf Thorne, who had joined *Vendetta* a month before the war. Thorne was also a Brit, born in Devon – that ancient cradle of English seafarers – but in the RAN since 1925 and now a stalwart forty-year-old who turned a willing, vastly competent hand to any job that seamanship and leadership required.

With *Ping Wo* in the lead, *Yarra* escorted them from Tanjung Priok on 17 February, out through the Kepulauan Seribu, the Thousand Islands, then west and south down the Sunda Strait that separates Java and Sumatra. The enemy left them alone and with Whitting and Lace standing watch on watch and the crew at cruising stations it was an easy enough journey in good weather south to Christmas Island, where *Yarra* passed them mail for Australia and bade them farewell on 24 February. They plodded on, day upon monotonous day, night upon night, boredom and the vile food their chief enemy, until they reached the Rottnest Island Lighthouse off Perth on 3 March, the dear sight of Australian soil at last. The faithful *Ping Wo* left them to take her golden cargo into Fremantle and the tow was passed to a tug, *castle*, to bring *Vendetta* into port.

This should have been the moment of completion, of fulfilment, of a welcome homecoming after the two-week journey from Batavia. Instead, it was the beginning of an agonising six weeks of peril and injury, of imminent disaster. The signs were not good from the start. Twice that evening the line to *Newcastle* parted. With heavy rollers sweeping in from the Indian Ocean, *Vendetta* began to drift beam on towards the surf breaking on Cottesloe Beach. It was not until midnight that they managed to reset the tow again, eventually berthing at Fremantle at 0320 hours the next morning.

There was a six-day break there, which allowed everyone a run ashore and some decent food at last. Then there were new orders and they were off again on 10 March. The destination now would be Port Phillip Bay and Melbourne, *Ping Wo* towing once more for the 3000 kilometres across the Great Australian Bight – 'the dreaded Bight', as Whitting put it for, as every sailor knew, that vast expanse of open water could turn on all the ferocity of the Great Southern Ocean stretching away to Antarctica.

The next day out, in the early afternoon, *Ping Wo* slowed to a halt for engine repairs, leaving the two ships wallowing helplessly in a nasty rising sea with strong south-easterly gales and rain squalls. In the dark of night, hoping to moderate the rolling, *Vendetta* struggled to put out a sea anchor on her port side.

*Ping Wo* got her engines going but her master suggested putting into Albany for proper repairs. They laboured on for another two days, reaching Albany after dark on 14 March, only to find the visibility too poor to hazard the entrance. For yet another sleepless night they tossed and pitched in high seas, squalls and bitter cold, at one stage fearing they might be driven ashore on the rocks of Cape Vancouver lying under their lee. It would have been a test for the Officer of the Watch of a fully laden destroyer, engines working, fuel tanks full, with 30,000 horsepower to call on. *Vendetta*, light and empty, was thrown around like a hollow log.

Eventually they anchored in Albany Harbour. T dirtier still. There they waited for yet another ten ship – a small coastal steamer of the British Phospl the SS *Islander* – arrived to take up the tow to Mel went again with *Ping Wo* accompanying them ar broke, to be recovered with back-breaking difficulty. The following morning, as they were veering out cable on *Vendetta*'s fo'c'sle, the ship lurched suddenly and a capstan bar came loose and broke Chief Petty Officer Thorne's right leg. They bound him up with makeshift splints from a milk crate and got him into a bunk where he lay tossing in agony as the ship continued to gyrate.

For the next few days it was a litany of the same as the ocean did its worst: an agony of tow lines parting, of the little destroyer thrown about like flotsam, of *Ping Wo* simply disappearing into the night, of misery and hunger, of three sailors suffering from badly infected cuts and bruises. Their only hope now was somehow to get into Adelaide. The *Islander* radioed for help on 3 April as they lurched on:

0700   Clear lower deck, rig hand capstan. Pick up tow from SS *Islander*.

1100   Tow recovered and secured on fo'c'sle. This was done after much hard work on the part of the twenty men on board, and the bad weather and beam sea didn't make their task any easier. We had been adrift in the middle of the Bight in a roaring gale, completely disabled at the mercy of the wind and sea for seventy-two hours, during which period we had drifted 102 miles ...[6]

An RAAF Hudson flew over them the next day and flashed a recognition signal, which meant at least that someone had noticed them, and the day after that, with the weather mercifully abating at last, the survey vessel HMAS *Moresby* hove into view. *Moresby* sent her doctor over in a boat to do what he could for Alf Thorne and the other sick men and on 7 April they finally made it to Adelaide. Thorne was found to have a serious compound fracture and was put ashore to an army hospital. The trip from Albany to Adelaide had taken fourteen days.

But it wasn't over yet. On 10 April, with the *Islander* towing again, they ventured onwards in weather steadily deteriorating, in seas steadily rising. The tow broke the next day, and again the day after that. For another four days they struggled eastwards until, shortly before midnight on 14 April, they were off Port Phillip Heads in bitterly cold wind and rain. Another tug, the *Tooronga*, picked up the tow to take them through the infamous entrance rip, beating the ebb tide by just two minutes, and then on into the bay. Lieutenant Whitting finishes their story:

0700    All hands on fo'c'sle to house port anchor and prepare for entering harbour.

1100    Tug takes *Vendetta* into Victoria Docks.

1330    Secured at No 18 Wharf. Our journey is at last completed. We have been towed approximately 5000 miles,[7] the distance from Singapore to Melbourne, and it has taken 72 days.

Whitting was determined that whomever read his Report of Proceedings should know of the privations of his crew, which he described in his final paragraph with simple understatement.

Living conditions in the ship throughout were not the best. There was no power in the ship, no sanitary arrangements, and only tinned food was available owing to the absence of any refrigerator or ice box. In addition, the mess decks were used as storerooms and there were no comforts of any description throughout the trip.

I have the honour to be,

Sir,

Your obedient servant,

W. G. Whitting, Lieutenant RANR

He also took the trouble to write to the Naval Board recommending three of his men for decorations. John Lace had 'never faltered and was a tower of strength when things were at their worst'. Petty Officer Thorne had 'set a magnificent example of courage and devotion to duty ... he never failed me even when things appeared hopeless'. Of Able Seaman Bill Robertson he wrote that '... at times when the point of exhaustion was reached, he rallied the youn͠ the ship's company and was a mainstay in times of trc

The Board wholeheartedly agreed. The wheels tui all three men were eventually decorated, Lace with the

Service Cross and the other two with the Distinguished Service Medal.

—

It took until September 1942 to refit *Vendetta*, first in Melbourne and then in Sydney. The rest of her war was mundane, the unremarkable tasks of convoying along the Australian east coast and up to New Guinea, anti-submarine patrolling, the occasional chance to bombard a Japanese position on some remote island. She was never in real danger again and not a life was lost. In September 1945 she was sent to Rabaul, where Japanese officers came on board to arrange the formal surrender of General Hitoshi Imamura, the South-East Asia Commander.

And that was it. *Vendetta* moved under her own power for the last time in October 1945, back to Garden Island in Sydney. Ingloriously, she was sold to a scrap metal firm in 1946 and her hull was scuttled off Sydney Heads in 1948.

—

After he brought *Stuart* limping home to Melbourne on her one good engine, Lieutenant Commander Rupert Robison took the long spell of leave he had earned after almost two years away as Hec Waller's first lieutenant in the cauldron of the Mediterranean. He passed a happy month in Sydney with his wife Betty and their seven-year-old son Richard.

In January 1942 he was back at sea again in his first full-time command, the familiar old crock *Voyager*, and for a few months it was the monotony of convoy work up and down the Australian east coast, a far cry from the Tobruk Spud Run. Then it was up to Darwin where, in September, the ship was given a job which required something out of the ordinary. *Voyager* would carry commandos of the army's 2/4th Independent Company to the island of Timor to reinforce groups of Australian and Dutch soldiers who had been fighting a jungle guerrilla war against the Japanese.

Simple enough on paper, the operation would be a twenty-four-hour dash north-west from Darwin to land the men and their gear † Betano Bay on the southern coast of Portuguese East Timor.[9]

In practice it would not be so straightforward. Betano was hardly a bay at all and still less any sort of enclosed harbour; more of a shallow, sweeping curve in the coastline about 4 kilometres long with a surf beach at its western end and a scattering of rocky reefs to the east. There was a narrow channel between the reefs to an anchorage of sorts, but there were no charts, nothing with soundings to indicate depths on- or offshore, and no navigation aids of any sort; lights, markers or buoys. The navy had sent supply boats for the soldiers before this, but only small coastal patrol craft, nothing so big as a destroyer. The captain of one of those patrol boats, Sub Lieutenant Alan Bennett, an RANR officer, would go with *Voyager* to provide what local knowledge he had and his hand-drawn sketch of the beach but, basically, Rupert Robison would have to feel his way in.

They loaded the army on 22 September, 250 officers and men crammed on the upper deck with some 15 tons of their weapons and supplies and eight flimsy barges for getting them ashore. *Voyager* left Darwin in perfect weather at 1800 hours and, all according to plan, arrived off Betano exactly twenty-four hours later as the sun was beginning to set in a haze over Timor's palm trees and purple mountains. Now came the tricky part. With Bennett beside him on the bridge, the echo sounder working and, as an extra precaution, a hand in the chains swinging a lead and calling the depths, Robison gingerly picked his way towards the beach. As he began the run in, the sounder recorded a depth of some 235 metres[10] but the bottom quickly and alarmingly shelved to just 45 metres.[11] When the ship was about 500 metres from the beach Robison stopped her and lowered his starboard anchor. When that seemed settled, he gave the order for the troops to get into their boats and head off to shore.

A few minutes later, just after 1830 hours, Robison noticed that *Voyager* was swinging to her anchor and shifting uncomfortably close to the beach. He decided to weigh and to move out to deeper water by what he thought should be the most effective method, of going slowly astern on the port engine. But by that time the soldiers getting into the boats were milling around the port propellor. Robison feared it might well chew them to pieces if he started it, but the more he tried to get them clear the more confused they became, not comprehending the order, catcalling and talking back as if it were some sort of game. There was nothing for it but to try to ease out of trouble on the starboard engine, which he began carefully to do, and for a while it seemed to be working. It was not quite 1900 hours, the sun dropping quickly. *Voyager* was free and heading seawards again.

'Half ahead both. Starboard 20 degrees. Ship's head clear of reefs.'[12]

The words were hardly spoken when there was a horrible, low grinding sound aft and *Voyager* shuddered to a sickening, heart-stopping halt. A first attempt at going astern moved her not an inch, and then nor would she shift ahead. Her two propellors had screwed themselves into the sandy bottom, and no combination of helm and engine orders could move her. Whatever the navigational advice provided by Sub Lieutenant Bennett, it had not been enough. All through that grim night, ill met by moonlight, the captain and the ship's company tried everything they could to shift her and float her, first with anchors laid out in an attempt to winch and haul her free, then by getting rid of anything moveable that might lighten her, including jettisoning the depth charges and firing the torpedoes. Nothing worked and, worse, a stiffening south-east breeze and a rising swell began to bump her closer to the shore in worrying lurches.

In the morning the low tide revealed the appalling truth: she was high and dry on the beach, wretched and forlorn, slumped over to starboard, sand piled over both propellor shafts, parallel to the water-line and a bank of sand built up on her seaward side.

*Voyager* would never move again.

But there was no time for regrets or recriminations. As far as anybody knew the Japanese were not on this southern side of the island but they were to the north around the Portuguese capital, Dili, and it could hardly be long before *Voyager*'s plight reached them by word of mouth. Rupert Robison ordered the ship's company to begin concealing the boats and other gear in the trees that fringed the beach and the soldiers of the 2/4th stayed around in case they were needed.

That afternoon, at 1.30 pm, the enemy discovered them. A recon-naissance aircraft and a Zero fighter emerged from nowhere. Aground though she was, *Voyager* was still a fighting ship and her gunners shot down the search plane but, ominously, the Zero escaped. A few hours later, the Japanese returned. This account is from Lieutenant Surtees Rothery, one of *Voyager*'s officers:

It was late in the afternoon. Aircraft were approaching from the west and by this time most of the crew were ashore, however the remainder scrambled down scrambling nets and scattered with others along the beach in both directions and into the jungle. Laying on the beach the bomb bays could be seen open as the three planes flew over and then out to sea, returning one by one to suddenly release the bomb load that would fall and turn, heading for the ground. One pattern of bombs fell to the west along the beach, the next onto the beach and into the jungle above *Voyager*; the last lot fell on the water's edge below the beach. As each plane passed over after dropping its load the tail gunners sprayed the undergrowth and peppered the barges that were together at the top of the beach west of the ship. The bullets whistled through trees, craters were left in the beach and trees lopped a foot above the ground by bombs, but fortunately there were only a few superficial injuries.

Two more bombers arrived before dark with the same tactics and with so much machine gunning by the tail gunners that it could be heard above the engine noise of the planes.[13]

A few men were scratched or lightly wounded by shrapnel, including the captain. That night he radioed Darwin that he would destroy the ship to prevent her falling into enemy hands and he asked for a rescue for his men. After dark they laid demolition charges in the engine room which blew open the hull and broke the ship's back. The next day, 24 September, the sailors – out of their element – and soldiers – in theirs – prepared for a possible land attack, described by Lieutenant Rothery:

The commando officers gathered the crew around them and explained the sensitive situation with do's and don'ts and if's and the challenge word which was secret. The word was 'sketa' which apparently Japanese have difficulty saying. They explained that if things got tough we would be directed to caves high on the side of the hills behind and to the east of where we were. Also, if we heard aircraft, we were to run at right angles to the track and shelter behind a tree as the plane passed overhead.

Moving to a small clearing west of the wreck we decided it would be a spot to sleep at night. We were eating out of tins landed from the ship. For a cup of coffee ... one had to crawl along a creek bed beneath a large clump of bamboo to where a small fire and a large tin of coffee was being kept warm beneath the bamboo, because the bamboo leaves dissipated any smoke by the time it reached the outside and cleared the clump.

For fresh water the commandos had devised a method of obtaining it by splitting a bamboo in half lengthwise, cutting out the division pieces, sharpening one end, then ramming it into the thick bed of leaves on the creek bank, allowing the water to trickle along the bamboo.

As the commando officers suspected, we were visited frequently by Zero fighters strafing the tracks, but we had been told to run at right angles and this we did ...[14]

Before dawn the next morning, 25 September, Rupert Robison and one of his sailors, Able Seaman Cyril Webb, began to set fire to the ship: the same 'Spider' Webb who had famously dived overboard to rescue the nurse struggling in the water at Nafplion during the Greek evacuation. By sunrise *Voyager* was well alight and she kept burning all day, the ready-use ammunition and her after magazine exploding in fits and starts, the ship her own funeral pyre. That night the ship's company was rescued by the corvettes *Warrnambool* and *Kalgoorlie* and by 27 September they were back in Darwin, seven officers and 145 men, without loss of life. One enterprising sailor elected to stay ashore with the commandos.

In due course, the navy set up a Board of Inquiry into the loss of HMAS *Voyager*, a clinical examination of the facts in a quiet room far distant from the stress and strain of action. It allocated a little blame everywhere: the naval authorities in Darwin had given misleading information about the quality of the anchorage at Betano Bay; the behaviour of the disembarking troops showed a lack of discipline and training. But the cruel sting in the tail was for the captain himself. Lieutenant Commander Robison had anchored too close to the beach, had failed to veer sufficient cable, and had 'failed to take immediate action for the safety of his ship when it became apparent the ship was being set bodily ashore'. Remarkably, the finding suggested that he should have gone astern on his port engine, no matter that it might have 'risked the lives of a small number of military personnel'. He had therefore incurred 'the displeasure of the Naval Board' and his record would be noted accordingly.

Tragically, the loss of his ship and the blame laid upon his shoulders seem to have destroyed him. With the clear light of hindsight we can recognise Post Traumatic Stress Disorder, but that condition was unknown then and Rupert Robison's service record notes only that he suffered 'a nervous breakdown'. To its credit, the RAN apparently did what it could to care for him. In January 1943 he was sent by air to the United States and then by sea across the Atlantic to Britain where, for a year, he was a patient at a well-regarded psychiatric institution, the Crichton Hospital at Dumfries in Scotland. In December 1943 he returned to Australia by sea, accompanied by a navy doctor who reported 'a considerable improvement' on the voyage. It did not last. Back in Sydney he relapsed and was committed to the Callan Park Psychiatric Hospital with 'acute mania'. In August 1944 he was discharged from the RAN: P.U.N.S., which meant Permanently Unfit for Naval Service. The Distinguished Service Cross he was awarded for the Battle of Matapan must have been cold comfort.

Curiously, there is one final line penned on his record which reads: 'After further consideration the loss of HMAS *Voyager* was unavoidable and this officer was not to blame.' There was no explanation for that apparent change in the official view, but perhaps someone belatedly recognised the inherent danger, even reckless folly, of an unrehearsed operation to place troops untrained in boatwork onto a potentially hostile and certainly uncharted, reef-studded shore by night.

If so, it was too little and too late. The damage had been done. In post-war obscurity, haunted by his demons, Rupert Robison – and his family – laboured beneath the crushing trauma of his naval service until he died in 1999. It was a dismal end to a good man who deserved much, much better.

At low tide, the rusted remains of *Voyager* can still be seen at Betano Bay.

—

HMAS *Stuart* went quietly, the ageing actress now reduced to supporting roles in provincial theatres. After Japan entered the war, the White Lady of the Mediterranean, the Hero of Matapan, Hec Waller's destroyer leader, spent the rest of her war in Australian waters, never venturing much further afield than New Guinea. Newer, faster, grander destroyers had taken her place. Her humble lot now was convoying and fetching and carrying, in between ever longer spells in harbour for refit and maintenance. Engine breakdowns became more frequent. There was the occasional flurry of excitement when someone thought he had detected a submarine, but it never came to anything and she never fired another shot in anger.

Most of 1944 was spent in Sydney where she was slowly converted into what was generously described as a 'fast transport'. She was given radar and some new Oerlikon anti-aircraft guns, but her for'ard funnel and boiler were removed, which gave her an ungainly, stunted appearance. She did not get to sea again until April 1945, almost at war's end. Her long-time chief engineer, Wal Rands, had left her years before, but he saw her again and wrote:

> Her grotesque pole mast and single vertical funnel stand out incongruously amongst the lattice masts and streamlined funnels of her sleek successors, but the old hull is sound and lines are clean and graceful, and her ensign flutters just as proudly as it did when she led the 10th Flotilla on the screen for Cunningham's battle fleet.[15]

In truth, she was old and exhausted. No one surrendered to her, no defeated enemy trod her deck. She made her last trip under her own steam in 1946 from Townsville to Sydney, passing unheralded through the Heads and up the harbour to Garden Island on 13 February. The war was long over. Nobody wanted to know anymore. In her final report of proceedings, her last commanding officer, Lieutenant Edgar Whish, recorded her vital statistics since the outbreak of war in 1939:

| | |
|---|---|
| Total distance steamed: | 242,269.4 miles |
| Total hours under way: | 16,736.40 hours |
| Average speed: | 14.5 knots |
| Total fuel expended: | 68,331.77 tons |

There was another statistic too. For all that the ship had done and endured in her long and crowded years, not one of her crewmembers had died through enemy action.

*Stuart* was sold to the breakers in 1947. For a couple more years she languished in a bay at Waverton west of the bridge in Sydney Harbour while her upperworks were slowly stripped. Finally, she came to rest alone on a mudbank up the Parramatta River at Ryde before the oxyacetylene torches cut her to pieces in the early 1950s.

*Sic transit gloria.*

# APPENDIX I

# CROSSING THE BAR

Sunset and evening star,
And one clear call for me!
And may there be no moaning of the bar,
When I put out to sea,

But such a tide as moving seems asleep,
Too full for sound and foam,
When that which drew from out the boundless deep
Turns again home.

Twilight and evening bell,
And after that the dark!
And may there be no sadness of farewell,
When I embark;

For tho' from out our bourne of Time and Place
The flood may bear me far,
I hope to see my Pilot face to face
When I have crost the bar.

Alfred, Lord Tennyson

Written in 1889, at the Victorian flood tide of Rule Britannia, Tennyson's poem resonated powerfully with those who went down to the sea in ships. Ever since, sailors of the English-speaking navies have spoken of 'crossing the bar' as a poignant metaphor for the death of one of their own.

The last of the Scrap Iron sailors – the very last, so far as I know – died as I was finishing this book. Leading Steward Melville Roy McMillan crossed the bar in the winter of 2021, three months shy of his 102nd birthday. Like so many sailors he was a boy from the bush, growing up at Castlemaine in Victoria's goldfields country but dreaming of going to sea. The navy took him on in February 1937 and, after his training at Cerberus, a year later he joined the crew of *Vampire*, serving in her throughout her time in the Mediterranean. After the war he settled down first in Bendigo and then in suburban Melbourne, where he raised a family of six children who in time gave him seventeen grandchildren and twenty-six great-grandchildren.

Mel was proud of his service all his life. 'Once navy, always navy,' he used to say. His family threw him a great party for his 100th birthday in 2019 and some young sailors from Cerberus, including a couple of newly minted stewards, were invited along to meet him and to carry the navy's good wishes. To pay tribute, really. His eyesight was gone by then, but his mind was as sharp as ever, and he held them respectfully enthralled.

'Gimme the boats,' he told them, the rallying cry of the old destroyer men. Perhaps they understood what he meant, perhaps not. The phrase is no longer heard. More certain was his description of the disaster of the retreat from Crete. 'The Germans had everything in their favour. It was hell on earth. When they come at you fifty planes at a time, you can't do anything. Nothing stops them. Multiple pom-poms, nothing.'[1]

The navy was proud of Mel and stood by him to the end. At his funeral his coffin was shrouded in the white ensign, a commodore in full uniform and a senior warrant officer were there to salute his passing and to present the family with the RAN Bereavement Pin, a lapel badge of the navy crest wreathed in gold. COVID-19 kept the numbers down, but those who came sang the navy hymn – 'Eternal Father Strong to Save' – and then The Last Post and Reveille sent him on his way beyond the bar.

—

There were more than three years of war still to come after the Scrap Iron Flotilla and the rest of the Australians left the Mediterranean. The men who appear in this book simply got on with it. Not all survived. Let's follow them a little beyond 1942.

**Les Clifford.** Clifford's next ship after *Stuart* was the cruiser *Perth*, which brought him home from the Mediterranean. Fortunately, he left her before she was lost in 1942 and he spent the rest of his war ashore. His book *The Leader of the Crocks*, published in 1945, remains an invaluable record of the Scrap Iron Flotilla. Still rated a signalman, he was demobilised in November 1945.

**John Collins.** For many, Collins embodied the best of the Royal Australian Navy at war and in the peace that followed. In 1942, though still a captain, he was Commodore Commanding China Force, supervising the scrambling Allied naval retreat from the advancing Japanese in the Netherlands East Indies. In 1943 he commissioned the cruiser *Shropshire* given to Australia by the British after the loss of the cruiser *Canberra* at the Battle of Savo in the Solomon Islands in 1942. Promoted to Commodore 1st Class in 1944, he commanded the Australian squadron operating with the US 7th Fleet in the Pacific. In October that year he was badly wounded when a kamikaze aircraft hit the bridge of HMAS *Australia*, killing thirty-one men. Back at sea in 1945, he was in *Shropshire* again and Australia's naval representative at the Japanese surrender in Tokyo Bay. Promoted to rear admiral in 1947, vice admiral in 1950 and knighted in 1951, he was chief of the naval staff from 1948 until his retirement in 1955. He served as Australia's High Commissioner to New Zealand between 1956–62 and died in Sydney, aged ninety, in 1989. The navy's Collins class submarines were named for him.

**Arthur Cooper.** The gunner's mate and keen diarist in *Voyager* was awarded the Greek Medal for Outstanding Acts by King George of the Hellenes in 1942. From 1943 he served in *Shropshire* as a chief petty officer, seeing action in the Pacific at Leyte Gulf and the Battle of Surigao Strait in October 1944, for which he was awarded the Distinguished Service Medal. He retired from the navy in 1948.

**Andrew Cunningham.** Admiral of the Fleet Andrew Browne Cunningham, 1st Viscount Cunningham of Hyndhope, KT, GCB,

OM, DSO & Two Bars died in a taxi on the way home from lunch at his London club in 1963. He had been the pre-eminent British fighting admiral of the twentieth century. He stayed in the Mediterranean until 1943 for the surrender of the Regia Marina that September, famously signalling the Admiralty: 'Be pleased to inform their Lordships that the Italian battle fleet now lies at anchor under the guns of the fortress of Malta.' A month later he became First Sea Lord after the death of Sir Dudley Pound. Churchill had hoped for a more pliant admiral but eventually had to concede that Cunningham was the obvious, standout candidate. He remained in the job until 1946, gathering honours and laurels as he went. The supreme commander in Europe, General Dwight D. Eisenhower, wrote of him that, 'He remains in my opinion at the top of my subordinates in absolute selflessness, energy, devotion to duty, knowledge of his task, and in understanding of the requirements of Allied operations. My opinions as to his superior qualifications have never wavered for a second.'

Most telling is an anecdote from Nicholas Monsarrat, author of *The Cruel Sea* and a naval officer in the Battle of the Atlantic. On duty at the Admiralty on 8 May 1945, the night of victory in Europe, he went to the top of Admiralty Arch that evening to see the ecstatic masses thronging the Mall below. Cunningham was there on the parapet too, and Monsarrat glimpsed, in the floodlights, that he was crying.

**Walter Enneccerus.** After the Mediterranean, Enneccerus was transferred to the Russian front as squadron commander of StG 77 in October 1942. He was removed from command for refusing to carry out what he believed to be a suicidal mission. He survived the war as a Generalmajor and in 1956 joined the Bundeswehr, retiring in 1967 as a Brigadegeneral. He died in 1971.

**Hans Heidtmann.** *U-559* remained in the Mediterranean after sinking *Parramatta*. In October 1942 the boat was spotted by an RAF Sunderland north of the Nile Delta and eventually hunted to the surface by destroyers. The crew scrambled overboard without destroying their Enigma codebooks and these were captured by the British, a priceless intelligence coup. Heidtmann spend nearly five years as a prisoner of war. Never a Nazi, he joined the Bundesmarine in 1958 as a staff officer and retired as a Kapitän zur See in 1972.

**Gordon Hill.** The diarist from *Vendetta* later served in HMAS *Perth* and the corvette *Colac*. From 1943 he spent the rest of his war ashore in Australia and New Guinea and left the navy as a chief petty officer in 1950. He later became an accountant in Brisbane. His diaries and a unique collection of photographs are a treasure at the Naval Historical Society at Garden Island in Sydney.

**Ean McDonald.** Uniquely, McDonald served in all five Scrap Iron destroyers. After that he was a signalman in *Perth* until March 1942, leaving her just three weeks before she was sunk to do an officer training course and then a gunnery course. From 1943 as a lieutenant he was the gunnery officer in the corvette *Shepparton* until the war's end. Transferring to the RANVR, he briefly commanded the survey vessel HMAS *Polaris* and rose to the rank of lieutenant commander. In civilian life he ran a poultry farm, became a prominent architect and city councillor in Perth and gained a Master Merchant Mariner's certificate. In late retirement he relaxed by skippering cruise boats on the Swan River. He died in 2011.

**James 'Copper' Morrow.** Another officer much liked and respected by the men he led, Morrow was given command of the new destroyer *Arunta* in 1942. He sank a Japanese submarine off Port Moresby in August that year, winning a DSC to join the DSO he had earned in the Mediterranean. At war's end he was executive officer of *Shropshire* and with her for the surrender ceremony in Tokyo Bay. As a captain, Morrow commanded the destroyer *Bataan* after the war, served as Australian naval attaché in Washington and then as commanding officer of the fleet flagship *Australia*. Promoted to commodore, he was chief of naval personnel in the mid-1950s but found staff work boring. He left the navy in 1960 and died of cancer in 1963.

**Andy Nation.** After *Waterhen* was sunk, Nation was posted to the new destroyer HMAS *Nizam* in the Mediterranean. In the Pacific War he served in the destroyer *Warramunga*. He stayed on in the navy and was a petty officer stoker in the carrier *Sydney* during the Korean War, which he found rather tame by comparison. He left the navy in 1952.

**Rodney 'Dusty' Rhoades.** After setting the record of thirty-nine trips on the Tobruk Spud Run – earning a DSC – Rhoades commissioned the new destroyer *Quickmatch* in 1942. From 1946 he had the frigate *Shoalhaven*, the destroyer *Tobruk*, and was the first Australian-born officer to command HMAS Albatross, the naval air station at Nowra in New South Wales. As a captain he became the Australian defence attaché in New Zealand and he finished as a commodore in charge of training at HMAS Cerberus in 1963. He went blind in later life and died in 1991.

**Walter 'Jack' Ross.** Luck sailed with Ross. He left HMAS *Sydney* in October 1941, just ten days before she departed Fremantle on her last, fatal voyage. He joined *Canberra* where, as a paymaster lieutenant, he was the captain's secretary and was in her the night she was lost at the Battle of Savo in 1942. The second Japanese salvo fired at the ship killed most of the bridge personnel and fatally wounded the captain but Ross had been sent from the bridge on an errand just minutes before and escaped the carnage. He spent the rest of the war ashore and retired from the navy as a paymaster lieutenant commander in 1951.

**Ennio 'Banana' Tarantola.** The man who sank *Waterhen* left Stukas and returned to fighters for the rest of the war. Tarantola was shot down near Sicily in late 1942 and was badly burned, but survived to return to the air. From 1944 he continued to fly with the so-called Republican Air Force loyal to the Axis, but was shot down again and burned again. That ended his war. He was credited with destroying ten Allied aircraft and was created a Knight of the Order of Merit of the Italian Republic. For a while he flew in an aerobatic team. Much, much later, when they were old men, he and Ean McDonald exchanged letters. When McDonald visited Italy in 2002, he looked him up but found he had died the year before.

**Norman 'Whiskers' Teacher.** *Stuart*'s popular navigator won the DSO for sinking the submarine *Gondar*. Teacher went back to the Royal Navy in August 1941. A year later, as a lieutenant commander, he trained as a commando in the newly formed combined operations unit run by Lord Louis Mountbatten at Hayling Island in Portsmouth. In 1943 he led a combined operations pilotage party, COPP 3, a team of canoeists tasked to operate secretly in enemy waters. Teacher and two other men were carried by submarine to Sicily where, in the dead of night, they paddled away to survey a beach in preparation for the

Allied landings in 1943. All three went missing, presumed dead, in circumstances never discovered.

**Terry 'Dutchie' Van Prooyen.** With his exploits on the Danube a closely held secret, Van Prooyen joined HMAS *Australia* in 1942, still an able seaman. He was with her as a gunner through the Japanese kamikaze campaign off the Philippines in 1944 and was credited with saving the ship by shooting down two attacking aircraft. After the war he worked on the Melbourne waterfront. His son Steve went into the navy as a raw recruit and retired as a lieutenant commander.

**Hector Waller.** After leaving *Stuart*, Waller took command of the cruiser *Perth* in October 1941. He was in her at the disastrous Battle of the Java Sea in February 1942, when an American, British, Dutch and Australian task group of cruisers and destroyers was soundly defeated by a Japanese force invading East Java. On the night of 28 February, *Perth* and the American cruiser USS *Houston* attempted to break south through the Sunda Strait separating Java and Sumatra. They encountered another Japanese invasion convoy of overwhelming force and, after a brave but unequal struggle, both were sunk early in the morning of 1 March. Hec Waller was last seen on *Perth*'s bridge, staring down at the silent guns on the fo'c'sle below him. It is likely he was killed by a bursting shell. In his memoirs, Andrew Cunningham paid a high compliment:

> Hector Macdonald Laws Waller will always remain in my mind as one of the very finest types of Australian naval officer. Full of good cheer, with a great sense of humour, undefeated and always burning to get at the enemy, he kept the old ships of his flotilla – the *Stuart*, *Vampire*, *Vendetta*, *Voyager*, *Waterhen* – hard at it always. Greatly loved and admired by everyone, his loss in HMAS *Perth* in the Java Sea in March 1942 was a heavy deprivation for the young Navy of Australia.[2]

If John Collins was respected by his crews, 'Hard Over' Hec Waller was loved. He was the RAN's greatest fighting captain, and many believe he should have been awarded the Victoria Cross as well as his two DSOs and his three Mentions in Despatches. A submarine is named after him.

**John Walsh.** *Vampire*'s captain left her in 1941 and after a brief spell ashore was posted as a commander in *Canberra*. He was in her at Savo in 1942 and was badly wounded in one eye. That injury kept him in shore postings for the rest of the war and afterwards. Awarded an OBE, he retired as a captain in 1961.

**Bill Whitting.** *Vendetta*'s temporary captain had more fighting to do. He was awarded the Distinguished Service Cross for 'courage, endurance and devotion to duty' in *Vendetta*, and was badly wounded as first lieutenant in the corvette *Armidale* when she was sunk by Japanese bombers off Timor in December 1942. Back on his feet six months later, he was appointed captain of another corvette, HMAS *Colac*. He left the navy at the end of the war but shrapnel remaining in his body moved and rendered him a paraplegic in the last year of his life. Lieutenant William Whitting DSC RANR died in 1984, an authentic but unsung naval hero mourned by his wife, Mary.

# THE LINE OF STUARTS

There have been two more *Stuart*s in the Royal Australian Navy since the first. HMAS *Stuart II* was an anti-submarine frigate, a sleek and handsome ship of 2700 tons modified from a British blueprint and built at Sydney's Cockatoo Island. She was launched in 1961 and became the first ship to carry the Australian-designed Ikara missile system. Nicknamed 'The Tartan Terror', she did some escort work during the Vietnam War but never fired a shot in anger before she was sold for scrap in 1991.

The third *Stuart* joined the navy in 2002, to be the fourth of eight Anzac class frigates built for the RAN to a German design, the Meko 200. At the time of writing, the winter of 2021, she is out of the water at the Australian Marine Complex, a hi-tech shipyard at Henderson south of Fremantle in Western Australia, where she is undergoing an extensive refit and upgrading of a range of equipment from radars and communications gear to her galley fridges and waste disposal. It is a renewal to give her another two decades of life.

—

So, let the imagination wander. Picture Hec Waller and his men stepping on board HMAS *Stuart III* when she is ready for sea again. They find her at Sydney's Garden Island – or FBE, Fleet Base East as the navy now calls it – alongside the very same wharf they farewelled in 1939. She towers above them, so much bigger than their little ship, like a welded wall of grey steel. Even their most ardent admirers would be hard put to claim the Anzac frigates are an elegant vessel of long, low lines. Rather, they have a tough, muscular look to them, broad-shouldered and purposeful.

Within that hefty frame the twenty-first century *Stuart* carries an extraordinary array of weapons, sensors and communications gear: missiles, guns, torpedoes, various types of short- and long-range radar and sonar, all to be controlled and fought not from any storm-swept open bridge but in an air-conditioned operations room filled with computer monitors and consoles. Staring up from the wharf, Hec's men see a broad flight deck aft and a hangar for one of the RAN's Seahawk helicopters, also armed with missiles and torpedoes. Rising amidships, supplanting the slender masts of old, is her most striking feature: a tall steel tower topped with a bulky, hexagonal dome and crammed with electronics including CEAFAR, a world-beating radar system designed and built in Australia to perform all sorts of top-secret miracles of detection. No more the captain leaning back in his chair on the bridge, salt-smeared binoculars in hand, scanning the skies for the black specks of approaching enemy bombers.

These old sailors will find some things astounding, even bewildering, and others warmly reassuring, untouched by time. The first surprise is the flag flying from the staff on the stern: the Australian white ensign with its blue stars of the Southern Cross replaced the British naval ensign with its red cross of St George in 1967. More familiar, at the foot of the gangway there is the customary ceremonial lifebuoy to welcome visitors, gleaming white with the name *Stuart* lettered in gold and mounted on a varnished timber stand known – for reasons lost in time – as a crucifix.

Captain Waller bounds onto the brow. As a ship's commanding officer his arrival on board is announced and acknowledged ceremonially by the shrill of the bosun's call, a naval courtesy centuries old. Nothing surprising there. But on deck he is greeted by *Stuart*'s CO, a female captain in her early forties dressed in her working gear of the mottled, olive-grey fabric the RAN oddly calls DPNU, Disruptive Pattern Navy Uniform. The four gold stripes of her rank sit on each shoulder. She wears not an officer's white uniform cap but a blue, baseball style cap, with the ship's name embroidered on it and *Stuart*'s pennant number, 153. The sailors with her are dressed identically.

A woman? In fact, in *Stuart*'s crew of 190 there are some forty or fifty women, officers and sailors. It is a vision unimaginable in 1939. And the faces on deck are different, noticeably. Almost to a man, the sailors of the Scrap Iron Flotilla were Anglo-Saxon or Celtic. *Stuart III*'s ship's company is woven from the ethnic strands of multi-cultural Australia. The officer of the day, a young lieutenant standing attentively behind his captain, is Vietnamese. There are Italians, Greeks, Chinese, Indians, Lebanese, Pacific Islanders and more. The duty quartermaster, a leading seaman, is from a First Nations family in the Northern Territory.

Hec will recognise the badges of rank, for they remain much the same, although engineers and supply officers are no longer distinguished by stripes of purple or white cloth separating their rings of gold braid; only the doctors keep their traditional blood red between the gold. A leading seaman sports a killick – the fouled anchor badge of his rank, unchanged – and a chief petty officer, with his crown and gold wreathed anchor, remains unmistakably and unswervingly a chief petty officer and not to be trifled with. Boatswain's mates, the navy's pure seamen, go on forever, and the chief bosun's mate is still 'The Buffer'.

Some jobs, though, are gone for good. The brawny stoker of old, never all that bright but hard working, always on the lookout for a beer and a brawl ashore, is now a marine technician, quite possibly a young woman with a suite of advanced engineering skills. Signalmen have disappeared too, although the communication and information systems operators who have replaced them still must be able to run up or read a flag hoist at sea in a gale. Combat systems operator, maritime logistics officer, electronic warfare systems operator, chef, avionics technician: the list of the new goes on.

Gunnery, once the naval officer's god, has faded to a lesser art. *Stuart III* has just one big gun, a 5-inch rapid-fire weapon on the fo'c'sle that can shoot twenty rounds a minute, all automatically. No more men sweating below decks humping shells from the magazine, no more director layers and trainers, no more range spotters or turret officers. These days the principal warfare officer, a senior lieutenant or lieutenant commander who has survived a gruelling, make-or-break course of specialist training, will fight the ship at the captain's direction.

Invited up to the bridge, Captain Waller marvels at the space, the unapologetic comfort of it all. It is fully enclosed and air-conditioned, bounded on three sides by wide windows of heavy glass, the weather kept at bay. No more water green over the bow, drenching the watch. No more squinting into the teeth of a howling winter gale in a sodden duffel coat, lashed by icy rain; no more stinking Red Sea heat, no more gasping for breath in gritty dust storms.

A few things will be recognisable, commonplace. A Pelorus* on its pillar still stands proud, a focus point at the very centre of the bridge, with another on each bridge wing, as there has always been. The captain's chair is prominent on the starboard side as ever, although its cushioned leather upholstery is a far cry from the plain timber stool of Hec's day. And there the familiar ends. The cluster of speaking tubes is long gone, supplanted by banks of internal communications switches and broadcast networks – Main Broadcast, Conning, Upper Deck Broadcast, Action Intercom, Command Open Line, Flight Deck Intercom …

More wonders are revealed. There is a charthouse below the bridge, but it's a rare day that a paper chart is laid out on the table for the navigator to plot and pencil his lines and angles. It's all downloaded now, displayed on screens here and on the bridge and in the operations room. The greatest surprise of all, perhaps: there is no wheel, no quartermaster to subtly keep the ship ploughing a straight furrow in a calm sea or to wrestle her back on track in a storm. A steering console not unlike a kid's PlayStation controller sits on the port side of the bridge, and there the ship is helmed either on autopilot or, if needs be, with the smooth turn of a wrist.

Going below, Hec's men find spotless passageways and ladders leading to air-conditioned mess decks where each sailor has his or her own bunk, or 'rack' as they call them. No more hammocks to be slung or stowed. No more rats, no more cockroaches. There are bathrooms and laundries aplenty for men and women. No more sluicing the body or washing the shirts with a bucket of water on the upper deck. Meals of a more than decent restaurant quality, with an inviting

---

\*    A fixed compass used for taking bearings.

range of choices, are displayed in a brightly lit self-serve cafeteria. No more boiled beef and spuds, no more tinned stew.

In the bowels of the ship, the engineers of 1939 marvel at the rumble of the gas turbine engine which starts at a computer's command. No more steam to be raised, no more filthy boilers to be cleaned. With a displacement of 3900 tons *Stuart III* packs more than twice the bulk of *Stuart I* but, curiously, despite the dazzling advances in naval engineering over a hundred years, she is not as fast. The navy, rather hesitantly, allows her 'more than 27 knots'. The little destroyer leader, in her heyday, could turn on 36.

But speed is not everything. There is that array of weapons: armchair fantasy, to be sure, but *Stuart III* could have taken out the entire enemy fleet at Matapan in a brisk hour or so, day or night, without the Italians ever seeing or knowing what hit them.

—

The sun is lowering west over the city and the Harbour Bridge, the shadows lengthening. This evening *Stuart* will formally welcome her distinguished visitors with all the well-burnished naval pomp and custom at her command. On the flight deck they are making ready for a ceremonial sunset, a hallowed display of naval theatre to mark the parting day. See the guard of half a dozen sailors in smart white uniforms now, rifles at the shoulder, as they wheel into position under the command of a ship's lieutenant with sword in hand. Listen to the roll and rattle of drums and the blare of brass from the RAN band lined up on the wharf.

'Five minutes to sunset, sir!'

'Very good!'

The gentle notes of the 'Evening Hymn' drift across the flight deck and Woolloomooloo Bay, broken sharply by the crack of rifles as the guard fires the salute; not with the long-barrelled Lee-Enfields .303s that Hec Waller knew, but the stubby EF88 Austeyr automatic assault rifle that is the RAN's individual weapon.

'Guard, ho!'

'Present arms!'

With due respect the Australian white ensign is smoothly lowered to the plangent song of a bugle, and then comes 'Advance Australia

Fair'. It would have been 'God Save the King' in Hec's day. The guard leaves the flight deck to the trills and flourishes of the 'Royal Australian Navy March' and the day is done.

—

*Stuart*'s formal wardroom dinner for Captain Waller tonight begins sharp at 1900 hours with the buzz of chatter as the officers gather over beers or wine. If you ask for a pink gin the steward will find you one, but that heady cocktail once brought home by Australian officers from the Royal Navy has long since fallen from favour.

As with almost everything else in the navy, the dinner has forms and rituals, custom and practice to be observed. The wardroom is the place for officers to wind down, relax. It is home. The iron rules of rank are eased a little, in a manner well put by John Paul Jones, the father of the United States Navy, in thoughts on the ideal officer:

> In his intercourse with subordinates he should ever maintain the attitude of the Commander, but that need by no means prevent him from the amenities of cordiality or the cultivation of good cheer within the proper limits. Every Commanding Officer should hold with his subordinates such relations as will make them constantly anxious to sit at his table, and his bearing towards them should be such as encourages them to express their opinions to him with freedom and to ask his views without reserve.[1]

Others were not so sanguine. The Earl of St Vincent, First Sea Lord at the Admiralty in Nelson's time and a ferocious martinet, suspected the worst:

> Discipline begins in the wardroom. I dread not the seamen. It is the indiscreet conversations of the officers and their presumptuous discussions of the orders they receive that produce all our ills.[2]

There will be no presumptuous discussions this evening. Men and women are in black tie – the women have a choice of black trousers or long black skirt – and, in summer, all are wearing white mess jackets with gold buttons and miniature medals pinned to the left lapel.

No one, though, has decorations so striking nor so hard earned as Hec's Distinguished Service Order with Bar and two of the bronze oak leaf pins of a Mention in Despatches.

Ruling over all is the mess president, not the ship's captain but *Stuart*'s executive officer, armed with a polished timber gavel to maintain order at the table as the evening gets more high-spirited, which it will noisily do. To help keep the show on the road he has a vice president, addressed as 'Mr Vice', almost always a junior officer with a quick tongue and a finely judged understanding of just how much cheek he can get away with giving to his elders and betters. Hec Waller was renowned for his love of a party, a social occasion. He will find all this agreeably familiar. The gavel bangs.

'Mr Vice! The Queen!'

As ever, they stay seated for the loyal toast, a privilege granted to the navy in the nineteenth century by King William IV who, as a young officer and a tall man, regularly smacked his head on the wooden beams on the deckhead above when he rose to drink to his father, George III. The dinner goes on, three courses at which the cooks show their stuff. No one is allowed to leave the table for any reason until the president gives permission: 'You may ease springs.' At which point there is a hurried scrape of chairs and a stampede for the head.

The chatter and laughter grow louder. The president and Mr Vice will impose mock penalties and punishments for sins of decorum and behaviour real and imagined. Almost certainly some young sub lieutenant or bold midshipman will seize the moment to quietly steal and hide the president's gavel, a well-worn but much-loved prank cheerfully anticipated and usually causing no end of uproar.

After the meal the traditional decanter of port circles to the left, explicitly slid along the table, not passed in the air. There are prescribed toasts for each day of the week. Of a Wednesday it will be the lurid 'A bloody war and a sickly season!' which, in Nelson's day, meant the hope of quick promotion. Friday's toast calls for 'A willing foe and sea room!'. This is a Saturday though, and Hec and friends raise their glasses not to the recently abandoned 'Wives and sweethearts … may they never meet!' but to the very much more respectable 'Our partners'.

The dinner ends with the cooks and stewards invited in to be thanked for their efforts. A good few of the hardy souls will hang on at the bar for a nightcap or three, then time to go. Captain Waller is farewelled over the side and back to the pages of history.

—

*Stuart*'s last CO before her present refit, Captain Luke Ryan, brought the ship back home from a deployment of nearly five months in South-East Asia and the Central Pacific. Dismally, with COVID-19 about, the crew were confined to the ship all that time; no chance for a run ashore in any port they visited.

'The nearest we got to it was when we berthed in Hawaii close enough to a McDonald's to use their wi-fi,' he told me ruefully. 'But the troops took it pretty well.'

Ryan assured me that the traditions do matter. The navy genuinely cherishes its past. Visitors to *Stuart* will be shown the battle honour board, elaborately carved and scrolled in lacquered teak with the ship's crest, a Scottish rose at its centre:

Mediterranean 1940.
Calabria 1940.
Libya 1940–41.
Matapan 1941.
Greece 1941.
Crete 1941.
Pacific 1942–43.
New Guinea 1942–44.
Middle East 2004–11.

Every officer and sailor joining his crew is given a ninety-minute induction course on the ship's history and the Scrap Iron Flotilla.

'And do they *get* it?' I asked him. 'Do they take it on board?'

He was adamant. 'Yes, they do, especially the younger ones. And a lot of the job is the same. They're still out of bed at midnight to go on watch ...'

Certain to say there will always be a *Stuart* in the RAN, of whatever type the future brings.

And each time that ship puts to sea her people will know that their forebears, those bold warrior mariners of long ago, are there on watch with them.

# NOTES

## Chapter 1: The Theatre

1 Voltaire, *Candide*, 1759, *'Dans ce pays-ci, il est bon de tuer de temps en temps un amiral pour encourager les autres.'*
2 Hemans, Felicia Dorothea, *Casabianca*, 1826.
3 Churchill, Winston S., *The World Crisis*, vol. 1, The Gutenberg Project.
4 navy.gov.au/hmas-ae2
5 Commodore Roger Keyes, a distinguished British naval officer.

## Chapter 2: Commence Hostilities at Once with Germany

1 *Sydney Morning Herald*, 31 August 1939, 20° Celsius.
2 *Daily Telegraph*, 31 August 1939.
3 But for one thing. To the chagrin of RN sailors on exchange, the RAN never adopted the sailors' daily rum ration. Perhaps the memory of the Rum Rebellion was too raw. On the other hand, the Australian pay was better.
4 The Australian white ensign, with the blue stars of the Southern Cross, did not appear until 1967.
5 The author was Captain Rhoderick McGrigor RN, who would eventually become an Admiral of the Fleet and First Sea Lord.
6 Officer's Personal Record, National Archives.
7 Admiral Sir Walter 'Tich' Cowan.
8 Clifford, L. E., *The Leader of the Crocks*, F. W. Cheshire, Melbourne, 1945.
9 The (E) stood for 'Engineer'. It is no longer used.
10 Quoted in Shirer, William L., *The Rise and Fall of the Third Reich*, Secker & Warburg, London, 1960, p. 720.
11 *Daily News*, Sydney, 2 September 1939.
12 He was right. They did, 3–2.
13 *Daily Telegraph*, Sydney, 2 September 1939.
14 *Argus*, Melbourne, 2 September 1939.

15 *Daily News*, Sydney, 2 September 1939.
16 Clifford, op. cit. p. 17.

## Chapter 3: Travelling North

1 Clifford, op. cit. p. 17.
2 One U-boat eventually made it to Australian waters. Sailing from Japanese-occupied Batavia, *U-862* sank an American freighter off Sydney in December 1944.
3 HMAS *Stuart*, Report of Proceedings, 3 October 1939, AWM, Canberra.
4 Ibid.
5 Documents of Australian Foreign Policy, vol. 2, 1939, No. 169. HMAS *Perth* was in the Caribbean on her way home to Australia.
6 Ibid. No. 214.
7 Ibid. No. 222.
8 McDonald, Ean, *Flip Side War*, Hesperian Press, Perth, 2005, p. 22.
9 Clifford, op. cit. p. 24.
10 McDonald, op. cit. p. 26.
11 Sailors from HMAS *Australia* at a British barracks were astounded when an RN captain ordered them to bathe once a week, whether they liked it or not.
12 Clifford, op. cit. p. 33.
13 For various reasons, the two promised cruisers never arrived.
14 Clifford, op. cit. p. 40.
15 *British Chivalry* was sunk by a Japanese submarine in the Indian Ocean in 1944. The Japanese captain machine-gunned her survivors in lifeboats.
16 en.wikipedia.org/wiki/Hans_Langsdorff#Death
17 *Australasian* weekly, Melbourne, 27 January 1940.

## Chapter 4: That First Christmas

1 Reeve, Bill quoted in *The Royal Australian Navy in World War II*, Stevens, David (ed.), Allen & Unwin, Sydney, 1996.
2 Clifford, op. cit. p. 51.
3 Lind, L. J. & Payne, A., *Scrap Iron Destroyers*, Naval Historical Society of Australia, Sydney, 1976, p. 31.
4 Hill, G. A., *My Naval Sojourn 1938–1950*, Naval Historical Society of Australia, Sydney, 2020.
5 Ibid. p. 27.
6 Cunningham, Andrew (Admiral of the Fleet Viscount Cunningham of Hyndhope), *A Sailor's Odyssey*, Hutchison & Co., London, 1951, p. 219. In 1946, Admiral of the Fleet Lord Tovey, celebrated as the man who sank the *Bismarck*, visited Australia. The men of the Scrap Iron Flotilla had been some of the finest crews we had, he told the newspapers. But they had bad material to work with.

7   McDonald, op. cit. p. 28.
8   Ibid.
9   NAAFI. The British Navy, Army and Air Force Institute. A worldwide civilian organisation that ran canteens and entertainment for the services.
10  Clifford, op. cit. p. 60.
11  *Naval Historical Review*, December 2017, Naval Historical Society of Australia, Sydney, p. 15.
12  Ciano diary, quoted in Shirer, William L., op. cit. p. 830.
13  Dymond, Ralph, *The History of HMAS Voyager I*, privately published, p. 52.
14  Ibid.
15  Clifford, op. cit. p. 64.
16  And worthwhile. Waller claimed salvage money. An able seaman collected £125 at the end of the war, a handy sum.
17  Lind, L. J. & Payne, A., op. cit. p. 40.
18  *Trocas* had another brush with Australian naval history. In November 1941, in the Indian Ocean, she rescued the first survivors from the German raider *Kormoran*, which had sunk the cruiser *Sydney* with the loss of 645 men. It was the first news the RAN received of the disaster.

## Chapter 5: 'A morning never to be forgotten'

1   Badoglio, Pietro, *L'Italia nella seconda guerra mondiale*, Mondadori, Milan, 1946, p. 37.
2   Gilbert, Martin, *Second World War*, Weidenfeld & Nicholson, London, 1989, p. 90.
3   Roosevelt, President Franklin Delano, University of Virginia Commencement Address.
4   House of Commons, *Hansard*, 13 May 1940.
5   Ibid. 4 June 1940.
6   Cooper diary, quoted in Lind, L. J. & Payne, A., op. cit. p. 44.
7   Hill, op. cit. ... several pages.
8   Ibid.
9   Lind, L. J. & Payne, A., op. cit. p. 45.
10  *The Royal Navy and the Mediterranean*, vol. 1, Appendix E, Routledge, London, 2002.
11  Lind, L. J. & Payne, A., op. cit. p. 48.
12  *West Australian*, 11 September 1940, p. 9.
13  Hermon, Gill, *Royal Australian Navy 1939–1942*, Australian War Memorial, Canberra, p. 159.
14  forumlive.net/Dentrolastoria/L_affondamento/Affondamento.htm
15  Dymond, op. cit. p. 68.
16  Ibid. p. 71. They were sent to POW camps in India.

## Chapter 6: 'You are going on a very dangerous mission'

1  Van Prooyen, Terry, private papers.
2  Ibid.
3  Ibid. and also Lardner, Robert, private papers.
4  Foreign Office Report on 1940 Operation, UK National Archives, Appendix C.
5  Clifford, op. cit. p. 62.
6  Ibid. p. 63.
7  Now Serbia.
8  Cunningham to the Admiralty, 22 November 1940.
9  Consul R. McRae to the Foreign Office, November 1940, UK National Archives, FO 371/29990.
10 Minshall, Merlin, *Guilt-Edged*, Panther, London, 1977. Regrettably, some writers have swallowed this rubbish at face value.
11 Van Prooyen, op. cit.
12 About AU$50,000 (2021).
13 Gibson, CMDR Alexandria, Report of Proceedings, 20 August 1940.
14 BBC summaries, Deutschlandsender, 8 April 1940.
15 Health of Romanian Special Service Party, 23 January 1940, UK National Archive.
16 Gibson, op. cit.
17 Clifford, op. cit. p. 95.
18 Brooke was a sub lieutenant RNVR in the Royal Naval Division. Unromantically, he died of an infected mosquito bite two days before the Gallipoli landings in April 1915.
19 Gibson, op. cit. p. 28.
20 Ibid.
21 G. B. Marshall to the Foreign Office, 2 October 1940.
22 Van Prooyen, op. cit.
23 Cunningham to the Admiralty, 22 November 1940.

## Chapter 7: Old Mediterranean Hands

1  Churchill, Winston S., *The Second World War*, vol. II, Houghton Mifflin, Boston, 1949, p. 205.
2  Ibid, p. 209.
3  Smith, Colin, *England's Last War Against France: Fighting Vichy 1940–1942*, Weidenfeld & Nicolson, London, 2010, p. 86.
4  Cunningham, *A Sailor's Odyssey*, op. cit. p. 246.
5  McDonald, op. cit. p. 28.
6  Churchill, op. cit. p. 212.
7  Letter to Robert Bontine Cunninghame Graham, quoted in *Joseph Conrad: A Biography*, Meyers, Jeffrey, Scribner, New York, 1991, p. 166.
8  navyhistory.org.au/captain-h-m-l-waller-dso-and-bar-ran/2

9   Quoted in *Cruiser*, Carlton, Mike, William Heinemann, Sydney, 2010, p. 342.
10   *Hec Waller, A Memorial Book*, privately published.
11   navyhistory.org.au/remembering-hec-captain-h-waller-ran/3
12   Captain Adolphus Huddlestone Williamson RN.
13   'Pusser' is elusive naval slang, hard to define. It derives from 'purser', the officer who provisioned a ship. It can be an adjective or a noun, meaning anything properly naval. Hence 'Pusser's rum', distilled to the Admiralty formula, or a 'Pusser's dirk', which was a sailor's knife.
14   National Archives, Collins Confidential Report.
15   Ross, Lieutenant W. H. 'Jack', *Stormy Petrel*, Paterson's Printing, Perth, p. 110.
16   Ibid. p. 111.
17   *RAN 1939–1942*, Official History, p. 162.
18   Post-war research found that Italian submarines had very large conning towers, making them much easier to see than U-boats or British subs.
19   Ross, op. cit. p. 120.
20   Ross, op. cit. p. 120.
21   Collins, Vice Admiral Sir John, *As Luck Would Have It*, Angus & Robertson, Sydney, 1965, p. 81.
22   conlapelleappesaaunchiodo.blogspot.com/2017/11/espero.html
23   Ross, op. cit. p. 128.
24   Naval Burial Service, Anglican Book of Common Prayer.

## Chapter 8: 'In the Royal Australian Navy things are slightly different'

1   Cunningham, *A Sailor's Odyssey*, op. cit. pp. 258–9.
2   As a lieutenant commander, Garside had spent two years in the mid-1920s on loan to the RAN, finishing as fleet gunnery officer in the old cruiser HMAS *Sydney I*.
3   Gerard, Francis, *Malta Magnificent*, The Specialty Press, Melbourne, 1944, p. 40.
4   *Stuart* chronicle, NHSA.
5   Ross, op. cit. p. 140.
6   *Stuart* chronicle, op. cit.
7   Cunningham, Despatch to the Admiralty, 29 January 1941, reported in *The London Gazette*, 28 April 1948.
8   McDonald, op. cit. p. 31.
9   Reeve, Bill in *The Royal Australian Navy in World War II*, Stevens, David (ed.), Allen & Unwin, Sydney, 1996, p. 56.
10   Cunningham, *A Sailor's Odyssey*, op. cit. p. 262.
11   Ciano diary, quoted in regiamarina.net
12   Cunningham, *A Sailor's Odyssey*, op. cit.
13   Ibid., p. 259.

14  HMAS *Vampire*, Report of Proceedings, July 1940, Australian War Memorial.

15  *Voyager* history, op. cit. p. 77.

## Chapter 9: 'Stand to the dawn'

1   *Advertiser*, Adelaide, 22 May 1937.

2   *Mail*, Adelaide, 24 August 1940.

3   HMAS *Vampire*, Report of Proceedings, July 1940, AWM, Canberra.

4   AWM history, op. cit. p. 243.

5   Navy Sea Power Centre, YouTube *HMAS Sydney (II) at the Battle of Cape Spada*.

6   Ross, op. cit. p. 152.

7   Collins, op. cit. p. 86.

8   AWM history, op. cit. p. 188.

9   Navy Sea Power Centre, YouTube HMAS *Sydney (II) at the Battle of Cape Spada*.

10  AWM history, op. cit. p. 191.

11  Ibid. p. 192.

12  Cunningham, *A Sailor's Odyssey*, op. cit. p. 266.

13  Navy Sea Power Centre, op. cit.

14  Cruisers in those days had a band of eight or ten professional musicians who wore uniforms similar to the British Royal Marines. They doubled as clerks, ammunition handlers and damage control crew.

15  Ross, op. cit. p. 167.

16  Collins, op. cit. p. 88.

17  Quoted in warhistoryonline.com/instant-articles/the-battle-of-cape-spada-crete.html

18  The Palais Glide was a dance popularised by the bandleader Victor Sylvester.

19  *Mail*, Adelaide 24 August 1940.

20  *London Gazette*, 26 July 1940.

21  *Courier-Mail*, Brisbane, 22 July 1940.

22  *Argus*, Melbourne, 25 July 1940.

23  *Dandenong Journal*, 24 July 1940.

24  *Cumberland Argus and Fruitgrowers' Advocate*, 31 July 1940.

25  *Courier-Mail*, Brisbane, 22 July 1940.

26  *Advocate*, Melbourne, 2 August 1940.

27  *Sun*, Sydney, 21 July 1940.

28  *Australian Women's Weekly*, 3 August 1940.

29  AWM history, op. cit. p. 196.

30  Ibid. p. 195.

31  *The Royal Navy and the Mediterranean*, vol. 1, Routledge, Abingdon UK, 2002, p. 49.

## Chapter 10: A Submarine Kill

1  The Maletti Group, named for its commander, General Pietro Maletti.
2  'E' for enemy.
3  A small, battery-operated lamp for close work.
4  From an old naval family. An ancestor, Admiral Sir James Saumarez, had been one of Nelson's captains at the Nile.
5  Ross, op. cit. p. 198.
6  *Voyager* history, op. cit. p. 80.
7  McDonald, op. cit. p. 45.
8  AWM history, op. cit. p. 222.
9  Clifford, op. cit. p. 119.
10  Toschi, Elios, *Ninth Time Lucky*, William Kimber, London, 1955, p. 32.
11  Ibid. p. 34.
12  Ibid. p. 36.
13  Ibid. p. 39.
14  AWM history, op. cit. p. 224.
15  Officially the QF 12-pounder 12-cwt gun. Also known as a 3-inch gun.
16  Ross, op. cit. p. 210.
17  *Voyager* history, op. cit. p. 84.

## Chapter 11: Enter the Luftwaffe

1  Quoted in armouredcarriers.com/operation-judgement-swordfish-attack-taranto-from-hms-illustrious
2  Cunningham, *A Sailor's Odyssey*, op. cit. p. 286.
3  Ross, op. cit. p. 226.
4  Ross, op. cit. p. 228.
5  *Ramb III* had an extraordinary life. Launched in 1936 she was first a 'banana boat', then the armed merchant cruiser. In 1943 the Germans seized her and converted her into a minelayer. The Americans sank her in 1944. Raised in 1947, she became the presidential yacht for the Yugoslav leader Josip Broz Tito, guests received on board included Queen Elizabeth II, Jawaharlal Nehru, Indira Gandhi, Gamal Abdel Nasser, Haile Selassie, Mu'ammar Gaddafi, Nikita Khrushchev and Leonid Brezhnev. Her sumptuous staterooms are now in a museum in Rijeka (formerly Fiume) in Croatia.
6  AWM history, op. cit. p. 235.
7  A big submarine depot ship.
8  Quoted in O'Hara, Vincent, *The Struggle for the Middle Sea*, US Naval Institute, Annapolis MD, US, 2009, p. 66.
9  Ciano Diplomatic Papers, London, 1948, p. 402.
10  *Fuehrer Conferences on Naval Affairs 1939–1945*, Chatham Publishing, London, 2005, p. 155.
11  Clifford, op. cit. p. 130.
12  Ross, op. cit. p. 254.

13   Nation, Andy, *A Stoker's Journey*, Slouch Hat Publications, McRae, Victoria, 2005, p. 15.
14   Ibid. p. 15.
15   About US$152 million (2021).
16   *Sydney Morning Herald*, 21 December 1940.
17   Ten shillings would be about AU$43 (2021).
18   *National Advocate*, Bathurst, 24 December 1940.
19   *Mount Barker and Denmark Record*, Albany, Western Australia, 23 December 1940.

## Chapter 12: His Name is Waller

1   Nation, op. cit. p. 17.
2   The McDonalds were a navy family; Hugh's twin Neil had joined *Stuart* as a midshipman at the same time. Their elder brother Ian was also in the Mediterranean, flag lieutenant to Admiral Pridham-Wippell in the battleship *Barham*. Neil would become an admiral.
3   The Queen's Own Regiment, a British infantry unit.
4   AWM history, op. cit. p. 290.
5   Long, Gavin, *To Benghazi: Australia in the War of 1939–1945*, Australian War Memorial, Canberra, 1952, p. 205.
6   en.wikipedia.org/wiki/Battle_of_Bardia#Casualties
7   Chapman, Ivan, *Iven G. Mackay: Citizen and Soldier*, Melway Publishing, Malvern, Victoria, 1975.
8   Collins, op. cit. p. 96.
9   Ross, op. cit. p. 277.
10   Cunningham, *A Sailor's Odyssey*, op. cit. p. 303.
11   Lamb, Charles, *War In A Stringbag*, Arrow Books, London, 1977, p. 128.
12   Jock Lawrance, interview with the author, 2008.
13   Cunningham, *A Sailor's Odyssey*, op. cit. p. 302.
14   AWM Long, p. 211.
15   Clifford, op. cit. p. 138.
16   McDonald, op. cit. p. 36.
17   Cunningham, *A Sailor's Odyssey*, op. cit. p. 308.
18   AWM history, op. cit. p. 293.
19   Sheedy and Nelson quoted in Carlton, Mike, op. cit. p. 186.
20   Clifford, op. cit. p. 141.
21   Menzies, Robert Gordon, *Afternoon Light*, Cassell Australia, Melbourne, 1976, p. 26.
22   AWM, Greece, Crete and Syria, p. 18.
23   Ibid. p. 17.
24   Cunningham, *A Sailor's Odyssey*, op. cit. p. 315.
25   Quoted in *The Second World War*, Beevor, Antony, Weidenfeld & Nicolson, London, 2012, p. 153.
26   AWM history, op. cit. p. 306.

27  Nation, op. cit. p. 18.
28  *Sun*, Sydney, 19 August 1941.
29  Menzies diary, op. cit. p. 53.

## Chapter 13: Destroyers Attack!

1  Gaudo being the Italian name for Gavdos Island.
2  Cape Matapan, a barren headland, is the southernmost point of mainland Greece. It lay over the horizon to the north. Italians use another name, *La Battaglia di Gaudo*.
3  Carlton, Mike, op. cit. p. 213.
4  Pack, S. W. C., *Night Action off Cape Matapan*, Ian Allen, London, 1972, p. 42.
5  Carlton, Mike, op. cit. p. 216. Thirty-four knots is optimistic. She would have managed 32 at best.
6  Pack, op. cit. p. 54.
7  Ibid. p. 67.
8  gunplot.net/main/content/hmas-stuart-battle-matapan
9  Cunningham, *A Sailor's Odyssey*, op. cit. p. 332.
10  *Daily Telegraph*, London, 6 April 2012.
11  *Stuart* chronicle, op. cit. p. 5.
12  Chenevix-Trench, Richard, article in *Quadrant* magazine, Sydney, June 2011.
13  *West Australian*, 10 May 1941.

## Chapter 14: Only the Navy Could Sustain Them

1  *Herald*, Melbourne, 3 April 1941.
2  *Daily News*, Perth, 14 April 1941.
3  *News*, Adelaide, 23 April 1941.
4  Quoted in *Tobruk*, FitzSimons, Peter, HarperCollins, Sydney, 2006, p. 209.
5  Ibid. p. 251.
6  Quoted in *Admirals*, Lambert, Andrew, Faber & Faber, London, 2008, p. 415.
7  Menzies diary, op. cit. p. 112.
8  Australian-born, in Manly, Sydney.
9  Quoted in Lind, L. J. & Payne, A., op. cit. p. 80.
10  Nation, op. cit. p. 24.
11  The raid was a fiasco. One of the commandos was the novelist Evelyn Waugh, who revealed all after the war.
12  Long, *Greece, Crete, Syria*, op. cit. p. 71.
13  Nalder, Rosemary (Molly), 2-5agh.org
14  Ibid. Initially, the Germans treated them very well. The hospital was moved to a new building near Piraeus, and dressings and drugs were provided. The Greek Red Cross helped with food and clothing. With other wounded prisoners brought in, some 1200 Allied patients were being cared for.

This ended in December, however, and all were sent to camps in Germany or Poland.

15  Dr Moore ended up in Stalag 383 near Nuremberg and was repatriated in 1944. There is a memorial to his memory in Bathurst.

16  Lieutenant Colonel Charles McDonald, www.2-5agh.org

17  *Voyager* history, op. cit. p. 83.

18  Ibid. p. 129.

19  Ibid. p. 134.

20  Heckstall-Smith, Anthony & Baillie-Grohman, Tom, *Greek Tragedy*, Anthony Blond, London, 1961, p. 146.

## Chapter 15: The Disaster of Crete

1  McDonald, op. cit. p. 37.

2  Ibid. p. 38.

3  Clifford, op. cit. p. 194.

4  Rhoades, Rodney, navyhistory.org.au/the-tobruk-run

5  A muscular bull of a man, Freyberg had been awarded a Victoria Cross in the First World War and was a Churchill favourite.

6  Quoted in *Cunningham*, Winton, John, John Murray, London, 1998, p. 210.

7  Long, *Greece, Crete, Syria*, p. 291.

8  Cunningham, *A Sailor's Odyssey*, op. cit. p. 384.

9  Carlton, Mike, op. cit. p. 292.

10  Ibid. p. 293.

11  For a full account of the bombing of HMAS *Perth* see Carlton, Mike, op. cit.

12  *The Naval Review*, vol. LI No. 3, July 1963.

13  They got three years' jail.

14  Quoted in Lind, L. J. & Payne, A., op. cit. p. 105.

15  They were the second RAN ships to carry the names. The first had been First World War destroyers. Two other sloops were built, *Swan* and *Warrego*.

16  *News*, Adelaide, 22 August 1929.

17  McGuire, Paul, *The Price of Admiralty*, Oxford University Press, Melbourne, 1944, p. 148.

18  The younger brother of *Yarra*'s captain, Wilfred Hastings 'Arch' Harrington.

19  Walker, Jefferson, personal letter.

20  Ibid.

## Chapter 16: Farewell to the Chook

1  Durrell was the press secretary at the British Embassy during the war.

2  An earlier *Pass of Balmaha*, a three-masted clipper launched in 1888, was captured by a German U-boat in 1915 and converted to a commerce raider, the *Seeadler*. Captained by Kapitänleutnant Count Felix von Luckner, 'The

Kaiser's Pirate', she sank fourteen ships before a tidal wave smashed her onto a reef in French Polynesia in 1917.

3   The 2nd squadron of Sturzkampfgeschwader 2 (StG 2), a Luftwaffe dive-bomber wing.
4   Walker, op. cit.
5   Ibid.
6   Ibid.
7   There is a treble meaning here. *Picchiato* also means 'crazy' and *picchiata* means to nosedive.
8   Nation, op. cit. p. 29.
9   *Mercury*, Hobart, 19 August 1941.
10  Nation, op. cit. p. 30.
11  AWM history, op. cit. p. 394.
12  One Australian was shot down and killed, Pilot Officer James Kent, of Sydney.
13  HMAS *Vendetta*, Report of Proceedings, July 1941, AWM, Canberra.
14  Lind, L. J. & Payne, A., op. cit. p. 96.
15  *Vendetta*, RoP, op. cit.
16  Lind, L. J. & Payne, A., op. cit. p. 97.

## Chapter 17: Thank God for the Navy

1   A naval anchor, and also the badge of rank for a leading hand.
2   Quoted in Carlton, Mike, op. cit. p. 314.
3   The captain, Commander George Stewart, pleaded guilty at his court martial, which heard that his wine bill for the day of his arrest listed fourteen glasses of port, thirteen tots of gin and five glasses of beer. He lost a year's seniority, was dismissed from his ship and severely reprimanded.
4   HMS *Collingwood*.
5   *Daily News*, Perth, 11 June 1941.
6   McDonald, op. cit. p. 40.
7   *Catholic Weekly*, Sydney, 26 March 1942.
8   Nation, op. cit. p. 27.
9   Quoted in Stevens, David (ed.), op. cit. p. 64.
10  Libyan Arab soldiers oppressed by Italy and allied with the British.
11  HMAS *Voyager*, Report of Proceedings, July 1941, AWM, Canberra.
12  Idriess, Ion & Jones, T. M., *The Silent Service*, Angus & Robertson, Sydney, 1944, p. 193.
13  Ibid. p. 194.
14  Ibid.
15  Including modern-day Lebanon.
16  Report, 24 August 1941, National Archives.
17  navyhistory.org.au/occasional-paper-81-recognition-for-scrap-iron-flotilla

18   Ibid.
19   McGuire, op. cit. p. 281.

## Chapter 18: Scared Stiff and Anxious

1   Führer Conference on Naval Affairs, 25 July 1941.
2   Ibid., 22 August 1941.
3   6.5 kilograms.
4   AWM, Army, Ch. 8, p. 310.
5   Quoted in *Churchill and Australia*, Freudenberg, Graham, Pan Macmillan, Sydney, 2008, p. 299.
6   An army inquiry, held months later, found that the soldiers had been told to wear life jackets but that most had not heard the order. In fact, there would not have been 298 spare jackets on board.
7   Field Marshal Helmuth von Moltke 1800–91. Usually abridged as 'no plan survives first contact with the enemy'.
8   Some were picked up by the tanker *Trocas*, which *Stuart* had saved from going aground in the Med in 1940.
9   *Courier-Mail*, Brisbane, 2 December 1941.
10   Cunningham, *A Sailor's Odyssey*, op. cit. p. 424.
11   navyhistory.org.au/hms-barham-survivors-account-of-sinking/2
12   The sinking was filmed by a newsreel cameraman and can be seen here: youtube.com/watch?v=YdrISbwy_zI
13   McGuire, op. cit. p. 296.
14   Ibid. p. 297.
15   Quoted in AWM history, op. cit. p. 455.
16   anzacportal.dva.gov.au/wars-and-missions/world-war-ii-1939-1945/events/war-sea-1939-1945/lost-sea/hmas-parramatta
17   McGuire, op. cit. p. 296.

## Chapter 19: The Destroyer Breaks up and Sinks

1   Kriegstagebuch *U-559*, 27 November 1941.
2   navy.gov.au/hmas-parramatta-ii
3   Ibid.
4   *Sydney Morning Herald*, 4 December 1941.
5   *Herald*, Melbourne, 8 December 1941. The attack on Pearl Harbor was 7 December Hawaii time, 8 December Australian time.
6   Curtin speech, 8 December 1941.
7   *News*, Adelaide, 20 December 1941.
8   Ibid.
9   *Western Mail*, Perth, 23 April 1942.
10   AB George Smith, of Scottsdale, Tasmania. Details are sparse, but he made it ashore near Bardia and was rescued by New Zealanders.
11   The Tysoe luck ran out. Harry died a POW in Japan in 1943 from beriberi. His wife did not find out until 1945, war's end. Fred stayed in the navy but

died of injuries and burns in an explosion on board the landing ship HMAS *Tarakan* in Sydney in 1950. Denmark today has a Harry and Fred Tysoe Park in their memory.

12 navyhistory.org.au/occasional-paper-35-loss-of-hmas-parramatta-ii-first-hand-accounts

13 *Smith's Weekly*, Sydney, 16 August 1941.

14 *Herald*, Melbourne, 27 December 1941.

## Chapter 20: Ships That Pass …

1 Now Sri Lanka.
2 *Vendetta*, RoP, op. cit.
3 Ibid.
4 Ibid.
5 About AU$8 million (2021).
6 *Vendetta*, RoP, op. cit.
7 8000 kilometres.
8 *Vendetta*, RoP, op. cit.
9 Now Timor-Leste. In theory neutral territory in the Second World War, but this was ignored by both sides.
10 128 fathoms.
11 25 fathoms.
12 AWM history 1942–45, p. 179.
13 *Voyager* history, p. 184.
14 Ibid. p. 189.
15 Lind, L. J. & Payne, A., op. cit. p. 149.

## Appendix I: Crossing the Bar

1 Tape recording, RAN Sea Power Centre.
2 Cunningham, *A Sailor's Odyssey*, op. cit. p. 308.

## Appendix II: The Line of Stuarts

1 To the Naval Committee of Congress, 14 September 1775.
2 Sir John Jervis, 1st Earl, for whom Jervis Bay is named, and Gulf St Vincent off Adelaide.

# BIBLIOGRAPHY

Admiralty, *Fuehrer Conferences on Naval Affairs 1939–1945*, Chatham Publishing, London, 2005.

Australians at War, Australian Government, Department of Veterans Affairs, anzacportal.dva.gov.au/stories-service/australians-war-stories

BBC, World War II People's War, bbc.co.uk/history/wwIIpeopleswar/categories

Gill, G. Hermon, *Australia in the War of 1939–1945*, Series 2 – Navy.

—— Vol. I, *Royal Australian Navy, 1939–1942*, awm.gov.au/collection/C1417313

—— Vol. II, *Royal Australian Navy, 1942–1945*, awm.gov.au/collection/C1417314

Hasluck, Paul, *Australia in the War of 1939–1945*, Series 4 – Civil.

—— Vol. I, *The Government and the People, 1939–1941*, awm.gov.au/collection/C1417302

HMAS (various authors), vols. I, II, III, IV, The Australian War Memorial, Canberra.

Long, Gavin Merrick, *Australia in the War of 1939–1945*, Series 1 – Army.

—— Vol. I, *To Benghazi*, awm.gov.au/collection/C1417306

—— Vol. II, *Greece, Crete and Syria*, awm.gov.au/collection/C1417307

—— Vol. III, *Tobruk and El Alamein*, awm.gov.au/collection/C1417308

Moyes, John F., *Scrap Iron Flotilla*, NSW Bookstall Co., Sydney, 1944.

Page, Christopher (ed.), *The Royal Navy and the Mediterranean*, Routledge, London.

—— Vol. I, *September 1939–October 1940*, 2002.

—— Vol. II, *November 1940–December 1941*, 2002.

Walker, Allan Seymour, *Australia in the War of 1939–1945*, Series 5 – Medical.

—— Vol. III, *Middle East and Far East*, awm.gov.au/collection/C1417325

# HISTORIES

Anon., *Chronicle of HMAS Stuart*, Naval Historical Society, Sydney.

Atkin, Malcolm, *Section D for Destruction*, Pen & Sword, Yorkshire, 2017.

Barnett, Corelli, *Engage The Enemy More Closely*, Hodder & Stoughton, London, 1991.

Bastock, John, *Australia's Ships of War*, Angus & Robertson, Sydney, 1975.

Beevor, Antony, *The Second World War*, Weidenfeld & Nicolson, London, 2012.

—— *Crete*, John Murray, London, 1991.

Carlton, Mike, *Cruiser*, William Heinemann, Sydney, 2010.

Cassells, Vic, *The Destroyers*, Kangaroo Press, Sydney, 2000.

—— *The Capital Ships*, Kangaroo Press, Sydney, 2000.

Churchill, Winston S., *The Second World War*, Houghton Mifflin, Boston, 1949.

—— Vol. I, *The Gathering Storm*.

—— Vol. II, *Their Finest Hour*.

—— Vol. III, *The Grand Alliance*.

Coulthard-Clark, Chris, *Where Australians Fought*, Allen & Unwin, Sydney, 1998.

Dymond, Ralph, *The History of HMAS Voyager*, privately published.

Eldridge, F. B., *A History of the Royal Australian Naval College*, Georgian House, Melbourne, 1949.

Firkins, Peter, *Of Nautilus and Eagles*, Cassell Australia, Melbourne, 1975.

FitzSimons, Peter, *Tobruk*, HarperCollins, Sydney, 2006.

Frame, Tom, *HMAS Sydney, Loss & Controversy*, Hodder & Stoughton, Sydney, 1998.

—— *HMAS Sydney*, Hachette Australia, Sydney, 2008.

—— *No Pleasure Cruise*, Allen & Unwin, Sydney, 2004.

Frame, Tom & Baker, Kevin, *Mutiny*, Allen & Unwin, Sydney, 2000.

Freudenberg, Graham, *Churchill and Australia*, Pan Macmillan, Sydney, 2008.

Gilbert, Martin, *Second World War*, Weidenfeld & Nicolson, London, 1989.

Gillett, Ross, *Warships of Australia*, Rigby, Sydney, 1977.

Greene, Jack & Massignani, Alessandro, *The Naval War in the Mediterranean 1940–1943*, Chatham, London, 1998.

Grove, Eric (ed-in-chief), *Great Battles of the Royal Navy*, Cassell, London, 1994.

Henshaw, John, *V&W Destroyers*, Seaforth Publishing, Barnsley UK, 2020.

Hinsley, F. H. & Stripp, Alan, *Code Breakers*, Oxford University Press, 1993.

Jones, Vice Admiral Peter, *Australia's Argonauts*, Echo Books, Geelong, 2016.

Lambert, Andrew, *Admirals*, Faber & Faber, London, 2008.

Lind, Lew, *The Royal Australian Navy, Historic Naval Events Year by Year*, Reed Books, Sydney, 1995.

—— *Battle of the Wine Dark Sea*, Kangaroo Press, Sydney, 1994.

Lind, L. J. & Payne A., *Scrap Iron Destroyers*, Naval Historical Society of Australia, Sydney, 1976.

Mackenzie, William, *The Secret History of SOE*, St Ermin's Press, London, 2000.

McGuire, Frances, *The Royal Australian Navy*, Brown Prior Anderson, Melbourne, 1948.

O'Hara, Vincent, *The Struggle for the Middle Sea*, US Naval Institute, Annapolis MD, US, 2009.

Pack, S. W. C., *Night Action off Cape Matapan*, Ian Allen, London, 1972.

Roskill, Stephen, *HMS Warspite*, US Naval Institute, Annapolis MD, US, 1957.

—— *Churchill and the Admirals*, William Collins, London, 1977.

—— *The War At Sea 1939–45*, vol. I, *The Defensive*, Naval and Military Press, London, 2004.

Shirer, William L., *The Rise and Fall Of The Third Reich*, Secker & Warburg, London, 1960.

Smith, Peter C., *Critical Conflict: The Royal Navy's Mediterranean Campaign in 1940*, Pen & Sword, Yorkshire, 2011.

Stavridis, Admiral James USN, *Sea Power*, Penguin, New York, 2017.

Stevens, David (ed.), *The Royal Australian Navy in World War II*, Allen & Unwin, Sydney, 1996.

—— *The Royal Australian Navy: A History*, Oxford University Press, Melbourne, 2001.

Stevens, David & Reeve, John, *Southern Trident*, Allen & Unwin, Sydney, 2001.

Toland, John, *Adolf Hitler*, Ballantine Books, New York, 1976.

## MEMOIRS, BIOGRAPHIES

Chenevix-Trench, R. B., 'Night Encounter', *Quadrant* Magazine, June, 2011.

Clifford, L. E., *The Leader of the Crocks*, F. W. Cheshire, Melbourne, 1945.

Collins, Vice Admiral Sir John, *As Luck Would Have It*, Angus & Robertson, Sydney, 1965.

Cunningham, Andrew (Admiral of the Fleet Viscount Cunningham of Hyndhope), *A Sailor's Odyssey*, Hutchinson & Co., London, 1951.

Doenitz, Großadmiral Karl, *Ten Years and Twenty Days*, Naval Institute Press, Annapolis, Maryland, US, 1990.

Gerard, Francis, *Malta Magnificent*, The Speciality Press, Melbourne, 1944.

Glen, Sir Alexander, *Target Danube*, The Book Guild, London, 2002.

Heckstall-Smith, Anthony & Baillie-Grohman, Vice Admiral Tom, *Greek Tragedy*, Anthony Blond, London, 1961.

Hill, G. A., *My Naval Sojourn 1938–1950*, Naval Historical Society, Sydney, 2020.

Lamb, Charles, *War in a Stringbag*, Arrow Books, London, 1977.

Lewis, Tom (et al), *Captain Hec Waller*, Drawquick Printing, Sydney, 2008.

McGuire, Paul, *The Price of Admiralty*, Oxford University Press, Melbourne, 1944.

McDonald, Ean, *Flip Side War*, Hesperian Press, Perth, 2005.

Minshall, Merlin, *Guilt-Edged*, Panther, London, 1977. (Entertaining, but a farrago of fantasy.)

Nation, Andy, *A Stoker's Journey*, Slouch Hat Publications, McRae, Victoria, 2005.

Nesdale, Iris, *Spin Me A Dit*, privately published, 1984.
Ollard, Richard, *Fisher and Cunningham*, Constable, London, 1991.
Poland, Vice Admiral Sir Albert, *Tobruk and Beyond*, Halstead Press, Canberra, 2007.
Ross, Lieutenant W. H. 'Jack', *Stormy Petrel*, Paterson's Printing, Perth, 1946.
Winton, John, *Cunningham*, John Murray, London, 1998.

## WEBSITES

Wikipedia has entries for most of the ships, prominent figures and battles mentioned in this book. It is a vast and invaluable resource, although occasionally its facts have to be cross-checked.
Gunplot.net: Informative and entertaining on the RAN, privately run.
Hyperwar. The Mediterranean and the Middle East. Vols, I & II, ibiblio.org/hyperwar/UN/UK/UK-Med-I/index.html
Naval-history.net
Regia Marina Italiana, regiamarina.net
Royal Australian Navy, navy.gov.au/history: The official RAN history site.
Royal Navy Officers 1939–1945, unithistories.com/officers/RN_officersA.html
U-boat.net: Excellent on U-boats, their commanders, operations and battles.

# ACKNOWLEDGEMENTS

This is my fourth book of naval history. Once again I have been fortunate to draw on help and encouragement from good friends and total strangers, a great blessing in these times when face-to-face meetings have been difficult if not impossible and so many museums and archives have been closed. The internet is a life saver.

My first thanks go to the sailors of the Flotilla themselves, most especially those who left memoirs or diaries or letters or photographs as grist for history's mill. Keeping a diary was illegal on board a warship, except for midshipmen, but quite a few people privately jotted away at it, and thank heaven they did.

Mr Ric McDonald of Perth, the son of Lieutenant Commander Ean McDonald, was very kind in allowing me to quote from his father's memoir and in finding photographs. Lieutenant Commander Steve Van Prooyen, son of Able Seaman Terry 'Dutchie' Van Prooyen, went to no end of trouble helping me with the mysteries of his father's trip up the Danube. Chief Petty Officer Melissa Roberts did wonders with that too. I am also grateful to the Dymond family for permission to quote from Ralph Dymond's excellent *History of HMAS Voyager*. The memoirs of Gordon Hill, now with the Naval Historical Society of Australia, were also invaluable. The Society is a treasure trove lovingly maintained and enhanced by volunteers. Many thanks to the president, Captain David Michael, Commander John Smith, and David Stratton, who were more than generous with their time and knowledge. So too the RAN's Sea Power Centre in Canberra, where

John Perryman – a great custodian of the navy's history – and his colleagues Robert Garratt and Petar Djokovic helped me immensely. In a quiet way, doing its job in the background, the Sea Power Centre is also a national treasure.

Other institutions were there to rely on, chiefly the Australian War Memorial in Canberra with its unsurpassed collection, and the Australian National Archives. And a special thanks to Trove, the brilliant online search engine for Australian newspapers since the year dot, maintained by the National Library. Thanks also to my friend Michelle Feuerlicht in London, who fought her way through the COVID queues to get to the British National Archive at Kew, and to Michele Colvin McKenzie, who helped with information on Midshipman Tony Synnot. The books of the Australian naval historians David Stevens, Tom Frame, Tom Lewis, John Henshaw and Vice Admiral Peter Jones are too many to mention here but they are always a rich resource, an unfailing backstop.

Navy people – some still in the service, others retired – have been kind and enthusiastic. Once again I am indebted to my friend Rear Admiral James Goldrick, a former captain of HMAS *Sydney* and one of the world's leading naval authors and historians, for his constant support and willing advice on matters big and small, again and again. James put me in contact with Kapitänleutnant Tim Döbler and Kapitänleutnant Paul Schröder, serving officers of the Deutsche Marine, who so willingly answered my questions on the Kriegsmarine in general and U-boat tactics in particular. *Vielen dank, meine Herren!*

Another great friend, Commodore Ivan Ingham, also a former frigate captain, read extracts from the manuscript and offered his expertise, his suggestions saving me from some clunking errors.

Other naval people there with help were Rear Admiral Lee Goddard, Captain Luke Ryan, and Captain Tony Raeside. Commander Greg Swinden was a mine of information and generous with it, and another friend, Lieutenant Commander Desmond Woods, stepped up once again with his endless list of naval contacts. The energetic Warrant Officer Marty Grogan and Commodore Greg Yorke both helped me track down the last of the Scrap Iron survivors, Mel McMillan.

Despite some dogged effort, finding and contacting the holders of copyright to books and memoirs has been difficult at best and sometimes impossible. I do thank Dr Keith Windshuttle for permission to quote from 'Night Encounter' in the *Quadrant* magazine edition of June 2011. Ivan Berryman, a distinguished British war artist, very handsomely permitted me to include his painting *A Tribute to Ennio Tarantola*, courtesy of Cranston Fine Arts. The striking drawings of HMAS *Stuart* and *Waterhen* are by Colin Harvey, an artist on the Queensland Gold Coast. They appear in respectful memory of his father, Stoker Frank Harvey, a young man from North Melbourne who served in *Stuart* in the war in the Pacific. More of Colin's illustrations of ships, trains and aircraft can be seen at charveyart.com. If any copyright holders do contact me I will be happy to acknowledge them in future editions.

Finally, my publishers at Penguin Random House – particularly Alison Urquhart and Catherine Hill – have been their usual delightful selves, encouraging me all the way. My elder son, James, has done wonders with the maps yet again. My wife, Morag Ramsay, and my younger son, Lachlan, have cheerfully tolerated my long absences writing behind a closed door. To all these people, my sincere thanks. I could not have done it without you. Any errors, however, are all my own.

# INDEX

NB Navy ships are listed under their HM (Her Majesty's) prefix.